CW00796541

Thank you for purchasing the Great War diaries of Stapleton Te mistakes or punctuation errors are shown as they were trans diaries.

Stapleton Tench Eachus was born in Stafford in 1889 and lived on Marston Road. (Cover Picture: Stapleton having signals training, far right)

In 1916 Stapleton was sent to France and over the next 3 years, he wrote in tiny notepads a set of 15 diaries about his adventures in the Great War.

These diaries contain over 150,000 words.

He was educated at St Austin's Catholic School, Garden Street, Stafford.

After leaving school Stapleton joined the post office where he worked until 1910, he then enlisted with the South Staffordshire Regiment before moving to the Warwickshire Yeomanry. Stapleton fought in Egypt with the Warwickshire Yeomanry before transferring to the Royal Engineer's Signals.

Each diary written by Stapleton was posted back to England via the French postal system. These diaries are a fascinating insight into another side of World War One.

Stapleton was married to Elinor and they had a son called Derek, he had 2 sisters called Gladys and Dorothy and a brother called Harry.

These diaries are dedicated to Stapleton and all the other brave souls involved in this futile war.

If you would like to use any quotes from this book for other publications please contact me at:

jonwick@live.co.uk

These diaries are available exclusively from:

https://www.amazon.co.uk/Great-Diaries-Stapleton-Tench-Eachus/dp/1535339977/ref=sr_1_1?ie=UTF8&qid=1469456128&sr=8-1&keywords=stapleton+tench+eachus

Stapleton's diaries also have a website, which can be found at: www.wardiaries.co.uk

Daily updates are also available on Facebook at:
https://www.facebook.com/Stapleton.Eachus.War.Diaries/

Happy reading Jon

© Jon Wickett 2016

The Great War Diaries of Stapleton Tench Eachus

A signalman at war

Written By: Stapleton Tench Eachus

Transcribed by: Jon Wickett

© Jon Wickett 2016

Table of Contents

24/5/16 Empire Day

Left the depot at Fenny-Stratford, Bletchley with draft no 95 for France. The R.E band accompanied us to the station. Left at 4.30 pm and arrived at Hitchin about 6.15 pm had half an hour's tedious walk to the camp loaded up with kit bag etc. Coming along by train I particularly noticed the flag of St. George and the good old Union Jack flying sincerely from the tops of numerous buildings. I was impressed with the fact too for my mind was reverted back to the early days of the war. When I remember people were flag mad at the time my regiment came through London on its way to Newbury in Berkshire, our progress all along the line was marked by continual bursts of cheering and every house was bedecked with flags of many colours. This was mad London's attitude then, how different are things now.

25/5/16

This morning and again this afternoon no 97 draft has been kept busy with kit and equipment inspections and fitting out. My dear wife Elinor came over in the afternoon and was able to spend the evening with her, also as I could not obtain a pass to do so I took the risk and stayed with her until she left the following morning. Have not seen "E" much since I came back from the Dardanelles last December and was very glad indeed to be with her even for a short time and was a relief from the dead weight of my present environment, which I appreciated with all my heart.

26/5/16

Luckily was not missed at all last night. "E" came back to camp with me at 6.15 am and then went to catch her train at 7.20 am. Paraded in full kit at 8.45 am, afterwards did a bit of gardening until 11 am. Wrote several letters. I miss "E"'s society very acutely. Have asked her to come again tomorrow for the weekend, which I hope sincerely she will be able to do.

27/5/16

Parades as usual, and more gardening until 12 noon. On armed guard at 5.30 pm for 24 hours. I always seem to drop in for this on a Saturday. The weather however is very nice and pleasant.

28/5/16

Feeling rather tired, but another grand day. No 95 draft left this morning. No letter from my wife, and in consequence am very disappointed. Cannot understand her long silence. Finished guard at 5.30 pm and very glad too. It has been awfully hot and tiring. Went into Hitchin with a friend in the evening for a walk round.

29/5/16

Another brilliant day, spent most of the morning on parade, fitting and adjusting equipment. The rest of the day we were free except for a "check" parade at 4 pm. Had hair cut short, razors sharpened. No 96 draft left for France this morning. Ours (No 97) is expected to go about Wednesday. Had tea in town with my friend. Received a couple of letters from my dear wife Elinor.

30/5/16

Fine warm day. Had a good hours foot drill in full kit. In the afternoon gas helmet drill, with a double round the field, which almost suffocated me. Tea and supper in town.

31/5/16

Very hot again. More foot drill in the morning. Check parade at 2 pm afternoon free for the day. Had tea and supper with some nice people in the town. Bath in afternoon at the Sun Hotel.

1/6/16

Dull and cloudy inclined to rain usual route march before breakfast. Company and section drill in morning in full kit, very tiring to me as am not used to marching and have never had the opportunity of learning infantry drill. It is not however very difficult. Handed in our overseas blankets, as they are not to be taken on this daft. We all had to stand by and were not allowed to leave camp, to be in readiness for an inspection by the camp commandant. He did not however turn up.

2/6/16

Weather more settled, usual parades, pay parade 3 pm.

3/6/16

Weather dull and stormy but warm. Commandants inspection, which lasted from 10.10 am until 12.15 pm, on the parade ground where all the drafts, cable section, airline, dispatch riders and scores of motor lorries, making a somewhat imposing spectacle. The commandant afterwards addressed us and presented three men with medals, two received the D.C.M and one, the St George, the latter a decoration from the Emperor of Russia. My dear wife Elinor arrived here (Hitchin) at 4 pm and after parade for issue of blue and white arm lets and sun flaps, I was able to spend the rest of the evening with her at Mrs. Birds, 71 Lancaster Road Hitchin. I was so glad to see my little son Derrick too, the little fellow is very dear to me and his pretty little face and loving eyes, I picture constantly with a clear vividness in my mind. We are now under orders for France and parade at 7.30 tomorrow morning in full kit to proceed to Southampton, do not mind so much that I am again going to the front, but I am happy indeed to have the opportunity of seeing once more my dear wife and little boy whom I love with all my heart. Elinor bought me a signet ring and I purchased a brooch, a silver Royal Engineer crest mounted on a rifle for her.

4/6/16

Had breakfast with my wife and then went back to camp to finish packing up. Marched to the station at 7.50 am and caught the 8.20 am from Kings Cross. Elinor had arranged to go by the same train but unfortunately owing to silly red tape I was unable to travel in the same coach. At Kings Cross I saw "E" again but only for a minute as we were marched off through London to Waterloo Station. I had expected Elinor to follow by tube but saw nothing of her or little Derrick again and we were soon on the road for the port of embarkation, arrived at Southampton at about 2.30 pm and marched to the docks in a heavy down pour of rain, which completely wet us through. I was extremely disappointed with my parting again from those I love. I shall never forget that when leaving Hunstanton for Egypt the police would not allow my wife on to the station, which caused me to curse them well. Now again it has been my misfortune to be sort of suddenly dragged away from my dear wife and child. We embarked at about 4 pm on the steam ship France a low lying grey two funnelled ship. It is a fast boat although an old one. We were directed below and crushed together in a small compartment where we were told to make ourselves comfortable until tomorrow morning. How such a thing is possible for nearly ninety men, must I think remain a mystery. There was nothing to eat or drink, except what we could manage to buy and a poor cup of tea cost 3d and 1d deposit being refunded when the cup was returned. We started away at 5.30 pm and very soon nearly everybody was taking a turn pumping out the contents of their stomachs. It is true the sea was very choppy and in consequence swayed considerably but what annoyed me was the fact that the men would not take the trouble to go up on deck, but apparently took a delight in repeatedly advertising right under ones nose the last meal they had had in England. I tried to get comfortable in a corner, but the sea which came sweeping up the deck and down the hatch ways, and bringing with it all the filth of the vessel, found me out and besides a wetting I was certainly dirtier in more ways than one, than when I first came on board. This going over seas again reminded me strangely of the occasion when I returned to England a day before Xmas on the Re d'Italia. The weather was cold and miserable then and rain fell in sheets. The trees and fields were not so green as now, but then I was returning to my dear homeland and it looked beautiful, in fact my impulse was to go down on my knees and kiss the ground. A great many things have happened in the meantime and I go away sad and disheartened. England has become the home of licentiousness of all manner of folly and vice. The leaders have lost their heads and in consequence the nation has gone mad. God alone knows how much deeper we shall sink, but for these reasons and others we shall never win this war.

5/6/16

Arrived Harve at 12.30 am and berthed up at 4.30 am after a fair night to rest in a very stuffy compartment. Tea, bully beef and biscuits for breakfast but could only get a few broken biscuits owing to the scramble, bought some however. Put back watch one hour to represent French time. Disembarked at about 9 am. I was one of the party selected to escort a batch of prisoners (20 odd) who were under arrest as absentees etc, to the field punishment camp which is situated at one end of the docks. On the way we passed a number of gangs of German prisoners doing all manner of fatigues, some of them looked fine well-built men, and their uniforms clean and a perfect fit. After handing over our charges we marched to the rest camp, which is also in the docks. Had a shave and a wash up as soon as I got rid of my equipment, but got pretty wet for my pains, as a heavy storm and piercing wind came over and swept through the wash house which is open on all sides. Had some lunch at the YMCA. They have nothing whatsoever to eat and have therefore to satisfy myself with tea and cake for all meals at the Y.M. They have no bread in stock many things are much cheaper than in England, in fact they stand at prices at which they could be obtained before the war, such as Golf Flake cigarettes 3d chocolate 1d per bar, boot laces 1d per pair etc etc. Should have left this camp at 3 pm to proceed up country but orders have now come that we shall not move away until 9.30 this evening. Bought half a loaf of bread 5d and a pot of paste 2d at Expeditionary Force canteen and made a decent meal out of it. We were not allowed permission to leave the camp but after tea another fellow and myself put on our bandoliens and boldly marched past the sentry. The town of Harve was however too far so did not attempt to go far. Went into a cafe and ordered a bottle of "export", conversed in French with Madam and her sister. The latter's husband she told me was an artillery man. They both said I spoke French "tres bien". Returned to camp about 8 pm. There have been considerable movement of troops here, mostly R.F.A coming in from England. Paraded at 9.15 pm and marched to the station. I find I cannot rough it now as of yore, in fact this short march in full kit almost did me in. After reaching the station we drew rations for the following day. Then we were all packed into cattle trucks which were marked on the outside "Hommes 36-40 chevaux (enlong) 8". Great gaps showed between the planks on the floor, through which the permanent way was plainly visible, a large amount of vegetable refuse covered the floor and the side of the trucks were open from half way up, with merely a number of them wooden lathes nailed across perpendicularly to serve as bars. This was not exactly a comfortable compartment in which to spend the night. The train started about midnight and jigged along at a terribly slow pace.

6/6/16

Did not sleep much or well and was up soon after 4 am looking out at the beautiful country through which we were passing, with its snug little villages nestling on the hill sides and in the valleys. I wondered how they would look had the sun been shining. Our train was most annoying it would not go at a decent pace at all, and repeatedly stopped, especially in tunnels. Passed through Rouen station through another tunnel, where of course we stayed for a while, then crossed the river, and had a splendid view of the cathedral. Here the line bends sharply round to the right and shortly arrived at a sort of goods station, where we pulled up and got down. Took of our kit in one of the big huts in which was congregated a number of soldiers belonging to different units. I adjourned into the next hut, which was equipped as a canteen and bought a couple of hard boiled eggs, a crust of bread and a bowl of tea, which cost me 7d. I also changed a 1 pound English postal order for which I received in French money 28f 55 c. I would like to note here that all the Y.M.C.A's I have been into so far over here are staffed with English ladies. They have to work all hours and very hard too. This type of English womanhood one cannot help but admire sincerely. They are the same that one meets, wherever there are British troops, sacrificing much to succour our wounded lads in distant lands and on the seas, how different indeed to their less devoted sisters at home. A short service was held in the canteen in the dinner hour and the men sang such hymns as "onward Christian soldiers" heartily and sincerely. It is very tiring waiting about so long, the men amuse themselves in a variety of ways but chiefly by playing cards and "crown and anchor". Entrained at 3 pm and left at 4 pm, but oh how we did crawl along and constantly stopped.

7/6/16

Had an awful night travelling found it was quite impossible to obtain any sleep or even comfort, owing to the fact that we were crammed into 3rd class coaches, with hard wooden seats and straight backs. The 2nd class are slightly better, as they enjoy the luxury of upholstering, the 1st class coaches are easily distinguished by their old English road coach appearance but of course such compartments are exclusively reserved for officers. Arrived at our destination "Abbeville" about 4 am and at 5.30 am we were marched off to the "signal depot" a distance of something like 2 miles. Handed in our ration bags and had breakfast, which consisted of bread and butter, jam and tea. Had a shave and wash then a nap until dinnertime. Wrote several letters in the afternoon. A popular game here, which is played by the troops, chiefly Canadians is called baseball. There are about 1,000 men in this camp "signal depot" but unfortunately there is not enough accommodation for so many and if one is unlucky in getting anywhere in the rear of the queue, which is obliged to form up in the open at meal times, the chances are that it is necessary to wait a considerable time before obtaining rations and also a seat in a marquee, on account of this I went without my tea and instead walked down to the town. I visited all parts of the town, which in fact is my usual custom. The chief object of interest so far as I am aware is the Eglise Saint - Vulfran, which although interesting enough in the interior is far more beautiful and picturesque to look upon from the outside. The "Monument de l'amiral caurbet" in the square is also unique and conveys to the looker on a sympathetic interest. La Somme as it passes on its way through the town does not present exactly much beauty. The canal between the Somme and the station is bordered on each side by pleasant walks, with tall trees lining its banks.

8/6/16

Experienced a cold night. Have only one blanket and the weather since we arrived in France has been exceedingly cold and wet for this time of year especially. First parade 6 am, when all our draft was issued with riffles. Breakfast at 7 am for which we had ham, bread and butter and jam and tea. Second parade 8.30 followed by section drill until 10.30, again paraded at 11 am and went on a route march, which was rather rough as we were completely tired out after the drill with rifles. The roads too are not as good as in England at least those I have seen up to the present would only be classed as 2nd class roads in the homeland. There are few hedges but what apparently appears to be the custom of planting trees on each side of the road helps considerably to relieve the monotony. I noticed women are freely employed upon the land, and that they go about their work in a most energetic manner, which fact so far as I have been able to observe is really very typical of these French folk. One thing which I particularly notice with regard to the "bonnes femmes de France" is that they do not need the aid of masculine attire to enable them to carry out their labours expeditiously and well. I may note here that I have been struck by the obvious large number of widows, many quite young, who may be easily recognised attired in deep mourning. After 2 o'clock parade we were dismissed, had wash shave and clean up. Tea 4 pm, paraded for pay at 5.30 pm when I received 5 francs, after went for a walk in the country. The first thing to strike my attention were large and small crucifixes, one large crucifix is erected in front of the church at the bottom of the road leading up to our camp, another I passed in a shaded nook by the road-side. They are to say the least, most impressive, as they represent agony surrounded by a world at peace and quiet restfulness. I wonder if their influence extends to the majority for any length of time, or merely lasts for a period, and that man becomes accustomed to the mute supplication, which enervates from the cross, and pass by without notice, even without awe. The French appear to hold to the peculiar custom of tethering their cattle by means of chains attached to the beast's horns. The only reason I can give for this is that in the absence of the hedges, particularly along the roadside, such a course is necessary to prevent the cattle from wandering. I must certainly make a note of a little surprise, which I experienced today and the odd way it came about. When on our way up country from Rouen and during a long halt on the line, another "R.E" and myself got into a conversation with some French military railway engineers. During the talk my companion was asked where he came from, and he replied Stafford. I told him that was my home too, but neither knew the other. Today however he told me that he could now recognise me, mentioned my Christian name, and the school I attended (St-Austin's) and in fact we both lived in the same road, but it must be quite 15 years ago since we met and were play-mates together.

9/6/16

Another cold night. Poured with rain all night, which has made the ground quite sodden. We have only one blanket and ground sheet per man and no wooden floors, which in such weather is both uncomfortable and dangerous for the men to lie down. Went on route march after the 2nd parade through the most beautiful country imaginable. The fair fields of France are fair indeed to look upon and are justly entitled to such distinction, for an hour I passed through waving corn-fields and rich pasture lands, all ablaze in brilliant colours, vivid red poppies, blue corn-flowers and flowers of countless hues, intermingled with the growing corn and spread out in all directions in picturesque patches on the cultivated slopes and in the valleys, Abbeville with its elegant spires and pinnacles could be plainly seen in the distance. It was indeed a truly glorious spectacle of peace and prosperity. Our path suddenly dipped sharply down into the valley of the Somme towards the village of Epagnette and upon gaining the main road, halted and adjourned into a cafe, where we indulged in some selections of light French wine. Arrived back in camp about 12 noon. Dinner 1 pm, parade at 2 pm, when we were tested in telegraphy which lasted until tea time, afterwards had shave and clean up and went down to the cafe where I called yesterday and conversed in French with Monsieur et Madame and their daughter. I remained with them until 10 pm partaking supper at their table, which consisted of steak, sausages and beans together with beer followed by a couple of eggs especially fried for myself and two cups of tea. The whole only costing me 1f 50c.

10/6/16

Warmer and more comfortable night. Hailed very heavily for a time after breakfast, but the sun came out and shone brightly soon afterwards. I paraded with the sick at 8 am on account that of my face breaking out in sores all over. I first became aware of it the day after leaving England, but cannot in any way account for the cause, found however that the sick parade had already gone to hospital as the time has lately been altered to 7.30 am, but no reference is made to this effect on the notice board. The R.S.M however excused me duty for today, merely telling our party of four to clean up the lines, which task we quickly accomplished. Had a nap, after diner lay down again for short while, then shaved and washed. Did not stay in for tea but went to Une Epiciere where I have been several times previously and conversed in French with Madame until 7 pm, when I left I visited a cafe higher up the road. Returned to camp at 9 pm.

11/6/16

Fair night, but weather looks threatening. Today being Sunday first parade was at 8.30 am, was on fatigue duty for short while, received three packets "Ruby Queen" cigarettes and one box of matches, which is the weekly issue to each man, or if tobacco is preferred the men receive a 2 oz tin instead of cigarettes. My face is still very troublesome with sore places, but there are signs now of them healing up for which I am extremely thankful. After dinner went into Abbeville and walked out into the country passing through a sort of park, whose chief claim to beauty however consisted solely of its avenues of trees. It also boasted a football pitch. Passing on there is a charming walk by the side of a fast running stream. Had tea at a restaurant. Afterwards came back towards the camp and visited a cafe where I stayed until 8.30 pm.

12/6/16

Fair night, weather cold and damp, foot drill in the top field, afterwards swilled and brushed wagons. Continual heavy showers and awfully cold, after dinner the operators adjourned into the practice school. After tea walked down to Abbeville with the landlady and her daughter. Returned to camp at 8.30 pm and indulged in a basin of coffee and some cake at the YMCA.

13/6/16

Very cold night, beastly weather conditions prevailed this morning. After parade bought a couple of eggs 4.5 f for breakfast, but waiting in the queue for tea and a slice of ham, caused them to go cold, also the tea. Went for a route march in morning, taking the same way as we did a few days ago. It was however very wet under foot and a cold wind blowing, stayed for a time at a cafe at Epagnette and drank coffee and rum. In the afternoon, operators marched off for practice in the "top" school. I did not do much of that however, but wrote a few letters and studied French instead. After tea walked out to Epagnette and stopped at a cafe for a time, came back to Abbeville and went into my favourite cafe to talk French. Returned to camp at 9 pm, found a letter waiting for me, which had just arrived from my dear wife Elinor. This was the first I had received and was very welcome indeed.

14/6/16

Poured with rain the whole night. The weather has been most atrocious since we left England, in fact one would think it was mid-winter instead of summer. It is nothing else but mud, mud, mud everywhere, and on this account I cannot obtain a good rest at nights, with only one blanket and a sodden ground sheet to provide comfort and warmth. Bought a couple of eggs for breakfast, which assisted materially in getting down the bread and butter. In practice school all morning, wrote several letters and studied French. Received 10 francs pay in the afternoon. Went to the cafe after tea and stayed until 9 pm, had supper there which consisted of a couple of fried eggs, bread and butter and tea, followed by steak chops and fried potatoes and tea, which cost me 1f 50c. Returned to camp, found a letter waiting for me from my dear Aunt Ada.

15/6/16

Weather still very cold and wet. French time advanced one hour last night. This makes the 2nd time have had to put on my watch 60 minutes. I may note here that I have been struck repeatedly by the large number of French women in deep mourning but contrary to my previous understanding, I am now enlightened to the fact that is the custom in France that when any member of a family dies, the women folk all go into deep mourning, which gives one the impression that they are widows and which in fact I quite thought was the case at first. After tea went down to the town and bought another dozen picture postcards. Afterwards returned and called at the cafe up the road, where I stayed until 9.15 pm, arriving at camp soon afterwards, found a letter from Dill awaiting me. It looks as though I shall be here for some little time yet, as the drafts are only small, which have gone up the line since I came and there are a large number of men in the camp.

16/6/16

Awfully cold night. I visited last night the "Eglise saint gibles", as I had heard that it was very beautiful in the interior. The choir which was composed of a number of boys and one priest were singing when I entered and added considerably to its impressiveness. The church is an old one and not by any means remarkable for its structural architecture at least that was my impression. It had however been elaborately decorated and the walls and pillars painted in divers hues. The painting, which were hung about the building constituted in my opinion the most remarkable feature to be seen in this place of worship. Perhaps however my vision in such matters may be influenced in a prejudicial direction on account of the fact that having had the privilege of visiting that most wonderful sumptuous church St-Johns at Valetta, Malta, one is apt to judge to readily and in so doing overlook the claims of those of less repute. After breakfast a few of the "O.T's" including myself who were not down for scheme or practice, went for a route march, taking the usual route and stopping at a cafe at Epagnette until about 12 noon. Upon reaching camp I heard that a big draft was being got ready, but at the time of going to dinner, no list of names had then come out. At 1.20pm however while having my dinner I heard my name mentioned as one selected for the draft, which had to parade at 1.30pm for medical inspection. Proceeded to the general hospital at 2 pm, we were kept waiting until 3 pm before the doctor was at liberty to examine us. Arrived back at camp at 4pm, where we were informed to parade again at 5pm. This meant rushing about a bit as had to fetch my washing from down the road, fight for some tea, draw equipment, including rifle, a couple of gas helmets, rifle sling, anti-gas goggles, 50 rounds of ammunition and can of rifle oil, also had then to collect my things together and pack up etc. Marched down to the station at 5.30 pm after shaking hands all round with my former friends. Entrained at 8.30 pm started shortly after 9 pm. We passed through beautiful country every yard of it a perfect picture.

17/6/16

Had a rough night and very cold. Do not know where we are making for at all. There have been the usual number of stops on the way, still there have been several hours of good travelling. Cannot remember all the places we have gone through but I remember "Longpre", Saint Roche and Amiens, all along the line there are obvious signs of big movements of troops. At the time I am making these notes we are halted opposite a sort of "Venice of kitchen gardens". Many acres of land have apparently been cut into allotments and separated by waterways. The gardeners may be seen coming along punting their gondola shaped boats, and others going away laden with vegetables and greens. These waterways are fed by a river, which runs through the centre of the allotments. Several of our fellows have made a raid on the radishes and lettuce etc. Our destination was "Hielly" but for some unexplained reason the train did not stop there, but went through to the next village called "Mericourt and Ribemont". This was unfortunate as we were consequently obliged to march back to first named place a distance of about 3 miles in order to report our arrival to the "R.T.O". It was hot work too, and the roads were choked with wagons, automobiles and dust. However did the journey in good time, and were told on arrival that a motor-lorry would be sent for to take us up to the 4th army, which is supposed to be about 9 miles away. In the meantime made a Dixie of tea, which was very acceptable. It was rather amusing on the way up to see the soldiers at every stop on the line leave the train and make for the nearest engine, carrying with them their canteens to procure hot water to make tea. It is a custom to get down on the line when the train stops and walk about. There is no fear of being left behind, as it is quite easy to catch the train when it starts and the men do not trouble to board it until it has really made a start. We boarded a motor lorry at 4 pm, which was laden with coal and had rather a rough ride for nearly 2 hours on the top of it. We passed on the road a poor young fellow in a motor-ambulance who had been knocked down by a motor-lorry and killed a few hours before. Passed through a place called "Carbie", and soon afterwards reached "Quarry", which was our destination. Reported to signal officer, then at orderly room in the village. Six men were told off to go on duty from 7 pm until 9 pm and again from 10.30 pm to 1 am. This was rather hard lines as we had been continually on the go for more than 24 hours. However we were conducted to our billets, which proved to be a tumbled down barn, with a rare supply of fresh air kindly provided, and infested with rats. The barn has been fitted up into a sort of bunk arrangement, one over the other, which are reached by climbing a permanent ladder. My kip is on the top story in the loft. Had a wash and shave, while waiting for our tea to be got ready, down by the stream, which runs close to the big chateau which is used as he headquarters for the 4th army. Made my bed about 9.30 pm which however only consisted of a ground sheet, as have no blanket and none are supplied here. Artillery firing is distinctly audible here and the buzz of aeroplanes overhead hardly ever ceases. At 10.15 pm a heavy bombardment apparently from our own guns commenced and continued for at least a couple of hours.

18/6/16

Had a very cold night. Got up at 6.45 am and washed at the stream, which passed by the bottom of the gardens to our billets. Breakfast at 7.30 am at headquarters. Paraded 8 am, very busy morning working up and down on 3rd army (C.A.R) circuit, also did a little on the 6th French army (B.O), off duty at 1.0 pm until 5.30 pm. Was on Amiens wire all the evening and very heavily pressed, with long priority messages. One having 611 words in it. Finished duty at 9 pm tired out. Had some bully beef and biscuits for supper then got down to rest. Tried another method of keeping warm, by lacing up about a couple of feet of my ground sheet at the bottom, to make a pocket for my feet and also by putting my feet into the sleeves of my tunic. In this way I managed to keep my lower limbs comparatively warm, but that was all for I spent a restless night on account of the cold. At 10.30 pm, our guns commenced a heavy bombardment, which continued for some time.

19/6/16

Dull morning, but not cold.
"French Signals"
a .-.-
a or a .--.-
ch ----
e ..-.
n --.--
o ---.
u ..--
understand ...-.-

On duty at signal office from 8.30 am until 1 pm, worked very hard indeed. Poor dinner of bad potatoes and burnt meat. Wrote a letter to my dear wife Elinor in the afternoon. Not much time off duty so cannot do much, had a shave and wash under the trees down by the stream behind our billet. It is extremely beautiful country all about this part. Our headquarters at the chateau are exquisitely situated, surrounded as it is on all sides by dense clusters and avenues of tall trees, many of our fellows spend their leisure time fishing in the stream, with improvised rods. There are but few of the original population left in the village, and most of the houses are mere mud shanties, quite untenantable never the less, one cannot realise very much that there is a war on here, except for the distant booming of the big guns, which is only faintly audible, and the heavy traffic on the roads, provide the only evidence of the hell further up the line. There is at the present moment much talk of a big advance, but personally I think that such rumours are exaggerated considerably, and are more or less the expressions of those who have had little or no experience of the true nature of the fighting line, and its gigantic significance. On duty at " S.O" at 5.30 pm until 9 pm. I approached our officers on the matter of blankets but they could do nothing for me. Have contracted a bad cold with only my great coat to cover me at night, in a very draughty barn, and extremely cold weather for the time of year, find however that nothing can be done, as we are not allowed to have blankets. This is what one has to put up with in the British army. I commandeered a bouton of straw from a neighbouring rick yard, which was certainly more comfortable to lie upon than the floor, but spent a cold night never the less.

20/6/16

Sun shining brightly this morning. Worked hard on GHQ duplex in the morning. Received a letter from Dill, which has been on the road since the 6th. The French have but three meals per day the first in the morning is called "edijeuner" the second at midday is called "le midi diner". They do not take tea but have a meal in the evening at 7 pm or 8 pm which is called "le soir souper". Things are indeed very slow here. The cafe's are only open to soldiers from 6 pm until 8 pm, my duties do not terminate until 9 pm so am completely cut off from all intercourse with the natives, which is unfortunate as had set my heart on making the most of my stay on French soil by learning as much of the language as possible. For this reason I approached the people who occupy the adjoining cottage to our billets, to permit me to go too speak with them. There is also a young girl there 14 years of age, who will probably assist me materially. Had a wash and shave by the stream in the afternoon and afterwards wrote a letter to my aunt Ada. Our office is a perfect hive of industry. There are three Wheatstone circuits and several punching instruments working all day long, after duty at 9 pm went with several more fellows next door, where we had a basin of hot milk each and I put bread in mine. Thought it was a good thing for my cold, and only cost 1.5 c. Stayed gossiping until 10 pm and then retired.

21/6/16

Cold restless night, but bright pleasant morning. I would like to make a note of one particularly English custom which has been adopted here, in the absence of street names in the village, English ones have been put up, such as "Exchange St", "Cannon St.", "Burton St.". The latter is where a billet is situated. Received a letter this afternoon from my cousin Ethel, informing me Isabel's husband had been killed in action, by a shell. The news affected me a great deal. It is so tragic "Billy" has done his duty it is true, he has done it nobly and well, but to what purpose? War has lost its glory. This is not war, it is a curse, a blight upon the nations of Europe, nay upon the whole world. It is a ruthless extermination of the best of our nation's manhood, for what? There is no answer. The chaos in which we find ourselves has been brought about by ignorance, by folly and other hellish intrigues and now mankind has deliberately taken up his abode in the devil's madhouse. When will enlightenment come? How long must this bedlam last before we are allowed to regain our freedom? Had hot bread and milk at neighbours for supper.

22/6/16

Better night, but still suffering from a cold and my left ear is extremely sore from recent breaking out on my face. It is a beautiful morning and will be apparently very hot during the day. I have ascertained that the "chateau" at which the headquarters of the 4th army are installed is known as "Chateau mon le conte dansle contarac" and that the owner is at present a prisoner of war although not a soldier. Had a swill in the stream this afternoon. It has been very hot all day and I feel rather done and tired out. Wrote a letter in French to my sister Doris and also one to Will. I regret to relate the unfortunate occurrence, which has befallen our comrades at the 3rd army headquarters at St-Pol. The town was bombed about 2 pm this afternoon by twelve taubes. Eight R.E's were killed in the camp and ten wounded, five of them had only been in France a fortnight and two had been to Gallipoli. A telegram arrived for one of the men who was blown to pieces, and which had been following him up the line for eight days. It contained the news of his wife's death. He would have gone on leave to England in the evening had he lived. I have noted these facts, as they represent in their tragic eloquence the terrible evil, which is rapidly visiting every home in Europe. Had some milk for supper, which was warm, coming straight from the cow.

23/6/16

Good night's rest. Another beautiful morning all the countryside is gladdened and peaceful. The birds who alone in this world catastrophe continue their peaceful avocations joyfully and with many melodious songs, undisturbed and unheeding, have proved a soothing delight to me in many places. Received a couple of letters from my dear wife Elinor and one from home containing one letter from my father and another from Doris. My father mentioned in his that he had visited among other places Abbeville. I wish I could tell him I had been too. I hope I shall have the opportunity of seeing many more places of interest in the near future. As our billet neighbours were very busy this afternoon I could not claim their assistance to help me with my French. Indeed the peasants here are nothing if not industrious, they do not believe in being idle and in fact they must indeed put their shoulders to the wheel, in order to live at all, at lease that is my impression. However I was determined not to waste the couple of hours, which is all I can get to myself each day, so went to another house and asked Madame to kindly oblige. Her son was there, just returned from Verdun, where nearly all his comrades had been killed. He was taking a rest before proceeding to the Vosges, where the fighting is less severe. He helped me a great deal and is a decent sort of fellow. It has been very hot all day and at about 3.3 pm we experienced a short sharp thunderstorm, which caused a captive balloon somewhere to break loose. Had deux sous worth of new milk for supper and then retired.

24/6/16

Fairly good night, except for a thunderstorm, which broke over us during the night, and of course easily penetrated through our flimsy shelter and dripped down upon our beds, I soon went to sleep again however. Had the misfortune to meet with an accident shortly after getting up this morning, while cleaning my rifle in the barn, another fellow up in the loft knocked down his mess-tin was heavily filled with different things, it fell upon my head and cut my scalp rather badly, which bled profusely. A couple of fellows kindly bathed it and applied borasic powder, which sufficed until I saw the doctor, my hair was cut off round the injury and bathed again. Have now got a large bandage across the top of my head. The doctor also inoculated me in my left arm, on account of having a head wound, as a precaution against lockjaw. He gave me too some ointment for the breaking out on my face, particularly my left ear. Went on duty directly afterwards. Spent a good afternoon with my friends from "Verdum". I find it by no means an easy task to make headway with my French, it is only by impudence and perseverance that I am able to pick up a couple or so words daily. Still I am satisfied, for although my progress may be slow and laborious, I know too that I make steady but sure progress. Had a short walk after finishing duty at 9 pm, passed the little cemetery just outside the village, it looked very quaint with its many crucifixes and low hedge which constituted its boundary, corn fields surrounded it on all sides. The firing lately at least the past few night has been almost negligible.

25/6/16

Good night's rest. Had my head dressed and bandaged up at the doctors. The weather is very close. Noticed a lot of troops being conveyed in motor vehicles through here, each conveyance carried about 50 soldiers and had roofs attached, probably to secure them against observation. Went to a cafe and had a glass of tea and picked up a few more French words. As I am writing this in the garden, at about 3.45 pm a number of British aeroplanes have passed over at a considerable height, going in the direction of the enemy's lines. Suppose they intend some mischief to our despicable enemy. It is a beautiful day and very warm. Heard this evening that three German observation balloons had been brought down in flames by our aircraft. Third army tell me they have had another tank raid but no casualties with them, although four operators are supposed to have been killed at 7th corps headquarters. Wrote a letter to Mr and Mrs Roberts at Southport, who were such good friends to me, while I was in hospital at that place. With regard to the above success of our aircraft over the enemy's kite balloons, I would like to mention that according to the official report on the matter the adventure was carried out by the squadron of aeroplanes, which I witnessed passing over this afternoon which occurred according to the said report "about 4 pm". Heavy artillery fire commenced early in the evening and continued most of the night. I was surprised upon returning to billet at 9 pm to find there several of my old friends of no 97 draft. They had just arrived from "Abbeville" and were under orders to proceed to one of our Divisional Headquarters on the morrow.

26/6/16

Rained during the night, rather close this morning. Had my head dressed, it is quite an operation to get the bandages off as they are fastened down by a very sticky plaster, and each time my hair is either pulled out or has to be cut off, this is extra hard luck considering the amount which I have. My first experience of a French box of matches was rather peculiar, finding that I could not get a light after striking a considerable number, owing to the fact that they apparently went out as soon as they were struck, I bunched several together and procured a light in that way. It became obvious to me then that the matches did not actually extinguish, but continued to burn for about half an inch up the stem. The flame however is almost invisible, except for the faint blue gas, which originates from the sulphur on the match stem. To obtain a light for ones cigarette from this is most obnoxious and in fact is really asking to be gassed. One is obliged to wait until the match proper has caught before attempting to get a light. The universal method of using paper money instead of coins is also pretty often a disadvantage, for instance I have with me a note for 0,50 centimes marked Ville D'abberville, which will not be accepted anywhere here. The same with a note marked "chambre de commerce D'amiens" would also be refused at Abbeville. The following is a facsimile of a morning report by telegraph from the Etat Major of the 6th (French) army to Etat, major 4th (English) army. ("Boves nr50 10.55.
to "Etat Major Querrieu
no 3934/2
Compte renu du 26 juin 1916. 9 heures.
Rie de particulier a signaler en dehors de l'activite des 2 artillies celle de l'artillerie enneme restant notablement inferieure a la notre de Etat Major Boves").
Our bombardment according to official reports is progressing favourably. Gas was released and went over successfully. One of the enemy's guns was reported by an airman to have been blown completely up yesterday by our 66 siege artillery. Enemy retaliated but with little effect. It has been showery all day and at times very heavy storms had bread and milk at neighbours for supper.

27/6/16

Much rain fell during the night. Cavalry movements continued a great part of the night, passed through Querrieu this morning, the roads were choked with traffic, motor-lorries etc, which were carrying large water-tanks. All day long, long columns of British troops have been marching through the village, together with their attendant paraphernalia. For the most part the men looked jaded and worn out. They certainly had lost all semblance of barrack-square smartness, and were without a shadow of doubt whatever, obviously inferior in every respect to the bright brave lads who compose or at least compose the front line regiments, both regular and territorial at the commencement of the war. They will not compare with those battalions of South Staffs (my countymen by the way) who came by as we were lining up behind "lala baba" on that, for us, memorial 21st August 1915, they were men of fine physique for the most part and marched regularly, they could not refrain however from a jesting mood, although there was death ahead for many of them, this fact however did not seem to trouble anyone and jokes and taunts directed against the wily Turk accompanied with a rifle or spade brandished in the air to give the effect to such expressions, were freely exchanged between us (the Yeomanry) and the infantry. The men I saw today were not of this sort. They will undoubtedly give a very good account of themselves because they are British. I hope good luck will follow them, they will have plenty of work to do. Have unfortunately broken the glass on my wristwatch and it is quite impossible to obtain another here, the nearest watchmaker in fact is at Amiens. Nothing very much to note occurred today so far as I am aware, with regard to the projected "great advance". Gas was let off at a number of points along our lines. The work of the artillery was also reported as satisfactory. A ruse adopted by the Germans is worthy of note. It appears that when it became evident that we had completely destroyed the wire entanglements, which protected a certain section of their trenches, the enemy immediately evacuated that particular portion. Our men were permitted to enter unmolested, but found that it had been blocked up on the right and on the left, the Germans from behind the barricades then opened fire and bombed our soldiers.

28/6/16

Weather dull and very uncertain. Was continually disturbed during the night by the noise of cavalry passing through. I presume it was an "Indian Division", as I was aware that there was one in the neighbourhood, also an Indian transport column had arrived here early this morning and is in a field close by. The Indians look curious wearing their steel helmets. They are not nearly so picturesque now that they have discarded their well-known head-gear. I took a party of three round the village in what seemed to be a vain attempt to procure some milk for them, eventually however was successful and I acted as interpreter for them. One Indian could speak a little English and I performed the post of a sort of medium between the Indians and their hostess, two of them declined to accept a cigarette from me, as it would be, so they explained, contrary to their religion. Extremely heavy storms have been the rule today, which is obviously unfortunate and might possibly have some detrimental effect upon the general plans of the allies. There are a great many troops in Querrieu now, mostly artillery and cavalry. Our billet has had a considerable increase of engineers as inmates. My head is getting better nicely although still attend the doctors for dressing each morning. The breaking out on my face has also quite gone now. Sent a series of 22 picture postcards to England. More infantry passed through today. We were issued with 10 oz of tobacco or cigarettes per man and a box of matches. Paraded for pay at 2.30 pm and received 30 francs.

29/6/16

Cold night, but bright sunny morning, changed however after breakfast to dull rainy day. Went to farmhouse in afternoon where I took the Indians to get some milk yesterday morning. Spent the afternoon talking in French with the daughter of Madame, who is however also married and whose husband is at present in the trenches. She has a baby a year old. I think now shall be able to make some headway as Madame is also desirous of learning English, where other people here are always to busy to indulge in such pastimes. The war news today is satisfactory, British shell torrent along a front of 60 miles, many more raids into enemy trenches, some hand to hand fighting and a few prisoners. The enemy however seems to be reserving their fire and even evacuating their front line trench as they are repeatedly found empty, but severely damaged by our fire. There are several divisions of cavalry in this neighbourhood, I cannot say definitely how many, have heard that there are six divisions altogether. That would mean 36,000 sabres, I think however that that number is too high and that three divisions would be more near the mark. A cavalryman was telling me today that they have been practising trench jumping for the last three months. It is a fact that there are many things, which point to a great stoke being under contemplation in the near future. I hope that the sacrifice, which will be necessary, will not be in vain as in all cases hitherto fore.

30/6/16

Cold night and dull morning. Spent afternoon conversing with Madame at the farm. The weather has now changed to very hot, hope it will continue. Troops and all the paraphernalia of war continue to pass through on its way to the front. Nothing much to note today.

1/7/16

Fairly good night, but cold, bright sunny morning and evidently will be extremely warm as the day advance. There appears to be great things on foot, but at present can gather nothing of a sound nature. In the afternoon went down to the lake at the bottom of our road. It is very deep and full of weeds. I did not go in but had a good wash down on the bank. While thus engage an old comrade from P.O, who was originally in the Worcestershire Yeomanry came up to me. It appears he transferred to the R.E's (airline) before our brigade went abroad. It is peculiar but wherever I have gone have always dropped across men from the P.O Birmingham. Received a welcome parcel from my dear wife Elinor containing such valuable articles as a box of cigarette, four boxes of matches and two tablets of soap. The first day of our advance apparently went very well at the commencement. The Germans it appears had in many places evacuated their front line trenches and probably certain sections of their 2nd line, all the Germans holding shell craters gave in. Several corps or divisions reached their objective during the day, but others were held up. One division was counter attacked and driven out of the trench they had captured and took up a position according to the report on the matter in "Station rd". The 8th corps towards the evening were all back in their own lines except one division which was still occupying the front line German trenches and two battalions which were left behind at a place called "Serre" but unfortunately cut off. The whole of the regiment staff of a Bavarian regiment were captured including one colonel, two captains and two lieutenants, am in ignorance of events at other parts of our line and can only speak of a few of the principal features which have occurred on our own particular front. Personally I do not like the situation in the least and in fact I have little faith in British leadership. The method of attack to my mind is obsolete and is unavailing against an obstinate and resolute foe.

2/7/16

Good night rather bright warm morning. Spent afternoon talking to a couple of Canadians in a farmhouse, who belong to the "M.T" attached to the Canadian cavalry brigade at present with our army (the 4th). Wrote letter to my wife and my friend Ope Day. Official reports are slightly more favourable this evening, it appears that only our 4th and the 6th French army are carrying out the present offensive. French 6th army report at 7.10 pm "French line and of Somme aaa, point 6000 all mereancourd wood 6486 tr riensi aaa inf progressing in Herbecourt beyond church aaa point 39 42 tr Brunechilde aaa Fighting in progress in Addevillers aaa Battery of 105 taken at point 6486 aaa 20th corps report fighting I B du chaputre this unconfirmed". Our 13th own reports considerable movements of vehicles from Contal-Maison in a N.E. direction. Our 3rd corps reports that the 19th own states we have captured La Boisselle and German front and support trenches to the S.E enemy putting up stout fight by bombing. It is to early to judge of general results but personally I should say that under the circumstances and in view of the fact that the Germans had little or no reserves at the commencement that on the whole our advance has been a failure up to the present. Our 8th corps has been checked and driven back and our losses elsewhere appear to be very great, although we have obtained no substantial much less decisive result at any point. Our artillery continues to hammer and grind away day and night. I hope it is to some purpose wish I could bring myself to cultivate a little faith in British advances, but unfortunately it is impossible. Our army is controlled and led by a horde of amateur officers whose one and only characteristic and relieving feature that they all know how to die. That is not war however, neither does it bring victory and we are losing this war for the one sole reason, which is obvious that we lack purpose, initiative, one point at which I aim, a bold head and a strong hand. Where is the soldier who could and would put all these specific requirements into effect?

3/7/16

Cold night, sky dull and overcast. War news still of a slogging nature heavy gun firing continues, a report from the 6th (French) army at 10.45 am says "Assevillers occupied aaa German batteries N.E Herbesourt destroyed". On our side we appear to be consolidating our positions, which we have lately acquired and arranging for fresh attacks. One of our kite balloons reports seeing low dust on two roads, behind the German lines, so that it is probable that the enemy are receiving reinforcements and severe counter attacks may be expected. Received a long letter in French from my sister Doris. Nothing of note to jot down today. I would like however to make a few remarks upon my surroundings, most of the houses in this village (Querrieu) which I may take I presume as a fair comparison to many other French villages, are nothing more nor less than mud huts, shapeless beams constitute the framework of the whole structure. Shoddy lathes are placed horizontally from three to four inches apart. Mud is then plastered into the intervening spaces and in that manner the walls are built. The French peasants are hard working, thrifty and self supporting community, they impress me however as being exceedingly dirty and unkempt. I have always entertained a great regard for the French people, but recently one unfortunate trait in the character of the French has revealed itself to me on numerous occasions. What is generally attributed the Jews, the British Tommy accuses the French and it is perfectly true, they are close, unobliging and ungenerous. To me however this is not so surprising, I came to the conclusion long ago that an Englishman was not liked by any foreigner, with the exception of the Italians and some Swiss it is my opinion that we English have not a friend in the world.

4/7/16

Dull morning. Received letters from my Aunt and Will, was much impressed by contents of letter from my Aunt, she wishes me to visit Carnoy near Albert to see the grave of Lt. Santler and tell her all concerning same. I wish sincerely that it were possible for me to go there, but the difficulties in the way are at present insurmountable. The distance from here is approaching 18 miles. It is necessary to obtain a pass to go from one place to another, also I am working greater portion of the day and am afraid it would be impossible for me to obtain the necessary time off. It is doubtful too if I could obtain the means of conveyance, I am very sorry that am at present unable to comply with my dear Aunt's request, as she is such a good friend to me and I feel that I can not properly repay her for all that she has done for me. I wrote however to the "G.R.C" "Graves Registration Commission", 2nd Echelon GHQ requesting that a photograph of Lt Santler's grave should be taken and forwarded to his wife Isabel. I gave them all necessary particulars. Very wet today. Violent bombardment commenced between 10 pm and 11 pm which continued uninterrupted throughout the night.

5/6/16

Dull and overcast. Nothing much occurred today. The 12th division however were reported pushed back into its own trenches. The French however appear to be doing well and I believe we are not far behind them, at any rate so far as captures go. There are several tremendous trench mortars lying in front of the chateau, which have been taken from the enemy, numerous batteries have also fallen to us. Each trophy is inscribed in paint with the name and particulars of the unit who have been the means of capturing same. One thing however which to me is very striking in so far as I personally understand the present situation, is that we have had a host of cavalry standing by since we commenced operations of an offensive nature but every day they have returned without incident, it is evident of course that they are here for a purpose, a particular purpose too, hence it would seem, since they have not been able to carry out any blow, that my previous calculations are fairly correct and that our offensive has been brought to a standstill and is held up for the present. Good news from the north of the Russian front came through this morning to the effect that they had captured 14,000 Germans. The 3rd division infantry passed through here late last night, with bagpipes, drum and bugle bands blowing their hardest. The men were all cheerful and it was a genuine treat to hear the familiar hurrahs of the British troops as they passed along.

6/7/16

Nice pleasant morning. Many more troops passed through in the early hours of the morning also during the afternoon. They were conveyed in motor buses, equipped for the purpose. Am feeling rather done up today, think it is mainly on account of lack of exercise. We are extremely busy in the office. Official reports of recent fighting are noticeable only by their absence. It looks very much as though the people in England have been deliberately hoaxed again for from the tone of the letters, which I have received it is quite believed in the old country that a great, complete and successful offensive is on foot.

7/7/16

Rather restless night. Sky overcast and threatening, heavy thunderstorms the order of the day. Received a couple of letters one from Mrs Roberts at Southport and the other from Miss Weeds. They were both very nice and cheerful reading. No news again this morning goodness only knows how the newspapers in England can justify their glowing headlines. They appear to have adopted without any reserve whatsoever exactly the same methods, which have made the German journals notorious. In my opinion this process is decidedly disastrous. It is moreover an obvious sign of weakness and is born of nervousness, which may become acute. It has a great share to in this race-suicide, which is now being enacted, to the disgust of the generations to come. Why in God's name should the government and the country's informants work to hard to gull the public. They know full well that things are not as they should be with us and that we are up against impossibilities, simply because we are ignorant of the rules which govern the certainty of victory and are not even acquainted with the chief elements, which constitute defeat. This war is being kept up mainly on hopes, not upon victories, and in this way may continue indefinitely. Wrote letter to my wife also to my aunt and enclosed some picture postcards.

8/7/16

Little brighter this morning. But nothing but mud everywhere. When it is fine however one is choked with dust. One of the cavalrymen at present in this vicinity was drowned in the lake at the bottom of our road a few days ago, through becoming entangled in the weeds and was buried with military honours. This morning's report of last night's fighting was unfortunately unfavourable to us, official report from 4th army headquarters is as follows "PEEL report situation unchanged aaa TROTT reports an attack was made by FANNY at 8 pm on QUADRANGLE SUPPORT TRENCH aaa The attack failed owing to enemy's barrage and rifle and machine gun fire aaa a bombing attack on the right was also unsuccessful aaa we hold CEMETERY in X.7.C aaa Enemy is holding QUADRANGLE TRENCH north of point X.22.b.6.7 no change in situation of HILDA aaa TRUMPER reports situation unchanged aaa addressed ADV GHQ and neighbouring armies and II corps". Enormous artillery still passes through here, a couple of these mighty weapons passed this afternoon on their way to the front, they were drawn by specially constructed steam engines on caterpillar wheels and make a big noise as they move slowly along. The official report this evening is much more cheering, which is as follows. "PEEL reports our troops now firmly established in southern portion of TRONES WOOD and occupying MALTZ HORN TRENCH as far as its junction with CHIMPANZEE TRENCH aaa about 130 prisoners captured in TRONES WOOD aaa strong German counter attack in mas on MALTA HORN TRENCH from east of TRONES WOOD stopped our barrage earlier in the day and suffered very heavy losses aaa TRUMPER reports AMY has occupied southern portion of CONTALMAISON aaa Our troops hold BAILIFF WOOD aaa addressed adv GHQ adv GHQ (1) and repeated neighbouring armies and 2nd corps, from 4th army 7.35 pm.

9/7/16

Official reports this morning of a favourable character. One report I saw stated that the Russian third arm had advanced to the stocked river and took 12,000 prisoners 300 officers and 45 guns. Very warm and close today. Nothing much to note day. It is rather amusing today being Sunday to see all the women folk of the village promenading up and down, especially the young girls, dressed out in their best clothes and gossiping at every opportunity. During the week all these women work very hard and when out of doors rarely if ever wear anything on their heads. These facts will probably account for the wizened appearance which becomes noticeable relatively early in the lives of the female portion of the peasant community, notice too that in almost every cottage and home, they possess a machine a coudre and apparently make their own clothes.

10/7/16

Nice pleasant morning. My duties however prevent me from enjoying same both in the morning and in the evening. In consequence I never feel exactly well. It is too much like the usual routine of office work, without any comfort and a marked lack of out door exercise, the same as I have been accustomed to until recently with the Yeomanry, also the food we get is of a very poor quality and little in quantity. I spend a good deal of my pay to obtain such things as eggs and milk. Had a long chat this evening with a person who is attached to the Indian cavalry and is a sort of an agent, who buys the provisions for the troops. He speaks English well and also French. He told me that his people were conquered by the Mohamedans about 1200 years ago and were driven from their native country Persia and settled in India. Their custom's or to be more correct their religion is rather reculiar but rigid. They are not permitted to marry out of their own sect, neither can an outsider be taken into their creed. The outstanding feature in their belief is purity in so far as it effects the health. They must not smoke because it is injurious. They must stop and wash themselves completely upon rising in the morning. It is compulsory to wear white linen next to the body and changed for clean immediately it becomes soiled. He told me that his sect was very rich as a whole and that they were called the Jews of India, he had not many nice things to say about our regular army in India and called them a lazy lot of fellows, neither did he speak well of the English middle classes he had met with and of course in this respect he is quite right, I have myself been positively disgusted with the behaviour of some of our amateur officers, who have obviously been born and bred in that most arrogant and ignorant section of the British social world.

11/7/16

Bright sunny morning. The war news this morning is on the whole very favourable and perhaps it will be interesting to note the official report which is as follows.
"PEEL reports ANGEL captured trench running from MALTZ HORN trench as far as S.50.a.5.4 and many Germans killed aaa advanced troops reported in TRONES WOOD where prisoners

have been captured and many dead Germans have been found aaa TROTT reports relief of FANNY by DAISY complete aaa we hold a stop just beyond junction of PEARL ALLEY and QUADRANGLE SUPPORT, but not clear who holds WOOD SUPPORT aaa a large howitzer and three guns captured aaa

Total number of unwounded prisoners captured by TROTT 13 officers 293 other ranks aaa HILDA holds within forty yards northern edge and eastern edge MAMETZ WOOD aaa TRUMPER reports AMY holding north edge of CANTALMAISON up to X.19.a.5.5. on the east aaa prisoners taken 5 officers including a battalion commander and 184 other ranks aaa SARAH pushed forward patrols in x.16.a and x.q.d aaa Enemy was encountered in open and after heavy fighting patrols had to fall back on our trenches aaa Enemy was counter attacked fifty yards from our trenches and driven back with loss aaa left brigade were heavily engaged by enemy aaa some prisoners taken aaa SARAH now holding trench line and situation is normal aaa". I received a letter from my wife this afternoon. Am still struggling but find it extremely hard as cannot get anyone to talk with me or assist me in any way owing to the fact that when I am at liberty everybody here are busy working. Two more captured German guns were brought this evening and added to the already large collection, which are ranged up in front of the chateau most of them have been captured by 18th division and a few by 17th division, several are quite old weapons and bear dates in 1870, some of the trench mortars are good specimens, but a couple although interesting are extremely cumbersome in appearance. They are about six feet long and large enough to hold a football. They are made of wood with a steel lining and rifling on the inside, on the outside they are bound closely round with steel wire, I cannot conceive how they were fired as there is no touch-hole observable. Wrote a letter to my Wife.

12/7/16

Dull threatening day. Saw no news of any importance except that apparently a large number of troop trains had been observed approaching the German lines, which may have in my opinion far reaching results on our particular front, however we shall see. Was paid this afternoon and received 20 francs. Weather fine but rather close. A number of prisoners mostly Saxon I believe have been brought here and are employed doing odd jobs about the grounds, which fact I am very glad to see as our negligence in this direction has been a positive disgrace on account of the shortage of labour, and we have certainly worked against our own interests in not usefully employing our prisoners.

13/7/16

Troop movements are still the order of the day and motor lorries pass and repass through our village unceasingly. Am still plodding doggedly with my French and hope despite all difficulties to break the back-bone of same before long, nearly every day am able to add about 15 fresh words to my vocabulary which is mounting up steadily, my object is to learn each word so that can read, write and pronounce correctly and without difficulty. There is very little news from the front lately, fighting seems to be for the moment more of a ding-dong character. I saw a long ammunition column pass through on its way to the trenches this afternoon, I believe however that many such have gone this way at different times, all the cavalry have gone up to the line including the Indian cavalry division. Received a parcel from my wife containing a box of cigarettes, one large cake and several small ones, box of cough-lozenges, packet of tobacco, and cigarette lighter. All very useful articles and much appreciated.

14/7/16

Very dull and close morning. It is interesting to note that that even in these times of revolutionary methods of warfare, we still retain some of the old conceptions. As for instance the use of pigeons as carriers. There is a loft of those birds at a place called Lavieville, which distributed them to the various divisions for communication purposes. It is reported this morning that we are in full possession of TRONES WOOD. Managed to obtain a postcard, which had been taken from one of the German prisoners here and which had been sent to him by another soldier. Rather an interesting souvenir. The news today is of a very favourable character. The India cavalry division has received orders to stand to and be prepared to move into action immediately. It is believed too by the general staff that the enemy is withdrawing his artillery and that no further reserves are coming up. One wireless report I saw stated that a large amount traffic had been seen moving east, also numerous parties of men. It would appear from this that the Germans are endeavouring to carry out an orderly retreat, probably to fresh line in the rear. Preparations are on foot for making big attack with several divisions conjointly tomorrow.

15/7/16

Beautifully bright and warm morning. Our artillery has been pumping away throughout the night and is still very much awake. Between 9,000 and 10,000 prisoners have been taken by us. I remember now that it was reported, that the enemy were giving themselves up freely yesterday. The batch of prisoners, which are kept here and employed about the grounds were taken this morning to the bath-house, some of them I noticed were quite young lads. Wrote another letter in French to my sister Doris and posted same. Received a letter also from my wife. I hear that our divisions which attacked today all failed. This is in my opinion very unfortunate as I looked for great eventualities from these particular operations. On Friday an address was issued to the troops by the G.O.C among other things it stated that the battle was now more than half won, at the time I said it was a deliberate falsehood and wondered how many more addresses of this nature were to be fostered upon the troops. I remember that prior to the battle on 21st Aug. at Gallipoli, we were told officially that we were about to see and take part in the greatest battle of the war. This great victory however never materialised and resulted in a crowning defeat from which we never recovered and in all probability never shall.

16/7/16

Several Taubes came over here last night between 11 pm and midnight apparently making for Amiens. They were flying quite low and could easily be distinguished, our anti-aircraft guns opened fire, and a couple returned almost immediately. I was struck however by the fact of the absence of searchlights, which would have made the hostile aircraft easy targets. I see by a report from the 15th corps that the divisions, which went into action yesterday, retired at dawn this morning as per orders bringing with them all their wounded. The same corps also report that we have suffered many casualties through gas. It appears that the enemy are using a shell, which however does not explode, but the base is blown out, which frees the gas contained in the shell.

Have ascertained that one of our cavalry regiments the Black Horse did advance the day before yesterday with the object of gaining possession of a wood, which was achieved with the loss of about 100 casualties. Received a letter from my wife also wrote one to her in return. Turned out very wet in the evening.

17/7/16

Dull close morning. Saw no news of any importance, but from accounts we are still slogging away and doing on the whole satisfactorily that is so far as the general staff are pleased to consider, but certainly not in my own personal estimation. Had a walk out to the village about half a mile way this afternoon called "Pont-Noyelle". It is very similar to Querrieu but I liked it much better. There are several objects of interest there too, which I went to visit. The first "L'Gosuaire" I found in a secluded spot on the left hand side of the road and surrounded by trees. It is the burial place of some of the soldiers of France who fell in 1870. Here I met two more of our signal office telegraphists and together we proceeded a little further along the road and ascended rather a stiff rise to where the "Monument commemoratif 1870" is constructed. It is a circular column and is composed of stone and bears such inscriptions as "in memory of the men who died in defence of their country". It was erected by public subscriptions. From this point a splendid view of the surrounding country is obtained, and the spire of the cathedral at Amiens can be distinctly discerned. I noticed bodies of troops drilling on foot down in the plain and from their formation I should say they were cavalry. Close beside the monument I noticed also a dug-out with a sand-bag shelter and the terminus of a telephone wire, which was probably the observation post of an anti aircraft station. Rain fell heavily during the evening. Our artillery is slashing away too. Saw a long column of good British guns this afternoon as they passed through here on their way to the front.

18/7/16

Our guns have been firing all night, it has been raining too very hard, and is still so.
It is very miserable here when the weather is so bad. Have been posted to no 2 relief commencing today and go on duty at 1 pm until 5.30 pm. This morning visited the Eglise at "Pont Noyelle", which is situated a little way from the road on the left. I noticed that the stonework has be liberally inscribed with the names and places of birth of soldiers who had been there, much to the mortification of the parishioners no doubt, as this pernicious habit is unpardonable and most offensive. I was glad to see that a notice had been placed on the monument, which I visited yesterday to the effect that mutilations of this sort would be severely dealt with, which is perfectly right. Had a walk round the lake, which is situated in the grounds of the chateau and it is to say the least a very beautiful spot. No official news of much importance except that the ding-dong fighting continues still. Our guns have been grinding and belching all day long and I suppose they will continue to do so throughout the night. Hope that these hammer blows are being well directed, otherwise all the might and strength of old England will be of no avail.

19/7/16

Our guns still bellowing at an enormous rate and am afraid too that the Germans are giving us an unwelcome reply. Last night after an intense bombardment the enemy succeeded in ejecting us from two points. This afternoon walked to Corbie which is about 4 miles away, we were fortunate in getting a lift for about 1 mile, which was a good thing as the day was hot and close. Arriving at Corbie we met a Scottish regiment marching through headed by a band of bag-pipes. My friend and I stayed at the corner by the church and watched the sturdy sons of Scotland march by. There were a number of A.S.E men collected at the same place and standing by their lorries watching the procession. I mention this as a remark by a Scottie to a member of the A.S.E is I think worthy of note. It was evident that the infantrymen were pretty well exhausted by their march and prompted the following remark "How would you like to be a soldier eh" to which no reply was forthcoming and the men of the A.S.E. felt their position rather acutely I'm afraid for the moment. We next visited L'eglise, which has not however much to boast of either exteriorly or interiorly. The main entrance is rather confucious by its immense height. Inside, the chief object of interest besides the paintings, was a large slab of a sort of slate composition on which were embossed what appeared to be the figures of a priest and nun. The latter wore a veil, which reached almost down to the mouth. The whole had however suffered mulilation and in consequence was difficult to distinguish the meaning or object of the figures. On a pillar in the body of the church, was hung a small box with glass front in which was exhibited a small cross encased in metal, at the foot of the box were the words "Vraie croix" (Truc Cross). In the chapel dedicated to Saint Colette, which is situated on the right-hand of the church, is a wax vase figure representing the above saint enclosed in a case on the wall and placed in position all round the aforesaid image, are a number of small slabs bearing such inscriptions as "Resonnaissance a saint Colette" and " J' ai invoque Saint Colette elle 1 a obtenn justice 9 mars 1867" and another reads "Dieu soit lone nous avons invoque Saint Colette an moment de danger elle nous a sauves 13 juillet 1887 D. D." I was well pleased with my visit there, after leaving the church saw two more English regiments march passed headed by brass bands. Bought a number of picture postcards, also was successful in obtaining a new glass for my wrist watch. Had some tea and a slice of bread and butter at a tea-room, and also a row with the good lady who wished to charge us 3d for a small cup of tea and the same price for cakes, which in my opinion was excessive, however we paid. On our return home, managed to get a lift for about a mile in a motor car which was tres bon. Got back about 6 pm and went to a cafe and had a couple of eggs fried. Went on duty at 9 pm.

20/7/16

Worked hard during the night and absolutely fagged out. Very heavy shelling went on all through the night and even shook our hut considerably. Damp and foggy morning. Felt very tired when I left off duty at 8.30 am. Lay down about 9.30 am at the billet and slept until about 1.30. Had no dinner. Received a letter from my wife and sister Doris. On duty again at 5.30 pm until 9 pm.

21/7/16

Lovely sunny morning, which potions great heat. On duty at 1 pm until 5.30 pm and brought on again at 7.30 pm until 9 pm. Not much official news except that we were pushed out of some trenches during the night. Read a letter from my aunt.

22/7/16

Foggy damp morning, but very close. No war news of any importance recently, except the usual shelling and trench warfare. This afternoon I set out alone to walk to a neighbouring village called Daours about 3½ miles from here. I started at 2 pm and reaching Pont Noyelle turned sharply to the right and walking a short distance turned again sharply to the right, at this point I noticed a clump of trees and completely hidden from view, amid the thick foliage was a crucifix erected upon an iron framework. Where ever one goes in this part of the country, one is struck by the long lines of motor lorries, some a mile or more in length, which line the roads, apparently standing idle. They are there for a purpose no doubt however. The countryside is now quite a picture. There is not an inch of soil wasted. The corn is rapidly ripening and yesterday I saw some being cut down. Every field of golden corn is ablaze with myriads of vivid red poppies, and the patches of outs proudly vaunt a bouquet of pale yellow flowers, what happens to the poppies when the wheat is cut puzzles me. I should imagine that they would not exactly add to the better flavour or nourishment of the flour. I trudged along sampling each crop en route, but could get no "lift" and was pretty footsore upon arrival at my destination. Daours is certainly the best village I have so far visited. It is well kept and the houses are good. Had a look inside the church but I saw nothing unusual or grand worthy of note, although perhaps I should say that the usual adornments and elaborations peculiar to the Catholic faith were of course the prevalent feature. I bought a series of 7 picture postcards at a cafe, but could not obtain a drink owing to the rigid restrictions, which are in force everywhere. Cafe's are only open to the soldiers from 12 pm until 2 pm and 6 pm until 8 pm. I started back on my return journey at about 3.30 pm, a little way out of Daours on the left of the road and adjoining the French civil cemetery is an English burial ground for fallen soldiers, who have apparently succumbed to their injuries whilst in the hospital at this place. They are buried in deep trenches and a small wooden cross with the name and regiment etc, embossed on narrow strips of tin nailed to the cross, this is all that marks the resting place of Britains gallant defenders. The crosses are placed close together in rows of 36 and there were five rows completed. Continuing my journey I walked for about 15 minutes when happily a lorry came along and I jumped into it and was carried the greater part of the way back. After tea, went to a little shop and stayed playing with the children and throwing my French at anyone who would listen. Went on duty at 9 pm.

23/7/16

Left duty at 8.30 am and felt fagged out. Official reports over night were of a disastrous character as we were repulsed at every point of attack, it is too painful however to comment upon. Until we fight the enemy in exactly the same way as he has done his best to teach us for the last couple of years, we cannot hope to obtain a decisive victory. Our worst enemies by far are to be found at home and in neutral countries, yet we permit such tyrants to dwell among us and even pamper foreign neutrals instead of fighting them, as Germans if in our place would have undoubtedly done at the very commencement. Lay down until 3 pm and had no dinner. Went down to the lake and had a good swill down. Went on duty at 5.30 pm where rather an unpleasant surprise was awaiting me. The signal master informed me that the last three batches of picture postcards which I had posted for England had not gone on as the names of the places had not been crossed out. He also mentioned that 2 of my letters had also been detained. I suppose on account of a few strong remarks, such as "Don't believe official reports" etc, which I remember having written, the censor thought he smelt a spy. It is amusing I must admit. They would however be doing far more good for their country if they exhibited more energy in routing out the real traitors, which may be found in high places both in the army and in the government. Off duty at 9 pm and went to an Epicier at Pont-Noyelle and had a couple of eggs fried and cafe for supper.

24/7/16

Dull morning. Heavy bombardment continued last night. The cavalry to Bivoua I heard also last night. Spent the evening in cafes at Pont-Noyelle.

25/7/16

Extremely heavy shelling last night. There was also a terrific explosion between 1pm and midnight somewhere on our front, but cannot ascertain the cause. Very dull morning, looks like rain threatening. Official reports of last night bear evidence of fierce struggles but can glean no outstanding success out of the whole sordid business. Am still struggling hard with my French, but I must add that I have not been able for some time to progress at the rate of more than perhaps five or six additional words daily, still it is satisfactory and what is more to the point it is sure. The German prisoners, which we have here are given plenty of work to do such as road mending and sweeping up refuse etc. They may also be seen daily in the meadow at the bottom of our garden, some lounging and other stripped diligently runting through their shirts, on duty at S.O at 9 pm.

Diary Number 2

26/7/16

Dull morning, left off duty at 8.30. Paraded again at 10.30 for pay and received 30 francs. Lay down from 11 am until 3 pm. Official reports this morning are by no means favourable. We were repulsed at one point during the night. Enemy heavily shelled some of our positions and blew up a brigade dump, no change reported by our other units. Was fortunately successful in obtaining a pass, which I applied for yesterday, for permission to visit Amiens tomorrow, Thursday. Passes have been stopped for some time, so consider myself very lucky as I am extremely anxious to make as much use of my stay in France as possible. Went to Pont-Noyelle after duty at 9 pm and had supper.

27/7/16

I made good use of my pass this morning, was up at 5 am dressed, shaved, washed and cleaned by boots by 6 am, when I sallied forth to meet a cart, which was coming through Uuerrier from Pont-Noyelle on its way to Amiens with milk. I sat at the back between a woman and a girl, while the latters two brothers sat in the front, driving. We reached the first barrier midway between here and Amiens in about half an hour and had to produce our passes for the guard to inspect, after passing the second barrier, just outside the place of our destination. We stopped for a short while at a café and had coffee and rum and biscuits all round, which, as there is a war on up here was rather expensive for me. Riding on a little further, I proceeded together with one of the aforesaid brothers to walk the remaining part of the journey. The first thing that struck me as we entered this town of ancient history, was the breadth of the roads, which was as is usual in France, sheltered by avenues of pleasant trees. The trams were running along the main centre road and on each side were also roads for other traffic, between these and the buildings was a spacious footpath. My friend left me by the cathedral and I immediately entered and walked slowly round. To say the least that is possible of one's first impression of this beautiful piece of man's handiwork also of one's final impressions may be summed up in the one word "magnificent". Unfortunately however at the present time it is necessary to protect the base of the structure on the outside by sandbags, which for some 12 feet or so were being covered with a black fluid, when I visited this noble edifice of France. Likewise all the exquisite wood-carving in the interior is barricaded with thousands of sand-bags. I had a peep at these things all the same and was struck by the exquisite workmanship displayed. There are numerous chapels situated all-round the cathedral as is the custom in the Catholic Church, for the most part there was nothing unusually interesting in connection with this, except that some large and beautiful paintings were exhibited. One altar which is placed in the centre, was of huge dimensions and constructed in a most elaborate manner. The background represented rolling clouds and the beams of the sun came up from behind, probably signifying fire also, intermingled with these objects of heavenly significance were the figures of angels and infants. The pulpit is also erected upon the same principle. Whatever may be said however on behalf of the interior it certainly is no match against the superb beauties evinced by the exterior. As one stands in the place opposite to the main entrance, one marvels at the patience and perseverance of man in creating so successfully, such a masterpiece of art. One thing which I should like to mention and which divides me very strongly in opposition against the obvious artificial embellishments which in places crowd out the things of real beauty. Certainly the object I wish to mention was not of great importance, but quite sufficient from my point of view. Close by where a sand-bag barricade had been erected was a sort of tomb, which had most probably served the purpose of an alter where the bags now stood, it was made of wood and broken in places. The outside being painted gaudily in many colours like an ordinary piece of furniture. I felt quite disgusted that it should be allowed to remain there, it was totally unworthy of the place and certainly most uncomplimentary to all that which was real and made of hard stone by the genius of super men. Afterwards walked into the town and stopped at a shop to buy picture postcards, where I also obtained some breakfast. Walked about until about 11.30 am, when I directed my steps homewards, was stopped once in the town by a "M.P" who wished to see my pass. I saw very few English soldiers but there were a great many French soldiers walking about. Amiens is a lovely town, very big, good buildings, and it is thoroughly French. I walked for about a mile and a half on the way home when was fortunate in getting a lift on a motor-lorry, which was going to Heilly, and got back just in time for work at 1 pm. Spent the evening in an epicier in Pont-Noyelle, talking French and drinking vin-blanc.

28/7/16

Sunny warm morning. On duty 8.30 am until 1 pm. Spent afternoon worrying different people with my efforts to learn French. It has been extremely hot all day and at 9 pm when I resumed duty again was feeling very fagged out. Perhaps it would do more good to have more rest, but I am so anxious to make the utmost use of my spare time, then I really dare not indulge in a moment's leisure which would seem to me to be a sad waste of time. I noticed that the sky to the East was continually lit up the reflections from our guns, and heavy fire continued uninterruptedly. We do not appear however to be making much progress.

29/7/16

Dull morning. I feel quite done in after the nights work. Bully-beef for breakfast this morning. The food we get here is simply abominable and infact makes one ill. Had a wash and a shave when I returned to the billet and afterwards lay down until 2 pm. It is frightfully hot and extremely trying weather. Received a letter from Miss Weeds and also one from Bill, the letter is anxious not hearing from me for some time. The fact is two at least of my letters were held back for some time, on account of some strong remarks which I had written. I know that my country is being sold by traitors and amateurs and this fact hurts me sorely. The official report this morning, which I saw was most unsatisfactory. The fighting is terrific from all accounts and I'm afraid we are getting badly whipped. On duty 5.30 pm until 9 pm, afterwards had supper at Pont-Noyelle.

30/7/16

Bright sunny morning and portends another day of great heat. A terrific cannonade is going on up at the front. Received a letter from Miss Dorothy Roberts, also wrote one to Miss Weeds, and my sister Gladys, sent Doris a souvenir card worked in silk represent the crest of the Royal Engineers, also a couple of engineers buttons. In the evening sent off a reply to Dorothy's letter. Spent the evening after leaving duty at 5.30 pm at an epicier at Pont-Noyelle, talking French and eating currents and other fruit out of the garden, which one of the little girls had gathered for me. The air line section which came soon after we did and took up their quarters in our billet left again this morning. I was fortunate in securing one of the beds, which had been left behind, it is made on the same principle as a stretcher with wooden sides and legs and wire netting placed over to form the bed. It is rather "cutting" however at present as it requires a little packing of paper etc. Still it is a vast improvement on the straw, which hitherto has served me for a couch.

31/7/16

Another stifling hot day. It simply gets hotter each day. On duty 8.30 am until 1 pm also on fatigues at 2 pm together with three others. Our work was to load a lorry with heavy logs of wood, and afterwards to distribute same to a number of places for cooking purposes. It was extremely hard work and was heartily thankful when our task was completed. Had a bath in the stream, which runs by the bottom of our billets garden, directly afterwards which was most refreshing. After tea spent the evening at my usual place at Pont-Noyelle, where I had a supper of fried eggs etc. Received a parcel from my wife, which contained lots of useful and welcome gifts including, box of cigarettes, box of Crompton hospital lozenges, packet of Three Nuns tobacco, copying pencil with holder, large cake, tube of lemonade tablets, my old Cavalry haversack and belt of Egyptian and Gallipoli memory. Good mascots both of them. Went on duty at 9 pm, but at 12.30 am was told to take up a split duty, so left work and returned to billet.

1/8/16

On duty at 10 am. Have had my hair cropped very short on account of the heat, which is still most depressing. Now that our offensive which commenced on the 1st July is exactly a month old. It would be interesting perhaps to make a few observations upon the work achieved, the objects gained and our present position. On the 2nd July it was even then plain enough to me that things were not going so successfully as they should and it became more and more evident, first that the work in hand, was more than we could cope with, which situation was brought about in great measure I believe by a very skilful reorganisation of the German line, which was quickly strengthened and well backed up by their artillery. The objects achieved are in my opinion decidedly nil, granted that it was never anticipated that we should attempt a general advance, still at the same time I believe that if our object was to draw a large enemy army to this front, that it has failed ignominiously. The Germans are undoubtedly great masters in the art of war, but did they not attempt exactly the same methods in the battle for Verdun, with apparently a similar object in view. They presumed no doubt that to attack France at her strongest point, which was of course at once her weakest too from a tactile point of view, by an overwhelming superiority of artillery would induce the French to gather together large forces of troops into a small area, whereby they may be reasonably expected to be able to inflict large and serious losses to our allies, and at the same time break the back-bone of any determined offensive by them elsewhere. Perhaps to a certain extent Germany succeeded in this new departure in war, as there seems to be little doubt that our comrades suffered very heavily. One very important factor however the Germans appeared to have entirely overlooked. The battle of Verdun was not to be fought between artillery on the one side and by men only on the other side. The French were also able to bring to bear a similar weight of metal, thereby neutralising the position. to imagine that because we have accumulated massive guns etc. in great numbers is going to carry us through is a terrible and unpardonable miscalculation for as I have pointed out the situation merely becomes neutralised. To sum up I maintain that our position up to the present stands at "work done", fairly good, "objects attained" practically nil, "present situation" neutral. I am moreover quite unable to understand why an offensive on this front was ever attempted. I am quite sure the Germans are confident that they can hold their lines and that they have also completed adequate arrangements to meet all eventualities. Personally I am inclined to consider their point of view as being the correct one. I am moreover strongly in favour of evacuating France altogether, that is to say merely hold strong points, and to strike hard and suddenly elsewhere, where I could mention, and where they are least prepared to defend themselves. I am conscious however that my country is being sold. It is being quickly devoured not by open enemies, but by the wretched traitors within our gates and by the host of hopeless amateurs whom they employ. I am still persevering with my French. It is however a hard enough nut to crack. There are so many difficulties to surmount not the least of which is the provincial dialect or as it is called "Patois". In our province of Picardy this "Patois" is noticeably very strong. On duty 7 pm until 11 pm. I heard that a certain woman at Pont-Noyelle has been caught by the French and English military police serving the troops with whisky, Benadicitine and other strong drinks. This practice is forbidden and defaulters are very severely dealt with, and made to pay a fine of anything up to 1000 Francs.

2/8/16

Still exceedingly hot. Spent the day in the usual manner. Half work, and half study, often when I should be resting and in fact while others are sleeping, am worrying people round the village and hoping to pick up one or two new words and think I am fairly successful on the whole.

3/8/16

Terrific bombardment broke out late last night and continued well into the morning. Received a parcel containing a cake from my Aunt Ada, also a letter from my wife. No official news of importance received for some time.

4/8/16

Another terrific bombardment throughout the night. But can hear of nothing done or of any unusual happenings. The sky was illuminated by the explosions as in fact is always is when the guns are at work, if only each shell accounted for one German it would be a happy shot for us. The enemy however appears to stand it all very well and give us back much that we give them. Today is the 2nd anniversary of Britains declaration of war against our hated foe, Germany. I recollect how glad we were that the great opportunity had arrived at last and also how hopeful we all were. Fancy two long years, which seem however but a few months since, have now elapsed since the commencement of hostilities. How many things have come and gone during that time, how many things have alas occurred. Looking back into the abyss of time one sees that it is filled to overflowing with uncountable failures, disappointments, which have been and will be means for creating bitter anguish. The earth and the seas are choked with our dead and the very air is corrupt with rank pollution. The minds of men have lost their balance and seek only to satisfy their insanity. The very foundations of society are being shaken and uprooted and the edifice of civilisation is rapidly being overthrown and crumbling into the dust, corruption and remorse have both found entrance across the threshold of every home in the land and have established their abode therein, all that was good, and true and noble has been taken refuge in death and the evil which is in the world, is now for the time paramount and predominant and stalks about the earth in monster shape from door to door, quite unashamed and unabashed. My own England is painfully groaning under the weight of incompetency and treachery. My poor country, which has no knowledge of war, of its precepts, or of its obligations and sacrifices, is now learning a terrible lesson. The price she is paying is the price of folly. Even now she is unfortunately content to submit to the punishment, which is necessarily entailed on account of the ignorance displayed of all the traditions of war by our leaders. Its usage, its requirements, and its necessities are all conspicuous by their absence. My poor proud England with all its power and mighty strength, its noble virtues and aspirations is nevertheless bleeding profusely even to death. Those who imagine that this war will not last much longer are fools to say the least. It is plainly obvious that in the end the battle will be a draw. The military situation at the present time speaks volubly in that direction. Even afterwards however there will be many fresh battles to be fought, new obstacles to be overcome and the blackest of outlooks in store for many thousands, nay millions to face. Perhaps I might be blamed for taking up so pessimistic an attitude but I note these things merely as facts as I see them myself. I have repeatedly noticed that many of our greatest blunders have been enacted by and originated in that most powerful enemy to success, which is called "options". It has proved a very good ally indeed to the Germans, who together with our own Government have, on many occasions, made prodigious efforts to foster in our minds a vain belief in ourselves and so to weaken the strength and number of our blows. Cannonading recommenced early this evening with great violence of course, the guns are never quiet, but at given times it rises to a great pitch and rolls continuously like mighty thunder. Felt rather sick when I finished work at 11 pm this evening.

5/8/16

Much cooler this morning with an overcast sky. Received a letter from my wife, and later replied to same. German guns still being brought here, and it is rather a unique spectacle to witness our prisoners diligently cleaning them. I wonder what occupies their thoughts while thus engaged. Perhaps however like ourselves they are too fed up with the whole business to allow themselves to dwell upon such matters. Can hear of no news again today. The artillery duels however continuing without abatement each evening reaches to a high pitch of intensity.

6/8/16

Bright sunny morning with clear sky. Since I came here I have been repeatedly struck by the apparent splendid organisation of our air-service and untiring energy. One hears the buzz of the engines from early morning until late at night and from what I have been able to gather our airmen have established a complete ascendancy over our enemies. They make a pretty picture too as they pass to and fro at high altitude upon their special work, nothing of note to mention today.

7/8/16

Dull and much cooler this morning. Received a reply from the "Director of Graves Registration and Enquiries", to the effect that the photographs of the graves of 2nd LT Santer will be taken if possible and a copy sent to Mrs. Santer. I am personally very pleased for such a favourable answer and trust that same will reach Isobel safely. My "great push" in French is still progressing slowly, am hammering away perpetually, but this language business has certainly strong defensive positions indeed, which require time and patience to surmount. My system may be rather amusing but it is the only one that I find to be practicable, as soon as I leave work and have had a wash etc., I make my way first to one house then another. Preferably however I sound one or two "Estaminets" in my search for gold. If I find a place where they are not to much occupied with their work, I take a seat and with a dictionary in one hand and my note book in the other, commence to take down notes of all words which I find I need for conversational purposes. Will afterwards get the words pronounced and endeavour to retain same in my memory. No doubt I am a big nuisance, but still I look at it this way, that I shall be decidedly the gainer "apres la guerre", and I owe nothing to anyone. Saw a report, which contained good news concerning our forces in Egypt. It appears that the 5th inst. a body of Turks about 14,000 strong attacked our troops on the flank, which was composed of mounted units. These withdrew upon the first attack by the enemy, who however became disorganised among the sand-dunes and being counter attacked were compelled to retreat leaving more than 2,000 prisoners in our hands. The report speaks well of our mounted troops, which were engaged, but only mentions the Australian and New Zealand contingents. Personally it would be interesting to know whether any English Yeomanry regiments took part including my old regiment. Received a letter from my Aunt Ada.

8/8/16

Pleasant sunny morning. Day passed without much incident worth recording. Heard however that eight Zeppelins were reported on their way to London.

9/8/16

Hot sunny morning. Received a letter from the daughter of my former landlady at Newport Pagnall. Very hot all day, apparently the spell of cyclonic weather with which we have been treated with for the past week or so is very loathed to leave us.

10/8/16

Raining and very dull this morning. Received a packet containing a letter and a couple of packets of cigarettes from Mr. Kendrick. The King visited the chateau here at midday today, created quite a stir for a time, there were numerous French officers present who were gathered around the front entrance. Sent letters to Mr. Kendrick and Miss Hedge.

11/8/16

Dull and very misty this morning but close. Received a letter from my wife. There seems to have been a lull in the fighting lately, but last night we captured a trench, and killed 20 Germans, a counter attack by the enemy was beaten off with heavy losses to the attackers, which was principally incurred by Lewis machine guns. Felt a bit off colour in the evening, but think it was due to the weather, which is very oppressive.

12/8/16

Thick fog veiled all things within its damp folds this morning. Reminded one of the rapidly approaching autumn, after breakfast however the sun shone through and quickly dispersed the unwelcome visitor and in its place our old friend "heat" has once more taken up his abode and reigns supreme. Mr. Lloyd George visited our headquarters during the evening, but I did not see him. Was allowed to go off duty at 10.40 pm instead of at 11 pm, owing to work being slack.

13/8/16

Dull and close this morning. Woke up with a slight sore throat. Very little news again today. We are apparently marking time again, and as the official report will have it so often, we are probably consolidating our positions, whatever on earth that may mean, still such is frequently the case, just as though it was an everyday occurrence and had come to stay.

14/8/16

Slight rain this morning, but still oppressively hot. Changed to another billet near the orderly room, which is a change certainly not for the better. Our bedrooms consist of tiers of platforms, which are reached by climbing a ladder. Between each floor there is not enough room to kneel and one feels stifled in them. The name of our billet, which is painted up in large black letters is most appropriate. It is called "Ot as ell". Start again today on no. 2 relief and commence duty at 11 am and finished at 5.30 pm which is "tres bon", spent the evening at Pony-Noyelle talking in French with different people. Rained heavily just as we left duty at 5.30 pm.

15/8/16

Cloudy and dull this morning. On duty at 8.30 am. Did not have a very comfortable rest last night. Everything is extremely awkward where we are and there is little or no conveniences at hand. It is necessary to draw our water from a well, which is some distance down the road, which of course takes time. We are also further away from our work, and also from the mill where we have our meals. Off duty 1 pm. Spent afternoon at Pont-Noyelle. On duty again at 5.30 until 1 am. Long tedious day.

16/8/16

Was awarded 3 day CB this morning by the Captain for being absent from billet from 9 pm to 9.35 pm on Monday evening. This was the first occasion on which a roll had been called since I arrived in France and of course I must be the one to drop unlucky. Ah well it's all in a life-time and I entertain no interest in my present station in the Army whatever. Think in fact this has something to do with the case in question as have abundantly earned the enmity of most of the engineers because I have at different times given them to understand a few home truths, which they do not relish in the least. Still it does them good occasionally for they are for the most part lamentably a poor type of soldier and very well paid for it too. They can all tell big tales of the great battles accompanied by a few interesting details, they have not of course ever heard, much less seen a gun fired and have certainly no idea of trench life, still perhaps they like to amuse themselves in imaginary contemplation's, although I have a very shrewd idea that principally their thoughts do not wander very far from the hoard of gold which they are piling up at home. Received a letter in French from my sister Doris. Worked hard all the afternoon with spade and pickaxe. On duty again at 5.30 pm until 9 pm. Had a row with the Sergeant because he would not allow me to get some milk and other nourishment and demanded to see the Captain tomorrow, which was agreed to. I have been through some hard times it is true but under the circumstances our treatment here is most atrocious. Have heard a good deal about German atrocities, but certainly in some respect the British are quite as bad and unintelligible, for weeks together we have not had a second vegetable, often none at all. Rice or pudding of any sort have only had at most on three occasions. We only have seating for 32 men where as a rule there are about 70 men to be fed, and in consequence we are more often than not obliged to partake of our food standing. Our blankets were taken from us when the weather was bitterly cold and I suffered in consequence for some time afterwards. We are crowded into old barns and sleep on the floor, there are 3 tiers with about 4 feet between each floor, and into this small compress 37 men who occupy our billet have their compartments. There is no drinking water obtainable and no effort has been made to procure any for the troops. I might add that for breakfast we rarely get more than a piece of bacon about 3 inches in length and about an inch wide. Our diet too, frequently takes the form of bully-beef and biscuits, now there is absolutely no reason for the greater part of all this. When the conditions are exceptional the case is of course altered materially. Hard times are only natural under war conditions and when they occur are always faced with equanimity by the troops at the front, both officers and men know full well what to expect and appreciate the fact as part of a soldier's life and no complaints are ever heard. But that they should exist here is inexcusable, that the men should be deliberately forbidden to buy things for themselves to fill up the big gap in the army rationing is a crime against justice, common sense, and decency and is contrary to the common understanding of soldiering, which is primarily and essentially a case of "give and take", otherwise efficiency and discipline become dangerously undermined quite unnecessarily.

17/8/16

Warm sunny morning. Our relief were given 1½ hours hard drill from 9.30 until 11 am in a neighbouring field, afterwards I had a good swill down at the lake. On duty at 1 pm to 5.30 pm. Received letters from my wife, Mrs. Roberts and Dorothy Roberts, also in the evening two parcels arrived, one from my sister Gladys containing two towels, three handkerchiefs, and a pencil. The other from my wife contained a nice cake, two small jars of jam, packet of tobacco, box of fifty Players cigarettes, a stick of shaving soap. All very nice presents and most welcome.

18/8/16

Dull and threatening this morning. On duty at 8.30 am until 1 pm. Received packet containing letter and a pair of socks both being most welcome. On duty again at 9 pm until 8.30 am tomorrow morning. This is the third and last day of my confinement to barracks and I am heartily glad too. I have thereby lost three good days, which I could have put too much better purpose. Three whole days is a great deal in one's life especially when one considers how short is a year of time. However I will make up for lost time somehow.

19/8/16

Rained very heavily from early morning until about 10 am. After leaving off duty at 8.30 am had shave and wash and then lay down until 12.30 pm. I could not sleep however and after dinner directed my steps to visit some of my old friends at Pont-Noyelle. They had missed me it seems and thought that perhaps I had been ill. I spent a very useful afternoon in conversation. On duty again at 5.30 pm until 9 pm, did not sleep very well probably I think on account of a cold, which has again attacked me.

20/8/16

Attended church parade this morning, which was held in front of the chateau from 9.30 am until shortly after 10 am. The weather is fine but rain threatening. War news lately is of a severe type, nothing much accomplished, but a great deal of sacrifices entailed. Received a nice letter from my aunt.

21/8/16

Day opened with a row with the Lance Corporal cook for which I had to parade at orderly room at 9.30 am, together with three witnesses. The case went against me of course, but was remanded until tomorrow to give me time to decide whether I wish to have a court martial or accept the reward of the Captain. Am confined today in the guard-room but shall agree to accept immediate punishment to get the business over and done with. I hear that the Lance Corporal in question has been removed from his job for which I am glad for the sake of the other fellows who have suffered long at his hand and will I know be heartily glad, now that he is out of the way. Today is the anniversary of our participation in the last big fight at Gallipoli, an unfortunate day for me apparently. It is too dark to write more. If things continue as dark too as they have done, life will not be worth living at all.

22/8/16

I was awarded 7 days field punishment No. 1 this morning. I am not going to make any references as to my opinion on the matter or my feeling either. In such cases it is better to take things philosophically. I knew before I had joined this branch of service that I could not do much worse, and since I have regretted it every day. However my work is now on roads, with pick and shovel. We work from 7.30 am until noon, when we break off for dinner, back on the road at 4 pm, an hour for tea and resume work again at 5 pm, which today consisted of digging out a big hole for the purpose of burying empty cans and tines, finished the days work at 7.30 pm and was quite done up. It is very hard and dusty work and my hands are extremely sore and all my limbs ache excessively. I have a beastly cold too, which is not improved by the hovel in which we are detained. The space provided is about 6 yards by 4 yards to accommodate eight men, we sleep on the ground, which consists purely of mother earth and composed of lime or chalk. I shall be glad when my time is finished to get away from this alone. The surroundings are certainly not healthy and it is very cold sleeping on the floor without a blanket.

23/8/16

Worked on the road repairing holes in the morning and afternoon, the weather is fortunately good and not too hot. Perhaps the outdoor life will do me good for I am not well by any means. It is a hard life however and it is quite evident that I was never cut out navvying, from 5 pm to 7.30 pm worked on the hole as on the previous day. Was tired out when the time came for knocking off, in fact I was long before. Had a good shave and wash up however on returning to our billet. One of the fellows finished this evening at 4 pm which leaves seven, of whom two are quite old men, one young fellow is the town commandant's chauffeur, another is from the airline section and one has been wounded twice and is a regular.

24/8/16

Did not sleep very well on account of the cold. Usual work on the roads, in the morning and afternoon. My limbs simply ache all over, but think it has done me some good as far as my health is concerned at least. This morning was working alongside a squad of German prisoners. I suppose I am now for the present a comrade of theirs. I do not mind that so much either as it is better than working alongside ones professed enemies, who are of a deceitful character and whom one is glad to get away from too. Finished for the day at 7.30 pm and right glad for the opportunity to lay down and rest. I heard one of my present companions' say that he had been a Sergeant in his battalion and had come down through drink, he is a docker in private life and a strong trade unionist. He is non the less a good soldier for all that, but like many more met certain individuals in the army who very quickly kill ones ardour for soldiering.

25/8/16

Weather still maintains its pleasant attitude. This marks my fourth day of durance, so am more than half way through thank goodness. We content ourselves with consolationery remarks such as "roll on", sometimes "Roll on Blighty", and "Roll on that big ship". What I am looking forward to for the moment however, more than anything else is a bathe and a change of linen and a decent meal. We start out each morning, noon and night, each man carrying a spade and pick; one man also carries a broom and another the water-can for watering our work, it also comes in handy for a drink when we are thirsty, which is pretty often. One man wheels the barrow, in which he carries a couple of heavy rammers and feeds us with stones from a heap at wherever we may be working. I am becoming quite a good hand in road mending and can finish off a repair quite neatly now, although at first I think the poor road must have absolutely groaned at being so badly disfigured. We experienced several showers in the afternoon and evening but had to continue working all the same. Had a shave and a good wash after finishing at 7.30 pm.

26/8/16

Rather cold when starting the days travail, and showers during the morning, another engineer came to us this morning. He had also been awarded 7 days field punishment No. 1 for being drunk in Amiens. He is very fortunate as there are men here who have to serve for 28 days for the same offence. The man who has been wounded twice left this afternoon at 4 pm having completed his term of confinement. We miss him too, as he was the witty man of the party and made things a little more lively, when enjoying our leisure moments, which however are but few and very far between. I heard rather a good thing this evening, it appears that the pictorial paper "The Sketch" published a photograph of a Sergeant here handing a cigar to a German prisoner and very nice too on the face of it. On the other hand however this particular Sergeant was accused by two of his men (detail men more or less broken in health on account of hardships and fighting at the front) for taking a packet of cigarettes from each of the men under him, about eight in all and issuing only three packets instead of the customary four. These two men have both had to serve long periods in this vile hole for their pains, at least the crime for which they were convicted was for being drunk, but the reason of course is obvious, they are both decent honest fellows but it doesn't pay apparently to be honest and straightforward nowadays.

27/8/16

Cold and much rain threatening. Between 10 am and 11 am infact it teemed down. A New Zealand transport column passed through at the time and they were simply drenched, a great number of troops on foot also marched through headed by drum and pipe bands. Indeed all the time I have been on the "road" tranport and troops have been continually on the move. Received a letter this morning from my wife, also a box of cigarettes from my good friends at Southport. By rights we should have been off duty this afternoon to enable us to have a bath and to wash our clothes. However the town commandant decided otherwise for we were dragged out on to the road again at five minutes past one, although we had only 35 minutes in which to get our dinner. We broke off at 4 pm and directly after our tea, we were marched to the bath house, where hot water sprays have been fitted up. It is the place too where the German prisoners, at least some of them are interned. I quite enjoyed my spray bath. One has to stand however as there is not room even to sit in the square shallow wooden troughs, which are provided. Afterwards marched back to our "billet" and had a shave and did a little sewing and straightened up as much as possible in readiness for my exit tomorrow. I am quite anxious now to get out and am looking forward to my approaching freedom. I have certainly not had a bad time, taking everything into consideration and at any rate I have been treated as a soldier, which is quite a change from what I have experienced in the engineers. Perhaps I might add a little of what my work has been these last four days. In the first place it consisted of repairing holes and worn places in the road. It is the duty of whoever is in charge to say what is to be done, but generally we mark out our own work as of course it is not a very difficult matter to distinguish what repairs are needed, knowing this we then proceeded to mark off a square or oblong with the pick. It is extremely necessary to do everything neatly, after fetching out all the earth and stone it is necessary before filling it again to sweep out all the gravel and also to separate the stones from the gravel. This done, a new bed is made by using new bricks in addition to the old ones, but utilising the former preferably for the edges. When an even surface has been made it is the practice to pour water over and then to ram it down. If small pebbles are available they are next put on and make a good road surface, but in their absence dry sand is used in preference3 to the old soil especially if it be wet. The road is then carefully swept around the repair and the dust cast over it. It is then well rammed down. This is my way of doing it but of course as I am merely an amateur it is not necessarily the correct method. Still I have found it satisfactory and sufficient.

28/8/16

Many showers occurred this morning. We were down in the front of the chateau gates repairing the road all morning, ah well it will not be long now to 4 pm when I shall walk out a free man again. I spent an hour and a half after receiving my liberty in cleaning myself up. Was allowed to break off a quarter of an hour before the proper time to enable me to collect my things together. Spent the evening at Pont-Noyelle, where I indulged in a good meal of eggs and coffee and also a fair amount of white wine.

29/8/16

Did not sleep very well and upon rising this morning my nose bled freely. I noticed according to last night's orders that I have been transferred to No. 43 airline section. I shall continue for the present at any rate to work at the signal office of the 4th army. We were drilled for an hour this morning in a neighbouring field, which made me very weary. On duty at 1 pm until 5.30 pm. Spent evening at Pont-Noyelle talking and learning French. I have of course lost a good deal of time in this respect and must now redouble my efforts to catch up again.

30/8/16

Wet miserable morning. Only a fair night's rest, am feeling quite run down and in fact I look ill. On duty from 8.30 am until 1 pm. On again at 9 pm and finish tomorrow morning at 8.30 am. Received letters from Miss Weeds, Miss Hedges and Bill.

31/8/16

Very cold this morning, a good deal of heavy firing during the night. Did not lie down after finished work this morning at 8.30 am, but instead cleaned myself up and spent the day at Pont-Noyelle also having dinner there. On duty again at 5.30 pm until 9 pm. Wrote letters to Miss Weeds and Miss Hedges.

1/9/16

Pleasant sunny morning. My duty is changed today from No. 2 relief to a split duty, which commences at 1 pm to 5 pm and 6 pm to 10 pm. I think I will copy here my letter to Miss Weeds as it contains a few ideas which I have been able to form, on account of long contact with the world and in that respect is interesting to myself.

Dear Miss Weeds,

Many thanks for your long interesting letter, yes I remember Mr. ---- well, quite a decent sort of fellow. I have always thought him to be too. No, I do not receive the Record now. Am afraid that am rather lax regarding P.G. affairs of late. I was greatly surprised to hear of the whereabouts of Mr. ---- and particularly his new appointment. I suppose his wife is with him too eh? It is very good of you to invite us to the?. Perhaps fortune will be kind enough to permit of the realisation of such a pleasure. Many thanks also for the photos, am returning all except yours, which I would like to keep if I may. Re the "Kitchins lines" I can only say that the sentiment therein expressed is really and truly the undisguised opinion and belief of every Arab indeed the same may be said of all natives and foreigners who live under British domain, with regard to your own very interesting lines of which you ask me to comment upon, I would like to say at once, that am afraid they touch upon a subject, which lies deeply buried and firmly embedded in the life and affairs of the human kind. I might indeed go further and add, even in the life all things which live. If only such a subject could be reached by all or even by a few, the world would at once become enlightened to an ideal state of existence. I am afraid I could not possibly give you much satisfaction if I attempted to probe the impenetrable darkness, which shrouds the source and workshop of life. Have you read "The Road Menders", as your lines remind me of the book, which is written is somewhat a similar vein. Personally I have no faith in maxims and set no store by them. They may all perhaps contain a germ of truth, but when two are placed side by side they jar horribly. There is no fixed order of things for any one of us, because there are no likes. In fact, but for this life would certainly be much more easier, as of course then we should e3ntertain a common understanding with each other. Those who meet with so called success in life are individuals who have been born in a grove of natural circumstances, particularly suited to their particular temperament and aspirations. Success obtained in any other way is unnatural and unreal. It is moreover merely apparent and is short lived, in so far as effecting materially the undercurrent of human affairs, although thereby they may be temporarily disturbed. I will not continue further as the subject is beyond me it is difficult to convey with coherence ones convictions on such a matter without explaining minutely and explicitly all the small details involved, which is a matter as I have said, quite beyond me". Etc. etc.

2/9/16

Dull close morning. Received a letter from my wife. Obtained a new pair of braces and sock yesterday evening from the quartermaster, need a new pair of boots also badly, but he has not my size in stock. My present pair I have worn through Egypt and Gallipoli. Spent morning at Pont-Noyelle. Wrote a letter to Bill also to my Aunt Ada.

3/9/16

My duty changed again today. It is now from 1 pm to 5 pm and 9 pm until 1 am. This arrangement permits me to spend a good deal of time with my French studies, in which profession am feeling my feet nicely now. Heavy firing continued all night and throughout the morning. Received a parcel of bountious gifts from my wife including a nice cake, large box of chocolates, tube of Colgates toothpaste, two bags of biscuits, pipe, box of cigarettes and a packet of tobacco. For all of which I am extremely grateful. On duty at 9 pm and was feeling quite done up when I finished at 1 am. No particular news of the war, except that the fighting continues very severe, and is of a slogging nature, which means about six of one and half a dozen of the other. Wrote a letter to my wife.

4/9/16

Raining heavily first thing this morning, in fact we have experienced quite a lot of same recently. A concert was held this evening in the recreation room of the B.E.F. canteen. My relief No. 2 was allowed to attend, but could not do so personally as was on duty at which time it commenced. Rained very hard again all evening. The bombardment, which is being carried out on our front was also excessive.

5/9/16

We appear to have made good progress in yesterdays and last night's fighting. Judging from casualty reports it would seem that we are paying dearly. The 14th division for instance had over 3,600 casualties. This total however is of course comparatively light in comparison to the heavy sacrifices of the 29th division at Gallipoli, which occurred again and again. In this evening report the French have made excellent progress, advancing as much as 500 yards beyond the original readily organised position on the whole of their front, they have also captured several thousand prisoners. We the 4th have also done well and captured a large number of prisoners. The signal office is kept continually very busy. Should have been off at 1 am but could not get away before 1.25 am.

6/9/16

As it is necessary to get up in time for breakfast, which is served up for the last time at 8.30 am, I do not get much rest, not leaving work until nearly half past one in the morning and in consequence feel very tired all the day through. I dare not lay down during the day, because it would be a sad waste of time, and I wish to make the utmost of my spare moments off duty. On duty at 9 pm. Was surprised to see a band blaring forth in front of the chateau, which was brilliantly lit up with lights. It would be hard perhaps to argue against such practices by those in authority, but it is not war. Before and after is the proper time for artificial, otherwise that which is done by the higher powers will invariably radiate all along the line, down to the lesser ranks, which under the circumstances is not conductive to solidity, energy and fixed purpose. The light hearted way in which we entered the war is a most lamentably characteristic attitude which we have apparently adopted in our prosecution there of right up to the present. In which direction shall we eventually be led I wonder is it to "Java" or is it to "Sedan"?

7/9/16

Did not leave the signal office until 2.15 am this morning owing to much pressure of work. Received a letter from my Aunt Ada. The cannonading which continues unceasingly is at times most fierce. This evening in fact the incessant rumbling and groaning is positively terrific. We used to think Chocolate Hill bad enough for shell fire, but it was in fact childs play in comparison to the heavy bombardments on this front.

8/9/16

Finished work this morning at 1.30 am. Large numbers of troops are continually on the move together with their attendant baggage. A great proportion of the troops which I have noticed lately, and especially this morning have been New Zealanders. Quite a find body of men too I consider them to be. It would perhaps be rather interesting to make a few notes of certain events, which have been able to ascertain took place when the Germans first passed through Pont Noyelle and Querrieu on their mythical triumphal march to Paris. From what I can gather the Germans only stayed about these parts for a day and night. Most of the inhabitants had departed before they arrived, only the old people remaining behind. Still I know personally several of the younger people who did not trouble to quit their homes. The Germans demanded everything while they were here, but paid for nothing. There were two cases of barbarism, so far as I have been able to ascertain. One occurred at a small village near, a French man who hid himself when the Germans approached was however soon discovered and shot "tout de suite". At Querrieu an old man who refused to oblige his countries enemies in any way, was promptly cut open down the middle with a knife. On the other hand am afraid that in many quarters noble France's most viscious enemy was unfortunately only too well received. Another little story concerns the chateau here, which at present is the headquarters of the 4th army (General Rawlinson H.S.). The tale dates back to the war 0f 1870. The gist of the story, which I will endeavour to explain, runs something like as follows. At the time mentioned the Germans were advancing successfully through France and a big battle was fought in this district. In fact there is a large grave and a monument had been erected to commemorate the fallen heroes who fell fighting for their country, just a short distance to the North of Pont-Noyelle. There lived at the chateau of this time, an old man and his daughter, who was about 18 summers of age. I believe the former was the Count. There arrived at this old mansion a young gallant cavalier on his charger, to visit his fiancée "Mademoiselle". Upon leaving the girl instructed Monsieur to take the road leading directly in front of him and in order to see him departing she herself climbed up into one of the four turrets, which it is said existed at that time, but of which the chateau does not possess a single one at the present time. She was however mortified that her "Beau ideal" did not observe her directions to him, but instead turned off to the right, which led to danger. Mademoiselle at once dispatched a servant to overtake the horseman, but it was all in vain for Monsieur had gone too far and ran straight into the arms of the enemy and was killed. This event had a depressing influence upon the chateau maiden who elapsed into a droll sort of person and, to continue the story as it has been told to me. Whenever a thunderstorm came over it was the practice of poor Mademoiselle to go up into the turret and look out for her servant, whom she would on such occasions send repeatedly on a similar errand as she did on the first occasion. The man would invariably return with the tale that he had redirected the gentleman on to the safe and proper route, which she had directed him to follow. There came a time however when the messenger too was killed by lightning and Mademoiselle who had turned her 60th birthday asked God to strike her dead too. Whereupon the room in which she was standing, was immediately shattered and so ended the life of this unfortunate woman.

9/9/16

Sunny pleasant morning. The guns are still booming maliciously. From reports however which I have seen of yesterday's fighting we appear to have suffered many unsuccesses. Am making satisfactory but dogged progress in my French. Lately have been able to add a great deal more words to my vocabulary and can converse with comparative ease, I find however that it is more difficult to follow the speech of another, than it is to make oneself understood. There was very good war news of today's fighting, we have apparently advance with good results at different points and captured a large number of prisoners, although at present the precise total cannot be ascertained correctly.

10/9/16

Finished work at 1.30 am and feeling very done up. Got up at 8.30 am for breakfast. Am feeling the effects very considerably from working until anything between 1 and 2 in the morning, with little rest into the bargain. I must however get up fairly early or miss my breakfast and also it generally takes me about 45 minutes to clean myself properly and shave, which I have to do every day. Afterwards depart tout de suit to Pont-Noyelle in quest of knowledge. A large number of French automobiles passed through here this evening conveying to the front many English soldiers, of course I do not see much that goes on during the day or night owing to being otherwise occupied, but I see enough to be aware that the movement of troops etc. on all the roads leading to the firing line, practically never ceases.

11/9/16

The weather is quite good of late, and should have a favourable effect upon the offensive operations which are or may be contemplated. Day passed as usual. The work at the signal offices continues to be very heavy and the staff employed quite inadequate to cope with it, which is responsible for the work suffering a big delay at times. However "c'est la guerr" I suppose.

12/9/16

Sunny pleasant morning. Very good news from the French today on our right, they carried out successfully practically all their objectives and even applied to us for permission to come into our area to enable them to facilitate their attack on another point. They took I believe about 1500 prisoners, at least that is one estimate. Am changed back from tororrow on to my relief for which I am indeed thankful.

13/9/16

Wet and dull this morning. Received letters from my wife and Miss Weeds, also answered my wife's letter. On duty 1 pm until 5.30 pm. Spent evening at Pont-Noyelle. Received this morning 30 francs pay. Nothing of note to jot down today. This afternoon the signal-master relieved me on the circuit I was working for purpose of transposing a telegram into French and afterwards transmitting to the French army by Morse, which I accomplished satisfactorily.

14/9/16

Sharp breezy morning but sunny and pleasant. I will endeavour to numerate a number of little episodes, what I have had described to me in French at different times, or which in some way become acquainted. A story I heard the other day was to the effect that the British and French troops who are at the present moment closing in on the village of "Combles" are killing the civilian inhabitants indiscriminately. It seems that in numerous towns and villages the local population have in some way or another assisted the Germans in their plans and designs against the allies, even perhaps firing on them. Combles is a case in point and now that the tables are reversed the allies are taking their revenge. I hear also that last winter an agitation of some extent began to be talked about among the French troops, which was to the effect of stopping the war by resorting to revolutionary methods. In consequence there were many soldiers of France shot. I wonder if this is a forerunner of revolutions to come, not only in France, but perhaps in other countries too. There is a great deal yet to be purged from all. This war is in my opinion the beginning only of the end of many things, which probably can only be abolished by the aid of drastic measures, which may yet be adopted as they have in times gone by. To wit it is very possible and indeed likely too that much wealth is finding its way solely into the pockets of a few, which after the war will be a factor to be considered and dealt with, as of course such a state of affairs cannot and never is understood or appreciated by the plebeian community, who will be more than ever greatly in the majority. I have been acquainted also that the chateau here, which at present is utilised by the Headquarters of the 4th army (British) was infact originally lent by its owner the comptesse, expressly to be used for the purpose of a hospital and that she was greatly disappointed in her desire, upon discovering that the English had taken it over for quite another object, I would like to mention that I have been positively astounded on many occasions to find what the true feeling of the French people really is with respect to their views of the war. They are generally very sick and absolutely tired and even hate the war. In conversation their first comment is invariably "La querre est trop long". They seem to think that six months or a year at most of war is quite sufficient. They appear also to entertain a very vivid impression of England's demands and designs for paying for the war afterwards. I found that some people have the idea that we shall even continue to hold the territory we now occupy and work the railways, which we have built, by erecting stations etc. There is by the way a single line railway running between Querrieu and Pont-Noyelle. I believe it comes from Frenchencourt and runs to Amiens. It was built by Royal Engineers, and the local people are very anxious that the line should be allowed to remain after the war. It would certainly be a boom to them as they rely at present upon incoming carts from Amiens and Corbie for all articles of commerce. I am afraid that in many quarters in France the people are extremely suspicious of Britains intentions after the war, although personally I do my best to dissuade them to the contrary whenever I get the opportunity. I cannot really say either that I admire the French for the attitude which they appear to have adopted, especially in respect to the obvious favourable good reception accorded to the Germans in many places. Still I love them their country and their history none the less. I believe too that the British government has never played fair towards our allies and that such is the case is probably in accordance with unfortunate German influence in high official circles, which has been responsible for assisting more or less our enemies to resist all the efforts of the allies and paved the foundations which will in all probability ultimately enable them to continue the struggle to a favourable issue for themselves, for this I am ashamed of my Country. The policy adopted has been the means of sacrificing not merely hundreds but many thousands of valuable lives. Those who are responsible should be dealt with accordingly at the first opportunity. To continue my observations I might mention that it would seem that the condition of affairs in France is much the same as that which exists in our own country and probably also in those of our allies. That is to say from an ethical point of view. I have personally met with some queer goings on, even in our little village. "It seems quite the custom for a girl and for many married women too for that matter to take unto herself a man providing she be sufficiently attracted to same. Who may bask at leisure in the sunshine of the smile of Madame or Mademoiselle, so long as he should remain in her favour. It is perfectly in order apparently and little or no notice is taken thereof. If the husband however should discover the relationship and should he be of a lasty disposition may in such cases shoot both the lovers "tout de suite", as in fact did occur recently in a similar case which was told to me. It may seem strange, but the husband in this particular instance was not convicted of the crime or punished in any way merely acting within his rights according to the French way of thinking. On the other hand as an alternative he could without risk or annoyance quietly leave his wife and possess himself of another spouse and here again he is not blamed by public opinion for doing so. I have heard it repeatedly mentioned that French girls prefer Englishmen even to their own countrymen. It is perfectly true that there have been quite a large number of marriages contracted between the "lily" and the "rose" and in addition a vast number of unsolomnised unions also. A case in point I may relate with accuracy, on account of being personally acquainted with the parties concerned and the facts relating to each. I will not mention the unit to which the soldier in question belongs, but he is not a Royal Engineer. He came to France with the ---- about a couple of years ago and made the acquaintance of a girl from ---- in the North of France. The man is married, but the girl is unaware of the fact and believes she will eventually go to England with her fiancé (that word fiancé and fiancée covers a great deal of sin). She has followed him from place to place, which at times has been a very difficult matter indeed, owing to lack of conveyance, passports and no knowledge of her soldiers whereabouts, when on several occasions he has moved suddenly for a distant destination, she has always managed to find him wherever he has gone and stayed with him in rooms obtained by her lover or perhaps secured by the assistance of a French interpreter attached to the British army. This is a very good representation of what in various ways occurs daily out here and is not exaggerated, but on the contrary is quite the reverse. The story is also only half completed for the girl has reiterated several times to me that if Monsieur ---- leaves her, she will follow him and shoot him with a revolver, or throw vitriol over him, although she is herself a wrong one, for in conversation she has told me of her many amours with British Officers at Bethune, Boulogne and Paris, she also writes to one officer now whose mistress she has been and whose address she says is at Bristol. Ah well "c'est la guerre".

15/9/16

Finished duty at 8.30 am after an extremely cold nights work at the S.O. Several of our divisions have made good progress including the New Zealand division. There are great things contemplated now I believe. In a warning telegram to the corps. It was stated among other things that one division would attack a certain position to enable the cavalry to push through. We are anxiously waiting for news of events. Received a letter from my Aunt Ada. On duty at 5.30 pm until 9 pm and slept well in spite of the cold.

16/9/16

Pleasant morning. Was on ration fatigue from 9 am until 10.45 am which is rather heavy work. On duty at 1 pm until 5.30 pm. Spent evening in Pont-Noyelle, where I had supper too, which consisted of tinned rabbit fried with butter and onions. Very little war news, but all there is of a satisfactory nature and we appear to be making favourable progress, although there is no news of our Cavalry taking part in the action.

17/9/16

Bright breezy morning. On duty from 8.30 am until 1 pm. Saw many wounded pass through in motor ambulances, not much life left in some of them I'm afraid. On duty again at 9 pm.

18/9/16

Finished work at 8.30 am after a busy night and am extremely fagged out. It has rained almost unceasingly and in fact continued all day. A very unfortunate accident occurred during the early hours of the morning, a Red Cross train, which from what I can gather was travelling at high speed and left the rails at the bend near Pont-Noyelle, where it curves very sharply. The train was of course wrecked but cannot say what happened to the wounded of which it was full. Little or no war news. The Cavalry have not been put through, for which I am thankful, it would have been a new departure in warfare and personally I have no faith in its success, and from the first have strongly deprecated any such attempt. The time is neither ripe for the adoption of such a plan and it is only a matter of common sense to credit the Germans with having made all necessary precautions and are prepared to meet all emergencies. In this case I fail to see what it would profit us. The enemy infantry have first to be beaten and beaten well before a project of this sort should be even contemplated.

19/9/16

Wretched weather this morning, everywhere deep in mud. Received a letter from my father and also my sister Doris. Spent evening in Pont-Noyelle in company with a couple of soldiers.

20/9/16

Raining heavily this morning. Still the guns are pounding away at a tremendous rate. Feel rather unwell probably due to cold and perhaps too an after effect of drinking some of the local wines last night, which are not altogether the best quality.

21/9/16

Finished duty this morning at 8.30 am after a very trying night, what with fatigue and cold. Did not take any rest however as it is not my custom to do so on this duty, but went instead to a house at Pont-Noyelle, where remained until 4.15 pm, when I left for duty again at 5.30 pm until 9 pm. The people whom I visited make me very welcome and there is a large gramophone which I used rather freely. This morning we were all startled to hear quite suddenly a lot of noise, which was occasioned by one of the outbuildings collapsing. The roof and walls came tumbling down in a heap of debris. The two children were playing close by at the time and they narrowly escaped serious injury. Their mother was terribly alarmed for the moment on their account. I suppose that the violent bombardments which have occurred in this region recently must be held responsible for the collapse although the structure was very old and the wood supports quite rotten. I have on several occasions had it in my mind to make a few observations upon my work at the signal office, in respect to its connection and bearing upon the war. The principle feature I think, which has struck me most is when on such occasions as that on which the artillery fires is so very intense and the work in our office continues quite uninterruptedly quietly and smoothly. While the guns are belching angrily and making the whole world tremble, the little Morse instruments continue to rattle out their metallic notes. While the wholesale destruction of Europe's manhood is being carried on heedlessly and relentlessly up at the line, the small meek voice of brass and iron does not in the least abate, but rather increases more and more in intensity its ceaseless efforts to arrange for further dispatches etc. of deluded artists to dance to the tune of hell's music, and for the sole pleasure of the devil, also to drink at his table the rich red wine, which flows close by his couch in abundance and is called the stream of life. The wires, which connect up every unit with the whole may be termed with justice, the veins and arteries of the army. Should they cease to flow or to throb the whole military fabric would become as though dead, it would exist only in like manner as a worm, which upon being cut into many pieces each part taking a different direction and moves about quite aimlessly.

22/9/16

Good night's rest, which I needed badly. Sunny pleasant morning. A great number of French automobiles and British too passed through here today conveying English troops, to some destination unknown. The Germans carried out an air raid last night and dropped about 8 bombs on Amiens, between 2 and 3 am this morning but apparently did very little damage. It is thought too that they visited other places including Abbeville during an earlier part of the night. Wrote a letter to my father. Seems rather quiet again at the front. I hear that the comp commandant has ordered that all prisoners including Germans must not discontinue working when it rains and are provided with ground sheets, which are to be place round the shoulders during a storm.

23/9/16

Lovely sunny and bright morning, makes one think and crave for the pleasures of a walk in the beautiful countryside in England, which indeed has no parallel anywhere else in the world. In fact a few miles of champagne in the dear homeland is worth more than all the rest of the world put together. A little ditty which it is common to hear all the youngsters in the village sing and the soldiers too for that matter is as follows. "Apres la guerre fini, tous les Anglais parti, Mademoisselle Francaise a pleure sauvenir un bebe" I have obtained however a song, which appears fairly well known. It is written in French and as it conveys an extremely good idea of life out here during the war I propose to enter it here, but do not intend to translate any part of same.

1 Complet

"C'est bien triste la guerre de voir des chose commeca, c'est triste jeune Francaise de voir ce quel font las soir et matin sur las chemin, on les voie las main dans la main, pour commencer a racracher les officier qui donne des souvenir anglais.

Refrain

Il n y a plus de lait pour jeune anglais, les demoiselles Francaise on tour pris ne sachant pas que. C'est leur marie, apres la guerre finie et les anglais partie, les demoiselles Francaise vont restie on lercant'leur bebe.

2nd Complet

Est t'al possible detre bete decoutez les anglais, aven tout leur promesses les trois cart sont marie, les femmes pesse pasque don eq mois et un petit bebe leur viendra il vont restez avec leur souvenir anglais.

3rd Complet

Voyais les jeune Anglaise earie a leur marie que les femmes Francaise leur font tans de chishe s'il elle savant las veritez elle neceserait de pleurer. Apres tout elle leur dit tout qui reste a France a c'est leur gout."

Fini.

Diary Number 3

24/9/16

Finished duty this morning at 8.30 am. It has been an extremely cold night and very unpleasant working conditions in the office into the bargain, as there are no stoves. Nothing to note today.

25/9/16

Lovely morning with brilliant sunshine. Witnessed an air combat about 11 am over our headquarters. Observation was very difficult owing to the power of the sun. There were great quantities of shells exploding in small white balls all around, and one could easily observe our own craft in pursuit. Did not see the termination of the conflict, but the Germans would have as warm a time as they could wish for I have no doubt. We are exceedingly stronger and superior in the air to our enemy and it is only on rare occasions that they so much as pass over the lines viz the trenches. On duty at 1 pm to 5.30 pm. The Germans made another air raid this evening between 9 pm and 10 pm. It was quite a picture to watch the numerous search light seeking out their prey and countless shells, bursting, as it were in the heavens was more picturesque even than the so called shooting-stars, which were easily out-vied. Cannot say what the enemy was trying to do, but apparently they were endeavouring to locate Amiens and Corbie as they flew over both these places, it has been officially reported too that in this morning's aerial conflict two enemy machines were brought down, but fell in the German lines. Wrote a letter to my wife Elinor.

26/9/16

Pleasant warm morning. From official war reports it is obvious that yesterday we made a good deal of progress and advanced a considerable distance. The 10th Corp reports that the total number of prisoners captured by them alone has reached over 1000. Today is the fourth birthday of my son Derrick and oddly enough I have only seen him for about half his life, perhaps not even that much. I sincerely hope that there is a prosperous future in store for him and that his life will not be vexed with many troubles and anxieties. He is a dear child and I trust that no harm will ever touch him. If his manhood is as unimpeachable as his character and appearance now betokens, there should be an uncommon future waiting for him to undertake. Derrick my boy, always be true to yourself. Be honest and straightforward and never fear the truth, make it a point of honour to fear nothing whatsoever, but rely always and solely for aid and assistance upon that higher power which never fails. Further appreciative progress has been made during the day and we have captured "Combles", "Fleurs" and "Thiepval", taking many prisoners and much booty. This afternoon while I was at a house in Pont-Noyelle, which place I might mention I visit daily for French instructional purposes, although Madam unfortunately cannot read or write (a failing with many French people living in villages). Still I am able to make good progress in spite of these drawbacks, as of course there is always a way out of every difficulty. To continue my little story, I have to mention that owing to the danger entailed by the fact that half the building which the other day partly fell to the ground, but the remaining portion was still leaning in a dangerous manner and there was great risk of this crashing down too at any moment. I got myself into a favourable position to swing the structure little by little until the whole thing fell with a crash of rotten wood, tiles, bricks, mud and dust. Madame was greatly pleased with my handiwork, which hitherto had been a continuous source of anxiety to her on account of the obvious danger to the children when playing in the court, also it was necessary to obtain water to go underneath the "toiture" in order to reach the well, Madame also took the opportunity to knock out a few bricks of a neighbouring house, which bulged out considerably and in consequence interfered to some extent with the turning of the handle of the well, when drawing water. Quite a large hole was the result, but Madame merely laughed with delight for it appears that no neighbourly love was lost between them. Later on when Madame No. 2 returned in the evening she of course supposed things "tout de suit" and accused Madam No. 1 of the damage done to her home, heated words at once passed between them. No. 1 called the other a thief and "une solope" upon which No. 2 retaliated with the accusation "putain" and having a Captain Fiancé, upon which No. 1 without the least hesitation simply grasped hold of some bricks and hurled them point blank at her antagonist, who retreated quickly through her own door. She came out again however and a right royal battle ensued. Two French men endeavoured to stop the combat but I said "ohmon il est tres bien", upon which some women who were standing outside the pailing watching the fray simply burst into laughter. However there were no casualties but Madame No. 1 lost her "alliance", I should like to add here one or two more of my observations, which I have seen practised. I have frequently been extremely surprised to notice with what little respect God and the Bible are treated generally. One might see for instance posted up by the side of a crucifix a number of picture postcards of an amorous character. Christ in my quarters is not believed in and a future life positively ridiculed. Perhaps the Catholic Church in France is responsible in great measure for much that has befallen this poor noble country. One hears on every side stories of the confessional and implications are hurled at the priests wholesale. The amour of the lather with married women are talked of freely also "les bonnes soeurs" are included in the above category. In the place of piety superstition naturally takes the place thereof and in a variety of forms shows itself. For instance Madame will never place a loaf of bread upon the table with the flat surface (bottom of French loaves) uppermost as that might bring "mal chance" before cutting some she will always draw the knife across the bottom of the loaf to form the "sign of the cross". On duty at 9 pm.

27/9/16

Finished duty at 8.30 am, not so cold during the night as on previous occasions recently. Nice pleasant morning. Paraded at 10.30 for pay and received 30 francs. On duty 5.30 pm until 9 pm. Not much news except that the fighting is for the most part entirely in our favour and we have captured a large number of prisoners, over 10,000 infact during the last fortnight. The French too have done well, but somehow they always do, which fact is rather unexplainable to me and in consequence I become at times exceedingly suspicious that something is sadly wrong with the British high Command, or more probably the blame may be justly attributed to our immobile Government. Slight thunderstorm during the evening.

28/9/16

Close sunny day. It is really beautiful weather. On duty 1 pm until 5.30 pm. Received a letter from my aunt with "R.E." numerals enclosed and a paper from Miss Weeds. Spent evening at Pont-Noyelle.

29/9/16

Close morning with drizzle. On duty at 8.30 am until 1 pm and again at 9 pm. Nothing to note of importance today.

30/9/16

I finished work at 8.30 am. Not a very busy night and had about 3½ hours nap, which was very welcome. Spent day at Pont-Noyelle. It is rather cold now but fine. Another enemy aeroplane made an incursion into our area about 10 pm this evening. It flew at a great height and did not remain hereabouts many minutes and not many shots were fired.

1/10/16

The clock was put back an hour last night from 1 am back to midnight, so had an extra hour in bed. Nice sunny pleasant day. Received a letter from Miss Weeds also replied to same. Heard a rumour that leave to British troops has been abolished for the duration of the war and that rest camps will be formed by the sea for NCO's and men. Only those above the rank of Sergeant Major will be granted permission to return to England. Under a special permit soldiers may be given a pass to go to Paris. All this may of course be merely a fairy tale, still it is feasible. French troops are however allowed permission three times each year with seven days on each occasion. In fact this is guaranteed to them. On duty 1 pm until 5.30 pm.

2/10/16

Dull morning, inclined to rain. On duty at 8.30 am until 1 pm, and in the evening, I clicked for the "joy wheel", which is in place of the all night shift and commences at 5 pm and finishes at 1 am, or as soon after that hour as possible, according to the quantity of work on hand, sometimes in fact it is 2 am before we are able to get away. Received a letter from my Aunt Ada enclosing one pound postal order, also replied to same.

3/10/16

Very wet and miserable morning. On duty 10.30 am until 1.30 pm and again at 5.30 pm until 9 pm. Much rain fall during the day and everywhere deep in slush.

4/10/16

Muggy and hot again today. On duty at 1 pm until 5.30 pm. Since the clock was put back one hour we have particularly noticed the difference in the evenings, especially when finishing work at 5.30 pm as it is quite a difficult matter now to see and find our food which is served up at the mill and is exceedingly dark.

5/10/16

Pleasant sunny morning but evidence of more rain in the sky. Nothing especially worthy of note lately, so must be content to record the weather.

6/10/16

Finished duty this morning at6 8.30 am after working all night. Weather brighter but close. Have not received any news from my wife for some considerable time. I expected a parcel quite a fortnight past and am rather upset that it has not arrived. On duty at 5.30 pm was permitted to leave the office at 8 pm instead of 9 pm on account of scarcity of work in comparison to the staff employed.

7/10/16

Nice morning but rain threatening. On duty 1 pm until 5.30 pm. Spent evening at Pont-Noyelle, where I had supper, I have one meal at least daily there and it is a very welcome change from army rations, although I must admit that the latter have improved considerably since the Bombadier was sent away after the affair with myself, which resulted in 7 days of field punishment for me. One hears frequently even now bitter complaints of our former arrangements, which were undoubtedly a positive disgrace.

8/10/16

Rained very heavily this morning, got wet through coming down from the billet to the chateau. On duty at 8.30 am until 1 pm. Spent afternoon and evening at Pont-Noyelle. There is quite a lack of interesting occurrences lately, except those which I have been reiterating time after time. There are loads of rumours as per usual, such as that the French will shortly retake the trenches which the 4th Army (British) now occupy, and that we shall proceed to Belgium to relieve the French troops there. It is a fact that our allies troops are congregating in Freakencourt not far from here, but personally I construe from this that possibly they are intended to support the British operations on this front. It is also asserted that leave to our troops has been discontinued indefinitely and that permission will only be granted for leave to be taken at rest camps in France. At the moment it is not possible to say if this is true or not. It is feasible however and even probable, considering the large number of troops now in France, which would necessitate rather a large amount of tonnage being reserved for the purpose of carrying leave soldiers to and from England. On duty again at 9 pm.

9/10/16

Fairly fine day but close. Finished work at 8.30 am and feeling quite washed out into the bargain. Spent day at Pont-Noyelle nevertheless. On duty encore at 5.30 pm until 9 pm.

10/10/16

Nice sunny weather today. What is puzzling me at present is the fact that I have received no news from my wife for quite a long while. I think it must be at least three weeks since I had her last communication. However "C'est la guerre", as usual I suppose to continue my narrative of little peculiarities, which I am able to observe and with which I come into contact at different times. One thing in particular I wish to remark upon, it appears to be quite a custom, at least it is prevalent hereabouts, for a child to address its parent by their Christian names, for instance a little girl may be heard to address her mother as follows, "mama, "Blanche", vous donnez moi deux sous s'il vous plais". To an English ear such practice does not at first sound well, but I am bound to admit that personally I am of the opinion that the custom is really "tres joli". The dialect of "patois" which is peculiar to certain provinces in France is particularly broad and coarse here (Picardy). In each province the local dialect or "patois" differs entirely from its neighbour, from what I am able to gather concerning the "patois" in vogue here seems to me to be merely a contortion of the French language, as an instance I may quote the word "Acheter", which in the local brogue is pronounced "ah-ee-tay", which is vastly different to the correct French pronunciation of the word. The post in the village is delivered by a woman, which may probably be the case in the big towns too. Bread is also delivered by the opposite sex, who make known their approach by blowing a whistle, upon hearing which customers ally out onto the road, which saves the Boulangere from leaving her seat in the voiture. On duty 1 pm until 5.30 pm, afterwards spent evening at Pont-Noyelle.

11/10/16

Dull close morning but fine. On duty at 8.30 pm until 1 pm. Was quite done up at the end of it too. There is more news of an approaching further determined offensive. Have seen more big guns going up to the front. One remarkable feature concerning our bombardments now is that they are not even audible to us here. Proving that the two monster weapons have been moved some distance further up the line. The last two or three nights have been quite beautiful, with a full moon and clear sky. The air too has been most delightful, something like an eastern evening in fact. As one walks down the road of the village one is a t once taken away into a world of romance and varied thoughts crowd into the imagination. One will meet with all sorts of peculiar incidents appertaining to the war, and the contrast with the peaceful slumbering villages of France is really most alarming. Perhaps some isolated cavalry will come jogging along and if they be "lancers", their long weapons look rather formidable in the vanishing rays of the uncertain night's lights. Then there is the never ceasing hum and rumble of motor traffic, and dispatch riders. Perhaps a cart of the "RSPCA" will come slowly down the road drawn by a couple of horses and containing a sick horse. Then one notices little groups of soldiers probably stragglers marching laboriously with their heavy packs in the tracks of their comrades who have left them behind. Still the moon continues to throw down upon the whole its brilliant light and in the stillness of the night it is difficult to believe that not very far away the very best of our poor world is slowly but surely becoming exterminated.

12/10/16

Dull but fine morning. At a general meeting last night it was decided to commence immediately arrangements for an especially good time this Xmas. A particularly interesting piece of work has just commenced at the mill, where our cook house and mess room is situated Captain Batchelor RE is superintending the job which is being carried out by German prisoners. The object in view, is the lighting of the mill building by electric lights, and the river which flows by, and was at one time used for the purpose of turning the big wheel, is now to be utilised for procuring the necessary power required for the projected electric lighting scheme. German bricklayers and mechanics and a number of labourers are kept busily employed making the best possible use of the materials at hand, as of course none other are obtainable for such a purpose, and the machinery of the old mill is being rapidly brought back to life again. My friend who came out with me from England is under orders to proceed to the 1st Division Headquarters tomorrow morning. I am very sorry he is leaving us. It was only recently that he bought a violin in Amiens and in leisure moments treated us to many lively tunes. Am the only one left here now of the draft which came out from the old country.

13/10/16

Dull and close. On duty 1 pm until 5.30 pm. Spent evening at Pont-Noyelle where I had a good supper also.

14/10/16

Fine but cloudy this morning. On duty at 8.30 am until 1 pm and again at 9 pm for an all night shift. Nothing to relate today.

15/10/16

Finished duty at 8.30 am this morning. Rather cold and bleak, in fact it rained all through the breakfast hour, which owing to the circumstances proved very uncomfortable as at present we are obliged to partake of our meals in the open owing to construction work at the mill being in progress. Spent the day at Pont-Noyelle. On duty again at 5.30 pm until 9 pm. The guns were speaking very volubly all the evening and night but they are decidedly less distant now than formally.

16/10/16

Sunny day but much cooler, apparently winter is now setting in and will continue to become less favourable so far as the weather conditions are concerned. The leaves are fast falling and probably in a very short time the beautiful trees, which are a positive glory in France, will become denuded of their glorious garments. Was paid 30 francs this morning, this amount soon vanishes however. Am still without news from England, I have of course a good idea as to the cause, but it is never the less rather a mystery why my correspondence has been stopped and furthermore is greatly annoying. On duty 1 pm until 5.30 pm. Spent evening at my usual place where I had also a good supper.

17/10/16

Sunny morning but cold, still the weather is very delightful and I like the brisk fresh air in the morning immensely, it is very healthy and creates vigour in one. On duty 8.30 am until 1 pm and again in the evening at 9 pm on the all-night shift. Commence to rain hard in the evening and continued throughout the night, heavy firing can be heard. The official reports have contained little of special importance for a long time. The fighting maintains a certain standard of severity but with varying success. Today is the anniversary of my departure from the Gallipoli peninsula, it is a day I shall never forget and was the turning point in my lifes career, the line of demarcation between two destinies, my former life I feel assured will never return in any one respect. It is so changed even now and the road which I now tread is more obscured and less intelligible to me.

18/10/16

Finished duty at 8.30 am and quite fatigued. Spent the day at Pont-Noyelle, where I had dinner. Blankets have arrived today and each man is to be issued with one only. It is a positive disgrace that British soldiers should have been denied this very necessary article for so long, German prisoners are not obliged to be without at any time. On duty at 5.30 pm until 9 pm. Official reports on the whole very unfavourable. The brightest spot was in reference to a "male tank" which entered the enemy's trenches and remained in action there for 25 minutes killing numbers of Germans, afterwards returning safely to our lines. The difference I might mention between a "male tank" and a "female" tank is I believe that the former is armed with a quick firing gun and the latter with a machine gun.

19/10/16

Very wet miserable day. A good deal of heavy firing is in progress up the line. Troops have been passing in automobiles for the front all day long and were still going through our village until late in the evening. On duty at 1 pm until 5.30 pm.

20/10/16

Very cold night, but bright sunny morning, it is frosty sort of weather. Spent the afternoon and evening in Pont-Noyelle. On duty at 9 pm until tomorrow morning.

21/10/16

An extremely cold night. Between 2 am and 3 am enemy aircraft paid us a visit and dropped a couple of bombs quite close to the chateau. One however was a "dud" but the other exploded about 300 yards from the chateau and midway between the building and the railway, which was most probably their objective. It made a large hole where it fell by the side of a big tree. I was working quietly on the circuit at the time and the sudden concussion was rather startling. It soon became very lively also as our guns began to speak without delay, the familiar rattle of our airmen in pursuit was also distinctly audible. I received a couple of letters today, so that apparently my correspondence has not been stopped officially, although even now I am quite unable to account for the continued silence of my wife and Aunt Ada. On duty encore 5.30 pm to 9 pm.

22/10/16

Bitterly cold night, but fine brisk sunny morning. Monsieur Frost had apparently paid us a very close visit during the hours of rest. Was on fatigues, drew rations etc. from 9 am until 11 am. On duty 1 pm to 5.30 pm. Wrote a letter to Mr. Kendrick also another to my Aunt Ada. I hear that there was a considerable number of victims during the air raid on Amiens the other evening. The rumour is that at train a Longeau station, Amiens was blown up, but it is controversial whether it was full of soldiers or empty. I have however ascertained that an oil store including about 36 tanks was destroyed.

23/10/16

Foggy dull morning with a little drizzle, it is however decidedly warmer. On duty at 8.30 am until 1 pm. Spent afternoon and evening in usual way. On duty again at 9 pm. War news of an unfavourable character on the whole. For the past few days there have been heavy movements of troops to the front including several Australian divisions, fine strapping fellows too, they all appear to be.

24/10/16

Finished duty at 8.30 am. Very busy night. Rained heavily nearly all day. Received a letter-card from a French comrade with the French army signals "mericourt" enclosing 3 francs with the request that I should obtain for him some "English tobacco and cigarettes". On duty 5.30 pm until 9 pm.

25/10/16

Very wet weather. Paraded at 10 am with gas helmets for inspection and received one new helmet in exchange. Also issued with one under vest, which however I shall not wear as I have no change. Bought a couple of tins of tobacco suitable for making cigarettes as requested by my French confrere. I found however that there is apparently some rule bearing upon correspondence between British and French troops. I overcame the difficulties however by explaining the matter to Lt. Stephens who kindly dispatched the packet by dispatch rider thereby saving me any expense for postage and obviating any difficulty which might otherwise have been the case. On duty 1 pm until 5.30 pm, afterwards spent evening in the usual manner. Heard today of the splendid success obtained by the French army at Verdun capturing about 4,000 prisoners.

26/10/16

Very dull morning, with drizzle. On duty 8.30 am until 1 pm. Received a long delayed letter, which I have been expecting for a considerable time from my wife. It came this morning as a great relief. Apparently Elinor has been unwell and that is the explanation for the delay in writing to me. On duty encore at 9 pm on the all night shift. Enemy aircraft again flew over us some time after midnight and paid another visit to Amiens, I hope that whatever destruction they may accomplish at that place that at all events no harm will be done to that beautiful monument of French art the "cathedral".

27/10/16

Finished duty this morning at 8.30 am., fairly busy night, very wet and miserable weather. Last evening I obtained a new tunic which fits me well and also a pair of khaki trousers. Find that it is not possible to get riding breeches, which of course are more preferable, also obtained a new pair of boots and puttees a short while back so am well off for clothes at the moment. My old riding breeches have had mended where they needed it and shall continue to wear them as I dislike the infantryman's trousers. On duty 5.30 pm until 9 pm.

28/10/16

Clearer weather, but rather windy. Hear that a fight took place between British and German destroyers in the channel and that two of the enemy were sunk, we lost so I hear one destroyer and an empty troop ship which grounded. On duty 1 pm to 5.30 pm. Visited Pont-Noyelle as usual.

29/10/16

Dull morning inclined to rain. On duty 8.30 am until 1 pm. Will here make a note upon a few more observations in which are included many things. A very odd and probably old custom still prevails at least in the villages of France, it is similar to the well-known advertising agency which is employed at all the seaside places in England. Instead however of the usual assistance of a pony and cart and the loud ringing of a bell prior to announcing the sailings of pleasure steamers and the times when concerts and performances are scheduled to commence. The occasion here is different. An old man may be seen marching down the street, beating a drum of medium size, after which he will make known to the inhabitants such news as for instance, that a large number of troops are expected to arrive in their neighbourhood and are to be well received by the civil population, or perhaps he has some instructions to impart as to the lighting of premises or the closing of "estaminets". The French divorce laws are apparently greatly dissimilar to our own, if the wife for instance desires a divorce she must appear before the tribunal together with her husband. Otherwise her application is of no avail and will not succeed, a woman may obtain a divorce if her husband is brutal and that she can show the marks of his brutality, a wife can also obtain a divorce if after two years of cohabitation with another man she applies on the grounds that she has a family by her fiancé who she is desirous of marrying. Further if a wife should be dissatisfied with her husband upon sexual grounds she may also appeal to the tribunal for a divorce, all she needs to say is that before her marriage she did not cohabitate with her husband and consequently was not aware of the fact that her husband was unlike other men. The judge may indulge in laughter naturally but the woman will be granted her request. These are some very reasonable and sane arguments in favour of a much disputed question, aptly adopted by the French to suit most probably their own national characteristics. I must not fail to make a passing remark upon the spirit of the daughters of France, which is really to the spirit of "La France noble", which I think I admire more than anything else, it is the spirit of a nation, of a people whose heart and separations are clearly defined through the will of its woman folk more than that which obtains in any other country. I have often heard it remarked that both men and women are born fighters, born to be soldiers. I think however that if it is true of the former they undoubtedly derive their marital instincts from the women whose sons they are. I have personally frequently remarked the display of this spirit of utter fearlessness and sublime courage, which is an honest and sincere trait in the character composition of the women of France. I know for a fact that upon certain occasion when bombs have been dropping all around, some females absolutely ignore the fact and, decline to be disturbed or to budge an inch from their beds. This is however merely an exemplification of the French women in the Crimea, who although her time was close for "couch" she nevertheless sallied forth to the trenches as usual to cook for the soldiers and in that place of danger her child was born and both were well. When they hate they do so whole-heartedly and in addition exhibit great stubbornness. On the other hand the feminine world are extremely affectionate and far less hypocritical in their mannerisms that I have found to be the case with so called staid English maidens. They moreover love devoutly and deeply, with extreme concern and without affection, at least not more than one must always grant to the opposite sex. I do certainly admire the spirit of the women and mothers of "la France noble". Above all things perhaps they do possess a strong perception of justice, which they are not slow to assert and I believe that if necessary very speedy way to lead the way. The French as a nation have a world-wide reputation for thrift, which in my opinion is truly well merited. There are no such objects of distress as work houses and I know of no charity institutions. It is no exaggeration to assert that practically one and all who constitute the plebeian community have amassed their 1,000 francs or thereabouts. It is unfortunate however a lamentable feature in connection with this national characteristic, as I have heard it frequently remarked by neighbours that even young women have been known to succumb from overwork, but perhaps principally their early death has been hastened on account of the fact that they have attempted at the same time to exist on quite insufficient nourishment in comparison to their daily heavy toil. It is literally true to say that the peasant women work in the fields and allotments until the moment that they lie down upon their death bed. One sees old women bent double proceeding daily either to the fields driving cattle or wheeling a "Brouette" (Wheelbarrow). To me this state of affairs is sad. These old women have completed their lifes long toil long ago, but I am afraid that the habits and usages of centuries cannot easily be effaced. There are certainly not many things much harder to kill and do away with entirely the people's customs, which in truth become part and parcel of themselves. A few remarks must certainly be made upon a few matters of a domestic nature. To begin with I might commence with the "poele" or stove, which is invariably almost the first object, which a stranger remarks, upon entering any French house. It is placed as a rule in the centre of the room or perhaps a little distance away from the walls. The smoke escapes by a pipe which is let into the wall. The fire, what there is of it, is entirely closed in, with the exception of a small hole at the bottom for the purpose of "attiser" (to poke) the fire with a "tisonnier" (poker), still a good heat is quickly obtained and there is apparently very little waste for almost anything will burn without much difficulty. In the absence of coal, which is at the moment an expensive luxury and also exceedingly difficult to procure for civilian consumption owing most probably to the fact that the military authorities commandeer the greater portion, the French peasants instead burn logs of wood, which commodity is by no means sparse. The logs are sawn into small chunks by a most necessary article of the household furniture known as a "scie" (saw), but it is totally different to

61

our well known hand-saw. It is in structure similar to that, which is used for cutting stone-blocks, but of course the "scie" is on a much smaller scale. One foot is placed on the end to keep it firm and holding it upright between the legs to steady while the branch or piece of wood is drawn up and down and at the same time revolving same until it is sufficiently cut all round to enable the piece to be broken off. Wherever there is a "poele" and French people there is also most assuredly a "cafetiere" upon that "poele". The French are devout lovers of café even more so perhaps than we English are of our cup of tea. They grind the beans themselves in a small square wooden box affair with a revolving screw down the centre. This inevitably little article is called "moulin a café" without which no French home is complete. It may seem almost incredible but I am firmly convinced that the air here is decidedly different to our English air, which in my opinion is appreciably more bracing and clearer. Personally I find that the atmosphere in these parts in generally more humid and relaxing. Perhaps too there is a slight mixture of the Eastern temperature. Only a short while back when we experienced a short spell of frost were my thoughts carried away to the brisk fresh air of old England for the first time since my arrival in France. I am of the opinion too that it is probably this matter of climate which has a good deal to do with the difference in temperament of continental peoples to ourselves, where we are so snug in our breezy little island. In conclusion I may remark that in my opinion I see many evident signs of approaching revolution, not only here but in other countries also. If this war does not culminate after this winter the women of French at all events will probably rebel. I think in fact, it is more than likely that only revolution will put an end to this insane struggle. It is no longer war, neither is it possible that we can obtain any other result than a draw with our enemy, no matter to what length of time we may keep up the fight, all the essentials to victory are in my opinion lost and have been deliberately thrown to the winds. Many of them moreover disappeared at the Dardonelles, never more to be regained. Germany has been permitted to root herself firmly and she cannot now be overthrown, at least in the manner, in which we in the first place set out to accomplish. For all this we have to thank alone the base traitors in our Government whom we should by all the laws of right and justice expel from office and oblige them to answer to the nation for their downright treachery. Again I say that the woman will not allow this madness to continue, it will be stopped and if necessary in a very dramatical manner indeed. On duty 9 pm until 8.30 am tomorrow morning.

30/10/16

Finished work this morning feeling very tired. Did not rest at all however during the day, as I am too anxious to take the utmost advantage of every moment I have to spare, and I prefer to spend my time endeavouring to pick up the language. On duty again at 5.30 pm until 9 pm. Was paid 30 francs.

31/10/16

Spent morning in Pont Noyelle. On duty at 1 pm until 5.30 pm. Nothing of much importance to note. The war continues it is true, just as usual, which fact is made obviously apparent in the evening, by the brilliant flashes which constantly light up the heavens.

1/11/16

Fair weather. On duty 8.30 am until 1 pm. Today is known as "La Toussaints" and before the war was a day of great celebrations. I am not very well up on church matters but I gather that this particular fete is in commemoration of the dead. It was the custom for the churches (Catholic) to organise grand processions and everybody took a holiday. In the villages round about however at the present time there is a great dearth in cures probably due to the fact the French Government oblige these members of the ecclesiastical profession to take their place in the ranks of the army. Hence there were no high jinks today but I noticed that the opposite sex could not refrain from putting on their Sunday robes. Bought a pair of slippers with rope bottoms for which I paid 2.25. It is quite a relief to put them on for a time and as I practically live at a house in the village I find them most convenient and practicable. Was also issued with a leather jerkin, which is certainly a most welcome article. It is well lined and splendidly warm and comfy also received a couple of pairs of winter pants and a pair of woollen gloves, for a soldier however this latter article of clothing is of little practical use, mittens are of great value and much more preferable.

2/11/16

Very wet night and apparently does not appear that it will cease raining during today. Finished work this morning at 8.30 am very tired too. The all night turns of 11½ hours which comes around every 3rd night on the relief is rather too frequent. As I wish to record anything and everything which might be of the slightest interest I will here give an accurate facsimile of a couple of casualty telegrams from two casualty clearing stations. There are of course quite a large number of them and they all send in their returns to the DMS 4th army and to the DGMS 2nd Echelon GHQ several times each day. "t3745 30/10/16 aaa admitted since last return British other ranks sick 1 Indian other ranks sick 2 aaa In hospital British other ranks sick 40 Indian other ranks sick 18 aaa ranks sitting 6 Indian other ranks lying 5 sitting 3 aaa from luck now ces B section". "T846 2/11/16 aaa admitted since last return nil in hospital officers wounded 5 aaa other ranks sick 25 wounded 3 aaa German sick 2 wounded 2 aaa for evacuation other ranks lying 2 Germans 1 aaa From 2/2 Lond Cen 17/16". On duty encore at 5.30 pm until 9 pm.

3/11/16

Fine morning but very muddy. Our relief paraded at 9.30 am under Lt. Stephens and we proceeded on a route march for an hours. We were simply a mess of mud when we got back. Received a letter from Miss Weeds, also replied to same giving full particulars of the print of my horse "beauty" and also of my horse Doris, to enable Miss Weeds to paint them for me. Nothing special to note, we appear to be massing large forces of troops on the front but with what object it would be difficult to conjecture at the moment.

4/11/16

Nice fine morning. On duty 8.30 am until 1 pm also down for the "Joy-wheel" much to my chagrin discomfiture, so instead of resuming my duty at 9 pm this evening I shall have to come on at 5 pm instead, which gives one very little time to oneself. I finished work at 1 am feeling done up. Have also rather a bad cold, which doesn't improve matters.

5/11/16

Very strong wind blowing today but fine and sunny. The leaves from the trees are fast falling now, making a thick carpet over the fields and roads. It will be so bare and bleak everywhere when the foliage has all disappeared. On duty at 10.30 am until 1.30 pm and again at 5.30 pm until 9 pm.

6/11/16

My duty altered today to commence at 1 pm until 5.30 pm and 6.30 pm to 10 pm. This duty will last for 10 days and at the moment it is looked upon with great aversion by all the members of the staff in view of the fact that we are habitually kept on over our normal hours. We have always been more or less understaffed and at the present time such is especially the case, all the split duties (about 18) are invariably retained on account of pressure. I was compelled for instance to remain on duty this evening until 1 am, working hard all the time. Our case is exasperated not a little by the fact that for 3 days and probably we shall continue for some time longer to be fed upon bully beef, also there has been no issue of butter. This shortage of food is attributed to the activity of enemy submarines in the channel. I saw a telegram also, which stated that no mails had been received from England at Bolougne today, which is probably due to the above cause. On the whole we have very little time indeed to ourselves, not half enough infact, considering that we work all days alike and never as is the case with some other units of which I am aware, are we treated to the luxury of a day off occasionally to relieve the perpetual strain somewhat. Between 10 pm and 11 pm a couple of Zepps were reported to have crossed the frontier. They dropped bombs at "Meaulte" which is used by the British as a dumping ground etc. The oil dump was struck and burnt furiously throughout the night, lighting up the sky with deep crimson. Just after 1 am the Zepps or perhaps Taubes returned and were over Amiens, a veritable battle ensued between the earth and the clouds, numerous searchlights strove to penetrate the mist with commendable perseverance in search of their obscure prey. The shells from our guns could be distinctly heard tearing their passage through the air. I cannot say what was the effect of our fire, as personally I could neither see nor even hear the enemy aircraft, but the mischief which they were doing or at least trying to do plainly discernible from where I stood.

7/11/16

Very wet day. Duty as usual but feeling rather fagged out as cannot shake myself free of a rather nasty cold, which has attacked me recently. Nothing of note today.

8/11/16

Weather a little better but continues showery and is becoming much cooler. The leaves lie thick upon the ground and will very soon all have dropped from the trees. The countryside has indeed already taken upon itself a very different aspect to formally. On duty 1 pm to 5.30 pm and again

6.30 to 12.30, had to stay on for 2½ hours over my time. There is a model male tank outside the chateau, which is used I believe for instructional purposes. It is of huge dimensions and not of a very proposing appearance. There are a couple of turrets one on each side with a sham quick fire protruding therefrom.

9/11/16

Sunny pleasant day. I will endeavour to give a short description of the formation and disposition of our (the 4th army British) signal office. The hours are divided into 3 groups, which are worked by three separate reliefs of about 40 operators in each relief. Each finds 5 men daily for what is commonly called the "joy-wheel", which however, few, if any one cares much about. The relief's parade outside the chateau ten minutes prior to the time scheduled for commencing work at the "S.O". Dress "drill order", with rifle and bandoleer. They march by the drive, which passes the front of the chateau, salutes the sentry and upon reaching the place of much toil are halted and drawn up facing the office. The officer in charge may possibly inspect the new relief, but if not the men are given the order to file into the cloakroom for the purpose of placing their rifles in the racks and hanging up bandoleers and caps. There are in all 30 circuits to be manned, 3 wheatstone sets working directly to Abbeville (ab), Rouen (m) and Haore (HR). The first named is also (yq) with Romescamps (rs), Etaples (tp) and Boulogne (bn). These particular sets are kept well supplied by three "punchers". The remaining circuits include 5th army (ear) formerly reserve army (zar), advanced GHQ (gcp), 15th corps (pco), 10th corps (rco), 14th corps (oco), 3rd corps (cco), amiens (am), General headquarters (GHQ), 6th French army (bo) including mericourt, cagny and villers brettineaux, albert (alb), 2nd Cav. div. (vb), cav. corps (zrc), corbie (cb), Tibemont (rb) other circuits include (ol), (oh), (auo), (hd) and (vt) attached to the signal officer there is also a very busy and important telephone exchange. There are approximately about 250 wires, which come into this office, including telephone, test and Morse wires. The total average of messages daily which are dealt with here reaches over 5,000 which is more than the other 3 armies put together. It is certainly equal also to ten or 12,000 telegrams in a civil office owing to the length of the great majority of military messages. It may easily be gathered from this that we never have a very cushy time. Hostile aeroplanes were active again in the evening. One dropped 3 bombs near Guillemont station at 10.30 pm, but no damage was done. It is decidedly cooler now.

10/11/16

Lovely sunny weather prevails today. Towards the evening our "heavies" commenced an extremely heavy bombardment, which is shaking the ground even here. An interesting scrap of news I noticed in a telegram, was to the affect that "Sixty chairs from the National Galleries were being sold to the commandant of the 29th divisional school for 5 francs 75 each. The "taubes" were again over this evening. They have done a great deal of damage at different places especially Amines, which always appears to be the chief attraction to the air marauders. Tonight they have destroyed a number of houses and large buildings, killing many people. They also dropped leaflets which were written in French, telling the inhabitants that they would return tomorrow night. I viewed the contest between 10 pm and midnight. It was a perfectly glorious evening, a cloudless sky, lit up by the stars and a bright full moon. The hum of the aircraft could be distinctly heard and also the rata tat tat of the opposing machine-guns away in the direction of the firing line, our artillery was pouring forth a weight of metal incalculable and as it seemed causing the whole world to tremble. From a romantic point of view the whole scene was probably unique, but from the point of view as I know it in connection with the elements, which constitute in my opinion the real meaning of war, the scene which was presented also bore a strong resemblance to a world gone mad and beyond even its own control.

11/11/16

Weather fine but dull. Artillery still actively engaged. Received a letter from my Aunt Ada, with a 1 pound postal order enclosed and also a pencil with holder and rubber.

12/11/16

Dull misty sort of weather. Wrote a letter to my Aunt Ada and posted it. Will now produce a correct facsimile of a reinforcement telegram, similar in fact to many which are received daily. This one is from Dadrt Etaples times at 12 noon to traffic Amiens senders no 9128 date 12/11/16 and commences "Reinforcment train d941 leaves by c144 at 14.40 today aaa JESSIE 6 officers 6 men MONA 11 officers 7 men OLGA 2 officers 30 men MARY 8 officers 45 men EDITH 4 officers PEARL 37 officers 52 men JOHNS 3 men DELIA 9 officers 4 men SYLVIA 1 officer 27 men ENID 31 men BARNES 6 men CHESTER 2 men RUTH 5 officer 226 men RADIUN HQ 5 men JANE 13 officers 122 men IDA 3 officers 10 men NANCY 20 men ROSES 5 officers 113 men NOYELLES 2 officers 400 men NORA 3 men". We had fresh meat for dinner today and also butter was provided at tea, which was very welcome after so much of the eternal bully beef. Finished duty promptly at 10 pm this evening as there has been a decided falling off of business during the day. Our bombardment still continues without intermission, and by the evening had risen to great violence.

13/11/16

Dull damp day. During the early hours of this morning our artillery preparation has become of extreme intensity. It was rolling out in a veritable tornado. One wonders how it is possible for anything, human or otherwise, is able to survive such a hurricane of fire and iron. At 5.45 am we attacked from the SCHWABENREDOUBT to a point about 1000 yards north of SERRE. The attack at the latter place failed, but BEAUMOMT HAMEL and ST-PIERRE DIVION were both taken and more than 2,200 prisoners have already been reported as captured, another report says south of the ANCRE the attack was entirely successful. North of the ANCRE an attack was generally successful up to about (k.35 central) over 2,500 prisoners taken. Am not feeling up to the mark at present and yesterday I had a return of last year's toothache, which caused me a good deal of pain prior to falling asleep last night. Am still persevering with the language of the French and have amassed more than 1800 words, which I have learned off by heart, have only been able however to do this dint of much perseverance and unrelaxing efforts.

14/11/16

Rather dull and close today. Received a letter from my brother Harry. Prisoners have now mounted up to 4,000 and will probably reach over 5,000 according to reports. Our artillery fire continues with much abatement. The Germans have retaliated very heavily in certain sections of our battlefront. I heard from a person today who was at Amiens during the recent air raids there, that the Germans had succeeded in killing and wounding a large number of people, apparently all civilians, including women and little children. One case I may note concerns a small family. It appears that the husband left the home upon an errand, the wife asking him not to be long away. When he returned however, it was to find both his wife and child killed, murdered by the monsters of civilisation, another incident was enacted in a cemetery, where bombs fell and unearthed the bodies of the dead. Still we do not retaliate. If we are not to destroy all the vermin of German birth I think at least that we might collect all the bodies of our barbarious enemy and place them altogether, until their numbers have risen to the height of a hill, which would hence become a landmark for the whole world to behold and to shun. It would be an enduring monument of all that is vile and corrupt and a lasting object for future generations to observe and remember the moral lesson, there exhibited for their guidance and welfare. I was surprised to see 3 lorries packed up with soiled soldiers linen this morning which included shirts and pants etc. I expect they were the belongings of the men in the trenches, who not being able to wash them where they are, it is done for them by the military. I know that there is a military laundry near Amiens at a place called "cagny" so probably that was the destination of the lorries I saw. According to the official report, which I saw this evening the Germans do not appear to be able at any price to restrain themselves from their refarious devilry. The report stated "among the ammunition captured in the German trenches was a number of explosive bullets aaa The machine gunner with whom they were found admitted that he had received order to insert one round in every twenty in the ammunition belt of his gun". Prisoners up to now amount to 5165 and it is stated that several hundred have not yet been unumerated. Finished duty this evening at 10 pm prompt, which was very fortunate. Tomorrow I resume on the relief for which too I am truly thankful. Wrote a letter to my brother Harry and posted it.

15/11/16

Frosty clear day. On ration fatigue from 9 am until 11.15 am. On duty 1 pm to 5.30 pm. Received a parcel from Elinor, which contained a couple of writing pads with envelops and pencils, enclosed two packets of tobacco, box of gold flake cigarettes, two long boxes of chocolates, two tubes of toothpaste, a very handsome protected mirror and a nice cake. I am sure I am indeed exceedingly grateful for them all. In the meantime the war still continues and our artillery fire does not seem to have slackened at all. It goes on growling and thundering day and night, it must be terribly trying for our valiant gunners. I trust that the enemy is getting his belly well filled with our very generous offerings and that he duly appreciates same. The roads are all becoming very hard and dry due to the frost. I hope it will continue as I find that this sort of weather suits me admirably.

16/11/16

Very brisk frosty weather again today. On duty 8.30 am until 1 pm in the afternoon. I played football on our ground, which is on the right of the Amiens road. Wrote a letter to Elinor and posted it. Commence duty encore at 9 pm and worked through until 8.30 am the following morning. The "Taubes" again paid us a visit this time paying their attention to a very great extent to Albert, it is not true however that these night marauders carry out their nefarious work with impunity. I believe for instance that two enemy machines were brought down about a week ago by our fire from the anti-aircraft gun at Senlis within the first twenty shots.

17/11/16

Frightfully cold night it was a difficult matter even to manipulate the instruments, in spite of the fact that I had a woollen jersey under my tunic, a thick well lined jerkin and my cavalry great coat over all. Spent the day at my usual place at Pont-Noyelle, where I partook of the luxury of an excellent hot dinner. On duty 5.30 pm until 9 pm. Still continues extremely cold. The clouds are also gathering in dark masses and the moon is only partly visible occasionally. Away to the front the shelling (probably by the enemy) lights up the density even of the clouds, as it would seem in perpetual sheet lightning and the reflection illuminates in vivid flashes the village roads.

18/11/16

Woke up this morning to discover that the earth was clothed in its wintry garments of snow. It is blowing an icy wind and slight rain falling, for this reason our usual parade at 9.30 am for a route march was fortunately cancelled. On duty 1 pm until 5.30 pm. The war news today is that we have captured another 1000 prisoners. The snow has practically all cleared away, but it is still miserably cold and dreary. Have been picked to play in a "DaR" team tomorrow afternoon, Sunday.

19/11/16

Dull threatening morning, and very muddy everywhere. On duty 8.30 am until 1 pm. A facsimile of a forecast message, which is similar to those received daily. This was handed in at meteor GHQ Hesdin and is timed at 8.40 pm, addressed to climate 4th army date 19/11/16 and commences "Forecast wind between S.E. and S.W. 15 to 25 miles per hour probably increasing later aaa some rain with fair intervals and at times bright aaa cool aaa fair visibility aaa". At a quarter to two this afternoon I went with others to the officers mess where a lorry was in waiting to take the football party (2nd team) to Daurs a village about 4 miles from here to play the 29th Divisional school there. The day was dull and the ground sodden. We changed into our football togs at the signal office and the lorry took us up to the ground. I had put on a pair of footers, the only pair obtainable, which were decidedly much too small for me and hurts my feet horribly. Still they were better than the heavy military boots for the particular purpose. We had a good team in the field and Kt. Blower of ours played for us on the right wind, as for myself I might mention that I have not played the game for many years, in fact not since my school days, except on a very few occasions indeed. It was hard running too, on account of the heavy ground, which was of course extremely slippery. We were all very soon covered in mud, our side was fortunate if drawing first blood and within the first 3 minutes play scored an easy goal, at the close of the match we were the victors by five goals to our credit as against one for our opponents. The lorry which conveyed us out also brought us back. The journey was spent in the usual manner of soldiers by singing sentimental songs of home and girls. Arrived back at 5 pm, had tea and a wash at the billet and then proceeded on duty at 6 pm. Finished work at 1 am feeling rather tired and stuffy.

20/11/16

Rather cold but fine. On duty 10.30 am until 1.30 pm. Spent afternoon at Pont-Noyelle and went on duty again at 5.30 pm until 9 pm. From a report I saw today we have captured more than 7,000 prisoners during the last week.

21/11/16

Dull foggy morning and very cold. Paraded at 89.30 and went for a route march with our relief for an hour afterwards, had a bath and general clean up. By the way I never fail to have a good scrub down once a week and a complete change of linen. On duty 1 pm until 5.30 pm. No English mail arrived today. Our fellows had a whist drive this evening, one half representing ladies, and the other half gents. Prizes were given and the whole thing was a complete success, beer was sold at 1½ f per glass. I did not attend as I wished to spend the evening at Pont-Noyelle, where I had a hot supper of fried potatoes and chops, which was followed by the usual salad and wine. I might mention that another soldier, who is the fiancé of a French girl from Amiens, also spends a good deal of time at the same place and we are a jolly party when together.

22/11/16

Thick fog and very cold this morning. On duty at 8.30 am until 1 pm. Have obtained a pass for tomorrow to take me out of our billeting area, as I have decided to fulfil my promise to my Aunt Ada, to visit sometime the military cemetery at Carnoy which is situated about 5 miles to the right of Albert. On duty encore at 9 pm on the all night shift.

23/11/16

Frosty foggy morning. Finished work at 8.30 feeling very done up. However after having my breakfast and a wash I felt much refreshed and at 10.30 am started on my journey. It had now become quite a beautiful day, brisk fresh air but sunny and pleasant. I have reckoned upon obtaining a lift but was obliged to walk some distance before a private motor car came along and took me as far as Lakoussoie. From which place it was not a difficult matter to get a lift into Albert. I mounted a lorry loaded with 8-inch shells upon which I sat and in consequence I trust that they will prove lucky shots. They were bound for Contalmaison so that upon reaching the well know town of Albert I had to descend and seek the road which was to direct me to Carnoy, but which no one seemed to know. However I got on the proper road eventually upon enquiring of a French interpreter, who gave me instructions from a map. I had a good look round the poor cathedral prior to departing upon my journey. The noble structure has been literally torn to shreds by shellfire, as in fact a large number of houses and buildings have unfortunately met with the same fate. Over the principle entrance to the cathedral is a large scriptural painting, which still presents to the people a little beauty in spite of the terrible destruction, which surrounds it. There are wide gaping holes in the walls, which are still left standing. The most astonishing feature however is the spectacle of the Virgin Mary, which has been knocked over and is leaning over from the summit of the tower, with the head pointing to the ground and over the road, which passes beneath. The image is holding the saviour child out in stretched arms, much as though the mother wished to show to the world how much the best of heaven and of earth have been called upon to suffer for the faults of man and the sins of the world by a rabid godless people. To continue I found that my progress from Albert outward, was of a most difficult character and extremely retardable. I was constantly jumping up into the lorries only to find that they were either going in another direction or stopped after a short run to discharge their loads. I was compelled therefore to do long distances on foot, upon a road too bad for words. The traffic too, along this typical artery leading to the front is so dense that one can only get along at a crawling pace. I should mention that as soon as I reached Albert German Taubes made their appearance and although our guns kept up a rapid fire, leaving huge clouds of smoke in the heavens, the Germans nevertheless continued to return time after time. I noticed that we had quite a large number of aeroplanes, carrying out so it appeared to me a sort of patrol work. These machines I constantly observed all along the route from Lahoussone circling to and fro and flying rather low. I noticed also that our aeroplanes never left the line of captive balloons, which encircled our battle front, of these latter agencies of observation I counted 24 silently carrying out their duties of watching the enemy movements. Our patrol machines (for such I choose to call them) reminded me very vividly of our vigilant little torpedo boats, which patrolled up and down the Aegean, when we were at the Dardonelles in order to safe guard our shipping from submarine attack. The captive balloons are certainly a most peculiar object to witness, especially from a distance. They look something like huge flies dotting the heavens. I don't think I have ever seen anything like the traffic even in London, which honestly never ceases upon these busy arteries leading to the front line. It is also of a most varied description, no procession ever formed could possibly be so interesting. Every step one takes is absolutely crowded with incidents, far too numerous to relate. There is no break at all in the long line of war appendage, which includes columns of lorries, batteries, dispatch riders, transport columns (horse), infantry on the march, motor ambulances, parties of cavalry and many single horsemen, Indians with their transport and colonials. All along the route on either side of the road have been constructed huge encampments in many styles and with varied materials. The road of which I travelled is in a beastly state of repair, it is remarkable that the traffic is able to make any progress at all. In the Crimea war we lost a big army from no other reason that that there was no good road. Yet although we have made use of this particular thoroughfare, practically throughout the war, no attempt whatsoever has been made to construct a new and better one. Even the graves by the side of this route are in many cases under water and crosses are leaning over in all directions. The tree which in better days ran along the roadside have all been cut down and parties of men are now engaged upon digging out the stumps. The woods to the front and rear are all in a badly battered condition and only the remains of broken branches remain upon the trunks, while others which are broken in half by shell fire, lie with the shattered portion resting upon the ground. Along the whole way from Querrieur there are large numbers of German prisoners in repairing it. I noticed too that a great many of them appeared to belong to the same regiment, which I assumed from the fact that they wore upon the back of their right shoulder a sky-blue ring of cloth. Passed Fricourt village on the left afterwards "Fricourt Sidings" (by the way a single line railway runs along the left-hand side of this road). Continuing straight on I passed by the "water point" (for cavalry) and afterwards I came to a rack, which struck off to the left and was pointed out to me as the nearest way to the cemetery at Carnoy. I took it and was at once over my boot tops in pure mud. However I stuck to it and presently struck the railway, where I met a "tank" ploughing its way through the slush. I have described this engine of war slightly on a previous occasion, but to watch its movements is most interesting. The monster rises and falls quite naturally as it negotiates the undulations of the ground. Like me it was simply covered in mud, from the quick-fire which protruded from its side turrets I concluded it was a "male tank". Continuing my journey along the railway I came upon two small cemeteries to the left of the line, but upon investigating I found that they contained French soldiers only, some of them with the familiar wreath of twisted wire peculiar to French graveyards hanging from the crosses. Moving on a little further I passed another small French cemetery to the left, opposite on the right of the railway and in a hollow, close to the wood is rather a large British cemetery, in fairly good order and neatness. I commenced at one to search for the grave of my cousin's husband, 2nd Lt. Santher. I began at the first grave and scrutinised each area carefully, walking up and down each row in turn. Was not however awarded with success until I had almost completed my search. Lt. Santher is buried apparently with 5 privates of his regiment all in one plot. Probably they were all killed at the same time. I made several notes and duly despatched them in a letter to my Aunt Ada this evening. I felt that I could not leave the graveside with the mere satisfaction inspection only and wished sincerely that I had been given some commission to perform by Isobel. I involuntarily said a few words of prayer upon discovering the resting-place of a brave soldier. I took upon myself the responsibility to inscribe in indelible pencil, upon the top of the left arm of the cross, the words "love from Isabel". I then commenced my return journey at about 2.30 pm. Retracing my steps via the same muddy track by which I came, was fortunate in getting a lift in red cross ambulance which dropped me about 2½ miles from Albert. I endeavoured to gain the Albert road along a route, which passed by a church with only the front left standing. The road however was nothing more nor less than a running river of undiluted mud, so I gave up the attempt and took another way, which was not quite so bad and which brought me to the main road again by a large military cemetery (British), which is also a perfect picture of neatness and order. Mounted a lorry which was going to Albert and quickly reached that place via the cathedral. Albert is sadly knocked about it is true. There are a large number of houses and buildings totally destroyed. The walls in many places are bespattered with shrapnel holes. Still I should have imagined that the whole town would have suffered far more severely than it has considering the close proximity of the Germans for such a length of time, and more especially in view of the fact of its supreme importance to the British army. Getting into another lorry I commenced the return journey to Querrieu along the Amiens road, which is perfectly straight all the way, in fact it would not be possible to imagine a straighter road anywhere. Passing over the well-known "sauet bridge", which spans the railway and according to the interesting information of a friend in the lorry, the Germans have repeatedly attempted to destroy it, which may be true enough. Before reaching Lahoussoie I was obliged to descend and get into another automobile in order to continue my journey. When passing through this village I noticed a band of Scotch pipers playing in the roadway, this and many other military spectacles may be witnessed up here at any hour of the day. I arrived back at 4.15 pm feeling rather the worse for wear, still I was not sorry as I had enjoyed the outing immensely and also I had fulfilled a promise which had waited already much too long. On duty at 5.30 pm until 9 pm. Received a letter from Elinor and also one from Doris.

24/11/16

Good night's rest. Dull day, paraded at 9.30 am for a route march, but instead Lt. Stephens took us up to the football ground, where we tossed for sides and played for an hour. On duty at 1 pm until 5.30 pm. Have managed to contract another bad cold again, which always makes me feel rather weak.

25/11/16

Very wet dull day. On duty at 8.30 am until 1 pm. Received last evening a parcel from my Aunt Ada, which contained a nice cake, two writing pads, an indelible pencil and a reading book, also received a letter from my Aunt Ada today, which contained another official document, requesting details of my wife's military allowances. Wrote back to my aunt to the postmaster of Birmingham. Spent afternoon and evening until 8.30 at Pont-Noyelle, when I proceeded on duty at 9 pm to work the all night shift.

26/11/16

Rained heavily all through the night. Spent a very uncomfortable time in the office, due to my cold, which is accompanied by a slight sore throat. Was extremely fatigued upon completion of my services at 8.30 am. After breakfast I visited the French "perruquier" for the purpose of having my hair cut and a shave, after which I proceeded to Pont-Noyelle where I stayed the day until 4.15 pm when I returned to Queirieu and paraded for my duty at 5.30 pm. It is really very fortunate for me that I have somewhere to go during my leisure moments, otherwise I could not possibly contend with the many unpleasantries of our billet, which is so dull and cold. Also I am afraid that my health is seldom very good, and that my constitution is by no means strong or even as it once was when I can remember that I often breasted many hardships and privations comparatively easily.

27/11/16

White frost this morning. My cold has slightly improved. From 9 am until 11 pm on ration fatigue, 1 pm until 5 pm on duty at the signal office, afterwards had hot dinner at Pont-Noyelle.

28/11/16

Bleak cold morning. On duty at 8.30 am until 1 pm. Spent the afternoon and evening until 8 pm in the usual way. Went on duty at 9 pm on the night turn.

29/11/16

Fairly good night on account of the good heating of the office. Finished work at 8.30 am feeling much less fatigued than upon the last occasion. Pay parade at 10.30 am at which I received 30 francs. Cold day which turned in the evening to a sharp frost. I should mention that leave commenced last week and that nineteen per week is our allotment for blighty. There are about 467 however attached to this headquarters so that personally I am afraid my turn will come in the far distance. In connection with the attempted electric lighting arrangements by means of the stream, which flows through the ground of the chateau. I might mention that up to the present it has proved a failure, the effort has not been dropped and a party of German engineers with the assistance of a few English are still doggedly persevering with the object, which they have in view. On duty 5 pm until 9 pm.

30/11/16

Cold sharp morning. Paraded at 9.30 am and marched to the football ground, where we picked sides. Ours won by 2 goals to 1 managing to net both goals myself. On duty 1 pm until 5 pm, afterwards wended my way to the next village where I had a hot supper. There is a good deal of sickness among our chaps at present due no doubt to the scarcity of nourishing food and continued exposure, which they have to contend with in their billets. We parade every third day for a route march or perhaps a game of football. This is done with the object of forcing the men to active exercise in order to keep them in good trim, am picked to play in the team tomorrow, my position being "centre forward". Wrote a letter to Miss Dorothy Roberts in answer to one which I received from her in the morning.

1/12/16

Very cold morning with slight mist. On duty 8.30 am until 1 pm. Played in a football match this afternoon. We had quickly 2 goals to our credit, but before the play was finished we had lost by 6 goals to 2. There were various causes for our defeat, amongst them being that some of our men were too worn out during the 2nd half and some of our opponents belonged to the 1st team of their respective unit. However such is war and the same applies in sport. I felt very stiff when I went on duty at 9 pm and had also received one or two slight hurts.

2/12/16

A very cold night, but feeling better. I finished work this morning at 8.30 am. Had a shave in the village and afterwards visited the "instituteur" who is an amateur photographer, for the purpose of having myself taken. Don't know how it will come out, but do not expect great results. It requires too much time however to go to Amiens. After my visit here I took at once the road to the next village and had a hot dinner, am feeling a bit seedy at the moment which is most probably due to rather a nasty cold. I will here reproduce the usual morning report of casualties, which is different from the others of which I have previously given examples in as much as this particular casualty clearing station states also the maladies of the patients. It is from OC 39 CCS and timed at 6 am of today's date, addressed to DMS/4th army and also to the DGMS GHQ 2nd Echelon, senders no 2335. Commences "Admitted since last return sick, officers three includes 1 suspect dysentery, other ranks 36 includes 12 suspect dysentery aaa in hospital officers sick 10 includes 4 suspect dysentery 2 measles aaa other ranks sick 326 includes 5 suspect C.S. - M 4 suspect diphtheria 3 diphtheria 30 suspect dysentery 4 dysentery 20 rose measles 12 measles 21 mumps 1 scarlet 1 suspect typhoid 4 suspect typhoid carriers aaa for evacuation officers lying 8 suspect dysentery sitting 1 other ranks lying 31 includes 3 dysentery 13 suspect dysentery 8 mumps 3 diphtheria sitting 10 aaa". On duty 5 pm until 9 pm.

3/12/16

Rather cold day and misty. Received a letter from my aunt and one also from my cousin Isabel. I received a packet yesterday from my cousin Ethel, which contained a pipe stick of shaving soap, three notebooks and a tablet of soap. My duties have been altered, commencing today for 10 days. My times will be 1 pm to 5 pm and 9 pm until 1 am. Have replied to all the letters which I have received today.

4/12/16

Bright clear and fresh this morning. Herewith are contained a few additional notes, which I have hitherto not mentioned. There are French "interpiretes" attached to almost every unit in the British army. They may be easily identified by the badge which they wear upon the collar of their tunics, one on each side. It is in the form of a sphinx's head, is made of metal and is yellowish in colour. In military phraseology these men belong to what is known as the "mission militaire Francaise attachee a l'armee Britannique". Their duties are varied but so far as I have seen personally their principle function appears to be to find lodgings and beds for the officers, when for instance a unit is on the march or in rest. Will now enter one or two more features of the first days of the war in so much as they effected our own immediate locality. It appears that the Germans were always pleased whenever they found that the inhabitants of a village or house had not decamped and for very obvious reasons as they had a once plenty of servants ready to hand to answer to their beck and call. One case in point however at Querrieu, where the family had quitted the farm-house, the Germans at once set the place on fire and indulged in a few high jinks around their handiwork. Another instance of their disreputable character, is shown in the case of an old man who still lives in the last house on the right of the road leading out of the village of Querrieu towards Amiens. The Germans killed one of his cows and the old man was so dismayed that he inadvertently made use of the expression "coahon" (pig), a German officer who was standing within hearing distance, overheard the remark and in consequence struck him several times in the face, probably much worse would have been the result, but for the timely interference of a friend who happened to be near at the time and who pleaded on behalf of his fellow countryman to the affect that he was an old man and therefore excusable. I must say that the common habits of the French people leave much to be desired and lack of cleanliness to say the least. In the first place no one could accuse the French of wasting water for the purpose of washing themselves, or for that matter soap either. In this particular respect too they fail totally to comprehend the English and our fondness for the bath. In one other respect too that although the "cabinets" (of a sort) are provided, the poorer classes do not even trouble to make use of them, but frequently squat down in any convenient spot outside the door. In this matter of cleanliness and hygiene I must certainly state as my personal opinion that I do not admire the French for their obvious laxity in some of the first principles of life. Another habit which I have observed is the practice of throwing any refuse upon the floor, such as the dregs of cups etc. However in the matter of dress I think the women of France could easily hold their own anywhere. Their clothes are spotlessly clean and well arranged. In short they dress themselves very "Chic" and what is more they know it too. I would like to add with respect to the above remarks that I do not profess or even suggest that they appertain as a fact to the French people as a whole. They do apply however to particular classes of which I have personally come into contact, but of which it would be rather a difficult matter to make distinctions by separating into classes and certainly not wise to attempt. I have ascertained that since the commencement of hostilities the French housewife has not been compelled to pay rent and that in practically every case she is not doing so. After the war however she will be called upon by the landlord to refund in full the total sum unpaid. This of course will be in the majority of cases an absolute impossibility. There will probably be a good deal of flitting from place to place in order to avoid the inevitable necessity of finding such a large amount of money as will be due and which in fact has already reached to a very high figure. I saw a funeral today and was struck by the familiar "Drapis des morts" which was carried by the bearers in exactly the same manner as for the same ceremony as I witnessed in Egypt. The French one however was different in colour, having a black background with a white cross down the centre and a white bouflette at each of the four corners. Whereas the Egyptian one, if I remember rightly was composed of many gaudy hues.

5/12/16

Cold day. Heavy artillery firing has continued throughout the day. Nothing of special note today.

6/12/16

Dull miserable sort of day. Am very glad indeed to see in today's papers that the Prime Minister has resigned. I have considered him to be for a long time the prime obstacle to victory. He should also be made responsible for our many blunders and calamities and pay the price of all such traitors. I noticed in an official telegram the other day that it stated that "no French soldier can join the British army unless authorisation be granted either by the minister of war or the General Commander in Chief". This particular telegram was in answer to a query from the French who had put forward an application by a French soldier who wished to join the British army. At the bombing school near Freckencourt a village close by a regretable accident occurred nearly a fortnight ago. From what I have been able to gather of the fact concerning the case, it appears that while handling a box of bombs, for some unknown reason they exploded and killed an officer and four other ranks. They have been entered on the top of the hill near to the above named village. I fancy that our casualties from a similar source must by now have amounted to a considerable figure and is obviously extremely lamentable.

7/12/16

Very dull and cold today. Everything appears to be at a standstill at present and there is nothing at all worth jotting down here. We shall soon have Christmas here but I shall spend it I presume in a vastly different way to the last. It is a year ago at the moment since I was travelling along the Mediterranean and out into the bay of Bis on my way to my beloved country. I remember we were all so happy on board the hospital ship and our hopes were running high with the prospect of spending Christmas at home in the dear homeland after our long Eastern travels. I shall never forget that most pleasant of all voyages as long as I live. It was pleasant in all respects and unmarred by the knowledge of facts, which I was destined to face.

8/12/16

Damp and foggy. The roads are all in a beastly state. I am not feeling up to the mark today, but am always badly affected by such weather. Obtained my photograph today, which was taken some days ago, but as I expected they are greatly disappointing and am vexed rather as I could not really spare the money for them. I demanded that it should be retaken, this time in profile but I have little faith in a good result even now.

9/12/16

Weather continues to be unpleasant. Very dull and heavy grey clouds obscure the sky. It is nothing but drizzle and mud. My boots too are almost off my feet, which makes matters worse, as it is necessary before one can obtain a new pair that the old ones should have little life left to them. This method is obviously extremely extravagant and unnecessary. It should not be a difficult matter to supply the 400 odd men here with a spare pair of boots so that when they begin to wear it would be possible to have them mended. There seems however to be much that is wanting in systems with the Royal Engineers. Received a letter card from Ethel.

10/12/16

Very damp and muddy again, no prospects of finer weather yet I'm afraid. Nothing of an unusual character worth noting.

11/12/16

Grey overcast sky and the usual plentiful supply of mud everywhere. Obtained a new pair of boots (brown) this morning and not before I required them either, was obliged to walk or attempt to do so upon my heels to prevent if possible my feet from becoming wet. I have always a nasty cough, which at times becomes rather severe and is most disconcerting and unnerving too. I should mention that last night I returned to our billet after leaving duty at 1 am. This is the first time I have not slept in a bed for some months, ever since in fact I finished my time on the road. It is strange rather that I was not pulled up and punished for failing to answer the roll. I have however been left entirely alone, stranger still is the fact that although all my comrades are undoubtedly a little jealous of my apparent select position, they nevertheless one and all appear to wish me well. I spent a very shivery night and have no intention of repeating the experience again. Had I not found a bed I am well aware that I could not have withstood the rigours of a life in a draughty damp barn as it is I hope to be able to stick it through now.

12/12/16

Weather continues murky and uninviting. My duty is changed again today and I resume on the relief. Finished work at 5 am for the day, which I certainly appreciated after the spell of 10 days going on duty again at 9 pm until 1 am.

13/12/16

Little brighter weather has made its appearance today. Commenced work at 8.30 am until 1 pm. On the "joy-wheel" in the evening from 5 pm until 1 am. This is an extremely tedious and irksome duty. It means that two days is practically spent working at the office. However "sa ne fait rien, c'est la guerre".

14/12/16

Miserable wet day encore. Received three letters this morning from my Aunt Ada, my sister Gladys and Mrs. Roberts. On duty 10.30 am until 1.30 pm and again at 5 pm until 9 pm.

15/12/16

No change in the weather today. No items of particular interest to note. It is very same from day to day. Short day at the office only working from 1 pm until 5 pm. The electric lighting arrangements at the mill are making rapid progress. News came through this evening that the French have achieved a notable success in the Verdun region, capturing over 8,000 prisoners and many guns. Several villages also have fallen to our allies and they have apparently advanced a distance of about 1½ miles on over a 7 mile front. I hope this will be a suitable answer to Germany's audacious and unscrupulous peace proposals, which filled the daily papers three days ago. Not that I believe that we can effectually crush our enemy by our methods of warfare but I do certainly believe that now we have disposed of some of our most formidable enemies in the Government that we stand a very favourable chance of hitting our foreign foe very severely indeed.

16/12/16

Frosty morning and not so much mud lying about. Received a parcel from my Aunt Ada today, which contained a plum pudding, box of sweets, pair of football boots and an undervest. My French studies are progressing very favourably. Have amassed over 2,000 words which I have learned by heart to speak. I have in fact laid a very fair conversational ground work, which is extremely satisfactory to myself. Wrote a long letter to my Aunt this morning, also dispatched 46 postcards all of Albert except 3, which were photographs of destroyed buildings at Carnoy.

17/12/16

Finished work at 8.30 am after spending a very cold night at the signals office. Received another parcel today from my Aunt Ada, which contained a box of gold flake cigarettes, a nice cake, and chestnuts etc., two cakes of chocolate, another undervest and a small cake. Hear that the prisoners now in the hands of the French as a result of their latest offensive have reached the grand total of over 9,000 and more that 80 guns. There seems to be also some artillery activity upon our front the last day or two. There is a rumour that a leave allotment is to be considerably increases, but as yet there is no official confirmation to that effect. During the late evening the artillery fire became rather vigorous. I hope that we are also preparing a suitable British reply to our enemy's barbarity and cowardice.

18/12/16

Muggy and cold today. On duty 1 pm until 5 pm. Spent an hour in the evening talking to some French people of my acquaintance in their home, afterwards proceeded to Pont-Noyelle. The artillery fire on the front is not diminished in the slightest, but continues to rumble monotonously through the night. There does not appear however to be any official reference to it. Wrote a letter to my sister Gladys.

19/12/16

Very cold frosty morning. Was nearly too late for parade this morning at 8.20 am, owing to my watch stopping, just managed however to snatch a morsel to eat and scramble on duty in time. Slight snow storm in the afternoon. Received our Xmas cards in the evening, which were ordered a few days ago. They depict on one side the village church and on the other the road which leads to Amiens with a transport column wending its way through the snow. They are both coloured engravings and make quite a suitable presentation to send to our people at home.

20/12/16

Finished work at 1 am this morning and returned to our billet to spend the rest of the night. It was frightfully cold and this morning there is a heavy frost. Received a small parcel from my sister Doris containing a plentiful supply of note-paper, a box of 20 BDV cigarettes and some chocolate, all of which I am very grateful to receive. On duty 10.30 am to 1.30 pm and again at 5 pm until 9 pm. There was a very heavy bombardment during the day, but the official report does not mention the fact.

21/12/16

Miserable wet day. Slept at the billet last night, as it is not possible for me to go to my room now, owing to it being occupied. I am very sorry indeed for this as I spent an extremely shivery night and did not feel rested when I got up this morning. Received a letter from my cousin Isabel. On duty at 1 pm until 5 pm, afterwards spent the evening until 9 pm at a little farm house close by talking French with the family. The master, Monsieur Dervios has served for 2 years in

Algeria with the French troops and was apparently delighted to tell me his experiences, which in many respects coincided with my own in Egypt with regard to the natives etc.

22/12/16

Beastly weather, nothing but rain, rain, rain and heaps of mud. Received a letter from my sister Doris. By a telegram which I saw today from DDS & T 4th army only sufficient plum puddings have been received to issue at the rate of a ¼lb per man. Issues at this scale will be made tomorrow. On duty 8.30 am until 1 pm and again at 9 pm on the all night turn. Wrote a letter to my sister Doris.

23/12/16

Blowing a gale today and very cold, a bessoneau shed at Chipiloy aerodrome which belonged to the 4th Bde RFC was blown down, but no machines were inside at the time. It has also affected a little destruction to our billet but No. 3 billet where I resided for some time when I first arrived here, was severely handled and is partly a wreck. After finishing work at 8.30 am this morning, I cleaned myself up and proceeded to my usual place at Pont-Noyelle where I stayed until dinner time. The afternoon I spent at my recent acquaintances down the road. On duty 5 pm until 9 pm. Might record here that about 4 weeks ago there was instituted a system of wireless interception stations in our army (better late than never I suppose). They are apparently doing a good deal of work and I will here reproduce a facsimile of a message from "wireless ?" of today's date timed 6.20 pm and addressed to Intelligence 4th army. It is written of course in German cipher senders number 36. Commences "Intercepted BB to Ba begins 0900 ZIF 12 FOQOB YPAHP AH ends aaa IC to IB begins 1345 CHI 20 SZYOB NFLAK QYBKY ESENP AM AP JAMMED ends".

24/12/16

Bright sunny day, the sort of weather which forces one to hope inspite of oneself. Bully-beef and cheese for breakfast, in consequence of the bacon being reserved for cooking with the turkeys tomorrow. Attended divine service with our relief which was held in the canteen and commenced at 9.30 am. General Rawlinson commanding the 4th army also attended and sat in front close to where I was sitting. He is a soldierly looking man and carries three rows of colours on his tunic. Afterwards visited Pont-Noyelle. On duty at 1 pm until 5 pm. All split duties and "joy-wheels" have been suspended for tomorrow (Xmas day) to enable everyone to take part in the local festivities. Received a parcel from Mrs. Roberts and Miss Cummins containing 300 cigarettes, which will keep me provided for some time. Spent the evening at the little farm just down the road. The French people do not keep up Xmas as we do. They have no knowledge of plum pudding and all the other Xmas luxuries so dear to the heart of the English. There are no decorations or preparations of any sort.

25/12/16

Fine but rather dull. On duty 8.30 am until 1 pm. I would like to note here that according to a telegram which I saw yesterday afternoon from GHQ Intelligence the Germans are still practising their usual atrocities. The wire states as follows, commences the sender no ta/25900 date 24 Dec "It is reported that British prisoners are being sent from Cambrai to work in the danger zone near hermos aaa Endeavour to obtain definite evidence on this point from German prisoners aaa". No letter or parcel mail arrived today. Spent the afternoon divided between my new place at Querrieu and my old at Pont-Noyelle. Only bully-beef for dinner, so that until 6 pm when we all gather together to take part in the Xmas dinner which is being got ready at "L'ecole des garcons", we must make ourselves believe that we are not hungry. It was however to say the very least certainly worth waiting for. When we entered the tables were decked out with spotlessly clean washable material and the room was gay with bunting and various sorts of decorations, the whole with the aid of brilliant electric lights, presented a very pleasing and inviting appearance. The first course consisted of turkey, ham and vegetables, which was followed by roast beef and vegetables. Afterwards came plum pudding with sauce. The drinks consisted of beer, grenadine, VIN rouge, a little whisky etc. all of which there was an abundant supply. We had as much as we could possibly eat and had a nice sort of comfy feeling afterwards. The colonel and officers called in during the repast and spoke a few words of cheer. The feast was followed by a concert, the singers being found from among the soldiers present. Nuts, apples and oranges washed down with divers waters, also cigars and cigarettes were freely distributed among the men. One and all there is no doubt whatever spent a thoroughly enjoyable evening, even in spite of the fact that there were some who must admit that they did not enjoy the best of health on the morrow. Unfortunately I had to leave the entertainment at a few minutes to 9 pm to prepare for duty at that hour. As the relief marched down to the chateau they gave vent to their hilarious feelings by singing along the route.

26/12/16

Finished work at 8.30 am. Did not feel so fatigued as usual, probably owing to the fact that I had had a good stomachful of excellent food the previous night to help me withstand the rigours of an all night service. Received a letter from my wife and brother Harry, also cards from Miss Dorothy Roberts and her mother also one from Miss Cummins and another from Aunt Ada. In an official telegram, which I saw today it was stated that "one more Russian prisoner came over from the West of St-Pierrevaast wood and is being sent with the other five to GHQ. One of the latter number is wounded". It would obviously appear from this that the Germans are now employing Russians for working in the danger zone. There has been a good deal of heavy firing throughout Xmas. On duty 5 pm until 9 pm.

27/12/16

After breakfast and clean up spent the morning at the little farm close by. Heavy artillery firing still continues and at about 3 am this morning there was a terrific explosion which literally shook the earth. On duty 1 pm to 5 pm. Wrote a letter to my dear wife Elinor, also received one from Miss Weeds. The weather is greatly improved today. Spent the evening divided between the neighbouring village and my friends here. It is freezing hard this evening.

28/12/16

Severe frost during the night. No cessation in the artillery firing, which became exceedingly excessive during the early hours of the morning and in fact kept me awake for sometime. On duty 8.30 am until 1 pm and again in the evening at 9 pm on the all night turn. Things seem exceedingly dull lately and it is hard to find occupation for ones thoughts. It is a blessing that I have my French studies in spite of their rudeness to enable me to pass away this lonely life.

29/12/16

When I finished work this morning I felt quite done up. It was a dull misty sort of weather which heralded the day. After breakfast I took my clean clothes down to the bath-house and there indulged in a comforting spray-bath. the water however was slightly on the cold side as I had apparently arrived rather too soon, still I could not allow my weekly ablutions to pass by and so must needs get the matter off my mind at all events. My duties have been changed today for a split, which will be for the ensuing 10 days commencing at 1 pm until 5.30 pm and 6.30 pm until 10 pm if I am lucky. I have visited a house today in the village for the purpose of obtaining a bed if possible. I shall know in a day or so if it will be at liberty for me. This procedure is of course I know full well contrary to the town major's orders but I am anxious to get as much comfort as possible and incidentally a little practice in talking the French language with my landlord and lady. Returned to our billet after finishing work at 9 pm did a little French study and then engaged in a sound sleep.

30/12/16

Got up too late this morning to go down for breakfast. It is very windy but drier. This sleeping in the barn seems to upset my stomach owing probably to the damp coldness of the place penetrating through my clothes. Spent the morning visiting different people including the place where I am desirous of securing a sleeping apartment and helped them to kill a rabbit. As a proof of the high cost of living I may mention that this particular rabbit cost eight francs and I believe that they cannot be obtained anywhere hereabouts under seven francs. I noticed that in the casualty reports, which have been going through recently, that they include Kaffirs, which is significant as it shows that we are at last making some little use of the Empires manpower, which of course is the strongest point and the principal feature, with regard to the ultimate issue of the war. France has already all her man-power in the field right down to class 17, but I believe that we have still quite a strong force in reserve and even untapped. Finished work at 10.20 pm. Wrote a letter to Miss Hedge.

31/12/16

Dully muggy day. No luck so far with my contemplated sleeping out affair, still there e is nothing like exercising a little patience, when in the army. It becomes in fact more or less a habit. There is no official news of much importance. For some time the chief item contained in the reports are repeated references to the artillery activity on both sides. Occasionally we indulge in short concentrated bombardments, which we direct against the enemy's trenches, and at times to some effect as we have observed the enemy carrying away his wounded. Wrote a letter to my brother Harry. Tonight is New Years Eve. I wonder what it will bring for us and for the world. I trust that at all events there are approaching brighter times, although at the moment I cannot see much that is worth looking forward to, but I suppose that in this gigantic conflict the proper attitude to adopt is a full and distinct disregard of all personal considerations.

1/1/17

Strong wind blowing and dull and damp. Things move along from day to day in the usual jogging manner. This evening the electric lighting installation at the mill, which is worked by the river, commenced operations and is apparently a laudable success, more3 lights will be obtained owing to its greater power as compared with the portable affair, which was hitherto the source of our electric lighting supply. A new hut is being built by the relief's in turn, each doing something daily towards its erection. This alteration has been made necessary on account of the mill being totally utilised for the above lighting purposes, and the new hut, which will also have the luxury of electric lamps, is to accommodate us for feeding.

2/1/17

Weather is very temperate at the present. On fatigue in the morning. Commence work at 1 pm and do not finish until 10 pm or after, which makes it a terribly long and tedious day. Received a New Years card from Miss Weeds on which she had painted a horses head and my thoughts at once reverted to my "Beauty".

3/1/17

Muggy windy day. Received a letter from my wife Elinor. No luck encore, re the bed which I am anxiously waiting to have the pleasure of sleeping in. I am boundlessly fed up with everything. I do wish it were possible to have a few days furlough in England. There seems not the slightest chance however and the whole affair of leave seems to have collapsed miserably, which is due absolutely to the usual English method of bungling up things. the men who have already been to blighty are all unanimous in the condemnation of the utter chaos, which exists all along the route and especially at the ports, where men are often obliged to waste several days hanging about. During the first days of leave for our army the men were also left without food, no arrangements having been made to feed the soldiers from the time that they left their units.

4/1/17

Received a letter from Miss Dorothy Roberts. In the afternoon the weather turned very cold and chilly which probably signifies a frosty night. German aeroplanes owing to the clear atmosphere paid us a couple more visits in our direction during the late evening.

5/1/17

A little more bright this morning, am afraid however that the exposure is slowly getting the better of me as am feeling rather low and several have remarked on my pale appearance. I am also terribly weary of all things. There seems nothing at all to expect or to look forward to and I know that this long war is ageing me to no inconsiderable extent. Wrote a letter to Miss Dorothy Roberts. Enemy aeroplanes were over Amiens quite early this evening and there was considerable shelling by anti-aircraft guns.

6/1/17

Very cold night, which greatly disturbed my sleep, weather still beastly, wet and muddy. Heavy artillery firing commenced in the late evening, cannot say however to what purpose or for what reason.

7/1/17

Roads all hard with frost. Spent a restless night and was much troubled with that most unwelcome malady tooth ache. This is the last day on a split duty and tomorrow I resume on the relief for which I am truly thankful.

8/1/17

Cold windy day. Reported sick in the morning for the purpose of having my teeth attended to as had suffered for 4 days with the tooth ache. Rode into Amiens in the Red-Cross ambulance lorry and was taken with others to the New Zealand hospital where I had a couple of bad teeth extracted. Also had a nice dinner which was of tender meat and bread sauce followed by rice milk pudding and prunes, but none of which was cooked in the orthodox military style. Started back about 1.30 pm and called at the 37th cas clearing station at Allonville to drop a man, who was suffering with diarrhoea, arrived at Querrieu about 2.30 pm and proceeded on duty at 3 pm and worked till 5 pm. A most peculiar object which I witnessed this evening with several more soldiers was the appearance of what looked like a small aeroplane in flames and flying with the wind, which was very strong towards the frontier. It was about 7 pm and of course quite dark and such a spectacle was most weird to say the least. No one could even conjecture what it might be and we watched it for sometime before it finally disappeared in the far distance amid the clouds.

9/1/17

Dull cold morning. On duty 8.30 am until 1 pm. should have recommenced work at 5 pm on the "joy-wheel" but persuaded a comrade to exchange duties with me for 5 francs which gave me the evening free. After dinner our relief was employed in erecting an Armstrong hut behind the mill for the use of the electrical mechanics. About 7 o'clock this evening I again observed the aerial fire this time flying in the direction of Amiens. I have ascertained that it is in truth an aeroplane, but until yesterday I had never observed the peculiar object which these machines present when illuminated in such a manner. A heavy bombardment is progressing upon our front without intermission, I have had another interview with the people with whom I propose to live that is for sleeping purposes, as I was undecided whether it would be better to return to my old place. I intend however now to take up my new quarters and may go into them tomorrow evening.

10/1/17

Cold dull day. Finished work at 8.30 am and after breakfasting proceeded to have a swill at the bath-house. The following are a few more points upon interesting observations. It is of course a well understood fact that the number of Anglo French marriages contracted in this country since the beginning of the war have been steadily but surely mounting up to a somewhat high figure, with regard to this I might mention that the French wife of an English soldier gains considerably from a financial point of view as compared with the "allocation" which she would otherwise receive if her husband was a soldier of France. The rate of pay is upon the same scale as that, which an English wife in England receives and in corresponding French money amounts to 2 f 50 c per day for herself and 1 f per day for child. The French rate of pay on the otherhand represents only half the above sum being 1 f 25 c per day for the wife and 0.50 c daily for a child. The French fold argue that the "allocation" is intended merely as an aid to subsistency and not meant to sustain the family and further that women without means are expected to work to gain a livelihood, which they undoubtedly do and work very hard too. Another point, which I might mention is the annoyance, amounting almost to bitterness among French soldiers, which is caused by the obvious preference of their own countrywomen for the English. It is an absolute and testified fact that "Les Demoiselles" of France appreciate to a far more considerable extent the attentions of the British than they do that of their own countrymen. This is singular and to me quite unexplainable, except for the fact that we are strangers and are presumably more tidy and clean in our habits, with a fame for beaucoup cash, as compared with our discarded though gallant allies. I may add too that in my opinion "les hommes Francais" are often rather negligent in their associations with women and girls in respect to a standard propriety, when in conversation with the fairer sex. They do not posses quite the same respect for females even of a modest demeanour as that which characterises fairly well bred English men. On the other hand the men are always very civil indeed to strangers, where as the opposite sex, which is perhaps more feminine in this country, than in any other in the world, are apt to become quite suddenly, extremely conservative and even insulting in the brusque straightforward dealings, especially if they fail to take a liking to one. I have repeatedly noticed one distinct difference in the social habits of the French in certain important directions, in comparison to our well worn and greatly tried British methods. It is obviously not considered necessary at any rate at the present time to contract marriage in order to live happily as man and wife. It is considered perfectly respectable for a couple to live together as lovers. This mode of life is by no means uncommon, as all women who can get a man get one, at least which is how it appears to me. Personally however I am of the opinion that this custom among engaged couples has its drawbacks and is not exactly profitable to the state as I believe it is true that parties united in such a manner are rather careful to avoid the necessity of children. A few notes upon the methods adopted by large numbers of small-holders for threshing their corn most common in these parts, might be of some little interest. ? of motor propelled machines the small farmers thresh their harvest by means of hand machines, while some who are more fortunate hire the aid of a peculiar contrivance which is worked by placing a horse upon an endless band and by ? The animal forces round the band which works the whole machinery. Xmas time is not apparently a season for holiday-making or grand feasting in France and such luxuries as Xmas pudding and mince pies are things entirely unknown. The New Year however is celebrated by the usual good wishes and in addition rather a profuse amount of kissing among friends. The salutation being given first on one cheek and then upon the other. Personally however I did not participate in this little bit of frolic although I believe it is true that a young swain is a t liberty if he wishes to kiss any girl and that his action upon this occasion is not contrary to the strict ethics of propriety, and that for this reason the liberty would not be resented in the least by the recipient. The guns are still banging away this merrily and those of high velocity are exceptionally active. I took up my new quarters this evening my room is not very big it is true, but I can stand erect in it, without fear of injury to my head, there are a couple of chairs and a small table for washing purposes at disposal, convenient shelves for putting my affairs thereon, and the bed is most cosy. There is also a small stove, which I may use if I so desire. On duty 5 pm until 9 pm.

11/1/17

Had a very restful and comfortable nights sleep. On ration fatigue from 9 am until 11.30 am. Snowing during the morning. On duty 1 pm until 5 pm. Spent the evening visiting different people and returned to my billet shortly after 8 pm. My landlord and lady together with their daughter had gone to Amiens for the day to be present at the wedding of their son, who is on leave from the Verdun front for 7 days. All French soldiers have 7 day "permission" every four months, which privilege is guaranteed to them, Mademoiselle is over here for a few days on leave from some place near Paris, where she is a school teacher. Beastly weather all through the day with snow and drizzle.

12/1/17

Good nights repose. On duty 8.30 am until 1 pm. Weather still dull. Received a letter from Miss Dill Lees. Spent the afternoon chatting to the daughter of my landlady. In the evening I invited a friend in the same relief as myself to take supper at my digs, had a good feast of steak and chips, washed down with VIN rouge and afterwards partook of the plum pudding which my Aunt Ada has so kindly sent me for Xmas. It was quite a pleasant little party, which personally I thoroughly enjoyed. Afterwards went on duty at 9 pm.

13/1/17

Finished work at 8.30 am feeling tired. Very cold wintry like weather. After breakfast and a cleanup etc. I felt however considerably better. The rest of the morning I spent in conversation with Mademoiselle at my billet. She went back to Amiens at 1.30 this afternoon, so that I shall miss my instructress, as she was very patient in her endeavours to teach me correct French. In the afternoon I betook myself to the home of the factrice, a kindly old lady, who lost her husband recently, as she asserts through the negligence of the doctor. On duty again at 5 pm until 9 pm.

14/1/17

Very cold night with snow. Had a good nights rest and did not get up until 11 am this morning. On duty 1 pm until 5 pm. Spent the evening at different places in the village. Wrote a letter to my wife Elinor. The guns are still showing considerable activity. A Zeppelin was reported flying towards our front shortly after 5 pm in the direction of Bapaume.

15/1/17

Good nights rest. It is quite a luxury to put ones limbs between clean sheets, although to begin with it strikes rather cold. It is very lonely also to be always alone. I am sure that after the war a woman will be more appreciated and more idolised than ever she has been before. It was quite cold this morning, when I looked out of my door but fine and dry, in consequence of a frost during the night. Artillery bombardment still in progress, to which the Germans reply on the whole in rather a feeble manner, although at times and at certain points, they pour their shell s upon our lines unsparingly. On duty 8.30 am until 1 pm, at 2 pm when on coal fatigue together with three comrades, to a village about 4 miles away. We filled over forty big bags with coal and afterwards distributed them round the village at a number of places. We managed to "win" a fair sackful for our billet after a good deal of manoeuvring. Knocked off about 5.30 pm feeling a little the worse for wear. I hope that it will be a long time before my turn comes round again, to do this fatigue which considering that we have the all night to do on top of it, it rather more than a joke. Received a packet from my wife Elinor which contained several extremely useful presents, including a tobacco pouch, pipe and 2 tines of tobacco. The first named came as a timely and most pleasant surprise, as only three days previously I had had the misfortune to burst my own right across. I had already posted a letter to my wife in the early morning and in the evening I dispatched another, also wrote to Miss Weeds. On duty again at 9 pm.

16/1/17

Off duty this morning at 8.30 am. Very cold night, and frosty. Received a letter from my wife Elinor. Spent the day visiting friends. On duty at 5 pm until 9 pm.

17/1/17

Good nights rest. Got up at 8 am and found that all the world was deep in snow. Attended pay parade at 10.30 am at which I received 30 francs. Six of which will have to go for my room alone. In view of the coming big battles which are expected to take place this year I have decided to make a note of a battle plan which I formed before Xmas and which I am of opinion would be the most suitable under existing conditions. I will go further and say that I believe that an attempt to break the German line in any other way whatsoever will meet irretrievable disaster. I have indeed often wondered why it is that our military successes are so greatly outnumbered by defeats, that we have suffered in all parts of the theatre of the present struggle and am bound to admit that it appears to me, even after making due allowance for the obvious malicious influence, which has undoubtedly been permitted to be directed by traitors who unfortunately hold or held positions of great importance in the state. I believe however that in spite of all this that the unpardonable failures of many of our military enterprises have been the result more especially on account of the fact that we English do not appear to realise the chief principles which govern the conduct of war and which never change. Without attempting to criticise any particular battle I would like to jot down what are in my opinion some of the chief factors in ensuring victory. The first item and above all the most important is what is known as "manpower". In fact a multitude of heavy guns and high explosives stand for nothing in comparison to the immense driving force of the human machine itself. As a battle plan for a future offensive I will lay down the following outline, "An army greatly superior in numbers to the enemy immediately in front should be massed upon a particular point, so that the enemy would be quick to see that we were threatening vital points in his system of defence and communications. The tail of this army should lie conveniently in the rear in order to be able to gain access at a moments notice to the artery leading to the real object of attack, which should take place not within a hundred miles of our threatening concentration. This tactical situation may be advantageously likened to the tactics attributed to the whale, his head may be large and awe inspiring, likewise that of his body also, but the chief danger is his tail. Artillery should be massed infront of this whales head unsparingly and a bombardment commenced and kept up for such length of time as it may take to cause the enemy to bring up in near proximity to the threatened area his maximum amount of troops in reserve. It would then be an opportune moment to strike suddenly and without any apparent prelude (which would only serve as a warning to the enemy), with the extreme end of the tail of the "whale", and carry out an attack principally by bombing, machine gun and small mobile cannon male tanks. I believe that by such methods as the above although only casually explained and after all the thousands and one contingencies arising therefrom have been properly and systematically accounted for and arrangements made to meet each particular case of difficulty, and by perseveringly following our plan by concerted action I do believe most sincerely that we could break through and smash our foe within a comparatively short space of time. By launching the attack from the first consistently and with vast numbers of men, rapid progress would be quickly established and the enemy's army cut in twain, would be obliged to make a general retreat or on the other hand be cut off and destroyed in detail. To obtain a sufficient number of men for this purpose I am of opinion that it would be necessary most of the white troops (of all arms), in distant parts and to fill their places with manpower which would be drawn from our Empire overseas. These troops I am confident would be able to maintain a good military standard upon the borders of our Empire, further it would be advisable to direct that in order to be able to follow up the "wedge", with ever increasing intensity that all except "strong points" should be systematically abandoned, so that the men thus freed, would add strength to the fighting power at our disposal. The enemy would not be prepared for such a manoeuvre and for that reason he would be unprepared to attempt a forward movement upon a large scale himself. Where as we should have gained the march from which the enemy would be forced to reel and could hardly expect to recover, as by a preconceived plan we should oblige him to fight upon a battlefield of our own choosing, or capitulate. I believe sincerely that the Germans could be beaten and at no great cost to ourselves, within a probable space of 3 months, if only a leader would come along and fight according to the rules of war in all ages, which never change, and which are really not changed now". There was a good deal of artillery firing throughout the night and during the early hours, it became extremely violent. Received a letter from Miss Hedge. My duty is changed to 1 pm until 5 pm and 9pm to midnight, which times I shall do for 9 days.

18/1/17

Good nights rest. Cold and miserably wet morning, with some showers of snow. Dispatched my wristwatch to England for repairs. There is still a good deal of artillery activity. Did not finish work this evening until 12.45 am.

19/1/17

Lay in bed until midday, so that was rather pressed for time to be on duty at 1 pm. There was only bully beef for dinner however and one potato per man. We are infact being indulged to some considerable extent recently in the above commodity and biscuits. Had my customary VIN rouge chaud and treated myself to a small packet of petit beurre biscuits to make up for the army's lack of nourishment. The ground is still partly covered in snow and the whole outlook presents a most dreary and unbecoming aspect. Finished work shortly after midnight. As there was no bread and butter for tea I bought 3 port chops and my landlady cooked one which together with a good plate of fried potatoes and a bottle of VIN rouge went down comfortably. Tomorrow shall have the same, but intend to share with my host and hostess. Freezing hard tonight.

20/1/17

Got up at 8 am. After breakfast and cleaning up, spent the morning writing. By the way I was brought a cup of coffee before getting up, by monsieur which was quite a delight. Very cold frosty day. Had supper at my billet before resuming work at 8 pm. Nothing of note to remark upon.

21/1/17

Lay in bed until midday. My host brought me a cup of coffee at 9 am. Still freezing hard and the roads are bound very hard. Had supper this evening composed of the usual French diet of soup followed by the well known dish of potatoes, carrots and cabbage and leeks with a little meat. Am feeling remarkably well in spite of all the circumstances such as the eternal bully beef and biscuits supplied to the army for consumption the last four days. Finished duty at five minutes past 12 am. It was a pitch dark night, I don't think I ever remember it so utterly black. It was necessary to find my way home to strike matches repeatedly in order to find the turnings etc.

22/1/17

Got up shortly after 9 am. Had shave and hair cut, afterwards short walk and called in at Epicerie for coffee and a couple of small cakes, also bought three mutton chops at the only butchers for many miles around. Shall have them for supper with my landlord and lady. Still very cold but towards midday a slight thaw set in. Wrote a letter to my wife Elinor.

23/1/17

Got up at 8.30 am. After breakfast at the mill I visited quartermaster store to obtain a new pair of boots in exchange for an old pair, which I had not handed in after receiving a new pair of boots sometime ago. It is most necessary to have change of footwear out here especially during wet weather, I have therefore like everyone else managed to wangle an extra pair. Still freezing, but beautifully bright and sunny. Bought some steak chops to have for supper this evening. Received a registered letter this morning from my Aunt containing 1 pound money order, which I was able to change into French money at the French civil post office at Querrieu and for which

I received 27.75. It is still freezing very hard. When I went down to breakfast this morning I noticed a dog lying dead upon the footpath obviously frozen to death. I wondered at the time if it was the same poor beast that followed me a short distance down the path between midnight and 1 am as I was leaving the Chateau grounds.

24/1/17

Hard frost still holds the ground, but it is beautifully bright and sunny in spite of the severe cold. My landlady had put a welcome hot water bottle in my bed and I did not rise this morning until 11 am. Had a clean up and shave and on my way to work a glass of VIN rouge chaud with the "fractrice" who happened to be in the same café. Received a nice long letter from my wife Elinor. This morning the roof of our signal office has been covered in canvas which was badly needed, owing to the draft which was always very uncomfortable, while we were working the circuits. An aeroplane has fallen on the summit of a hill near Corbie and its tail, which is of immense size, can be distinctly discerned from here, although it is probably more than 3 miles distant. I cannot say what was the cause of the machine falling there. Wrote a letter to Miss Hedge. Artillery is still very violent upon our front, indeed the groaning of the guns does not cease night or day. In addition the several bombing schools and musketry schools round about fill the air incessantly with loud explosions. In fact at times the concussions are so violent that we are unable to read the Morse sounders.

25/1/17

Another frosty day, but also bright and sunny. Got up at 10 am. Had a short stroll and basin of coffee, en route bought three beefsteak chops, which cost me 2.25, am spending a good deal of money upon the important function of eating. They will go down very nicely however this evening with the aid of a bottle of wine etc. Artillery extremely heavy this evening. Did not finish work this evening until 1 am owing to the pressure in the office.

26/1/17

My duty is changed commencing today back onto the relief. On duty 10.30 am until 5 pm with a break for dinner from 1 pm to 1.45 pm. Bitterly cold this morning owing to keen driving wind. Had some sausages for supper with fried potatoes and a bottle of VIN rouge. This wine is now 2 francs per bottle (litre). Frightfully cold day. Artillery bombardment still very heavy at times.

27/1/17

On duty at 8.30 am. Beastly cold again. Leave has been yet once more stopped for the poor Tommies, on account of congestion of the French railways. Staff officers and some other grades are however allowed to go to England on leave. The bully beef which we had for dinner was quite frozen and covered in ice. Bought some beef steak chops and had them for supper with my landpeople before going on duty at 9 pm. The 29th Division obtained a complete success this evening capturing more than 300 prisoners.

28/1/17

Finished work at 8.30 am feeling rather fatigued. After breakfast and wash up went for a short stroll. Very cold still and the wind blows more and more bitterly. On duty at 5 pm until 9 pm. Was soon into bed and fast asleep.

29/1/17

Got up at 11.30 am. Extremely cold still. Received a letter from my landlady's daughter, which was written in French, she speaks well of my effort in letter writing. The soldiers here find a good deal of amusement skating and sliding on the lakes round about, which are thickly coated with ice. A census has been taken of all the soldiers here, it is thought that a weeding out process is contemplated. On duty 1 pm until 5 pm and again at 5.45 pm until released, which fortunately happened to be about 6.45 pm. Artillery firing still rather heavy. The Germans have bombarded heavily our newly captured trenches. The reason why they did not do so immediately was I should imagine because our little offensive came as a complete surprise to them.

30/1/17

Got up at 7.30 am. Washed in warm water, which my landlady brought me. Very cold and there was a slight fall of snow during the night. On duty 8.30 am until 1 pm, on the "joy wheel" in the evening, which commences at 5 pm until 1 am. When finished work at this late hour it was snowing rather hard and beastly cold. Bombardment continues heavy.

31/1/17

Got up at 9 am after a welcome nights rest. Snow made a white carpet over all the world, it was awfully cold. Visited the French barbers for a shave and then returned to my billet for a wash etc. On duty 10.30 am until 1.30 pm. Bully beef again for dinner. Spent the afternoon in a small epiciere drinking coffee and eating chocolate. Afterwards collected some small pieces of wood for my fire, which I intend to light after leaving off work tonight at 9 pm in order to heat some water to "bath" myself in. I was fortunate in finding a gas mask, which I utilised, as a receptacle for my firewood. After work at 9 pm I collected the sticks, which I had laid aside during the afternoon near the Chateau. Made myself a fire and boiled some water, with which I had a good swill down before getting into bed. It was rather a cold job all the same as my compartment is separated from the house, and in consequence does not get the advantages of a fire during the day. The walls are infact glistening with frost.

1/2/17

Got up at about 8.30 am. Had an excellent nights sleep. Had breakfast and cleaned up. Bought some beefsteak for supper this evening. On duty 1 pm until 5 pm. A slight thaw has set in today, but do not think it will last long. Received a letter from my wife Elinor and one also from my sister Gladys. Freezing again very hard in the evening. The bombardments during last night became very intense indeed.

2/2/17

Good nights repose. Artillery firing considerably relaxed. Still freezing rather hard. On duty at 8.30 am until 1 pm. Spent afternoon drinking coffee, then bought some beefsteak for 2 francs which is the price I usually pay, and is sufficient for my landlord and landlady to partake with me. It is fried and together with potatoes also done in the same way and a bottle of wine or beer, makes altogether a pleasant little feast. I also get the advantage of considerable conversation in French, which is what I desire more than anything. On duty again at 9 pm on the all night shift. Artillery activity again today renewed with vigour.

3/2/17

Finished work at 8.30 am. Beautiful sunny day but frosty. Indeed it would seem that it had come to stay. After breakfast and a clean up, spent the morning drinking coffee and a little talk, after dinner visited an "estaminet", when I stayed until 2 pm. Afterwards more coffee. Later collected a sackful of small pieces of branches and transported them to my billet for the use of my hostess. Wrote a long letter to my wife Elinor, also another in French to my landlady's daughter, to whom I shall transfer it, for transmission to the said mademoiselle. On duty 5 pm until 9 pm. Very heavy artillery firing throughout the day.

4/2/17

Good nights rest. The roar of the artillery never ceases, and at times is of a most violent character. Got up at 10 am, had some coffee and biscuits and afterwards proceeded on duty at 11 am. Finished work at 5 pm. It is piercingly cold, but bright and sunny during the day. Weather reports, forecast a continuation of our cold friend. I should consider myself very fortunate indeed in having the luxury of a bed, a fire is lighted in my little retreat each night by me landlady for about an hour, and a hot water bottle placed in my bed. I wear a pair of socks (for sleeping purposes only), and soon after getting between the clean sheets I am comfortably warm and sound asleep. It is indeed an enormous contrast to my less fortunate comrades who sleep in barns. Spent evening in an "estaminet" drinking VIN rouge, which is more like water nowadays, although it is costly enough, being 4 d for a small glass. Was in bed just after 8 pm. Had the misfortune to kick my hot water bottle out of bed, which cracked it badly. The 5th army made an attack last night at 11 pm, after a most violent bombardment and captured all objectives except one strong point, which we surrounded. Our captures included 1 officer and 200 other ranks, also 3 machine guns. Heavy artillery firing continued throughout today and became intense in the late evening.

5/2/17

Up at 7.30 am. On duty at 8.30 until 1 pm. Freezing still very severely. Spent afternoon in usual manner walking round to different places and drinking coffee. Received a French elementary grammar book from my landlady's daughter, which is of a decidedly useful kind and will undoubtedly aid me considerably in my studies. Received also a couple of parcels from my dear wife Elinor containing my large black infantry kit bag, wrist watch which I had despatched to England for repairs, box of gold flake cigarettes, box of Turkish delight, box of chocolates, box of fruit drops, packet of tobacco, cake and a large pork pie. All of which gratefully delighted me and am more than grateful for them all. A new French English dictionary was also included in the above and a large mince pie. Bought some beef steak which I had for supper with fried chip potatoes at my billet. Am making very good progress with my French conversation too. On duty at 9 pm.

6/2/17

Finished work at 8.30 am this morning. Rather fatigued too but after a wash, shave and clean up felt considerably improved. Still freezing severely. Several immense guns have passed through our village this morning from the front. Indeed for sometime past there have been similar movements of artillery from the direction of the front. Had a game of chess before dinner which I lost. I was reminded of the old days in Egypt where I played the game twice or three times daily. On duty 5 pm until 9 pm. Was soon in bed and fast asleep.

7/2/17

I have been temporarily attached to No. 3 relief commencing today. Got up rather late and in consequence had to rush about somewhat in order to be on parade at 8.20 am. Managed to scrounge some bacon and bread, which I put in my pocket and consumer later in the office. Finished work at 1 pm. Leave was opened again I believe last night. Freezing still but not all unpleasant in the sun. Spent afternoon with a short walk and a little French studying. On duty again at 5 pm until 9 pm. Rather vigorous bombardments during the evening. Hostile aeroplanes again visited Amiens in the late evening doing some damage, from a French source I gather that two houses were demolished and 2 or 3 persons were killed. Extremely cold night, I collected some branches of trees in the chateau grounds after leaving off duty at 9 pm and carried them to my billet. In fact almost daily I procure something to take to my land people, which takes the form sometimes of wood, and sometimes bread and cheese which I obtain from our mess. In consequence of the high price of sugar in the village, which is also a difficult matter to obtain I buy a couple of pounds a day from our canteen, at two pounds for one franc, just half the price for the same quantity at the shops in the village.

8/2/17

Very cold morning, but warmer later on when the sun got high in the heavens. On duty 5pm until 9 pm. Am changed onto No. 1 relief today. More movements of artillery from our front. Very cold night.

9/2/17

Good nights rest. Still hard frost. On duty 10.30 am until 5 pm. Bought some beefsteak in the evening, which I had for supper with some fried potatoes and cider. Heavy artillery still trekking throughout our village. The bread which we had had issued lately has been so frozen that it can only be cut with great difficulty, even with the stoutest of knives. Enemy aeroplanes reported their visit to Amiens and other places last night and were employed dropping bombs from 8 pm until about 4 am the next morning. The casualties in Amiens up to the present and not including tonight's performance, are one civilian killed and two wounded, six horses were also killed and several houses wrecked during the last few nights. It is rather a difficult matter to get to sleep during these idiotic visits.

10/2/17

Still very cold and freezing. On duty 8.30 am until 1.45 pm. Spent afternoon writing and studying. Bought 2 francs worth of beefsteak and together with my two hostesses I had a good supper prior to going on duty at 9 pm on the all night shift. During these occasions I might say that I have the advantage of considerable conversation and in addition I always manage to acquire a number of fresh useful words.

11/2/17

Busy night. Very white frost this morning, not quite so bitterly cold today and a beautiful sun is shining. After breakfast and a wash up, spent morning writing and studying. Dinner at my billet, being the guest of my land-people. Spent afternoon in conversation. Very fatigued, as am much in need of sleep and rest. On duty 5 pm until 9 pm.

12/2/17

Good nights rest but rose this morning to find I was not quite up to the mark and my head was full of cold. There is a decided change in the weather today, which in fact first became noticeable yesterday. It is still freezing slightly but is by no means as cold for which everyone is extremely thankful. My duty is changed today to a split, which will last for probably 9 days commencing at 1 pm until 5.30 pm and 6.30 pm until 10 pm or later if required. This evening managed to get away at 10.10 which is not a bad start and I trust that this time will keep up for the duration of the split duty.

13/2/17

Got up at 8.30. It was less cold now, but the frost still holds its own and binds the earth in its strong grasp. I did not however have to break the ice this morning in order to wash. The sun is shining brightly and except for the groaning of the artillery, which became rather intense early this morning, it would be difficult to believe that there was a war on, everything seems so peaceful and content. Spent morning writing and studying. Am back on my own relief today, which commenced at 1 pm until 5 pm. Spent evening drinking the ruby VIN rouge, but I may add I did not drink too much as in fact that would be a difficult matter nowadays.

14/2/17

Rose at 7.30 am. Drank a cup of coffee, which was kindly brought to me by my landlord. On duty at 8 am until 1.45 pm. Paraded for pay at 2.30 pm at which I received 30 francs, also received 1 pound money order from my Aunt Ada yesterday, which I changed into French money at the local civil Post Office. It is a nice bright day but still freezing. Received 3 French books this morning from my sister Doris, which will be very useful indeed, also had an official notification from the Postmaster at Birmingham that to the effect that the amount of 41 - 10 - 6 which it was asserted had been paid to me in excess refunded and enclosed a receipt for same. It was for this reason which decided me in joining the Royal Engineers and giving up my rank in the Warwickshire Yeomanry in order to pay off to the Department in as short time as possible this large sum of money. Spent this afternoon reading and studying. On duty again at 9 pm. Wrote a letter in French to my landlady's daughter also another likewise to my sister Doris. Bought 3 mutton chops and had them with my host and hostess for supper prior to going on duty in the evening, acquired a number of fresh words and had a very useful conversation in French.

15/2/17

Finished work at 8.30 am. It is quite a beautiful bright sunny day and not at all cold. Spent the morning drinking coffee and studying. The afternoon I spent in the same way. On duty 5 pm until 9 pm. There appears to be some changes on foot, as outstations such as Albert have come to Headquarters, which increases our staff. In consequence all extra duties have been abolished from tomorrow. This is indeed a great improvement for which we are all truly thankful.

16/2/17

Got up at 8.30 am. Had a good nights rest. Received a couple of letters one from my wife Elinor and the other was a specimen of my little boy's handwriting. It is cold and dull today. It has however commenced to thaw in earnest. On duty 1 pm until 5 pm. Bought 3 pork chops and transported them to my billet. Spent evening in conversation and learning many words. Went to bed at 9.15 pm.

17/2/17

Rose at 7.40 am. On duty 8.30 am until 1 pm. Very dull with a misty sort of drizzle. Everywhere is becoming very muddy again as of old, which is most undesirable and makes on think that after all the frost is preferable. General Nivelle Commander in Chief of the French Armies visited our Headquarters at midday today. We were informed of the fact yesterday, but warned that the visit must not be spoken of either publicly or amongst ourselves. I know however that the news did leak out, as it came back to me, in consequence of one of our number giving away the secret which goes to prove that man and woman have the same weakness in that respect. The band of the Royal Engineers headed the guard of honour, which was composed of picked men of the Grenadier Guards, and all were of the same height. It was quite a pleasing spectacle to witness the machine like accuracy of all their movements in obeyance to the orders of their officer. It is on such occasions that one is proud to be a British soldier and feels that there is yet strength and vigour in our poor country. The guard presented arms upon the approach of the General and the band started off with Marcellaise, which brought every officer to the salute. "God Save the King" followed the officers again standing at a salute. The General himself is of a sturdy build, and extremely active in his movements, but his gait would appear to be affected from the habit of riding. Spent the afternoon studying and in the evening bought 3 port cutlets, which I had for supper at my billet. On duty 9 pm.

18/2/17

Finished work at 8.30 am. After breakfast and clean up went for short stroll and did a little studying afterwards. Had dinner with my hostesses and spent afternoon in conversation with them. On duty at 5 pm until 9 pm.

19/2/17

Got up shortly after 9 am. Very dull weather and wet under foot. Spent morning writing and studying. On duty 1 pm until 5 pm. No English mails yesterday and again today, which is probably due to the thaw precautions which came into force early yesterday morning and which provides that lorries must not be allowed to run on the roads, in consequence of their destructive propensities to the road surface during the period of the thaw. Had supper at my billet, which consisted of pork chops and pancakes, good deal of useful conversation. Wrote a letter to my Aunt Ada.

20/2/17

Very wet miserable sort of morning. On duty at 8.30 am until 1 pm. Spent afternoon studying. No English mail again today. In the evening supper at my billet and a good deal of useful conversation. On duty 9 pm on the all night turn.

21/2/17

Finished work at 8.30. Had a busy night and feeling rather exhausted. It is a very damp misty morning, after clean up spent the morning writing and studying. Received a letter from my dear sister Gladys, with a pair of socks enclosed in a packet, she had kindly knitter for me the socks herself and will be very useful. Also had a long nice letter from my Aunt Ada, and another from Miss high of New Pagnall. In the afternoon I worked at my French studies. On duty 8 pm until 9 pm.

22/2/17

Got up 9.30 am. Very dull misty morning, mud everywhere. Studied a little in the morning. My duties are changed today from the relief to a split, which is 1 pm to 5 pm and 9 pm to 1 am. The sergeant gave me the choice of duties, as the five other men detailed for split duty are newcomers. I chose this duty as it is considered by all to be the best and further I am free in the evenings to pursue my studies with my hostesses, which to me is of primary consideration. Had supper at my billet and beaucoup conversation prior to going on duty at 9 pm. The supervisor released me at 12.30 as we were not very busy and the staff ample to carry on the good work.

23/2/17

Rose at about 8 am and had a good "bath" in hot water, which my landlady brought to me. Afterwards changed into clean things and feel nice and comfy once again. I change by the way all my underclothes once every week for clean ones. It is awfully dull and miserably damp today. Received 3 letters from my Aunt Ada, Miss Dorothy Roberts and my wife Elinor respectively. On duty 1 pm until 5 pm. I will now give my adventures or at least some of them for the rest of the day and the following morning. In invitation had appeared in last nights "orders" inviting officers and men of the British army stationed hereabouts who understood French to attend a lecture by Germain Bapist on "Britains effort in the air" to be held at the "Cinema omnio, ue des vers aubnois Amiens", commencing at 8.30 pm. The idea struck me to make some endeavour to attend and with that view I approached the signalmaster upon the subject as it would be necessary to be relieved from duty in the evening. The signalmaster gave me his permission to be absent and I thereupon request at the orderly room that I should be given a special pass for the above purpose, which was also granted. Owing to the fact that automobiles are forbidden to run upon the roads at present owing to the thaw precautions still being in force. I had in consequence the prospect of a long walk in front of me into Amiens, a distance of about 11 kilometres, which is by no means a small feat during these days of poor and insufficient rations. As luck would have it however I managed to pick up a Red Cross ambulance, with a load of parcel mails, which was going in my direction and was soon whizzing at between 30 and 40 miles per hour. We reached Amiens shortly after 6 pm, although I did not finish work until 4 pm, and had changed my clothes, had tea (piece of bread and butter and cheese) and was obliged to wait sometime for my pass. Walking down the principle streets of Amiens, I was astonished at the large number of prostitutes. In fact nearly all the women and young girls appeared to be in the streets for no other purpose. I was personally accosted continually. One woman grabbing hold of my sleeve, really would not let me go, at least for somctime. I went into a flash sort of dining room and found therein rather a good looking girl and well dressed, another woman who was with her and who owned the place, was a little older. Almost the first question put to me was a proposition of familiarity with Mademoiselle. I admit that I thought the idea a good one, but I did not intend to accept all the same. I explained that I had come into Amiens to attend a conference and that at the moment I needed something to drink. I asked for tea, but was persuaded after they had numerated a list of strong wines to accept Benedictine. I was well aware of course that this type of woman (enjoleuse) merely want money and nothing else and I was determined to give them neither. I noticed that the wine was indeed strong even possibly drugged. A thimbleful was in fact sufficient to mount quickly into the regions of my brain. It was time to be looking for the place of meeting, so paid my bill at the rate of one franc per thimbleful of Benedictine, and departed much to the disgust of the females. I was lucky in passing three British nurses who by their remarks I gathered that they too were bound for the same place as myself. I heard one say "Thank goodness there is a lecture on tonight", which gave me the impression that the nurse was very fed up like the rest of us. I decided to follow them as otherwise it would have been a difficult matter for me to find my whereabouts owing to the darkened streets. Nearly everyone carries a flashlight, especially the women who wish to sell their favours. They flash their torches continually into ones eyes. I did nearly come to grief against a lamppost in the middle of the road. Entering the cinema I found that only a few had arrived, but later the building became quite full. The audience was composed mostly of French officers some with their wives and families, a number of British officers also attended, but I was the only "Tommy" present. A score or more French nurses came to listen and I thought that on the whole, the gathering was a good sample of French society. Monsieur Germain Bapist wore plain clothes. He is of slight stature, with a comparatively wide but receding forehead. He uttered each word clearly and distinctly and I was able to follow a good deal of his speech in spite of an abundance of coughing, which very frequently drowned his remarks to my ears.

He spoke upon a large number of subjects, most of which are already familiar to Englishmen, a few others I might mention such as that every British regiment has a Drapean, which is the emblem of honour, he enumerated in their order the names of the battles, which one regiment bore upon its banner, and which passed in review before the late field marshal Lord Roberts during his visit to the troops in France. He solemnly declared that it was the duty of the officers of the Republican army to salute the standards of British valour. He spoke of our 3,000,000 volunteers with the highest esteem. Three million men he declared who were not forced to serve in the ranks, was a revolution and that in all the history of the world there was nothing to approach such a magnificent display of patriotism. He stated that had we not entered the war at all, we should have merely acted within our rights and that no nation could have accused us of treachery. That we went to war for the sake of Belgium and the oppressed. He pleaded that as England was now giving her all to obtain the victory both in men and money and that by gigantic efforts France would again renew her old national borders and freedom. He very solemnly warned his hearers that it was the duty of his countrymen, never to forget the loyal support of their ally, and impressed upon them the facet of France's obligations to L'Angleterre. He mentioned our national characteristics of tenacity, which was likened to the grip of a bull-dog. He reminded his hearers of the occasions when they too had found themselves in that same grip. He spoke of the late Lord Kitchener as a man possessing an exceptionally powerful character. The whole of the speech was in fact positively full of praise L'Angleterre and L'Anglaise. He reminded his hearers of our valuable assistance upon the "aisne" and the "marne". He stated further that in the absence of our timely intervention in the war, it would have been over within three months. He stated that we were finding fabulous sums of money for all the allies including themselves and that our workshops and factories were turning out ammunition and war materials at a rate and in abundance truly gigantic. He referred to our artillery as having no superior in the world, our command of the sea, he asserted was still decidedly unchallenged in spite of the fact that the Germans claimed a big victory at sea and that they were still chained down by the fleet, which they had vanquished. The speaker spoke indeed so fervently but at the same time in a severely sober and careful strain, that although one must acknowledge his sincerity and profound knowledge of his subject, the thoughts nevertheless involuntary occurs to one as to the sum such an able speaker would receive as salary from the British Government. A few remarks such as his reference to the fabulous sums that we have and are still advancing to the allied nations is not in my opinion logical. In view of the fact that by following the old Babylonian and Carthaginian principles of hiring mercenaries (other armies) to do their fighting is obviously disastrous. The cause and object may be just but the principles involved are necessarily threatened with disaster. Other nations too must feel very acutely that we hold a strong hand over their affair, while they are under such vast obligations to ourselves. However this aside at the close of the meeting a British staff officer mounted the Tribunal and spoke a few phrases in the venicular, which were most cordially received by the French. The meeting coming to an end I went to the "hotel du Marc d'or" and put up for the night. It was quite impossible to go back to Querrieu on foot at that time of night, although it is contrary to the PM's regulations that any soldier should spend the night in Amiens. I was not aware of this however so slept in peace.

Diary Number 5

24/2/17

Got up about 8.30 am. Directed my steps at one towards home. Bought a number of artistic post-cards en route. I was fortunate in picking up a lorry about a mile out of Amiens, which was going in my direction. We were however very shortly turned off the main road owing to repairs etc., and were obliged to turn and take another route via Daours and Corbie. This was very unfortunate, as it was a route in an extremely bad condition, at one point we were stuck in the mud for some time and was only extracted after considerable exertions on the part of the engine and assistance of a gang of German prisoners. Passed Daours and eventually reached Corbie where we had the ill luck to break down, owing to the fan band breaking. I was therefore compelled to walk the rest of the journey, a distance of more than 3 miles. Noticed that a large number of British troops were engaged in war exercises in the neighbourhood of the latter place. Arrived at Pont Noyelle at midday and called at a small epicerie for a café but was informed that the youngest child which had had an operation for an abscess behind the ear and had been very ill for some days had died early of the preceding day. I was shown the little mite, he lay arranged in white serenely peaceful a white veil was placed over his face and reaching down over his small hands, which were slightly curled and almost touching, at his feet lay some lilies of the valley and upon a small table nearby there was the usual paraphernalia associated with the Catholic church, including candle sticks etc. Bully beef for dinner. On duty 1 pm until 5 pm. Supper at my billet which consisted of mutton chops, macaroni and cider. On duty again 9 pm until 1 am.

25/2/17

Got up at 9 am. Rather cold and foggy. Spent morning writing. Yesterday received a parcel from my wife Elinor which contained a cake, half a dozen packets of cigarettes and a pair of mittens. Sun appeared about midday which greatly improved the temperature. On duty 1 pm until 5 pm. I was the guest of my landpeople at dinner today. Feeling the effects of my walk yesterday rather acutely. Had supper in the evening at my billet. On duty 9 pm until 1 am.

26/2/17

Rose at about 9 am. Spent morning studying. It is a beautiful fine spring morning. According to reports from our front yesterday the Germans appeared to be moving further back to a considerable depth and upon an extensive front. From reports of captured prisoners it appears that the enemy had been slowly moving to the rear for several days and their orders were to take up another line of defence in front of Cambrai by the 25 inst. The object is of course obvious, but at the same time this ruse will undoubtedly affect our future offensive operations in no minor degree. On duty at 1 pm until 5 pm. Do not feel quite so well today. Wrote a letter to Miss Dorothy Roberts and received a small parcel from Dill enclosing a pair of socks and a short note. Supper at my billet. Had some practice in writing French from dictation by my landlord, and managed it fairly well. On duty 9 pm until 1 pm.

27/2/17

Got up at about 9.30 am. It is quite warm now and the roads are drying up nicely. Spent my time in the morning writing and studying. On duty 1 pm until 5 pm. After tea went for a cycle ride to Corbie and returned shortly before 8 pm. A little study before going on duty at 9 pm until 1 am. The heavy bombardments which commenced the other day, when it was found that the enemy was retiring still continues with vehemence.

28/2/17

Got up at about 9.30 am. Paraded for pay at 10.30 am I received 30 francs. Also cashed a postal order for a sovereign at the Civil Post Office. It is rather dull today but fine and dry. On duty 1 pm until 5 pm. Wrote a letter to my Aunt Ada. Feeling better than yesterday. Bombardments still heavy upon our front. A few more successes are reported and one reverse which later occurred early this morning. The 29th division (I believe) being forced to evacuate a village.

1/3/17

Got up about 10 am. Very pleasant sunny morning. On duty 1 pm until 5 pm. Not feeling well again today. Wrote a letter to my wife Elinor. Supper at my billet. On duty 9 pm until 1 am.

2/3/17

Rose rather late. Feel rather ill. Very nice pleasant weather. On duty at 1 pm until 5 pm. I have much much uneasiness and concern. The life which I have had to lead for nearly 3 years is son unnatural and I live in a sort of fear of the consequences perpetually. Supper at my billet. On duty 9 pm until 1 am.

3/3/17

Rose late. Am still feeling ill. It is a dull cold sort of day. On duty 1 pm until 5 pm. My duties are changed on to the relief today. Our dinner consisted of stew, which was quite a change from the eternal bully beef and biscuits which has been our lot for a long time. We sadly miss vegetables however. For tea yesterday we had one slice of bread per man and a handful of dirty currents. This is the sort of food which we have had to endure for some time now. Supper at my billet and plenty of French studying, including dictation and conversation. Had a "bath" prior to getting into bed. The guns are roaring incessantly this morning.

4/3/17

Got up at 7.30 am. It is a sharp frosty morning, but sunny. On duty at 8.30 am until 1 pm. We are still on bully beef diet, but today we were privileged to one potato per man. What makes things worse for the troops also is a new regulation, which forbids bakers to sell bread to the troops. This is really quite in order as before the bakers and others had declined to sell bread on very many occasions to the civil population as they preferred to sell to the English by reason of their willingness to pay a higher figure for same, than that which is the standard according to French law. On duty again at 5 pm until 1 am.

5/3/17

When I finished work this morning at 1 am I found that the ground was covered in snow. Got up shortly before 10 am. On duty 10.30 am until 1.30 pm. Snow lies about 4 inches thick upon the ground. I am not well at all and am afraid that the hospital will be my ending which however I am very desirous of avoiding if possible. On duty at 5 pm until 9 pm. Collected some long branches in the Chateau grounds and transported same to my billet.

6/3/17

Got up rather late. Good nights rest but still very down in health. It is rather a nice day, but the snow has not yet cleared away. On duty 1 pm until 5 pm. Spent evening at my billet studying etc. Had a good supper of steak and chips. Retired shortly after 9 pm.

7/3/17

Rose at 7.30. Calm but cloudy morning. On duty 8.30 am until 1 pm. After midday the weather changed quite suddenly to freezing. Spent afternoon studying and drinking chocolate. Had supper at my billet. Am feeling considerably worse however and quite shivery. On duty at 9 pm on the all night turn. Was burning and shivering alternately all the time.

8/3/17

Finished work at 8.30 am feeling very exhausted. After breakfast went to bed and stayed there until nearly 4 pm in the afternoon. Received a letter from my wife Elinor and a parcel from my Aunt Ada. It is still freezing hard. On duty 5 pm until 9 pm. The parcel from my Aunt Ada contained a letter, 12 notebooks and a lovely cake.

9/3/17

Rose late. Had a good nights rest and am feeling somewhat better in consequence. Received a letter from Mr. Kendrick. It is still freezing, but after midday there was a sudden change to snow. On duty 1 pm until 5 pm. One of our comrades has been awarded 21 days 1st field punishment for stating in a letter certain truths respecting the poor and shocking state of the food, which has been our lot for sometime, and also making some severe remarks concerning leave, which apparently is an institution merely arranged for the benefit and convenience of the officers. Had supper at my billet, some useful conversation and French dictation, which latter I accomplished very well.

10/3/17

Not a very good nights rest. Got up just before 8 am. On duty 8.30 am until 1 pm. It is a cold damp morning. It might be interesting to note that German prisoners are now employed in digging and planting all the gardens in the village, which is obviously a most useful and beneficial occupation. Spent afternoon drinking chocolate and I did also a little studying before going to work again at 5 pm on the "joy-wheel".

11/3/17

Left duty at 12.30 am this morning instead of 1 am. Had a good rest until 8.30 am. When I got up had breakfast, shave and clean up. On duty 10.30 am until 1 pm. It is quite a pleasant sunny day and extremely mild temperature. There is a scent of spring in the air and as it were a new note of joy and hopefulness fills all the world. I am feeling considerably better in myself today and trust that this improvement will continue to make progress. It is such a pleasure to feel well and strong and without care. In the "Daily Mail" of the 9th inst., I read with much shame the findings of the majority and minority reports by the Commissioner, who was elected to enquire into the Dardonelle fiasco. I feel that I must make a few personal observations and remarks upon same as I do not think I have ever read such a jumbled conglomeration of unintelligent statements. Characteristic in fact merely for their utter ignorance of the subject in hand, lack of common sense and void of clear vision. In short a truly remarkable "English" document, moreover I have little doubt that the whole will be easily swallowed by the English and not a word of resentment or of protestation uttered from Land End to John O'Groats. The impression which one may naturally drive from the perusal of this "modest example of English knowledge and judgement upon the laws of war" is that the men concerned in drawing up thereof were unfortunately born with brains on one side of their heads only. Wholesale attacks are directed against the only man (soldier) of our generation, by men to who, if they were all grouped together would not be equal either in common sense or power of judgement to Lord Kitchener's big toe. I do not suppose that any one of those who had "had the honour to attach his signature to this scroll of infamous rigmarole could even state what should be the height of the parapet or the proper depth of a trench. Yet we the great British Empire will sit still and tolerate quietly these weak brain waves, which emanate from such hopeless befaggled intellects. Although it may be that they are feeble enough, still nevertheless, such perfidy is calculated to interfere in no minor degree, if not to utterly destroy the foremost principals which are essential in successful conductorship of that most important factor in the life of a nation, which is known as "war". Further it is not to commissions that we must look for the truth concerning the Dardonelles. The officers and men who went through that campaign will not be befooled by any false statements by commissions and they will certainly not be hoaxed into any false belief that Lord Kitchenor was responsible for the ultimate result of that campaign. The failure may have been due either indirectly or directly to the dictates of our foreign policy in the East, which at that time at any rate we had little or no desire to relinquish even for Russia. Why I would also ask should K of K be so jealously attacked by inferiors in all departments, simply because he possessed in himself the same characteristics as the German's claim and we attribute to Hindenburg. The latter is reverenced by his countrymen, why then are the English to positively short-sighted as to condemn Lord Kitchenor for these same characteristics which are only worthy of a great soldier. The fact of the whole matter seems to be that poor England is groaning under the weight of a tyrannical and most disreputable lawyer gang, which perhaps only a revolution will shift. On duty again at 5 pm until 9 pm, was allowed to leave work however at 8.15 pm as we were slack and had plenty of staff.

12/3/17

Good nights rest. I am feeling quite well again at least almost so. Rose at 8.15 am. Had breakfast, hair cut and shave. Had a few drinks (chocolate) and did a little studying. On duty 1 pm until 5 pm. We had what the soldiers call a "bon" dinner today. For some weeks our food has been so terribly poor and scanty, that without buying a good deal for ourselves it would have been impossible to exist. It is rather dull and extremely mild weather. Had supper, which consisted of eggs at my billet. Afterwards had a bath and a change of linen.

13/3/17

Had a fearfully bad night, think that I caught a chill while swilling myself down last night, my whole body simply burned and perspired excessively the whole night through. Got up at 7.30 am feeling slightly better, but suffering from a severe pain in my right side and generally very weak. It is a mild but cloudy day. On duty 8.30 am until 1 pm. Got into bed at 2 pm where I stayed until 5 pm as I did not wish to report sick. Sgt. Drag of my relief kindly gave me permission to stay in my billet, for which I was extremely thankful, as had I gone on duty at 9 pm to work all night I should have become very ill indeed afterwards of that I feel certain. Managed to procure a little milk, which my landlady boiled for me, mixing there with the yolk of an egg. She also made me a basin of tea and mixed a couple of eggs therein. A favourite drink of the French for a patient was prepared and put into a bottle, which I kept close beside me during the night and in that way was able to keep it from going cold.

14/3/17

I had a slightly better night, but never ceased to sweat. It simply poured out of me in fact, I do owe a great deal to the kindness and attention of my landlady. This morning I had a hot basin of milk with two eggs broken into it, at midday a basin of chocolate with a little bread soaked in it. I got up at 3 pm feeling slightly better but still very weak and the pain in my right side still in evidence. Had a shave at the barbers. On duty at 5 pm until 9 pm. I was permitted to leave work at 7 pm owing to the fall off in our work and the additional staff, which we have at present with us. It was raining hard when I left off and I went straight to my billet. Had a basin of milk with an egg. My landlady made me a bottle of drink for the night, which had in it amongst other things, a certain amount of honey, which I bought for the purpose at the canteen this afternoon.

15/3/17

Good nights rest, but perspired a good deal. Feeling a little better but still weak and have no appetite. Got up at 8 am. Had breakfast at the mill. Prior to this however I had had already a basin of chocolate with bread soaked therein which my landlady brought me about 7 am. It is rather a nice day but cloudy. Received a letter from my wife Elinor. On duty 1 pm until 5 pm. Supper at my billet, which consisted of veal cutlets and fried chip potatoes and tea. Followed by a little studying. There is a good deal of heavy artillery firing this evening.

16/3/17

Rose at 7.20 am. Cold frosty morning. On duty 8.30 am until 1 pm. Did a little studying in the afternoon. On the "joy-wheel" in the evening, which commences at 5 pm until 1 am. Many reports came through during the night of Zeppelins on the wing. Finished duty feeling very fagged out.

17/3/17

Got up at 8.15 am feeling much refreshed. Had breakfast, shave at the barbers and general clean up at my billet. It is a very pleasant sunny morning. On duty 10.30 am until 1.30 pm. A Zeppelin was brought down in flames near Compiegne last night, which is a little item very pleasing to hear about. The news came through this morning that British troops had entered Bapaume at 7 am and occupied the place after a fight at the old factory, also Achiet le petit was taken and our troops appear to be making considerable headway. Fighting is proceeding at certain points. On duty again at 5 pm until 9 pm.

18/3/17

Got up at 7.30 am. Have still rather a bad cold but it is now leaving me gradually. Attended church parade at 9.30 am. Short walk and a couple of chocolates afterwards. It is a lovely bright sunny day. Our troops are still making some headway and have occupied Peronne. On duty 1 pm until 5 pm. Supper at my billet which consisted of pork chops and fried chip potatoes. French study including dictation and reading. Got to bed at 9 pm.

19/3/17

Got up at 7.30 am. On duty 8.30 am until 1 pm. It is rather cool and cloudy this morning. Am still a little off colour. On duty 8.30 pm until 1 am. The weather turned extremely boisterous towards the evening. Our troops are still going forward and today 40 more villages have fallen into our hands. This number added to yesterday's figure, which was 60 villages, makes a grand total of 100. It appears the enemy are leaving behind the civilian population and even causing them to flee from behind their own lines. They are in need of groceries and medical comforts, which however will be provided by the French authorities (see the 21st).

20/3/17

Got up at 8.15 am. Am still unwell. It is very windy and cold. Paraded at 10 am to have our overcoats inspected as one man had lost his from the cloak room. On duty 10.30 am until 1.30 pm. Not much news today of any importance.

21/3/17

Rose at 8.20 am. Breakfast and clean up, including my rifle. The latter however I do everyday. It is a cold bleak morning, but the roads are dry, which is a great deal. On duty 1 pm until 5 pm. I wish to note here the conclusion which I came to on the 19th inst. regarding the recent developments on the western front, but which I have not had time to enter up before. The main feature seems to be in my opinion that the Germans are reverting to their original order of battle, which of course they should never have relinquished, at the moment however we appear to be on our side in total darkness as to the intentions of the enemy. One thing my be and is in my opinion an established certainty that supposing the enemy is rearranging his "order" of battle it is naturally to fit in with his future plan of battle, which is I presume being formed upon the basis of heavy concentration of troops upon and behind points of strength and strategical importance. Presuming this to be correct then we in our turn must do likewise, otherwise we risk disaster in detail be reason of our extended formation. Moreover what the Germans have done is very similar in substance to my own plan of about 3 months ago, which I suggested was the course that we should adopt. Supper at my billet in the evening, which consisted of liver and mashed potatoes, followed by the usual French study. Went to bed about a quarter to 10 pm.

22/3/17

Rose at 7.15 am. There is snow on the ground from overnight and it is freezing. On duty 8.30 am until 1 pm. Received a letter, which was written in French from my sister Doris. Paraded in the afternoon at 2.15 pm with our new gas helmets and marched to the anti gas school at Pont Noyelle for the purpose of instruction in their use and also to try them by putting us, a dozen at a time into a gas chamber in which was sprinkled tear gas. This new pattern box helmet is a considerable improvement upon all that I have ever seen before. It is quite easy to breathe in it and one could live through the most deadly gasses, which either side could use. On duty again at 5 pm until 1 am.

23/3/17

Rose at 8.20 am. On duty 10.30 am until 1.30 pm. It is a brisk frosty morning and sunny. Received letters from my wife and Miss Dorothy Roberts. Am still feeling rather unwell. There are many rumours going about that we shall soon leave this place for a more advance position, at the moment however it is hard to say what will be done. I shall be sorry to go away as am well contented where I am and should prefer to stay.

24/3/17

Rose at 7.30 am. Had breakfast and afterwards had a walk as far as Corbie. It was a beautiful fine morning but very windy and the roads were hard with frost. I noticed that piles of trench sticks had been placed all along the route at intervals of about 50 yards. I am sure of the correct distance as I measured several while walking along. It was rather a unique sight to see the plough working in between the rows of trenches, which are dug along the fields on the right of the highway to Corbie. It was a peculiar mixture of war and the common employment of man. I enjoyed the walk immensely and ate a good dinner when I got back. There are plenty of troops in the town of Corbie including "jocks". I saw several companies of the latter marching in grand style. On duty 1 pm until 5 pm. In the evening I invited a friend Lt. Richardson to take supper with me at my billet. We had pork chops, fried potatoes and pineapple chunks and spent on the whole a pleasant evening. Tonight at 11 pm all the French clocks are to be put forward 60 minutes and the British army in France has orders to do the same to conform to French time. Shall lose one hour in bed in consequence.

25/3/17

Rose at 7.30 am. On duty 8.30 until 1 pm. It is a most magnificent day. There is a strong touch of spring in the air, which is so delightful that one wishes sincerely that it were possible to remain out of doors all day long and to drink in the fragrant and refreshing air which passes lightly by ones face. On duty again at 5 pm until 1 am. We have had a great deal of work to cope with in the office lately. I should mention that the 2nd finger of my left hand, which I managed to cut a piece out of the other day while cutting myself a morsel of cheese is now healing up satisfactorily. I am still however rather on the jady side of health and am looking forward to the time when I shall feel quite well again.

26/3/17

Got up 8.20 am. On duty 10.30 am until 1.30 pm. It is a miserable wet cold and windy day with fierce hailstorms at times. Wrote a letter to Miss Dorothy Roberts. On duty again at 5.30 pm until 9 pm.

27/3/17

Rose at 8.15. Bright and sunny during the early morning but changed later to cloud and cold. Obtained a new pair of khaki trousers from Q.M. Spent morning writing at my billet. Received a letter from my Aunt Ada. On duty 1 pm until 5 pm. I saw a telegram today, which stated that the French had captured an agent who had in his possession certain things which were intended to spread disease among horses especially among the cavalry. It was to be put either in the food or in the water, which was given to the animals. It might also have been used by placing up the nostrils after causing an abrasure with some sharp rough instrument, such as a wire. The effect would be to cause glanders. I presume that the individual in question was left behind by the enemy in the evacuated areas and there are probably more such reptiles still at large with similar purposes to carry out. Wrote letters to my Aunt and sister Doris. Had supper at my billet and some French study afterwards.

28/3/17

Rose at 7.30 am. On duty at 8.30 am until 1 pm. Received a letter from Miss Hedge of Newport Pagnall. It is rather a cold day but at times beautiful bright intervals. There was considerable heavy firing of artillery about 5 am this morning. On duty in the evening from 5 pm until 1 am. Am still somewhat on the wrong side of normal health.

29/3/17

Rose at 8.10 am. On duty 10.30 am until 1.30 pm. Very wet miserable day. On duty again from 5 pm until 9 pm. Slightly more fit in myself today.

30/3/17

Breakfast at 8.30 am. Afterwards clean up including my rifle. Obtained a new pair of puttees from the quartermaster. On duty 1 pm until 5.30 pm and again at 6.30 pm until 10 pm. My duties have been changed today for the above times, which will continue for 9 days. It is a cold wet sort of day. It seems pretty evident that we shall be quitting here for more uncivilised parts in the near future. Malheuresement.

31/3/17

Got up in time for breakfast at 8.30 am after which I went for a short stroll along the Corbie road. It is a fine morning, but threatening rain clouds are hovering overhead. In a telegram which I saw the other day but forgot to make a note of it here at the time stated that 32 men, 121 women and 138 children had been evacuated to hospital in Bray. It would seem that the inhabitants in the recovered areas are in a pitiful plight, from want of attention and nourishing food. I will now add some further notes to my already somewhat large collection of same. I find for instance that burials are arranged in five classes, for each of which there is a fixed price allotted as follows 1st class 200 francs, 2nd class 140 francs, 3rd class 100 francs, 4th class 75 francs and 5th class 40 francs. The cercueil (coffin) 5th class 15 francs. The fosse (grave, to dig) 5th class 8 francs. I really think that many suppliers of articles to the Army, should be very summarily dealt with indeed. For instance the pencils which are supplied by B. S. Cohen Ltd. of a plain colour and marked 2H are absolutely useless for multiple addresses and are not suitable to make more than 2 copies at a time, without breaking. H.B. pencils of the same plain colour and manufactured by the same people are even worse. Being either too soft or too brittle even to sharpen. This sort of thing is responsible for a great deal of waste. Then again the tobacco which is supplied to the troops is of a very poor quality. I have known tins of the same to be covered in green mould upon opening, owing probably to the cases having been badly sealed. The cigarettes are for the most part unsmokable. Such firms as are guilty for this most unpatriotic treatment of the country's soldiers should be brought to book for such obvious grasping avariciousness, which is daily, practised upon the troops. A few remarks upon the "British officer" might be worthy of note. To begin with I do not think that the individual in question has a counterpart in the whole world. In the first place he is not elected upon any of the especial grounds, which are vital and necessary in the making of a soldier, such as service, experience, instruction or intellect. The latter in fact is notably absent in the British officer of the new armies. In fact British officers have the reputation of a notable lack of all the foregoing qualifications amongst the civilians in France, it would appear that they are looked upon as a sort of useless ornament with too much money to spend. I have heard many remarks to this effect and have even heard it said that the British officer is only fit for searching for the bodies of women. Which latter remark is of course based upon a good deal of evidence. I could myself write a good deal upon this subject as I am personally acquainted with some astonishing facts in this particular direction. It is better however to leave such topics to look after themselves. I will now speak of the positive disgrace, which attaches to officer's messes behind the lines. I think infact that it might be called a crying shame. The food that is consumed in these cosy retreats is out of all proportion to human requirements, even of British officers. The local BEF canteen caters practically exclusively for the above mentioned nonentities. It is in fact very frequently indeed a difficult matter to approach near the counter in consequence of the huge orders for goods, which are being tendered by mess orderlies. This too in such time of shortage of food and when the ordinary "Tommy" finds it hard to exist at all. One mess of which I am acquainted with and therefore can speak with truth, it is also probably similar to many others. The one of which I speak has 8 men and a woman to look after 7 officers. Yet it is said that we are still in need of men for the Army. Another little item before I close down is the damnable conceit and ignorance generally displayed from a sub-lieutenant upwards, as an example. I may say that I have never once seen a motor car stop to give a "Tommy" a lift, if it contained an officer. The latter are constantly dashing about the country upon their own amusement and apparently imagine that the vehicles have been supplied by the country solely for their own use. One may meet tired "Tommies" at all times of the day upon the roads and weighted down with kit, scores of cars may pass, but the Officer, probably a Sub-Lieutenant who is the only occupant of the handsome cars, merely looks out for his salute.

1/4/17

Rose shortly after 7 am and after breakfast I proceeded on foot to Corbie for the purpose of buying a wreath to place on the grave on 2nd Lt. Santler the late husband of my cousin Isabel Brown. I reached the shop at about 9.45 am and after inspecting a number of wreaths I chose one composed of roses of a celluloid composition. The colours include cream, white, pink (light and darker) shades, red and deep red. These are the best descriptions I can give of the colours. A rosette of red, white and blue ribbon about 4 inches in width is attached. The inscription which I requested be affixed to the wreath is composed of aluminium characters of between 1½ and 2 inches in height are arranged in four rows across the wreath in the following manner "2nd Lt. SANTLER FROM HIS LOVING WIFE ISABEL AND ALL WHO LOVED HIM". My landlady has presented me with a young rose tree, which stands about 2 feet high and bears red blooms also she has given me 2 small sprigs of white lilac all of which I shall take with me and plant at the graveside either tomorrow or the day after if possible.

2/4/17

It is a very cold wintry sort of day with frost during the night. As I do not feel well I am not attempting the journey to the cemetery at Carnoy today, but wish to do so tomorrow whether I feel well or not. There has been a continual stream of troops passing through here today, with their respective bands playing. There was a band also placed against the chateau gates, which struck up a tune as each battalion came up. Scotch tunes for the Jocks and English ones for the Tommies. I was particularly struck by the fine physique of the troops, especially the Scotchmen. We appear to be massing at some particular point, which I am personally very glad to think is being done. I noticed too, by a telegram a few days ago from the 4th Army commandant, which asked if it was true that a certain battalion had arrived from Egypt in Khaki drill. This little fact going to prove that some at least of my suggestions which I made sometime ago in my journal and elsewhere are being carried out. I am feeling very down in health indeed this evening. Received a letter from my wife Elinor which contained the unfortunate news that Derrick was ill with the measles. I received a money order also for 1 pound, which I cashed at the local civil post office. Have obtained permission from the signal master to be absent from duty tomorrow from 1 pm but that I must make up all time which I am away after that hour. After I concluded my duty at 10 pm so goodness knows when I shall get away. Have also got my pass put forward to the orderly room, which will entitle me to visit the cemetery at Carnoy and be in that neighbourhood until 4 pm. I am to call at the orderly room tonight after 10 pm when the pass will be returned to me. We have had a good deal of rain today and snow too, it is beastly cold. In the evening I was ordered by the signalmaster to conduct one of our fellows to his billet and see him safely in bed as he was not feeling well.

3/4/17

Rose about 7.20 am. Had wash and breakfast and then started immediately upon my journey to the military cemetery at Carnoy near Albert. I was to begin with rather unfortunate with respect to "lifts". Some distance passed Pont-Noyelle I got a ride in a French brewery lorry which I overtook, and had a long talk with the driver. This vehicle however although drawn by two horses, made very slow progress. We passed La Houssoge and Franvillers before a lorry came along, which I transferred into. It was rather comfortable arranged inside for these particular type of vehicle and the journey to Albert was quickly accomplished. I noticed that the front petition was profusely decorated with postcards of French women in the nude and in other characteristic attitudes, which is a custom familiarly practised among British troops in France. The walls of billets and bivouacs are always decorated with this sort of feminine attraction. From Franvillers there begins a recurrent system of defence, which consists of trenches protected with as many as four rows of barbed wire entanglements. From Albert to Carnoy I was obliged to traverse practically whole distance on foot. Along this route I was particularly struck by several distinct changes, which had taken place since my last visit in that direction. In the first place there was a total absence of traffic, and only a few solitary soldiers, employed at different jobs. The whole scene was one of quiet and terrible desolation. The road, which before was more in common with a ploughed field and bore little resemblance to a thoroughfare, now presented an even and firm surface. In fact a steamroller was still working laboriously upon it close to Carnoy. The whole area looked as though it had been thoroughly cleaned up, and there is only the rust huts and turned up earth remaining, which still bears evidence of the British occupation. There are dumps for salvaged timber etc. and tins and other rubbish have either been disposed of or collected into heaps. I arrived at the graveside about midday. Snow still partly covered the earth. The soil upon the grave was somewhat disarranged, which looked as though small heaps of earth had been tumbled upon the whole plot. I did my best to rearrange the surface with my hands, which was however not an easy matter, owing to the clayey nature of the soil, which was at the time quite water logged in consequence of he thaw, which had set in during the morning. I hung Isabel's wreath upon the cross by means of a hook, but finding that the wind would probably ruin it entirely in a short space of time, by blowing it about, I bound the wreath to the cross by means of some thin cable wire, which I fortunately found close at hand. The rose tree I planted at the head and the two sprigs of lilac at the foot, one at each corner. I completed my work at about 1.20 pm and then commenced the return journey. Again I was unlucky in "lifts" but eventually got a short one into Albert where I arrived very tired and footsore. On the salt bridge just outside the town on the Amiens road I managed to get a ride in a side car and was rushed along at a grand pace for about 9 or 10 kilos when I was obliged to descend as the motor cyclist took another route. I caught a lorry however, which brought me the remaining distance to home. During this latter ride I had for a companion a dusky youth from Ceylon. He could speak English well and in addition was acquainted with a plentiful supply of bad language. He told me that he had only been in France a fortnight and had come over from his native country with six others, who had enlisted in different British regiments. He himself was a motor cyclist in the ASC. This was his first trip to Querrieu from Albert and his machine had broken down and in consequence, was doing the journey in the same way as myself. He said that he had been obliged to pay his own passage from Ceylon which had cost him 75 pounds, but of course this statement must be taken for what it is worth. I got back about 4.30 pm. Had a bowl of chocolate with an egg beat up in it. Afterwards had tea and went on duty at 6 pm instead of 6.30 pm. The signalmaster ordered me to stay on after 10 pm to make up for the time I had been away during the day which I thought was not quite reasonable or justifiable. I was not released until 1.10 am next morning, although I could not hold myself up on account of pains in my stomach and all around my waist. This however does not matter in the least, I have paid them back their paltry hours. While on the other hand I am glad with all my heart that I have been able to carry out so small a mission on behalf of those who are so good to me.

4/4/17

After breakfast had short walk. I am in a very poor state of health. Went to the doctors at 6.30 pm and was given some pills for indigestion. I was obliged however to ask to be released from work at 8 pm as I was in some pain. My landlady made me some tea into which she put an egg. She also made me a special drink from herbs, which I have never tasted before and I retired for the night.

5/4/17

Rose shortly after 7 am. Feeling greatly relieved and much better generally. I saw the doctor however at 9 am, he gave me some more pills. I was surprised to find that Mademoiselle Humel had arrived home for the Easter vacation when I returned to my billet this evening. I did not expect to see her for another day or so. I shall have plenty of French studying to do now and I am hoping to make a decided progress in the language before she leaves again to return to her duties.

6/4/17

Got up shortly before 8 am. Had breakfast and afterwards shave and clean up. Spent morning studying French with Mademoiselle Hunel who was very patient in her efforts to assist me. Had dinner with the family at midday, which consisted of fish (breme, brocket and peche), all fresh water fish, which had been caught in the lake close to the village. This was followed with pancakes, but I was obliged to go on duty before I had had time to take my fill of those latter delicacies. It is a bright warm day and I trust sincerely that the bad weather has gone for good. Am feeling much better in myself now.

7/4/17 -   Made a bet

Got up at 8am. After breakfast at the mill I had a swill down in a small tub at my billet. Rest of morning spent in study with Mademoiselle Hunel. On duty 1 pm until 5.30 pm and 6.30 pm until 10 pm. This is my last day on a split duty and commencing tomorrow on my relief. It is rather a dull and cold day, but with occasional bright intervals.

8/4/17

Sharp frosty morning but bright and sunny. After a good wash and clean up spent the rest of the morning studying. Have bought some beef steak, packet of patter cakes, tin of pineapple and large packet of tea for my landlady, with whom I shall have supper this evening. Have been changed from no. 2 relief to the new no. 1 relief together with a number of others, which will come into effect as soon as the old no 2 moves out to the report centre, which is being established apparently somewhere near to Peronne. Finished work at 5 pm and afterwards spent a pleasant evening at my billet talking upon a variety of subjects with my hostess until 10 pm when I retired.

9/4/17

Rose at 7.30 am. Very miserable wet day. Which is a considerable change to yesterday's glorious weather. In fact one felt glad to be alive and one experiences particularly upon such delightful occasions a great desire to be fee and at liberty, even so as are the birds. Commenced duty 8.30 am until 1 pm. Am very much improved in health. There is great news today, the 1st and 3rd armies (British) went over the top sometime during the last 12 hours. They have captured all objectives and the first reports spoke of over 4000 prisoners, which in the evening had increased to over 8000 prisoners and between 40 and 50 pieces of cannon, which the enemy had abandoned. Spent the afternoon studying French at my billet. On duty at 5 pm unitll1 am. Sent a letter to Miss Winnie Hedge in reply to one from her.

10/4/17

Ground was covered in snow when I turned out this morning at 8.30 am. On duty 10.30 am until 1 pm. Spent afternoon studying at my billet. On duty again at 5 pm until 9 pm. Our captures have now mounted up to 11,000 prisoners, 100 guns including some 8 inch, 70 machine guns and 80 trench mortars. After finishing work at 9 pm I was invited to sit awhile with my hostess and stayed chatting until 11 pm before retiring for the night.

11/4/17

Got up at 8 am. Had breakfast and bought some pork cutlets, a tine of pineapple and a packet of patter cakes for supper this evening. Received a letter from my wife. Spent morning studying French at my billet. On duty at 1pm until 5 pm. Spent a pleasant evening at my billet chatting and a little study. It is a terrible retched evening outside, snowing, hailing and raining alternately and very sloppy underfoot.

12/4/17

Hard frost during the night and this morning snow lay upon the ground. On duty 8.30 am until 1 pm at which time the sun became rather strong and it commenced to thaw rapidly. Received a packet from my sister Doris containing a bundle of note paper and envelopes and a short letter, also a picture postcard from my cousins Isabel and Ethel who are at present enjoying a holiday at the Isle of White. Spent afternoon at my billet doing a little studying and chatting. In the evening had supper with my hostess and also the fiancé of Mademoiselle who had arrived shortly before 5 pm. He will stay here, with his fiancée until she r4turns so that I shall have less opportunity now of her assistance in my studies, malheuresment. On duty again at 98 pm on the all night turn. The evening reports were good upon the whole of our front, but in my opinion they are only at the moment of local nature and probably meant to deceive the enemy as to our future intentions.

13/4/17

Finished work at 8.30 am feeling rather tired out. It is a bright frosty morning. All our attacks which we attempted during the night were successfully carried out. After breakfast and clean up lay down upon my bed for a rest until 1 pm. Had dinner at my billet and afterwards spent the afternoon chatting and a little study. On duty 5 pm until 9 pm. Tomorrow the new no. 1 relief commences and the old no. 1 leaves for Villers Carbonnel. I shall therefore be on duty at 8.30 am instead of 1 pm.

14/4/17

Cold day but bright and sunny. My duty today and probably continuing is 8.30 am to 1 pm and 3 pm until 8 pm., with a tea relief from 4.30 pm until 5.15 pm. By the way while mentioning meals I might say that such only exist in name. It is very rarely that we have bread for tea or meat for dinner. We exist almost entirely upon bully beef and biscuits, except for what we ourselves buy. This however is considerably more difficult now owing to the new French regulations which forbids the selling of eatables and drinkables until after 4 pm. We are not even allowed to enter any sort of shop until that hour. Wrote a letter to my Aunt Ada. Have put in an application to draw all the money, which at present stands to my credit with the army. Have also asked my Aunt to stop sending me the usual remittance. I received a letter this morning from my cousin Isabel in which I was very glad to note that she appeared to be well pleased with my little task, which I have had the honour and the pleasure to do for her. It has been a beautiful day with a strong scent of the coming summer in the air. Were I not so troubled and uncertain of what the future holds I could be so happy and content, as it is the hard life and much unpleasantness, which has been my lot since the commencement of the war is fast telling its tale upon me, my health and strength are not what they were, and the lines and wrinkles are making obvious encroachments upon my face.

15/4/17

On duty 8.30 am until 1 pm. It is a dull morning with drizzle. There are unmistakable signs of all the 4th army flitting. Several lorries are employed at the chateau this morning in taking away all the office furniture. The guards have already gone and some of the military police. Our own men are leaving in driblets every day, so that it may not be long before we have all gone elsewhere. Finished work at 8.30 pm and soon afterwards retired to rest for the night. Wrote a letter to my cousin Isabel.

16/4/17

Cold but not unpleasant weather today. The chateau looks quite deserted, everything and everyone having cleared out. Mademoiselle Hunel left yesterday with her fiancé to return to her duties, so that my studies with her have also come to an end. The French have today commenced an attack upon a large front, but as yet cannot gather what results have been accomplished. Have little news of any importance. The artillery activity, which was at one time our daily and nightly forcible reminder that there was a war on has long since ceased to disturb our tranquillity. The majority of the heavy artillery having gone elsewhere. Went to bed shortly after 8 pm and was soon in a land of peace and contentment.

17/4/17

Very bleak morning and strong boisterous cold winds, which apparently, has been the order throughout the night. On duty at 8.30 am. It seems an awfully long day to the time when my travail is finished at 8 pm. It is a most uninteresting life that one is compelled to lead at the present time, which is made considerably more tiring by the quiet unchanging life customary to a French village. There are too very few soldiers left in the two villages of Pont Noyelle and Querrieu. The thoughts of worse to come and the loneliness of villages made desolate by the ravages of war without civilian population and without the slightest possibility of securing a few civilised comforts, our items, which I have personally no longing desire to encounter. I am aware that my health as it is at present will not stand the test of much hardship or the strain, which lack of a few comforting commodities imposes. I shall however as always leave everything to chance and to good luck. After leaving work at 8 pm went for a short stroll and then returned to my billet, blacked by boots for the morrow and made some preparations for leaving so as to be ready to depart when the order is given. Afterwards got into bed and slept well.

18/4/17

During the early hours of this morning I could distinctly hear the rumble of heavy firing and the shock of explosions, which were perhaps conveyed to my notice through the medium of my iron bedstead as I lay in bed. I have in fact frequently observed that the firing at the front, appears to be especially distinct, when I have been lying in bed, which I attributed to the carrying properties of the earth in connection with my bedstead. It is a putrid sort of morning, cold and drizzle. I am feeling rather better however in health than usual, for which I am indeed exceedingly thankful and glad. Many of the huts, which have been built for the headquarters staff and adjoin the chateau along an avenue of beautiful trees, are rapidly being dismantled, prior to transportation to their new quarters. The men who are at present undergoing field punishment are engaged upon clearing out the billets situated in the chateau grounds and carrying out other work of a removal nature. It is amusing to observe the manifold articles, which have been collected by the men during their sojourn. It would be impossible to imagine piles of rubbish so deserving of the name, every item of which however undoubtedly served some special purpose and every bit of tine, wood, cardboard or bottle had its especial purpose and significance to the late possessors. The British Tommy no less than others is adept at making all sorts of contrivances, out of what material he can lay hold of and the result is always "satisfactory". In the short intervals of fair weather, which we have been so fortunate to have lately, between the gusts of hail, snow and sleet, it has been a pleasure, even soothing and grateful relief to hear the welcome songs of the birds and to see the trees and bushes throw off their sombre aspect and clothe themselves in light raiment's of budding leaves, all the world in such moments seems filed with great joy and with but one object, one aim in view, that of pure happiness. After leaving off duty, spent an hour and a half chatting at my billet before retiring for the night my landlady kindly made me a bowl of tea into which she mixed a couple of eggs.

19/4/17

My duties are changed today back onto the relief. My hours being 1 pm to 5 pm with 9 am to 1 pm extra. Had a very poor night's rest. I looked at my watch every hour until 3 am, when apparently I fell asleep. All night long there has been a most furious artillery bombardment upon some of the points of our front. I was of the impression that we here had become far removed from this particular evidence of a terrible war, but was obviously greatly deceived. The groaning and dull thuds of the heavy pieces are still audible as I make these notes. It is a very dull and miserable sort of a day. After 5 pm and when I had had my tea I started on foot to walk to Corbie as I was especially anxious to get a few presents for my sisters before leaving here for more desolate climes. I was very fortunate however in getting a lift in a lorry before I had gone very far upon the road. For my sister Doris I got a rosary mounted on silver and had a medal, (struck in honour of Sainte-Colette which is apparently the patron saint of Corbie) also affixed, a larger medal but similar I sent to my sister Gladys. They are rather small gifts it is true but they were the best I could obtain. For my collection I bought a relief of the Virgin Mary and a few picture postcards. Had a walk round the town after all my articles had been tied up and duly addressed, called at several places for a drink of tea or cocoa. In one place, where there were a couple of rather decent looking girls, and several soldiers belonging to the guards division (at present at Corbie) the usual topic of conversation was in progress and I was informed that 5 girls at Corbie had married English soldiers, and that they had all a baby each. By the way in view of the fact that it seems to be a generally believed conception that the women of France are more frivolous and possibly more loose in their actions that their English sisters. I will state here my version upon the point. So far as sexual matters are concerned there is of course no difference whatsoever between the two. Human nature is exactly the same all the world over. Otherwise the human race would indeed be a peculiar sort of animal world. It follows therefore that granting the aspirations or if such an expression should be distasteful to some, we will call it degradation, are the same, then all women no matter of what nationality must be equally alike. Moreover I may say that this is so. What I do believe however is that where as French women are on the whole more open and straightforward upon such matters as the aforesaid the English women on the other hand, although not adverse to talk about this particular subject, especially if between themselves as it appeals to their amorous senses just the same as to any other female of another nationality. Still never the less there is a certain amount of reticence observed which does not favour broaching the topic in too open a manner. This slight difference in character, which is probably more apparent than real is responsible for a very noticeable breach between French and English women. The former in their open heartedness throw off all attempts to disguise their true feelings as they prefer to be natural. While on the other hand the English by reason of their more sober characteristics makes them extremely clandestine in their actions, which tends to reduce all intercourse to merely a vice instead of a free wholesome enjoyment of the society between man and women which is the premier of all earthly favours, and which lies in the full possession of a partner, the one for the other and not one without the other. On my journey outwards I noticed that the field of corn are already green with life. It was becoming dark when I began to retrace my steps back to Querrieu and before long the night had completely enveloped all. I met nothing or anyone upon the road and truth to tell I felt so sadly lonely. As I looked up at the sky which was full of threatening clouds my mind wondered back to other skies which I had loved to watch in foreign lands. The heavens at night in Egypt were a source of pure delight and tranquillity to me. They seemed to posses and to convey so much, so very much. I have indeed many times found pleasure and contentment while observing them in contemplation when I have been lonely. The beautiful sunsets of Gallipoli would always bring vividly to my memory my dear ones at home in the West just where the last beams of light shot out of their fair reflections of hope and good cheer beckoned me to have patience and bids farewell. But now as I gaze into the blackness which encompasses the bright stars of hope and fortitude. I become oppressed with a great weight of misgiving and of future ill forebodings. My future does in fact seem so full of unpenetrable darkness. Upon my right in the direction of the front there are, it is true occasionally bright flashes, which momentarily light up the gloom of the night, but alas they are the flashes of death, of sorrow, anguish and pain. These little flashes however I often feel that I would prefer to face again than walk into the night, which has no dawn. Arrived back at my billet about 10 pm feeling awfully tired and foot-sore, was soon in my cosy little bed and fast asleep.

20/4/17

On duty 8.30 am until 1 pm. A rough sort of day with showers. The canteen has closed. There are only a few soldiers left here now. Expect we shall be moving away in a day or two. Spent the afternoon writing. In the evening I bought 2 large woollen shawls and a small one, which I have sent as a little present for Derrick. The other two have dispatched to my dear Aunt Ada and my wife Elinor. Have also sent off some picture postcards of Corbie. Had supper at my billet and at 9 pm proceeded on duty to work all night. Received at about 11 pm a letter, a very nice one from Miss Dorothy Roberts. It had apparently been sent up the line to our advanced signals prior to arriving here. Artillery bombardment still maintains a very high intensity.

21/4/17

Nice dry morning but somewhat cold. Had a good swill down with hot water shortly after 7 am in my little room. On duty 9 am until 5 pm. The signalmaster allowed me and another to go out for a walk from 10 am until 11 am, as there was not sufficient work for all the staff on duty and several of us are doing extra hours. Am feeling quite all right now in myself and more like my former self. I had supper at my billet in the evening and afterwards a little French study. Artillery bombardment very heavy. Went to bed about 10 pm.

22/4/17

Up at 7.30 am. Fine bright day, but rather cold wind. Artillery extremely heavy all through the night. Some time this morning the 3rd, 1st and 5th armies launched an attack, which was proceeding satisfactorily, when I left off duty at 1 pm. There should be plenty of good news shortly. If only we had a good leader on our side I am of opinion that the task before us should proved far more cosy to accomplish than most people imagine. A great deal depends too on whether the numerous traitors at home have been disposed of in such a manner as to totally debar them the possibility of intrigue and undue interference in the nations cause. This afternoon had a walk which I thoroughly enjoyed. Afterwards wrote a letter to Miss Dorothy Roberts and another to my Aunt Ada. Had supper at my billet prior to going on duty at 9 pm to work all night. I wonder how much longer this terrible existence is to continue. It is a hard life indeed, with little prospects of better things, even at the end of it. The fighting today has apparently been of a severe character. Over a thousand prisoners are reported through our cages which however is nothing to boast about especially considering the heavy days and nights of bombardments, which preceded the attack. We have however been more fortunate in the air, where our aeroplanes have accounted for quite a large number of enemy machines at comparatively small cost to ourselves. We have also destroyed 7 kite balloons. Had supper at my billet and afterwards paraded for duty at 9 pm to work the night through.

24/4/17

Had a very busy night and feeling rather fatigued. After breakfast and clean up I lay on my bed until 1 pm. It is a most glorious day, by far the best that we have had this year. In the afternoon I betook myself for a walk, which was exquisitely delightful. On duty 5 pm to 9 pm. I have now come to the end of my 5th diary. I wonder how many more I shall fill before I may close down for good not that I have truly noted all my actions and experiences for I have not done so, not by half or even one quarter but perhaps enough.

Diary Number 6

25/4/17

Rose at 7.30 am. Had breakfast at the mill afterwards shave and clean up. Managed to get a "pull through", some 4 by 2 and a pair of laces from the quartermaster. I am now complete in every detail and ready at a moments notice to quit, which however I am not in a great hurry about. Here I have a nice comfortable bed and I am able to keep myself clean and tidy, considerably better than in a barn. Received a parcel yesterday from my good old Aunt Ada, which contained a pleasant surprise in the form of a cake. I ate a little this morning, but found it rather a difficult matter to resist the temptation (which became strong after the first bit) to consume the whole of it at a sitting, and risk an attack of indigestion afterwards. On duty 1 pm to 5 pm and 6 m until 10 pm.

26/4/17

Had a good night's rest. On duty 8.30 am until 1 pm. It is rather dull and cold today, but towards midday and afterwards it became quite warm and cheerful. After dinner I did a little studying and then went for a stroll. After tea spent an hour sitting in the garden at my billet and pegged away at my French. During the last few days of fine weather the French civilians have been working with feverish haste at digging their gardens and planting same with sufficient vegetables to last them another twelve months. The country people and villagers do not believe in buying what they can grow, and although potatoes and the like are I hear practically a luxury in England at the present time, while here where the war is close at hand and even been under the feet of the invader, the people have a plentiful supply still of these essential commodities. In fact they constitute I may say with truth, their staple nourishment. It is rather a remarkable picture to see khaki clad soldiers assisting in this form of toil I have done a little myself, but only a little. On duty 9 m until 8.15 am.

27/4/17

Had a very busy night again felt quite fatigued and weary when I left the bureau at 8.30 am. After breakfast lay down until 12.45 pm. After dinner a short walk and did a little digging in a garden. Spent a short while sitting in the garden at my billet before preparing to go on duty at 5 pm. There are strong rumours that we shall all be away from here in another three or four days time, which I hope however is not true. I can't say that I like the idea of tent life, which is our prospect when we quit this place. I shall sadly miss my tiny chamber and cosy little bed. Artillery still heavy.

28/7/17

Up at 8.15 am. After breakfast and clean up at my billet, did a little studying and afterwards spent the rest of the morning out of doors. It is rather dull, but nevertheless very pleasant in the open air. On duty at 5 pm. Had supper at my billet and a long conversation in French afterwards and a little study. Had just settled down to the latter however, when a friend of mine knocked on the door to inform me of the unwelcome news that I was in orders to parade on the morrow at orderly room at 9 am with full kit to proceed to Villers Carbonnel for duty. I had half expected this on account of a row in which I had been implicated a couple of days previously with the

Superintendent and the signal master, when I completely lost my temper. Finished packing up my things before retiring for the night.

29/4/17

Rose about 7 am. My landlady brought me a nice refreshing basin of chocolate in which was soaked some bread (after the French style). Had wash etc. and then bid goodbye to my kind hostesses, who I was really and truly very sorry indeed to leave. Still what is must be and so must make the best of it. Collected a few more things such as my jerkin, haversack, gas helmet and blankets from the official billet of my relief. Had breakfast and then reported at orderly room. Received a long king letter from my dear Aunt Ada. With a comrade who was down together with myself to proceed to advanced signals, we started in a lorry, which was filled with telegraph poles and all manner of signal stores. The day was gloriously fine, a perfectly ideal summer's day. We were very soon covered from head to foot in white dust. Passed through Corbie and later touched the outskirts of Villers-Bretonneux, where we turned into one of the straight broad national roads peculiar to France. We passed four large aeroplane hangers on the right then a very large French ammunition dump and a little further we ran through our growing dump "R.E" at La Flaque, where a goodly number of German prisoners are kept busily employed. We now entered a country which words alone could describe but very poorly, desolation, devastation, extermination are some of the words, which are impressed and written deeply one would think ineffaceably upon every inch of terrain, upon the threads of timber and twisted iron. Lying among this wreckage are the graves. The solitary graves of soldiers, men, nay super men. These battlegrounds of 1915 are so churned heaped up and rent as to resemble in an extremely remarkable way the heavy rolling toil o f an angry sea. No landmarks are visible amidst this eruption of Hells torrents. Coming into the vicinity of Villers Carbonnel (our destination) we enter an area recently evacuated by the enemy. He has only been gone from these parts in fact a matter of about 6 weeks or so. Our fighting line now being probably 9 miles further north. We arrived at advanced signals about midday. Had dinner and short rest, managed to get a place in a tent, where there were already 9 occupants. As my friend and I were not warned for any duty we thought it wise to betake ourselves out of the way, so started off on a tour of investigation and chance our luck of discovering something either interesting or useful. The ground everywhere is pitted with shell holes of all sizes from a tub size to a pond, which in fact many are. What struck me however was the total absence of rifle bullets, I did not see a single one. Whereas at Gallipoli these deadly little devils were everywhere strewn about upon the ground. We directed our steps in the direction of the Somme canal, which we quickly reached, we skirted one ancient chateau protected by a moat. It is called the chateau of Happlincourt, a British officer was engaged at the time in sketching the edifice, which now however presents a sad spectacle indeed. Bearing of to the right along the canal bank we visited several dug outs but owing to the reason that we had omitted to bring along a flash light or candle we were perforce obliged to relinquish for the time being the idea of entering same. From here we reached a large gap, the handiwork of one of our high explosive shells. The day had been extremely hot and I suffered in consequence with rather a bad headache, which is a very unusual complaint with me. After tea however I felt considerably relieved and instead of lying down to rest as I intended to do started off once more with my friend upon another expedition. This time taking with us a flash light and a candle. First of all we visited the wood which was honeycombed with deep dugouts but all unfortunately blown in or burnt out, which made them to unsafe to enter, even had it been possible to do so. There was a good deal of feminine attire, chiefly underclothes, hardly soiled lying about although an attempt had been made to burn them. French civilian beds are quite a common sight lying strewn and badly battered upon the ground. As an instance of German tirelessness in his efforts to bring to perfection all that he undertakes. I may mention just one. In order to cover up the white chalk tops of his dug outs here from aerial observation he had placed a thick covering of long sticks each neatly bound together with wire. The same sort of thing was placed as a sort of palisade around the edge of the wood, but in this case the sticks were not bound closely together. This wood like everywhere else, where the Germans have occupied was crowded with empty bottles. There are plenty of dud shells lying about too. Continuing our journey we presently came to the same dug outs as we had visited previously in the afternoon, but where very disappointed to find that all without exception had been so damaged by fire and bombs as to make it an impossibility to enter. I picked up here a couple of small fragments of glass with thin wire enclosed therein which had been used for the door of the dug out. I brought them back with me in lieu of anything better as mementoes. We walked on along the embankment, visiting scores of dug outs but all in vain. Passed through the late site of a battery of artillery and entered a hamlet comprised of one big farmhouse, a couple of cottages and a small church. The Germans had even dug into the bowels oft the earth through the stable floor and taken elsewhere all the earth thus excavated. Mattresses and beds lay mutilated everywhere, also a good deal of feminine attire. The tombs in the churchyard had been badly knocked about by shell fire, an iron cross with the crucified saviour, (an object so common in France) which stood at the corner of the road close by had been bent right over. The German signposts indicating direction and the names of the roads, to which they had given names were still standing. Going up to the porch of this small village church we found the entrance blocked with a mattress. Inside, our gaze was met with a spectacle of utter destruction, most of the images had been knocked down and were lying upon the floor. One of the Virgin however on the right and another of Christ of the left, were still hanging upon the walls. The head of the infant Christ or of a cherub had been replaced upon a niche and was truly a touching object as a harmless victim of brute remorselessness. At the rear of the church are the graves of five German soldiers. Passing on the rear we came to several small cottages in which too the enemy had burrowed deep into the earth to provide himself with sanctuary from the shellfire. In other words funk-holes. On the door post of one cottage was painted the German national colours. Passing through the gardens of the departed peasants (where several British Tommies were busily engaged digging up plants of all sorts with the object of replanting same in their own little plots which they have dug by their tents or to garnish the surroundings of some particular hut). We arrived upon the canal bank again. Three German steam engines, which had been blown up by our fire, lay in all directions across the line and towing path. Immense barges blocked up the waterway. Timber lay about in profuse quantities. In fact there is a fortune to be had in the amount of wood which the Germans have left behind. The same might also be said concerning the vast litter of barbed wire, which is still intact in front of the different systems of enemy lines. All the German dug outs and funk holes are boarded up the sides and across the roofs with stout planks which are additionally secured by means of long flat iron bars about 2 inches in width, with slit apertures about 1½ inches long. By this means it is an easy matter to affix them to the walls with the aid of wide staples. All this and more will of course be recovered by us in due course. We managed to get over the canal by way of some floating timber and by scrambling over a barge which latter the Germans had used as a base for a bridge, which they destroyed upon leaving. The connecting bridge upon the opposite side was however still intact at any rate, for some distance as it passed through a wood and hence across the marshland, which had been rendered impassable on account of the enemy blowing up his bridges and in so doing had demolished the canal banks, which caused an immediate flooding of the low lying country beyond. As it was getting late we turned our steps homewards and arrived back about 8 pm. I had a shave and afterwards retired for the night.

30/4/17

Rose about 7 am. It is another glorious day. Was ordered to go on duty at 8 am. Our signal office is a spacious Nissan hut. Everybody seems to some extent happy and contented in spite of the long hours (12 hours daily). The food is good enough if only we got sufficient. Water was turned on last night, so that now we are alright in that respect. The canteen however as usual is very backward (except of course with respect to catering for officers) no matter what we require it is always the old cry, "sold out". Finished work at 2 pm, after dinner I took advantage of the nice weather to do some washing and afterwards betook myself away from the camp and sat down to do a little study. After tea I went to a little dug out where there was a bed made of sticks and wire netting. Using a biscuit tin as a desk I spent the rest of the evening writing my diary. On duty again at 8 pm to work all night.

1/5/17

Finished work at 8 am feeling rather done up. After breakfast had a shave and clean up. Bought several things at the canteen including a bottle of lemon squash. Lay down in the tent until 1 pm. Am now in another tent, which has just been erected, at present there are only 3 occupants including myself. On duty 2 pm until 8 pm. The weather is still gloriously fine and I trust sincerely that it will remain so for a long while. There was a report of a thunderstorm at Nancy yesterday. I trust that it will not pay us a visit. I am not anxious to see what this place looks like when it rains. Had tea in the office. After finishing work at 8 pm had my hair cut off with the clippers by the Corporal in charge of the cookhouse. It is surprising what a difference it makes to ones appearance. I prefer to be quite bald, however on this job and especially when the weather is warm. I always kept my hair (what little I have) in fact closely cropped all the time while I was in Egypt, it is much cooler, cleaner and last but not least there is less to do before going on parade. My washing was completely dried and aired by this evening. Received a ration of rum before retiring. Received a nice letter from my dear wife Elinor during the evening.

2/5/17

Was woken this morning by heavy bomb explosions close at hand and machine gun firing at about 6.30 am. Still beautiful fine weather which portends great heat during the day. Several more tents have been erected next to ours, my tent mate and I moved into one of them before breakfast as the one we were in was torn and full of holes that we judged it better not to wait until the bad weather arrived to find out its bad points so took the opportunity of selected the best that we could find, not an easy matter as they are all well worn. Transferred our floorboards into our new abode and otherwise arranged same for our convenience before the arrival of expected newcomers. On duty at 9 am until 2 pm. After dinner, which was by the way quite the best that I have had for sometime, it consisted of boiled mutton, desiccated vegetables and cauliflowers with bread to mix with the gravy, it was both good and liberally supplied, after devouring this sumptuous repast I walked over to Villers-Carbonnel, which lies to the rear of our camp. I observed that several heliograph stations had been established in this neighbourhood and were working. I stopped to read one message, but the receiving operator was rather a dud and the sending station in consequence was obliged repeatedly to send words several times before he got the acknowledgement signal, one dash. Passing on into the village I immediately entered an area of complete wreckage, everything blown up several times so to speak. Portions of skeleton framework of houses and cottages standing out above the heaped up debris in a gaping sort of manner, is all that is left to meet the gaze of a reckless world. Turning sharply to the left I walked down what was once a street, against a round tower (at least what is left of one) I noticed rather a large sized well, on which was a notice board and painted in black letters "required chlorination 2 measures" another well which I passed bore a similar warning in the following manner "dangerous water, unfit for use". Lying upon the refuse of what was at one time a large house, probably a stores, I picked up a small grocery account book, which I brought away with me. At another place upon the floor of a dwelling I picked up a photograph of a bridal couple, which I also added to my curio collection. In different places I found a couple of small enamel basins which although badly dented and rusty make very useful additions to our tent furniture. I came across several books but only possessed myself of two, they being the least battered and muddy specimens of French literature. I would really love the job of salvaging books. It seems such a pity that these, probably the best product ever accomplished by man in all ages should be allowed to go to rot and perhaps even lost, entirely to civilisation, in a somewhat similar way to that which happened to countless priceless and precious literature of the ancient Chinese who were ordered by a foolish leader to bring out all their books to be burnt upon piles in the public squares, death was threatened to all who attempted to hide any of these brightest jewels of mans creation and genius. A New Years card was when I discovered it in a shell hole completely covered in mud. After washing it when I returned to camp a pretty little girl proved to be the subject upon the reverse side. Picking up and opening what at first sight seemed an unobtrusive piece of paper. I thought at first that I had discovered a valuable not belonging perhaps to the bank of France, especially when a long official looking stamp dropped off. Upon closer investigation however it proved to be merely a receipt for 30 francs 50 from a fire insurance company, still it was yet once more a little item for my already very large collection of scraps for my album in prospective, providing always of course that I am able to get them safely over the water. I now wended my way home. Passed through the grounds of the village church and on through the demolished wall which skirts the northern side of this unfortunate edifice. It was quite a relief too to leave behind such a tortuous bewilderment of mans terrible handiwork. After tea wrote a letter to my dear Aunt Ada. Have also sent off all the above finds and in addition the two small fragments of wired glass, which I picked up the other day. It has been a very lovely day and I am feeling personally rather well in health. On duty at 8 pm to work all night.

3/5/17

Instead of working until 8 am this morning the superintendent released half the staff including myself at 1 am, so that I got in a fairly good nights rest. Got up at 7.30 am. Had breakfast, which consisted of bully beef, bread and tea. Started off immediately after with a chum to visit the scene of a severe fight which had taken place some distance away on our left. We walked a long way, but unfortunately failed to locate the actual battleground for which we were in quest. We traversed many lines of French (later British) and German trenches. Also came across a number of dead, both French and German, who were lying in most grotesque positions, nearly all having been kill by shell fire. They little resembled men, their hands and faces seemingly reduced in size and perfectly black. Some portions of their bodies lay scattered about between the lines, having been completely blown to bits or the head detached from the trunk. Soldiers had been buried even in the midst of wire entanglement, just where they had fallen. Coming across a British salvage party, we stopped to make enquiries. One of them volunteered the information that in his opinion the French had walked into a veritable death trap in these parts. I do not give his statement as proof of any fact however, he made it merely upon the ground of the enormous number of French rifles and quantity of ammunition, which he said had been left behind by our allies. I hope to make another visit shortly to other parts of the field of contention. Arriving back in camp I bathed my feet and washed out as pair of socks, then a shave and clean up. Wrote a letter to my dear wife Elinor, also despatched several personal articles to my aunt Ada, which I hope she will receive safely. We are still enjoying lovely summer weather. On duty at 2 pm until 8 pm. After leaving off duty in the evening knocked 3 post (which I scrounged this morning) round our tent and attached a clothes line (rope) there to, which I had been fortunate to "fined". Extracted the bullets out of a number of German cartridges, which I wish to keep in their clips as souvenirs. Read one of my French books for about an hour, before extinguishing my candle to repose.

4/5/17

Got up at 6.30 am. Had an excellent nights rest. Was awakened early by the arrival of most of no 2 relief who had started by motor lorries from Querrieu at 3 am. It is lovely warm weather and yesterdays weather report forecasts from 75 to 80 degrees temperature for today. On duty 8 am until 2 pm.. Yesterday morning early the 5th army launched a big attack against the Hindenburg line. In places the attack was successful although I am unable to say to what extent. At others we failed and our troops were very shortly back again in their own lines. It would appear at least in my opinion, that although we commenced our offensive some time ago in a business like manner I am afraid now that we are making some terrible blunders as of yore. This should not be at all, especially when one considers that it is absolutely necessary to strike soon, and vitally too. If we do not succeed in dealing a crushing low to the enemy very quickly smash him up and take 2 or 3 million prisoners then we shall not deserve much less expect to see the end of all this frightfulness this year, further more there can be no excuses for failure now. We have had nearly 3 years to mobilise the British Empire and bring all its vast resources to bear against our foe, in a preponderance absolutely overwhelming. I repeat therefore that if we have thus failed in duty to ourselves and to our allies, then we do not merit the victory, as we shall have been overmatched by a people who have proved themselves to be greatly our superiors, which follows therefore according to the rules of sport, and fair play that the honours go to the victor if not by reason of a knockout, at any rate on points. I have no patience at all with deliberate procrastination, especially when a nation's destiny is at stake. Wrote al letter to my sister Doris in the evening. On duty at 8 pm to work all night.

5/5/17

Finished work this morning at 8 am feeling positively worn out. After breakfast shave and wash I started alone to walk to the village, which lies to our left and in the neighbourhood of which there has been a good deal of fighting, not very long since. Its name is Barleuse. The sun was becoming intensely powerful when I started off and it was not long before I felt in no small degree its overwhelming effect. It must be understood that in order to go anywhere it is always necessary to pass over very rough ground, to take a zig zag course to avoid the thousands of shell holes, which deface the whole earth at intervals of about 10 yards or less. Also one is obliged to be continually trench jumping and negotiating barbed wire entanglements. Even to go so far as our canteen from the camp a double row of trenches have to be crossed. With regard to the enemy's retreat from these parts, there are distinctively two outstanding features of noteworthiness. The systematic orderliness and obvious ease with which or foe characterised his retirement and on the other hand we undoubtedly surprised him by the way in which we carried out our forward move with undisputed agility which was both effective and successful. It was a masterly retreat, in which the Germans unfortunately scored several strong points in their favour. I cannot think that they were able to do so much preparation to evacuating all this territory, without our gaining some knowledge of their intentions. The task was considerably greater than the evacuation of Gallipoli, where we had no dug outs to blow up, or much artillery to get away. In fact almost everything was left behind including stores. At Suvla-bay too there was the salt lake, which would be flooded at the time of our departure and would afford excellent protection from immediate following up in force. Another very remarkable thing, which I have noticed is the excellent condition of all the roads. It would seem that we had purposely spared them from destruction by our artillery fire. Our engineers are still busily engaged with the important business of searching for mines. Working along one section of the line at a time. They are proceeding too in a methodical manner to blow up all dangerous dugouts. Big explosions do note at intervals, that they are duly carrying out their crusade against these inhuman habitations with some purpose. However I had better return to my original theme. Entering the village I was met with the usual sight of wholesale destruction. The hallmark of war is written deeply upon all the towns and villages that have had the misfortune to lie within range of gunshot. I commenced to search among the debris, but found little of interest. I came across a thick portfolio of German "daily orders" and procured a few pages for myself, as of course it was impossible to bring away the whole complete. At another place I picked up several picture postcards and a couple of books. Walking in the direction (over the tops of the houses) of the church, which I was able to recognise by the substantial bricks of a small portion of a wall still left standing, I came upon the residence of the priest. The wreckage was strewn with books of an ecclesiastical nature, vestments and artificial flowers. I took none of these I had hoped to find something extra special, so to speak, but was disappointed. It is hardly feasible perhaps to expect to find much as of course the Germans will have had long ago the best of pickings. What they might have left, British salvage parties and others, would be quick to acquire. I passed on to the church, but it was merely a mass of jumbled bricks, timber vestments and statues. From her I cut across the open to the road and made my way back to camp, where I arrived shortly before noon, feeling utterly exhausted, I lay down for an hour. Had dinner and then on duty at 2 pm until 8 pm. We worked without jackets in the office on account of the stifling heat. We are also extremely busy. Received a letter from "Dill". Did a little reading before settling down under the blankets. It is decidedly colder tonight and inclined to rain.

6/5/17

The night has been very stormy, much to the discomfiture of many as most of the tents are decidedly obsolete, the cavas of all is easily porous and full of holes, or the doors are hanging in tatters. When I turned out a bitterly cold wind was blowing which pierced to ones bones. On duty at 8 am until 2 pm at least this was my term of work according to schedule. I was however destined to be up against it again very shortly after arriving at the signals office. It was in this way: I posted for censuring three separate packets to my Aunt Ada to avoid being over the weight for letter post 2nd. Lt. Black however thought otherwise and quickly brought them back to me, with the remark that they <u>must</u> be made up into one packet and paid for. This silly attitude on the part of an officer was of course rank impudence, originating from a paltry mind steeped in ignorance and stupidity. I have in fact (like every Tommy) come up against quite a lot of this particular sort of childishness, which is unfortunately one, of the chief characteristics of a certain type3 of individual who it would seem have all got commissions in the army. I took them back of course, but promptly re posted on of them. This was apparently too much for such weak brains to stand and after a conference of officers I was instructed by the aforesaid Black in a voice almost out of breath with excitement to "go, pack up my kit, and be ready as soon as possible to proceed to Peronne". A boxcar was already waiting outside to take me there. This by the way was just what I deserved or something like it for several reasons. Outstations of this sort are considered decidedly preferable to larger formations and units, upon very sensible grounds too. In spite of the fact that Peronne is a very heavily pressed little office, still, no matter there are other items to be considered of perhaps of greater importance as the effect ones health and happiness and are worth at least weighing fairly in the balance. The rationing here is a thousand times better and as much and more than one could eat, while at the army Headquarters, one lived a life of semi-starvation. Conveniences are better and last but not least one has considerably more freedom. In fact we are completely free from humbug and are simply allowed to carry on in our own time. I arrived at the "Exchange" Peronne about midday. Had my particulars of service etc. noted in the orderly room, was shown a place to sleep, on the 2nd story of our signal office. Had my dinner and went straight on duty until 4.30 pm. After tea I looked about for a bed. I found a large door, with wire netting already placed neatly across it, the panels having previously been knocked out leaving only the framework, a small chest of drawers minus the drawers I placed it upon its side and discovered that in this position, it served admirably the purpose of bed legs. Coming across a neat little affair with two shelves I placed beside my bed, which makes an excellent little cupboard for my cleaning, tackle, washing materials and other odds and ends. In spite of all the fearful wreckage, not a single house or building remains unscathed from the blast of war and the depredations of the Germans. Still there is a little left, which testifies to the prosperity and well being, which the inhabitants of this unfortunate town enjoyed in pre-war days. I shall have more to say I hope about this later on. After fixing up my bed etc. I went out to the rear of the house, climbed over the rubbish (I noticed that server dug-outs had been dug in the garden) and crossed the road to get to the moat, where I spent over an hour writing my diary, sitting in a dilapidated arm chair, which sported a quartet of near brick legs. It was very comfy none the less. On duty again at 8 pm to work all night.

7/5/17

Had a very busy time in the office until 2 am, when I was left by myself and shortly afterwards rolled up in my blankets and settled down for a short nap. I had placed a bell by my head, which had wired up to a couple of cells and the Morse circuit, so that should the army start calling I should get a loud ring in my ears. Nothing happened however until 5.30 am when the telephone bell rang, and was kept busy afterwards until I was relieved at 8 am. After breakfast and clean up, I went with a friend to have a look around the old fort, which is surrounded by a moat. The enemy had honeycombed the steep sides of the latter with dug outs and shelters. Thence proceeded to visit the cemetery, which was indeed a most pitiable sight to witness. Practically all the tombs had been blown up and iron, stone, marble, granite and wreaths literally littered this last resting-place. I noticed that probably most of the tombs were dug very deep, the walls being built up of brick. One could see the leges which represented the spaces allotted for the reception of each coffin, one about the other. The only object which appeared to have escaped unscathed is a tall crucifix of the saviour, which is situated at the far end of the path running through the middle of the cemetery. To the left of this at the far corner is the site of the German burial ground. I was surprised at the large number of graves therein contained, I have never before in fact seen so many graves of the enemy at one place, rather a large proportion too of the wooden crosses bore in facsimile the vaunted iron cross, even in death the Germans flaunt their military pride. I do not however blame them for this. It does seem indeed a great shame that even the dead have not been permitted to rest in peace. Their bones have been ruthlessly thrown up again to witness the hell in which their children have come to live, as though it would seem that the blame was upon them for the present corruption of man and of the world. Received a letter and postcard from my wife Elinor, and a packet of notebooks from my Aunt Ada. Several of my old friends from the 4th army headquarters came over here this afternoon and paid me a call, I took them round our billet and they had tea here. By the way it is my birthday today. I am 28 years old, so that I have lived in this hell for just 28 years. On duty at 2 pm until 8 pm. Felt dog tired when I had finished. Before retiring I wrote up my diary and did a little reading, also "scrounged" a trestle, and something else of a similar sort, a nice board completed a useful table by my bed side. The little affair (or, as they say in the French, when in ignorance of the proper name of anything "une petite machine") which I found the other day with a couple of shelves, I have placed at the back of my little table, which give the whole appearance of a neat and useful bureau.

8/5/17

Commenced to rain in torrents during the early hours of the morning and came pouring through the many holes in the roof ad lib, several fellows had their beds well wet and their boots etc. which were upon the floor got nicely watered too. Just round where I sleep the rain did not come in at all. So that I have something to be very thankful for. On duty at 8.30 am until 2 pm. Spent the afternoon walking about the ruins looking for "anything". Going over one street at a time. I picked up several articles of varied descriptions but too numerous to mention in detail. They included letters, (one written in English) photographs and postcards. My wanderings took me up to the church, which is entirely demolished, all but the pillars on the right hand side, which are miraculously left standing. The place of the high alter is also only partly damaged, amid all this chaos a British band was playing in a house with the front practically blown away, its selections were in rag time and so forth. A fiendish contrast I thought with the surroundings, but then, this is war. I was compelled to stop and listen. It is surprising to what an extent music affects one, no matter of what kind. Here especially its reverberations soothes the nerves so to speak and is to say the least very acceptable indeed. In one street I passed a "modes" shop, where, suspended from the balcony above was an effigy of a woman. She was complete in frock, blouse, false hair and hot. Probably it was a little bit of German humour. Not far from here I was almost caught under a shower of debris that some soldier was pushing from the floor above. It was rather amusing to see our men climbing over heaps of fallen masonry, dragging along with them a chair or two, or some other useful article for their personal comfort. After tea spent rest of evening making up packets, (which perhaps will not be allowed to go by post) and writing. I seem to have no time at all these days for studying or anything else, which to me is disappointing. I never waste my time either at least I do not believe myself that I do. On duty again at 8 pm on the all night touch.

9/5/17

According to arrangements, which we have come to between ourselves, instead of two remaining at work all night, we take it in turns to go off as soon as we clear up the work. By this arrangement I was able to go to bed at 1 am. Got up at 8 am. After breakfast I made a fire at the back of our place and boiled a large tin of water, which I drew from the moat, for the purpose of washing my linen. Looking about the ruins of the neighbouring house I found a marble slab, which served admirably as a washing board. Boiled my hairbrush along with my washing and used it to scrub my clothes with, which proved satisfactorily effective. This method also had the double advantage of less labour and at the same time will keep my hairbrush clean. Not that at the present it is of much use to me as I have no hair to arrange, but funny thing, I could not possibly wind up my toilet without brushing my "hair". I should feel all the time that I had omitted to do something due no doubt to that freak, the force of habit. Afterwards wash and shave. Spent the rest of the morning on my diary and just a wee bit of study. On duty at 2 pm to 8 pm. Our officer Lt. Watson, as I expected, he declined to forward my packages, an order too has been issued that only one letter per day will be allowed to be posted. Things are indeed looking up somewhat. They seem to become more "English" every day. This hallmark of foolishness, will receive a very startling awakening and perhaps at on distant date too. After 8 pm I lay in my bed reading until after 11 pm and finished my French novel before blowing out my candle. I received during the day a parcel from my friends at Southport, which contained a packet of gold flake cigarettes, some sweets and a beautiful tin of assorted biscuits.

10/5/17

Nice morning, which became later in the day extremely warm. On duty 8 am until 2 pm. Afterwards went for a walk along the road, Mt. Saint Quinton passed over two different sets of metals, which we had built. I would like to add that without doubt there is no word good enough for the great work accomplished by that almost unheard of Department, which is known under the insignificant title "R o D" (Railway Ordnance Department). The labour to be done is of heavy, extensive and gigantic proportions. No task seems to be too great however and the men of the "RoD" may be seen always carrying on with their work with precision and in a methodical manner. I walked as far as the top of the hill, which rises up midway between Peronne and a village to the North. I did not go very far over the brow as I felt too fatigued, on account of the intense heat which was really scorching. I stood for a time regarding the "psysage", with its little villages, amid a wilderness of barrenness. I endeavoured too to piece together the various systems of trenches. Ribbons of smoke were issuing from the vicinity of the mortally wounded villages, which was an evidence that British troops were in occupation. From the eminence upon which I stood thus occupied in weaving around the objects of my notice, numerous idle dreams of fancy. I was able to look across immense tracks of rolling plains. To see with my eyes upon the spot, a portion of the stage, upon which has been acted the greatest drama in history. May God forbid that such, the world should witness again. Out there where foe has met foe with all the sordid devices known in hell and improved upon by Christians, lie the carcases of many men, their bodies still exposed to the heavens. Do they need burial, perhaps not, for they are become like the earth upon which they lie. There is a remarkable resemblance, the men which were are gone, and only death and earth remain. The chief features along the route were the usual German dug outs, which were sunk into the embankment on the left-hand side going from Peronne. The whole landscape resembles nothing but desolation, and in very truth god forsaken.

What were once brilliant fields of smiling purity are now transformed in to a brown rusty sort of colour, which is spread across the intervening valleys to the crest of the heights beyond, which rise up in the distance in a protective manner around the flat fertile plains. German "troop tracks" were distinctly observable running in all directions from and to the lines of communication. Upon my return journey I was hailed by a fusilier who was working on the roads. He called out "Hello sonny, how's the game, come and tell me what you think of things". I accepted the invitation of course. I offered him my cigarette case and we opened a tete a tete there and then. He told me that he had left his wife and family more that 18 months ago at Charing Cross station and had not seen them since (this is a very common complaint among the troops in France). He was o f the opinion that the war would collapse this year, but that we could not win by force of arms etc. etc. After tea I obtained a big bowl of water and had a good swill down with it. It is most necessary to keep as clean as possible, even thought the means are limited. Spent rest of evening reading new French novel, called "Monsieur, Madame and Bebe". It has run into a great many editions, the one I have is the 189th, it is a book which some people would call "warm" but it is nevertheless very true of life. On duty 8 pm. There has been a very heavy thunderstorm this evening. I forgot to bring in my clothes which I had washed and they have gone through the whole storm. Read my book at intervals between work during the night.

11/5/17

I had a fairly "bonne" night, was clear of work at about 1 am, so lay my weary limbs down upon the floor where I stayed until nearly 6 am, with the exception of a call shortly after 2 am, when a telegram as handed in over the counter. After breakfast, shave and clean up I spent the rest of the morning until dinnertime writing and studying. On duty at 2 pm until 8 pm. I have heard from the orderly Corporal that all my packets had been sent off by the post, which I hope proves to be true in spite of our officer's threat to stop them. They contain a good deal of miscellaneous rubbish it is true, but after making a careful choice from this collection of odds and ends, which I have picked up I imagine that they will add richness to my scrap album, if not in wealth, then surely in pure valuelessness. I wonder if that is a good express. As I have nothing to talk about today I will endeavour to describe "OUR BILLET". In the first place it is a house in the main street. Its proper name is Doignt Road I believe, three or four houses to the right of the road which goes to Mt. Saint-Quentin. It has been expressly chosen on account of the fact that it has still four walls standing and a roof except where there is none. It is a good solidly built type of structure and its former tenants were obviously raised somewhat above the ordinary everyday sort of people. We enter the house by a hall with rooms situated at each side, our signals office is upon the right hand side, a blue and white flag flies proudly in the air from one of the little balconies above. This is of course the emblem of the signal service. The front rooms on the 2nd floor are used as bedrooms. The rear of the house is entirely destroyed and could only be described by seeing it oneself. The whole of the buildings behind and the garden present a spectacle beyond the ability of my pen to describe. The room in which I live is high and spacious. There are two portrait paintings hanging upon the walls in oval frames, both unfortunately have been pierced by bullets or stabbed with some sharp instrument. Our cookhouse has been fixed up at the rear; tables and chairs have been scrounged for its enganishment. We have even flowers in neat little glasses upon the table, which little feature is most pleasing and pleasant and probably encourages a poor appetite and increases a good one. We eat our food upon china plates, just like officers. Our cookhouse would certainly not be completed if I failed to mention that a pair of swallows are at this moment busily engaged building their home behind one of the beams. They have a good deal to say too, at times I sincerely hope that they are a happy couple and that when they give vent to their exceptionally high notes that they are not really quarrelling, but are quite agreed upon the best method of erecting their abode. We are fortunate in having an extremely gentlemanly and obliging cook, whose name is "Tate" nothing seems to irksome for him and he cooks really splendid meals. Now about fires, I have heard the French people remark often that the British Tommy is as destructive as Fritz, which perhaps is not fair comparison. I know however of several buildings at Querrieu which fell down and for which, our fellows were responsible, through having withdrawn timber for making fires, here our Tommies exercise no distinction whatsoever and in consequence all manner of expensive woods, such as solid mahogany etc. are all burnt indiscriminately. I grant of course that every article of furniture, whether large or small, all bear more or less the marks of mutilation, nevertheless the wood of which they are composed, could be easily and well utilised by the French its rightful owners upon their return. Getting into my blankets at about 8.45 pm I read my novel for an hour or more before turning over to sleep, by the way I must not omit to mention that one of our orderlies is an orchestralist, in fact he is a "band master" therefore he has obtained a violin and regales us often during the sultry day, with all sorts of music including classical pieces, which he renders exceptionally well. I will finish off with a short reference to our friends the rats. There lives about these parts an ever increasing community of the above named tribe, in the trenches their runs may be distinctly seen, running from dug outs to some other place of frequency. Here these "camp followers" abound in vast numbers. As soon as the evening begins to set in, they come slinking out and as the dusk advances, their numbers gradually increase. One almost treads upon them in the yard and garden of our billet, as they go skidding about upon their several ways much the same as a populace in a large town goes shopping.

12/5/17

Rose at 7.30 am. Another extremely hot day. On duty 8 am until 2 pm. Spent the afternoon down by the moat sitting on the grass, writing. We have four more telegraphists come to assist us, which is a good thing, as this sort of work is too tiring altogether for ones nerves. One of our men in fact did break down completely a short while back and I replaced him here. During last night and throughout the day, there has been heavy movements of troops through this town in the direction of the front. Spent evening reading and writing. Sent off one letter to my father and another to my wife Elinor, also received two parcels from my wife which contained a glorious cake, two packets of 50 gold-flake cigarettes, three lovely apples, a bag of chocolate, large tin of acid drops, some pencils, a couple of packets of three nuns tobacco and a birthday card. Instead of going on at 8 pm to work all night I was released and the fresh arrivals put to the wheel. I lay down on my bed and read my book for an hour or more. Got between the blankets about 11 pm and fell asleep.

13/5/17

Up before 8 am. Breakfast, shave etc. The morning is rather dull and close, with slight rain at intervals. Spent morning reading and a little study. It is rather peculiar but since I arrived in France nearly 12 months ago I have to a very great extent, spent my time, in study, which reminds me of the days under Gustavus Adolphus the Swedish General who came to battle in the plains of Germany. His soldiers did not require in those days so much time given for the purpose of instructions and training. They were however employed in the improvement of their minds and were to be seen even, thus engaged upon the battlefield itself. Schools were formed and teachers provided. Soldiers who came to fight in this manner, do not come to destroy, but to exalt. They are of men wise in their generation and the lessons which they teach with their good swords, have wide and far-reaching effects, for the advancement of civilisation and of all mankind. On duty 2 pm until 9 pm. I must say a few words about the houses neighbouring ours. The house next door on the right, has apparently been used by the enemy as a small salvage dump. The front room is filled with exploded shells and pieces of iron. The room behind and the yard are both heaped up with metal taken from the houses in the town and include lead tubes, baths, tanks, pies and sheet coverings. The back of the building has suffered a good deal more than the front portion. I mounted up the staircase however, which was a mass of fallen debris and extrememly shaky, and managed to reach a small room, which presented rather a striking spectacle amid such terrible surroundings. It was full of bottles and apparatus of an experimental nature. In the wall opposite was an oval aperture, which served the purpose of a window I did not tarry long in this little laboratory affair as I judged it best to exercise a little prudence and leave such things severely alone, harmless though they may appear to be. I passed on into another room which had obviously served the purpose of a "study". The floor was at least a couple of feet deep in paper etc. There was a beautiful massive porcelain vase, lying on the table fixed in the middle of the room. By its side lay a "male" bust, slightly damaged, as indeed was the vase, a piece having been chipped out of the mouth of the latter. The bookshelves although badly knocked about and the contents dispersed in all directions, nevertheless they still contained some really valuable specimens of early French literature. I have got the plunder fever awfully bad. As I handled them I was filled with a deep desire to squeeze them all into my "pocket". Some of the books included for instance "Histoire et description du japon d'apres de p de charlevoise 1839, ouvres de Monsieur de Fontenell des acadamies Francoif, des sciences, des belles lettres, de Londres de Nancy, de Berlin and de Rom. m. dcc lxvii, Lettres de Madame la Marquise de Sevigne, a Madame la Countesse de Grignan, sa fille. m. d. cc lxxx" of this latter I have about 15 "tomes", "memoires sur Napoleon, l'imperatrice Marie Louise (de 1810 a 1814) 1828". I got hold of a drawer and filled it to its utmost limits with these treasures. Among them I discovered an album which was filled with photographs of some well-known celebrities. It contains also a few private photographs. This is forsooth a tres bon souvenir but oh how I wish that it were possible to get them all safely over to England. Our officer however tells me that I could be shot (presumably at Dawn) for taking these things and that in fact a soldier was shot at Albert for a similar offence. Still life without risk would be unbearable, it would not be worth living. I shall not give up hope however of saving just a few of these books. All is fair in war they say and there is every possibility that everything of value, which might still be left in this town, may at any time be lost by fire or by the process of demolition. One has always to exercise caution, when visiting these broken homes (which is by the way strictly forbidden by the Town Mayor) in order not to tread upon anything dangerous and to be, on the alert for trailing wires, which might be left for the unwary to trip over, and which might have something unpleasant at the end of it. Several such wires do still exist and are treated with due respect by the troops, among the papers lying on the floor I discerned a bomb, but religiously bore the fact in mind, so as not to unwittingly disturb its repose. The adjoining house to this had been used as an officers mess (British) and soldiers billet, several pieces of good furniture are there and a couple of damaged oil paintings even now. These houses must have been very beautiful homes before the war. They are all 3 or 4 stories high. For some reason of which I am unaware they have beneath them very deep cellars, and in this particular case of which I am speaking there are thousands of rounds of German cartridges and bombs. Before retiring I read my book for an hour or more, when my candle extinguished of its own accord.

14/4/17

There has been a violent thunderstorm during the night. I was awakened at 3.30 am by the men who were sleeping on the other side of the room, frantically running about and dragging their beds and belongings out of the rain, which came pouring through in torrents, I was obliged to smile, it was so funny. Outside, the lightning illuminated most vividly every detail of the gaping wrecks of houses on the opposite side of the road, while inside our home, the men in all the rooms were creating such a pantomime running here and there in their shirts making frantic efforts to rescue all they could from the flood. In the morning I found several lying crouched upon the floor around my bed. On duty 89 am until 2 pm. Went to my favourite place in the afternoon, down by the moat, where I have found a little shaded place upon the embankment, here I write and study unobserved and in perfect seclusion, solitude and quietness. I was however compelled to return indoors very shortly owing to rain. After tea we paraded with rifle and gas helmets for inspection, which was followed by pay, I received 30 francs. A division of dismounted cavalry has arrived here and we see once more the familiar figures of our Indian comrades. On duty at 8 pm to work all night. Wrote a letter to Miss Weeds.

15/5/17

Had a fairly decent sort of night, but rather weary when I finished at 8 am. In accordance with the possibilities, which have arisen on account of the recent substantial increase in our staff, it has been arranged that the man who works the night shift should be free from duty on the following day. Hence today I am liberty. Had my breakfast and afterwards while is was engaged in the customary morning ablutions I bethought myself how best I could spend the day, which was at my disposal. I thought of my cousin Isabel and my promise to her to visit the resting place of her husband and in a way look after same, whenever the opportunity afforded to allow me to do so. When of course anything comes in to my poor head, I am bound to carrying out to the best of my ability. Putting on my oldest pair of boots I started off at once upon the road, taking the route to Mt St Quentin, I turned to the left down the "Avenue de Quinconce", which is indeed a pretty walk at the moment, inspite of the fact that enormous shells have plunged mercilessly into the beautiful wood which borders the right hand side of the road. Turning again sharply to the right, I took the road, which leads to Clerg sur Somme. Before very long I was overtaken most fortunately by a boxcar from the signals of the 4th army headquarters at Villers-Carbonnel, which at once stopped and picked me up. More fortunately still I found that it was bound for the same direction as myself. It was a dull bleak sort of morning and felt rather chilly as I had only the other day discarded my cardigan and vest. Towards Clery the ground was heaped about and bore the only too visible signs of the fierce struggle which took place in these parts between our indomitable allies and the cunning enemy. On the left as we entered Clery (alas blown clean out of existence) are large stretches of water and running between them and the road (which is considerably higher) is a railway, a large number of railway wagons lie totally destroyed near the permanent way, which is now the highway for the work of the "RoD". The village itself is completely effaced and the only thing of note, which attracted my attention was an unpleasant smell which hovers over the place. Leaving Clery some little distance behind we turned off to the left and descended a hill into the little village of Curlu (of which there is now hardly a trace) for the purpose of dropping some signalling stores for the uars Division, who are in Nissan huts at this place. Having duly deposited these things, we turned back upon our original route and soon afterwards came to Maricourt (which also exists only in name) and almost immediately passed through plateau the site of the big ammunitions dump fire, not long back a German airman during the early hours of one morning descended to an extremely low altitude and dropped three incendiary bombs upon a train loaded with explosives, which was standing on the rails running through the dump. I have it on very good authority that due warning was circulated to all the dumps to expect an aerial attack twelve hours before it actually took place. That rifles were fired at the enemy machine, yet he was able to compile his work successfully and got safely away himself. The fires that the bombs caused lasted several days until they had eaten their way through the entire dump. I saw a few twisted and distorted pieces of zinc and other metals lying in heaps as the only evidence of the catastrophe. A little further on I reached my destination and descended the declivity to the solitary graveyard of the brave. I found everything satisfactory. Isabel's wreath was still on the cross intact, but the flowers and ribbon had faded somewhat. The little rose tree bore evidence of life, in the fact of a few budding leaves a little way from the ground. The two sprigs of white lilac were both thriving, a little tuft of green leaves adorn the tops of each. Long grass is quickly covering up the whole plot. The letters "G.R.C.", which I had previously observed written in pencil upon the cross mean "Graves Registration Corps" as distinct from "G.R.U.", Graves Registration Units", a small button fixed to the top of the cross, which resembles the head of a screw, bears also these mystical letters, which is to show who was responsible for its erection. The "G.R.U" crosses are identified by the letters being impressed upon a small strip of metal, which is nailed to the cross. A party of 5 soldiers are at present engaged upon tidying up the cemetery and putting each grave into a picture of neatness and order. I got into communication with one of them, who explained to me several things of interest. It is intended to divide the cemetery at Cornoy into three parts, 2nd Lt. Santlers grave would probably be in the first portion. It is also proposed to erect a monument in every military cemetery, with the names of all inscribed thereon. My informant mentioned that "ever so many had said what a nice wreath it was, the writing like" he said and added "his wife will be always thinking of him". It would seem that he although unknown to her, had divined my cousins goodness and honoured her, an English wife in a soldiers way. I found that he knew the grave by name, when I first approached him and upon my departure, he promised "t" do his best to make it look nice"." I should mention that in comparison, this cemetery is only a small one, it holds so I was told about 900 graves, but personally I do not think there are quite so many. My luck was indeed in today, I had not been long upon my journey back, when I got a lift in a lorry, which was going to Peronne. I had more than half expected to have to walk greater parts of the journey, as there is quite a scarcity of traffic upon these particular roads now. I noticed two large French cemetery's at Maricourt, one on each side of the road, both were beautifully set out and arranged. The cemetery on the left was simply ablaze with the "tricoleur", a rosette in the colours of the French republic hung upon every cross. Even those lonely graves which are scattered about the plains and hills are honoured with the colours of France. Between Curlu and Clery the Coldstream Guards, the Grenadier Guards and the Scots Guards, were lining up, when we passed, as they were to be inspected by the King of the Belgians, a platform from which flew the Belgian colours had been erected by the roadside. I arrived back at Peronne about 1.30 pm and was not too late for dinner. Spent the afternoon writing. Have sent a letter off to my cousin Isabel. Spent evening also writing and some reading, across at my little retreat by the moat. Afterwards went with a friend to look through some houses, including a bank, could find nothing however except books, and it is useless to carry them off as I am not permitted to send them away by post. Got into bed about 9 pm and read for about 2 hours.

16/5/17

Good nights rest but overslept myself. I was on duty at 7 am, but did not "show a leg" until 7.45 am. On duty until 2 pm. Have despatched a parcel to my sister Doris containing all my French study books, for which I have no requirements here, and also to relieve to some extent the weight of my kit bag. It is a very dull cold day, with slight rain. In the afternoon, although it was raining I went for a walk round the town starting at the "grand place", at the further end of the square is a great mound of debris sticking out from which one recognises, a conglomeration of broken bedsteads and all manner of now utterly useless household utensils. This is a sight, which meets the eye almost at every step along the streets. A number of Indians were employed when I passed, clearing away obstructing rubbish by the roadside and from the footpaths. Reaching the far end of the "grand place", I turned down the road upon the right, which brought me to a solid looking building upon my left and which turned out to be a fort. Indians were billeted in its strong towers and at this time were occupied outside the walls carrying out such occupations as that of preparing their food, while a couple were hard at work endeavouring to saw up a large tree, which they found to be a task not easy to accomplish, on account of the wood being wet. A couple of English Tommies volunteered to show them how to do it but failed, rather badly too, in consequence of the state of the wood. I noticed a tall Indian standing in an embrasure, which had been made in the thick hide of the fort. These dark soldiers from our Indian Empire are really very handsome men. One is struck by the similarity in type of their well cut uniforms which the majority possess. The individual in the doorway presented to my mind a remarkable picture, as he stood there, dressed in khaki military uniform with pugaree turban, and quietly regarding all that was taking place around him. This soldier from the East conveyed to me a hundred thoughts as I looked at him, encompassed by the framework of wrecked medieval Europe in the background. At the back of the fort in the bed of the moat (now dry) a shooting range had been placed and consisted of 4 targets. I noticed a large quantity of British ammunition (empties) lying upon the ground, a large trench had been also dug along the base. Completed my tour and re-entered the road, taking a direction to the right. A particular feature, which always strikes me as rather extraordinary, bordering in fact on the marvellous, when walking in to the country through the village or in a town, where the blight of war has swept, that nowhere does a single house remain untouched. The searching propensities of modern high explosives have visited all and everything and written indelibly upon the whole face of the earth in large dreadful characters, the wrath of God upon the world. Carlisle has it in his "French Revolution" that "bricks and mortar cannot be destroyed". It is true that the revolutionists had vowed that nothing should remain standing, which had been polluted by foreign occupation. Toulon for instance resisted successfully all the efforts of the avowers to complete its demolition. But then Carlisle spoke of his day "seulement". The world has lived alas to see and to witness the impossible accomplished. I turned down or rather up a street to the left, called the "Rue de Vierges". I ascended a flight of cobbled steps, which brought back to my memory, that glorious old world town hall of Malta. I looked into a house on the right nearly at the top of the steps and "stole" a few "pieces of paper" which I thought worth keeping, or to put it better, I wished to "save" them.

131

Diary Number 7

17/5/17

Finished work at 1 am. Got up at 8 am. Very miserable wet day. With a comrade I went to fetch water, which we obtained from a pump on the right hand side of the main entrance to the church. We carried the cans upon an old "drum barrow" for carrying cable. As I write these notes a battalion of Grenadiers with band playing and followed by their baggage train is marching past and have taken the route to Clery where a Brigade of guards is in rest. On duty at 2 pm until 8 pm. Read my French novel for a couple of hours or so before blowing out my candle.

18/5/17

Rose shortly after 8 am. Have bought several little ornaments from a "scrounger" for 5 Francs. One is a beautiful brass flower-vase mounted upon a base of marble. I shall have to run the risk of getting them away. The books, which I have packed up to send to my sister Doris, our officer has refused to allow to go on, so that I have quite a small library on my hands. Another battalion of Grenadiers has just marched by in companies, with drum and pipes playing lively aires. Yesterday the 4th division of Cavalry (Indians) marched by but in the opposite direction. Troops are always marching to and fro, they wear an expression of much "fed-upedness", methinks too that they cast rather envious eyes upon those of us who appear to have what they would call, "soft jobs" or "staff jobs". Had a stroll over to Doigt before dinner, a little village about a mile or so away. One has to pass over a couple of wooden bridges erected by our engineers in place of the originals, which the enemy destroyed. The road which passes through the centre of the village is paved in the same way as the principal street in Peronne, all the houses have of course been destroyed, about a mile to the rear there are some beautiful woods, which surmount the surrounding hills. The German trench system covering this point can be plainly discerned. Here is also a strong system of trenches lying between Peronne and Doigt, it would seem that the enemy has cut up the ground at certain intervals all the way to his rear. It is not possible to go many yards without meeting evidences of his defence. Four new men have come here to work from the Army Headquarters to relieve the four who were here, when I first came, and who have been attached to the Cavalry Corps, which is taking over the 3 rd corps area. Spent afternoon washing my clothes also had a "bath" in a basin. Wrote a letter to Dill. After tea lay upon the grass behind our billet and read my book, to the accompaniment of violin music. On duty at 8 pm until 1 am.

19/5/17

Dull but fine morning. Received a letter written in French from my sister Doris. I had wished to write a short description of Peronne, but in my search for the necessary material, have dropped across some valuable notes of this old town and will paste them in here, included also are a few details concerning some other places I have visited. (Written in French - See pages 642-644 in diary no 7). I must admit that these particular cuttings I have taken from the pages of a great work in the form of an encyclopaedia. There are several books of immense size and weight allotted to each letter of the alphabet. I felt really ashamed of my self to deliberately mutilate such costly works, but I felt that I could not resist the temptation, which presented itself, and it seemed to me that they will all soon be to rotten and mildewy to hope that they might be saved and ultimately preserved. Together with hundreds of books, they must take their chance, and remain lying upon the floor in one confused mass of literature, defiled by the feet of all who wish to pass over them, and a prey to those most pernicious enemies the rain and damp. On duty at 2 pm until 8 pm. Posted a letter to my sister Doris. The march of troops has resounded through the mortally wounded streets of Peronne, throughout the whole day. The pomp of war is maintained to the uttermost, even here, where it has bitten so deeply into the core of civilisation and tortured the heart of a nation with the deep red blood. The notes martial music come fiercely upon the air from the distance and go reverberating through every hole and gap of this poor town in mocking laughter, in most derisive contempt, but stay perhaps I am deceived, it is not that the wardens of the "right and liberties" of men and of Christians are due to arrive. Methinks I hear the voice of the "British" clarion, which heralds the near approach of "le vengeance". Ma belle France, you shall yet be awarded with "la victoire glorieuse". Read my book a little while after undressing.

20/5/17

Rose at 7.15 am. Very warm day. On duty 8 am to 2 pm. Troop's still passing lead by their respective bands of drum and pipe and brass bands. Spent afternoon down by the moat reading. After tea wrote a letter to my sister Doris, and read a chapter of my French novel. On duty at 8 pm to work all night.

21/5/17

Fairly busy night. Artillery rather more active than usual. The French yesterday retook into their charge part of the line, which we were holding. After breakfast and clean up I spent the morning writing and reading. H handed in my jerkin, one blanket and a pair of gloves. These articles constitute part of ones winter clothing, and have now been returned to the base, for storing and perhaps cleaning, I do not know exactly. I would like to reserve a small space here to mention in words a few thoughts in connection with our new feathered acquaintances, who have, or a least, who are taking up their summer abode on the side of a rafter in our cookhouse. They are an exceedingly tame pair and are not in the least shy or perturbed by the close proximity of our presence. They "carry on" in just the same manner as though the greatest of all animals in the form of man, were entirely absent or in fact extinct. For one day or thereabouts after the unfortunate collapse of their first efforts, which was found upon the floor one morning, we were disappointed to find that the birds themselves had departed. They returned however and are now making rapid progress with a still more beautiful home than the first. Yesterday they made considerable headway, working desperately hard from early morning until dusk, at first I was of opinion that it was the female bird, who was doing all the building, while her lord, ledged himself upon a perch and sang sweet melodies of spring or perhaps of love, I know not which. They always fly away together and return "ensemble" almost at the same instant. I notice now, owing probably to the pressing urgency of getting on to the completion of their cosy little villa, that both of this interesting couple share the distinction of builders. They appear to have no time at all for anything else save for the particular task, which they have in hand, and in consequence I imagine that they are "tout les deux" becoming somewhat thin. I think we could all learn to our advantage a few things from these little creatures of the universe and of God. They are patient and persevering, they do not quarrel and their sweet notes do not in the least convey even the semblance of "mauvois" or words unworthy. Their "civilization" is represented by complete equality, no distinction of class exists among them, while their friendship for each other is sublime concord, which is irreproachable. There code of manners and morals are similar and prompted by like instincts. They are all of one class unique and not dissimilar in their habits and customs, in their work is exhibited a model of exactness, carefulness and perfection. Their whole life is spent in the accomplishment of their especial mission, which is decided by and for themselves, without recourse to violence, without fear of evil and ignorance of guile. These little feathered friends of man, would seem to have long since the acme of a life ideal, to which the poor human mind so often soars, alas in vain. After dinner I lay down upon my bed until tea. At 6 pm I went with a friend to the cinema (3 rd corps), where I spent an enjoyable time. It was simply packed with troops and officers and awfully hot, almost stifling. Wrote a letter to my aunt Ada and read my book for a short while before turning over to sleep.

22/5/17

Very wet morning and our billet is simply dripping everywhere with water. On duty at 8.30 am until 2 pm. In the afternoon I went on a scrounging expedition and brought back with me several old documents written on parchment, among them are included letters from the King of France and stamped with the royal seal. I discovered whole portfolios of these documents, but owing to the impossibility of taking them complete, and also on account of the wet mouldy condition in which they were in, I selected a few copies only. Opposite is a condensed history of the beautiful old town of Louvain. (Written in French - see diary no 7 - pages 654-656). I discovered also quite by chance a most remarkable photograph, hundreds of feet both of foe and friend, must have passed over it, at first I could not make anything of it myself owing to the dust and dirt in which it was enveloped. By brushing it carefully I perceived little by little a truly remarkable and astonishing picture present itself. The spectacle which became unfolded by degrees was to me most astounding and I wondered whether that which I held in my hands was evidence of some particular event in history, I am strongly of this opinion. The subject of my curiosity is an aristocratic prisoner. The scene is in a dungeon, he is apparently an old man and is quite nude except for a cloth, which lies across his legs, as he is seated upon the floor with his legs bent double beneath him. His hands are bound behind him in a strong vice of an iron lock, which is attached to a heavy chain fastened to the wall of the dark cell. Beside him up on the old mans left there is a beautiful girl (probably his daughter, or may be his wife). Her dress in front is loosened from the neck revealing in this place of horrors and sordidness a bosom of white purity and beautiful maturity (in this respect I have it in my opinion that I believe woman is the keeper of probably the most sacred of all blessings bestowed by god through her upon man. In as much that to the newly born babe the mother holds the secret of life - or death). The girl (I cannot call her "woman" she looks so young) has turned away her head and appears to be regarding the door. Her right hand rests lightly upon the shoulders of the tortured man, her left is upon her bosom. While the man, his visage encased with thick unkept locks of hair of flowing white, leans over to her and in haste, obviously perceptible, for perhaps the time is short and goaded by the remorseless pangs of hunger, the starving man drinks from her breasts the nourishment of life, which he must take-or die. In the evening I read my book until 8 pm. When I went on duty for a spell of about 5 hours work.

23/5/17

Got up about 8.30 am. It is a very hot and close sort of day. After clean up etc I betook myself off to the moat, where I spent the morning reading and writing. On duty 2 pm until 8 pm. Nothing of note to record. Read a chapter of my book before retiring. The bantoms of the 25th Division marched away from here today.

24/5/17

Got up at 8 am. Sunny day and very warm. It is my turn for morning off and spent some of my retreat down by the moat. Spent afternoon at the same place and wrote a letter in French to Monsieur Hunel a Querrieu, Somme and another to Miss Dorothy Roberts at Southport. To Monsieur Hunel I enclosed a photograph, which I picked up sometime back among the debris of the little village of Barleux near Villers Carbonnel. The portrait in question is an exact likeness to his son, and I am hoping that my find will prove to be the same as I imagine it to be. Leave opened again about 3 weeks ago and is working steadily down the list. It has already reached the men who have been out here for 14 months, so that even yet all may get a chance of going home. In a few more days time I shall have completed 12 months in France, how time does veritably fly, and how the number of ones experiences becomes augmented, and for what? In the end death takes unto itself all even as the earth and sea take unto themselves the flesh. Were it not better after all, that the womb of woman should instantly become barren. That the songs of birds in the air and the birth of spring upon the bosom of the earth, should all perish and pass away into oblivion, extinct for ever more. That the sun itself should nevermore ascend to offer welcome, to bring cheer and to animate a world so utterly void of good, so deep in guile, so dark within itself. These thought came into my mind after listening to the discourse of one of our number, who has just returned here from leave. He has many amusing anecdotes to relate, but many too of a nature to say the least regrettable. He tells of wives leaving their homes to go off with soldiers and leaving small children behind, of young girls lost beyond recall. This state of things sprung up immediately war was proclaimed and increased at an appalling pace, until now, that which was once a crime finds a place upon the same level as most people take all that happens nowadays. Such a terrible upheaval in the life of our nation, has apparently come to be looked upon indifferently and with little of no concern at all. Such matters are merely ordinary events and quite matterless. I believe however that I can see further the natural results, which will ultimately arise among this chaos and frightful disorder are being sown the stronger seeds of revolution, which will also run its course in a mad insane effort to level things down again to normal conditions. We have not suffered more in this respect than the case among other nationalities, for human nature differs not in kind or in acts. This war is the product of a disorganised, immoral, licentious world, which truth is now laid bare to the light of day for all to gaze upon. The state of the world before 1914 was so corrupt, degenerate and sick that there could be but one outcome ---- war. No further proof is needed than all that has resulted up to the present and there is (but God forbid) much more to follow yet. This is not war, for war holds in itself something charming, something holy. It was and is the birthright of the great, and noble, the chivalrous and the honourable, although no doubt to little men, with minds of smaller scope, it is a nightmare, now war is reduced to wanton devilry to hopeless degradation, to the mutilation, defacement and humiliation of all things noble, grand and good. This is not war, but rather an achievement originating from the most base, unscrupulous, diabolical and cunning minds, to overthrow, nay more, for their purpose is in verity to exterminate, by all means mechanical, physical and scientific the image of god himself, which man has admittedly so greatly dishonoured. On duty at 8 pm until midnight. Received letters from my wife Elinor and one from Miss Hedges of Newport-Pagnall.

25/5/17

Got up at about 8.30 am. Bright, but very hot day. Spent morning writing and reading at my usual retreat. Artillery activity is still rather more than normal. I might mention that a couple of days ago or so one of our telephone operators, discovered a little kitten in "la mansarde" of a house, which had recently been evacuated by troops, who had apparently taken along with them the mother and unwittingly abandoned the little mite. He brought to our billet and endeavoured all he could to sustain its life, he kept the kitten in a box, in which he had arranged a little bed. It was too young and weak to stand upon its feet and had to be fed by means of a spoon. Condensed milk however is no more the natural nourishment of a kitten tan it is of an infant. This morning the poor thing was obviously more dead than alive, in spite of the fact that for warmth the little creature had been placed in the oven of the cooking range to pass the night (some device that). The "foster mother" in consequence decided to deliver the sufferer from more pain. I saw him later in the garden digging a small grave. The march of troops goes on unceasingly from morning until night, as I make these notes a couple of battalions of the Northumberland Fusiliers are marching by, to the strains of their band which is playing "the sons of the brave" (or is it grave). In the evening after leaving of duty at 8 pm I went for a stroll round by the moat in the direction of my solitary retreat without cap and in my roped soled slippers. In fact I hardly ever put on my boots hear. It was a lovely evening, with a strong scent of spring impregnating the still air, passing out by the back of our "house" and over the garden wall and iron gates I turned to the right. A badly damaged garage and the remains of the home of a paperhanger and letter gilder I pass upon my left. Thence walked across some waste ground, pitted with shell holes, until I came to the outer breastwork of bygone fortification which are represented by earthworks situated upon the northern side of Peronne. On the other side hidden between deep declivity's lies the sulky and ever slumbering moat. It is partly covered with a greenish herbitage usually seen upon the surface of ponds, but the sun is rapidly turning this to a dingy brown colour. I turned to the left, down a gully with "knocked-in" dugouts at each side, an arch of bricks is built into the bank on the left, which the Germans had turned to its utmost use. On one side is a compartment which has evidently used as a place of rest, articles of household descriptions, litter the place, at the opposite side these human ants had dug a deep dug-out through the wall into the bowels of the earth. Following a stretch of that very common article, which is used extensively out here, as a protection from the necessity of walking in the mud, which one might call a "ground ladder", I came to the top of the bank, where the cunning enemy had placed a machine gun. It was composed of a little shanty with several rows of wooden shelves, which I presume, was where the bands of ammunition were kept. Two small holes, the right one being covered with a piece of glass looked out over the moat and commanded most admirably a large tract of the country. The roof, which was composed of a couple of sheets of zinc had a layer of earth over them and level with the top of the bank. It could not possibly have been distinguished from in front. Long grass now covers the whole. Directly underneath this deadly little corner, a dug-out descends into mother-earth, shell holes are still plainly visible dotted over the bank and some had come very near indeed to striking this hornets nest. Turning back again along the top I descended several steps, which the Germans had kindly made, and which are very useful to me personally, as this is the route to my "retreat" which lies along the side, beneath a few low bushes. A little further along is a solitary telegraph pole, which the Germans had dismantled before leaving. The ends of wires hang down in distorted shapes from the cups. The test-box is open and the wires similarly severed, a small ladder still rests up against the pole, a big shell has struck the ground within a few inches of it, but why should I talk about such little items. One has only to go a few yards to find much material for though and meditation, every yard of this poor country has much of history to relate, which perhaps it were better to endeavour to forget. Read my novel for a while before retiring.

25/5/17

Another tremendously hot day. The usual tramp of troops and the blare of bagpipes and brass and silver instruments penetrates the sultry air. On duty at 8 am until 2 pm. I posted a letter to Miss Hedges at Newport-Pagnall. Spent afternoon down at my resting place. It was my turn to be off in the evening and I betook myself to the bank against the moat, where I stayed until 8 pm. Over on the other side, but too low for me to see, there is another strip of water, where judging from the noise which went on there, a large number of British Tommies were enjoying a splash and swim. Their ringing cheers and laughter was vibrating in the air incessantly. It was good to hear the full, frank, whole-hearted laughter, which accompanied their sport. I myself am too much on the wrong side of good health. It was not from want of desire or wish that I am so overcome with lethargy. My spirit is naturally tireless and active but as usual I am a victim of bad luck.

27/5/17

Still beautifully sunny weather, with a pleasant moderating breeze. Quite by chance I discovered that today is Sunday and moreover that it is Whit-Sunday. Was doing fatigues this morning, which is a new advent into our life here. Three are told off each day for the purpose of fetching water for the cookhouse, sprinkling crisol throughout our billet and sweeping out same. At the back we have had an incinerator erected, were all rubbish is deposited, and this has to be "set going" each morning with the aid of much paraffin, after completing this task, had a shave, clean up and a bath. On duty 2 pm until 8 pm, afterwards went for a stroll and returned after about an hour. Paraded for pay at 1.45 pm in the afternoon and I received 40 francs.

28/5/17

I decided to report sick this morning. It is beautiful weather and glorious to be alive to those who are enjoying good health. I will give a description of my passage through the day, which might be somewhat interesting and I do not think I shall forget soon this Whitsuntide bank holiday. In the first place I am more than disappointed to have to leave Peronne, where I have become nicely settled down, and where we were in receipt of such good rationing and plenty of it, but the fortune of war is varied and I must perforce think of my state of health at the moment in anticipation of the future which god willing, I trust to enjoy a good time after all this sordid business has mercifully come to a definite end. At 9 am I got a sick report and went to the 1st S.M.F. amb(T), which has its quarters at the maternity hospital, a large building in the town, which has not suffered to such an extent as one might have expected from the allied bombardments. Saw the M.O (medical officer) at about 11 am, who marked me down for evacuation. Had my dinner there and had to wait until after tea, before any ambulances were available to take us to the main dressing station (no 105 field ambulance at Fins). Here there was a continual stream of arrivals and it was not until about 8 pm that my turn came to see the M.O. I was marked off for evacuation to the CCS (casualty clearing station) another long wait ensued for the necessary conveyance. One arrived about 11 pm and myself together with three others were put into it. Spaces for 2 stretcher cases being reserved inside. An officer of the M.G. corps (machine gun corps) was at this moment brought in and 2 of my companions were obliged to get out again, to wait for the next ambulance in order to make room for the officers kit and his orderly. One man badly wounded in the back and his face swathed in bandages, was raised upon a stretcher into the ambulance. He was in terrible pain and his moaning was piercing and unceasing. It must have been nearly midnight when at last we made a start. The poor wounded fellow on the stretcher was unfortunately compelled to undergo excruciating agonies through the jolting of the car. Although the driver drove his car at a steady even pace. He was in truth mad with pain. He would cry out "oh my poor back, what shall I do, what shall I do, it is burning, burning oh my" "hush" the hospital attendant would say, who was himself merely a young lad. "Try and stick it chum", "yes chum, I know, but I am suffering agonies, I can't help it" the sufferer would reply. "My belly is burning, can't bear even my shirt to touch it, oh, oh, can't we stop, are we there yet, oh my God when will this journey end, shan't we ever get there, oh my God it will drive me mad", "yes chum, it won't be long now, this part of the road is a bit bumpy but it is better a bit further on, you are sticking it very well chum, there are some sisters at the CCS, who will do everything for you, try and stick it out chum". Kind words of this sort continued throughout the journey. I learned, or perhaps it would be more correct to say that I did not learn, knowing already. But here, not far behind the battle line, cramped in the dark (there was no lamp) enclosure of an army ambulance, in the midst of much pain and suffering it was my lot to witness the enaction of a great truth most of us, probably all in fact, have been brought up to believe, right from our cradles, that women are the embodiment of love and kindness. But I have personally on more than one occasion observed the contrary to be the case. I have on several instances observed a male, in the form of man display unreservedly the real genuine article, and in a deeper saner sense than a hundred women put together could ever hope to attain. I have never yet heard a female in the form of a woman, either in hospital or out of it, speak one word of kindness or encouragement, which was not made with more or less and effort. What words could any woman possibly substitute for one single phrase of this hospital orderly, such as for instance "Hush chum, try to stick it chum". These are words which come spontaneously to his lips and are uttered with feeling, springing as they do from the depths of a man's sincerity, to which the nerve-racked and tortured hero at one responds. "I know chum, but I can't help it, I'm suffering agonies, give me a little cold water". I don't know whether it is because I am unfortunate, but as a casual observer, the only love worth calling such that I have seen bestowed by a woman, is that of a mother for her son. All other loves of which the female breast is simply stuffed to an enormous extent, come always to the same thing in the end, which amounts to one big "self-love". Yet we cannot do without the dear creatures. Hence the masculine blindness and indifference, which characterises the male community. The fairer sex, with their angle faces are so distinctly opposite to ourselves in the major and the minor respects too, especially when they dress themselves up in nice clothes, which makes them appear, so soft, bewitching and delicious, that one forgets at once all their many faults and short-comings, and one becomes

138

imbued with just one desire, which is ---- well, just to love and ---- and to eat em. We arrived at our destination (no 34 CCS) about 1.30 am the next morning absolutely dog-tired. The M.O came in soon afterwards. He first attended to the officer who had come along with us, ten approached the next table were our badly wounded comrade lay, he asked in kindly tones "well laddie and what has happened to you'. I was shown my place of rest for the night. An orderly brought me a nice hot bowl of cocoa and a piece of bread and butter.

29/5/17

Was awakened about 7.10 am by an orderly with a ham sandwich and another who brought the tea round. There are not many patients in this tent, which like many others is large and constructed by joining five or six hospital marquees together. Had shave and a wash. Spent morning writing. For dinner we had boiled meat and bread in basins, and afterwards boiled rice and uncooked figs. Spent afternoon writing etc. In the evening did a little studying and read my French novel, which I still have with me. Am also trying all I can to take along with me a number of French books and papers, which bear some historical interest. Am wondering if I shall succeed, I do hope so sincerely. It struck me that not being far from Peronne, only about a kilometre, I might be able to persuade someone going in that direction, to do me the favour of calling at the Signals Office there and enquire if there were any letters for me. While waiting with that intention, in the road outside the hospital, one of our dispatch orderlies came along on a bicycle and I requested him to do me the aforesaid favour. In due course a letter arrived from my cousin Isabel. Had a walk round our encampment. I see that there are two CCS's no.s 34 and 55, and they take it in turn, every other day, to receive patients. The railway runs along the side, there being several pairs of metals at this point. A long khaki coloured hospital train, all spick and span, came into the siding this morning and will stand by I presume, until there are sufficient patients for evacuation to the base, to fill it. There are 18 nurses here 9 in each CCS and several more are on the train. A derelict German light railway passes through the centre of the camp. There are dug-out's and shelters everywhere as per usual. Some shelters facing the hospital railway siding are covered in with thick walls of cement. The dug-out's which descend underneath the road are having all their timber extracted and then filled up, as of course at present they constitute a menace to the solidity of the road.

30/5/17

Dry but cool morning. Time seems to drag horribly. Enforced inaction is always very tiring to me. During the morning I swept up together with a comrade, the floor of our huge marquee, which is covered wit tarpaulin. Two other came along in our wake with mops and buckets and scoured it with a solution of disinfectant. It was a hard task, I was in consequence exhausted for the rest of the day. The hospital train, which was standing in the sidings moved away about midday, to pick up patients further up the line, so that we a doomed to hang on here until its return. Spent remainder of the day studying. reading and writing. Wrote a letter to my aunt Ada, enclosing a number of photographs etc, which I had picked up among the debris of the ruined houses of Peronne. Saw the M.O in the afternoon. The weather became oppressively warm towards the dinner hour. I am now drawing to the close of the French book that I am reading, and which has proved to be both interesting and instructive, in as much as that it is written true to life, to a remarkable degree. I have admittedly been rather a long time in reading this book, but that has been on account of the fact that I have at the same time endeavoured to commit to memory every word that I did not already know. In the chapters upon children, or I should say to be more correct, on the subject of boys, as there is not a single word, which refers to girls, my mind was taken back in a manner very vivid to the early days of my own little darling. I saw him passing through many stages from his first appearance in to the world. I could picture the little love as he lay quietly sleeping in his cradle, which I had made for him out of a orange box, which I had dropped around with some material of green stuff, speckled with roses and mounted upon a pair of rockers, which likewise had formally served as the partitions in the orange box and where of oval shape at the top. Then his darling little limbs grew too long for the cradle, which became a thing of the past. His long golden locks, which encircled and cast a halo around his girlish pretty face, constituted always a source of pure delight, of delicious unutterable happiness. Then there came the black times too. My little darling mite, suffered a good deal with those beastly little teeth. During those periods of his unconscious sufferings, and the merciless distortions of that worshipped little body which I was hopelessly powerless to relieve, even for a moment, I was tortured grievously in my heart. I have known no greater fear in life, or felt more pain of mind, than that, which thrilled through all my being on these occasions. War broke out and the glories of home life, came to an abrupt end. I have only seen my darling baby for a few hours, since the 4th Aug 1914. His precious little love I have not gained or even shared. He must be a big boy now, his tiny petticoats are now discarded, which made my baby look so charming as down the garden path he would run, myself in hot pursuit while playing hide and seek together, a game he loved to play, his bursts of glorious, frank and hearty laughter, when he had found me, or I had discovered him, was sweeter than the songs of birds and grander, greater, deeper than the depths of the sweetest music. My little darling baby I love you truly and sincerely, now as then and more my little love. My heart is aching, burning, breaking to embrace you just once again.

31/5/17

Pleasant sunny day. Spent the morning writing. We have all gone into another marquee, as the one we were occupying has been condemned, together with its neighbour. In the afternoon I strolled away from the hospital, crossed the railway, where I notice several Irishmen, in civilian clothes, working on the line. These individuals came up about 3 weeks ago and are receiving a contract wage, which no doubt the British Government can well afford to pay, although I have not heard that the ordinary common British soldier has been awarded an increase in his army pay. I suppose that the thoughtful Government takes into account, the great privilege which is accorded the Infantryman, to die for his country, and which is not placed within the reach of these particular Irishmen. Turning to the right along the canal bank, I walked to the nearest temporary bridge, where I crossed over. The bed of the canal is only covered with a foot or two of water and men who go there for a bath, do not go deeper than their calves, upon the opposite side of the canal are extensive stretches of swamps, across which the Germans had constructed improvised bridges, which we now however destroyed. Walking some distance along the bank, I sat down in the tall grass by the side of a bush, which offered a little shelter from the rays of the sun. Here I studied French for a time, and afterwards stretched myself out for a nap. After tea read my French novel and also commenced an English one called "Heart of the world".

1/6/17

Another broiling hot day. The hospital train no 30 came back into the sidings yesterday. Spent day as usual. An Indian "CCS" is rapidly nearing completion upon the opposite side of the road to ours. An Indian who came up on horseback to me that his brother had been killed yesterday. He wore upon his epaulets the numerals "9 hh" and spoke English rather well. It is rather surprising that practically every Indian one meets has some knowledge of our language, although the French tongue seems to be more familiar to these dusky worriers. While I was speaking to him, a comrade in arms. A younger man, approached and they saluted each other in that customary manner. The younger soldier placed his arms about the other a touched his body with his own first on the right side then on the left and again for the third time on the right. To carry out each of these movements, the head and body is swung from one side to the other. They then clasped each others hands, just as we do with the right hand. It is peculiar the different forms of salutation adopted by natives of all climes. Elsewhere I believe I have noted the form of greeting which is practised by the Arabs. Near to our hospital and close to the railway are about a score of German graves, with the customary tall and well designed crosses, placed at the head of each. Two are decorated at the top with the well known "iron cross" to signify I suppose that these emblems of the devil in the form of culture have gone down with them to hell. Behind this row we have commenced a new one and a couple of German soldiers who have died in hospital are already interned there small plain British crosses with their names, number and regiments inscribed thereon, indicating the spot of their last resting place. Another feature, which I have noticed in connection with German graves is that in a great many instances, a border of stones is placed around each grave. One of the however, which I have seen today, was typically Hunnish and more in keeping with the traditions of their barbarous stock. The border in this case is composed of empty wine bottles. Some of the graves had been planted with forget-me-nots, which are flourishing at this moment in abundance.

2/6/17

Warm pleasant weather still, but rather cloudy and threatening. Still nothing doing in the way of being shifted. Short sharp showers during the day.

3/6/17

Rather a cold night, but sunny and very warm during the day. Have been warned for evacuation to the base today and expect to start sometime after dinner. Today is the anniversary of my departure from England for France and now after exactly 12 months. I am about to depart from the scene of my labours of a year. God alone can tell what will betide me in the future, my life course has been so strange and varied, that part at least, of it, which I and no other know but myself, that there are probably still a great many more waiting for me in the dim future. A mention might be made before leaving the neighbourhood of Peronne, I had it from a source, which I consider reliable that dug underneath the vicinity of one of our aerodromes, which is situated a little further along the Peronne road in the direction of Villers Carbonnel, the Germans had excavated a huge place, which they used as a hospital, with sufficient capacity for the accommodation of 2,000 patients, I have not seen the place myself, so cannot vouch for its accuracy. I may add too that I have endeavoured to quote only incidents of truth all though my diaries, otherwise I could have written books upon hundreds of miscellaneous subjects of an inauthentic character, in connection with the war and other things, but on account of insufficient evidence I have consistently deemed it better to avoid even so much as mentioning same. I left the hospital as about 2 pm. We passed through and by several villages, of better times, which now however are no more. Nearing Villers-Brottonneux, we came upon the evidence of civilisation in the form of civilians, men and women working in the fields. The landscapes through which we passed were of ever changing beauty, which one never tired of gazing at, in contemplation and with much interest, much in the same way as one regards the reeling out of a fascinating cinematography film. I do not think I have ever before seen such ravishingly pretty sights as those that passed in endless succession before our eyes, and I was filled with even greater longing and desire to make this beautiful land my home of the future. It was a treat of great deliciousness to leave behind the terrible aspect of a blasted earth, where the claws of war had despoiled so mercilessly the beauties of Gods creation and to view in contrast these delightful scenes of indescribable magnificence. The pretty little white villages, by which we passed, so clean and prim, resting in solitude and peace upon the sides of the hills and in the valleys, all cloaked with glorious dense woods of various types, but all clothed in vestments of a vivid emerald green, were a true delight and a divine blessing to behold. There were several kindly nurses on board. One who brought round a big dish of chocolates, a small morsel for each patient, was of a very friendly turn of mind. She happened to knock my tea by accident, with her foot, which I had placed upon the floor, and a little was spilt. She exclaimed " Oh I nearly put my foot in it" I replied "well sister, if you had, I should drink it all the same". She was a good sort of sport and obviously intent upon being agreeable. She asked use how we were enjoying "so of the Sergeant Majors" and used other terms too, which she explained, were what the Tommies had named the tea of different "calibers". She admitted that there was a good deal that she had yet to learn from soldiers, before leaving the army. The journey was extremely tiring to me. We were packed in ten to a carriage, eight sitting and 2 lying upon shelves above our heads. At a pinch there was also room for another to scramble on to a shelf, which practically touched the ceiling of the carriage. The men who were sitting changed over at intervals, with those lying upon the shelves. Other portions of the train, were on the London tube principal, the patients sitting in long rows down the side of the train. We arrived at Rouen (our destination) about 1.30 am and we were put into big motor busses almost immediately. It was about 4 am before the stupid hospital routine had done with us and we were allowed to go to rest. Coming through the streets of this ancient city of Rouen I was unfortunately much too fatigued to take much notice of the places that we passed, although the night was fairly light by the brilliant rays of an approaching full moon. I was in agony too with my stomach, which groaned away and I felt sick and dizzy. I must mention one thing, which struck me particularly while doing this motor journey. It has to do with architecture, which although I am admittedly quite ignorant upon such matters. I though that in spite of the fact that the French appear to be strongly divorced from erecting building of the heavy solid type, still all that I saw presented to my imagination a fineness and elegance, which rather appealed to me. Also I was struck with the many lovely avenues of trees, which gave welcome shelter form the sun to all who should be obliged, or desire to walk abroad during the heat of the day. As there is nothing of interest worth noting in hospital life I have reluctantly decided not to keep a diary. Instead I wish to make the most of my time here to rest and recuperate. I have finished reading my French book, which is called "Monsieur, Madame et Bebe" today.

22/7/17

I left the convalescent camp yesterday and come into the 3rd I.B.D (Infantry Base Details) in the evening, where I am at present. Reveille at 6.30 am. Breakfast at 7 am, which consisted of a sort of bully-beef hash. It is beautifully sunny weather, but rather too warm, for work. I am waiting together with about 50 or 60 soldiers to be sent to our own particular bases I hope too that I shall be sent off without delay, as it is certainly anything but pleasant in a camp of this sort. Was hanging about all morning. Walked into no 3 I.B.D to look up an old hospital chum in the 3rd South African Regiment, I failed last evening to find him, as he had quitted the camp. I met him this morning however just prior to his departure on draft for the front. Son sac a dos, all ready for marching. After dinner I strolled out of camp, and walked as far as the Con camp, which is only a short distance down the road, I stayed here watching a cricket match until 3.30 pm, when I retraced my steps back to camp. After tea went for another short walk and sat down under the trees by the roadside. It is impossible to secure a pass into Ouen. In fact we are forbidden to leave the precincts of our camp. Neither are soldier (except officers) permitted to go anywhere for a walk, but must keep to the main roads. The soldiers (except officers) must not go into the woods and forests or even across waste ground. This I know from experience this afternoon and by the myriads of large signboards stuck up everywhere. There is quite an army of "red caps" both on bicycles and on foot, scouring the environs to see that these rules are strictly observed so far as soldiers are concerned (but not officers). Returned to camp shortly after 7 pm. Had a couple of small pieces of cake in the church army hut and also a cup of tea. Bought a mess tin full of beer, which was divided among my tent mates. Paraded at 9 pm for roll call. There are a large number here now, waiting for transference to their respective bases, about a score have been warned to proceed by the first train tomorrow morning to Havre.

23/7/17

Got up at 5.45 am. Had wash, breakfast at 6.30 am and shave afterwards. First batch left camp at 7.30 am. It is a beautiful sunny morning and the skylarks are singing gloriously in the heavens. Am feeling quite well in myself, during my spell in hospital I put on more flesh than had had for years, I had become greatly run down and what with acute dyspepsia and general disability I found the rest truly acceptable. No means of getting out of this camp this morning, so lay down until midday in our sweltering tent. Am under orders to parade at 12.45 pm and to proceed to Abbeville. Had a good dinner before leaving, was issued with rations, which consisted of a tin of maconicie, tin of jam, plenty of tea and sugar and a small slice of cheese. As I had no ration bag, and heaps of things to carry besides, I gave the entire issue to my tent mates. I was the only one for Abbeville and was given my own papers, according to which, I was to call the roll and conduct the party to our unit at the front. I was therefore alone responsible for myself and of course I was duly present at the roll call. We had about 8 kilometres to march to the station. We had first to report at the camp office concentration parade ground at 1.45 pm, where I fell in with a party of R.A.M.C bound for Abbeville, who were lined up opposite a notice board, which bore the name of the above town. As luck would have it the C.O decided that all the bags should be taken down to la gare in a waggon so that I was mercifully relieved of my heavy sand bag, which was full of books and souvenirs. The march proved very trying indeed, especially to the R.A.M.C men, some of whom were "P.B". It was a blessing that the familiar trees which border all the military roads in France offered a welcome shade from the blazing sun.

The train moved off at 4 pm. We were 8 to a carriage, and the journey long and tedious, only broken by frantic efforts to secure boiling water to make tea from neighbouring engines when we stopped upon the route, which, as usual was a frequent occurrence. Arrived at our destination at about 1 am. I went to the Y.M.C.A and purchased a packet of biscuits and 3 bowls of coffee, afterward lay down upon the floor outside to sleep until dawn. There was no room inside, all the bunks and the floor being occupied with tired troops.

24/7/17

At about 6 am I wended my way from the station to our depot. Left my kit at the guard room went into the dining hut for breakfast, which consisted simply of a slice of bread and butter and jam and a dixie of tea. Paraded at orderly room at 8.30 am to report myself and supply the necessary particulars. At 11 am paraded at Quartermasters stores to get small kit, blanket and ground sheet, which latter article by the way, is made to be used as a mackintosh also, having a collar inserted on one side at the middle. I did not attend the usual afternoon parade, being a newcomer, instead I indulged in a nap. Directly after tea I went straight to the little cafe which was my familiar resort, when I first came to this place about 14 months ago. I was recognised at once, even before I had crossed the road. Here I spent the evening in conversation, with soldiers and the family, and drinking beer. It has been extremely hot all day. Arrived back at camp at 9.30 pm.

25/7/17

Rose at 6.30 am. After breakfast, wash, shave and clean up, paraded at 8.30 am. Fatigues until midday. Have met several of my former office acquaintances in civil life, who are at present in this depot. Paraded at 2 pm for pay. I received 40 francs, which was the amount I had previously asked for. Had my hair trimmed. Applied for leave at the orderly room, but was informed that it could not be granted, as leave for England from this depot could only be sanctioned in favour of men appointed to the staff of this base. After tea when to my usual rendezvous, taking with me, all my French books and documents, which I had brought along with me from Peronne. I also deposited for safe keeping with my friends a German knife in sheath, which is used by the enemy for fighting at close quarters and resembles in shape a small bayonet, a pack of German playing cards completed the list. Spent evening talking and drinking beer. Returned to camp at 9.30 pm.

26/7/17

Rather dull today but fine. Working all the morning emptying reservoirs of putrid offensive smelling water in our camp. Quite a job for Germans I should think. For lunch I had three slices of cake and a bowl of tea. In consequence I could eat very little dinner which consisted of Bully-beef etc. Last night I bought a nice piece of embroidery work for a cushion and dispatched same to my dear sister Doris. Afternoon same fatigue as in the morning. After tea betook myself to my favourite place and took with me the rest of my souvenirs, consisting of a large official map of the Somme and French and German bullets. I'm sure that I have well merited many congratulations for having successfully carried all my relics up to this point. I think that now I have delivered same into safe-keeping until such time as it may be convenient to reclaim them.

144

I feel considerably lighter too, besides the fact that there will be less to look after and less to carry. Posted a letter to my aunt Ada this morning.

27/7/17

Morning dull but very close. Posted a letter to my sister Doris. Fatigues all morning in the staff mess hut. Was fortunate once more at dinner today, which consisted of extremely palatable rabbit. Fatigues in the afternoon as in the morning and again after tea. In the evening went down to the town to buy some picture postcards of Abbeville and dispatched same by the French post to my father. It has been terribly hot all day especially this afternoon. I feel very languid and aged, I have no time whatever now to study and in fact small desire to do so. Returned to my particular cafe after visiting la ville and returned to camp at the usual hour. Bringing with me my washing, which had been done there.

28/7/17

Another very warm day with thick mist. Light fatigues today. Received letters from Miss Weeds and Miss Hedge, which had been following me for more than a couple of weeks. Spent evening at the cafe down the road.

29/7/17

Heavy thunderstorms can be distinctly heard coming from the direction of the sea, it is very dull, a heavy storm is threatening. As we were about to parade at 8.30 am the storm burst with all its violence and continued extremely heavy for an hour. Our tent became very soon quite drenched, lightening did some damage to a tree and a building near our camp. Did not attend C.E service as went to sleep instead. After dinner walked into Abbeville sent a selection of picture postcards of Amiens to my father. Had a walk around the town, and shortly after 4 pm had tea at a restaurant, which consisted of a couple of boiled eggs, bread and butter and a pot of tea. The whole cost 2 f 25. Saw several khaki girls as they are called by the Tommies. Indeed several came into the same place as I was in accompanied by the latter. The girls look very chic in their new clothes. After tea returned to my usual place of rest where I stayed until the evening.

30/7/17

Dull morning. Paraded at 8.30 am with the party for the gas school. Spent all morning until 12.30 pm going through all the stages of gas instruction, fitting and testing, passed into the gas chamber twice, first through tear gas and the 2nd time through ordinary gas. My clothes smell abominably in consequence. Had a walk in the evening prior to visiting my little cafe.

31/7/17

Dull morning. Paraded at 8.30 am with towel and marched with the "operators" to the bath house, which is situated on the bank of the Somme canal near the bridge, close to the station. Afterwards fatigues. Passed close to where the "khaki girls" are billeted, I should think I passed on the road quite three score of girls, I was struck by their obvious youthfulness, the great majority could not have been out of their teens. They do look smart, I must admit and their somewhat short dresses permits a display of a great deal of "leg" as it is called, besides well turned and very pretty ankles. The French especially the women are never tired of looking at and whispering little things about the anglaise. It is rather a shame however that English women have come to this country. Ever since the war commenced the Tommies have never tired of eulogising their countrywomen to their French acquaintances, some of the most far fetched stories ever created have been freely circulated by the Tommies. Many times indeed I have been asked if such and such were true, now, the French are able to learn for themselves the answers, which they sought. Nurses especially have earned such complete notoriety that the Tommies themselves have named them "officers remounts". Perhaps it is hardly fair of me to make such statements, still nevertheless they are unfortunately true. Those only would deny the accuracy who are themselves, or who are not competent to make any statement whatsoever.

1/8/17

Rained hard all night and all morning. I feel very lazy and am quite unable to fix my attention on anything in particular. I have had no patience for sometime either for studying or reading. I don't think that I have had at any time in my life fewer wishes or less hope, my days are spent in what seems to me an endless captivity, I live in a sphere, which is foreign to my nature and my misfortunes would seem to have no end. There was rather good news today from the Flanders front. I hope sincerely that it will prove the preliminary to an end decisive and triumphant for the war worn allies. Rain continued throughout the day, my clothes are all wet and very uncomfortable. This concludes my seventh French diary; I wonder what eighth will have to say. Life is so uncertain and ones experiences so varied nowadays, at all events I hope and trust that long before I reach the last page of my next book, that this awful catastrophe, will have terminated, for the lasting good and blessing of all the world and for all time. May god will that this might be.

Diary Number 8

2/8/17

Rained all night everything and everywhere quite wet through. Rain hardly ceased for a moment all day. After tea went into town to buy several souvenirs, which included a couple of china vases, one for my cousin Isabel, who like myself takes an interest in things china, also procured a couple of small framed pictures, one of the cathedral and the other of the statue in the square. The shop people kindly packed and dispatched by post for me, afterwards returned and visited my usual place of rest until 8 pm when I returned to camp. It was still raining heavily.

3/8/17

Rain poured down all night and continued this morning. It is certainly hard luck on our offensive in Flanders. It would be difficult to imagine more miserable and uninviting type of weather. Nothing of note to record today.

4/8/17

Another rainy night and morning. Today we enter upon the 4th year of war. How different too is the state of weather now to the first few months of war. The 1st anniversary of this gigantic conflict I spent in Egypt, sailing for the Dardanelles a week or so later. The 2nd and 3rd anniversaries spent in France. Three precious years have gone by, years that can never be regained, all that I had before the war I gave freely, that I may be able at sometime to be able to serve my country. Now all is gone. I have lost all that I had, which was good to have, and everything that I loved and cherished are hopelessly gone out of my life. The country that I had learned to love so dearly has betrayed and robbed me, just the same as many others in like circumstances. It is full of dishonest men and women from the government downwards. Vice and corruption are the only Gods worshipped more especially by women. In the whole of Gods earth, there has never been a land so fair, and so beautiful, so outrageously despoiled, so teeming with vice, so sick of soul and unchaste. My poor country you have yet to suffer untold agonies and miseries. It is merciful that you are ignorant of you fate. Went for a short walk in the evening and afterwards visited the usual cafe. The people at which are dispatching by the French civil post to my aunt Ada, a pack of German playing cards and a large French picture, which I brought from Peronne.

5/8/17

Wet weather continues, during the morning the clouds gradually broke and the sun graciously presented itself for the first time during the whole week. Today being Sunday, we are allowed out of camp after dinner. I went for a walk along the left bank of the Somme. It was a most delightful walk and I enjoyed the fresh pure air immensely, there were a goodly sprinkling of fishermen lining both banks of this dreamy peaceful river, including a large number of Tommies. Boats full of happy occupants were out rowing, and in the air, which was very calm and still the musical notes of children's voices resounded from out of the tall grasses and among the proud and stately trees, which guard and protect the solemn waters.

Meeting two Mademoiselles I spent the remainder of the afternoon and evening with them. Having a French supper at 6 pm at a cafe in the village close by. I was rather amused at a little piece of rivalry, which ensued when a khaki girl with a soldier friend entered, my French acquaintances seemed quite eager to retain all my attention upon themselves. They kept up such a vigorous conversation at high velocity speed and in a low tone that I was truly hard put to, to keep pace with them.

6/8/17

Nice morning and the air pleasant and bracing, there is however an autumn mist hanging over the fields. This afternoon the garrison sports are to be held in an open space, which is surrounded by trees, and is situated in the centre of the town. The whole arena is bedecked with flags and everything neatly prepared. Two o'clock parade has been suspended for today to enable the troops in our depot to attend. I left camp at about 1.30 pm, but at 2 pm an extremely heavy thunder storm broke out quite suddenly, which lasted until 4 pm, I managed to get wet through to the skin before I could gain cover. When the storm had subsided I met one of my friends of yesterday and together we walked into the country. Had tea in a cafe and returned along the Somme. Left my friend at 8 pm and returned to camp, she is a bright sort of girl and an intelligent conversationalist. During my walk my clothes had dried, but to make matters worse, upon entering my tent I discovered that the rain had simply poured through and that water lay in pools upon my bed, still there is ever but one thing to do, which is to make the best of it.

7/8/17

Dull morning. Went with operators to the bathhouse. As the only towel I posses was quite drenched I had perforce to dry myself with my pants. The sports which were booked for yesterday have been cancelled until next Sunday in consequence of yesterday's storms. After tea I went for a short walk and then to my customary rendezvous, where I spent the evening.

8/8/17

Pleasant sunny morning, rather a favourable opportunity I should imagine for gathering in the harvest, a considerable amount of which lies flattened on the ground by the torrential rains, and may quickly become rotten in the husks. Well my "petit cahier gris", it is some considerable time since you and I indulged in a heart to heart talk. I have told you at different times many things concerning myself, of others and of this "tres drole" world of ours in which both you and I have been placed for some particular purpose, which, for my part however I should find extremely difficult to determine, as to what particular sphere, what course and the especial duties, which have ever been consigned to me to pursue and to carry out. On the other hand even you my little friend know and understand clearly your position in life, also your destiny and the functions which you are expected to fulfil during your career, your existence is regular and without misgivings, while mine varies unceasingly. I am subject to many changes, in position, thought and health. At times too am forced to embark upon weary journeyings, along the intricate and uneven paths of life, whereon indeed my steps are dogged by many shadows, my tired feet bruised sorely by the roughly edged stones, and my body buffeted and maltreated by the untamed elements.

Even to you, no, not even to you my faithful little cahier is it possible to divulge one only secret of the multitude, which lie hidden in this world of cruel barbarity. You are as I know as a rule very well informed but there are many things which it is wise to leave unsaid, even between you and I. To look upon our world is fair, and beautiful, inviting and alluring, but in reality not very deep beneath this cloak of peace and love, the world as it is lies hidden in a shroud of gloom, despair and barrenness, devoid of soil or heart it lies not dead, but forever slumbering in its dark depths, awakening at intervals, only to drag down into the strong bosom, the soaring covetousness and the proud designs of men, all that was, is, and is to be, must in due time be brought to nought, for so surely will the hand of destiny pluck all and everything in the end to itself. I must take up you again "mon petite cashier gris" for another little chat. I have just arrived back from an evening with a dozen or more old soldiers. Yes I have had a drink too of course, in fact more than one, a drink to comrades, a drink with soldiers for whom you know I have a very deep respect. One cannot be more happy or enjoy a more glorious time than with soldiers. They are the best company in the world. I love them infinitely more than any woman, even though she may be the prettiest ever born, "c'est vrai" and as you know my petite cahier, I have my very good reasons too. There is no prouder title in all the world than "soldier", who wants to be anything else, but the base selfish dregs of humanity, you and I know full well what else the world contains. Three things you say, oh yes I can guess-easily what they are, soldiers, wine and women, yes indeed my faithful cahier soldiers first always, then wine, and then women who of course rank last in the category of animals, but why mon petite ami do you think that women should take the last place, will you tell me please? Oh indeed, because they are the most dangerous of all animals, either in the air, under the water or upon the earth. Well yes I am disposed to agree with you entirely. Women are the angels of hell and right nobly do they perform their arts of witchcraft and other satanic devices to subdue mankind, and how truly do they bring about his ruin. Can you give me any proof mon cher petite cahier of the genuinely of your opinions. Oh, I see you have learned that married men are returning from leave suffering from all sorts of atrocious diseases contracted from their wives, that former sweethearts are also doling out the same venomous poisons to those who had trusted them that women have come since the war into their own and are revelling in a life of prostitution. Oh my friend what terrible things you say, what awful indictments. Surely there must be some mistake, you really do not believe all this to be true, come tell me honestly. Oh well if you take that line of response, that only the ignorant and foolish would attempt to deny it, then of course I cannot dispute the veracity of your assertions. Mais, n'en parlons plus, and listen, the last plaintive notes of the trumpet is sounding lights out, the day is ended, and in just such manner, must our own poor short lives terminate, when the call is sounded by the fast fleeting breath.

9/8/17

Bright sunny morning but cloudy. Short walk in the evening and then returned to my usual place, where I had some supper consisting of fried tomatoes and chip potatoes. Returned to camp at 9.30 pm.

10/8/17

Morning fine with spells of bright sunshine. Weather still maintains a threatening attitude. Fatigues today included peeling potatoes and onions, scouring dixies etc. Rain managed to keep off fortunately. Spent evening at usual place.

11/8/17

Weather this morning similar to that of yesterday. Fatigues during the day in the sappers cookhouse, and was pleasingly compensated at dinner, with a good supply of well-cooked and tender roast beef. In the evening I went to a cafe, where I met my soldier friends of a few nights ago. We supped together until 8 pm, singing, talking and making merry, the while I had had a little more than enough of our national beverage by the time we were obliged to leave, also a heavy storm broke at this moment and I was compelled to seek shelter in a house for a while. On my way back to camp I called for my washing and stayed chatting for sometime. Owing to the lateness of the hour, when it would have been difficult for me to reach camp without being interviewed by the M.P.'s, I was offered a bed by the old gentleman and his lady. Thus it came to pass that I spent the night in their bedroom, in a nice clean, comfy little bed. I returned to camp next morning (Sunday) between 11 am and noon after having eaten a breakfast which consisted of boiled eggs.

12/8/17

After dinner I went to see the garrison sports. The place was thronging with people. Such an occasion is quite a novelty to our French allies. Everything passed off very well indeed. Our own band (the signal depots) provided a good selection of music from their elevated position in a much beflagged bandstand. Returned to camp at 9 pm.

13/8/17

Sent with the operators to the sports ground of yesterday, where we were employed, in pulling down the bandstand, grand stand and other stands, tents, marquees etc, which occupied the whole morning. In the afternoon went with the above section to the bathhouse and afterwards a long march. Arrived back at camp at about 4.30 pm. Spent evening at my usual retreat.

14/8/17

Nice pleasant morning, the air is perfectly sublime. Day passed as usual. Shortly after 5 pm heavy black clouds gathered overhead and we were very quickly treated to a drenching thunderstorm. Spent the evening at my customary cafe.

15/8/17

Cloudy threatening morning, stormy in the afternoon and evening. Received fifteen francs at pay parade this afternoon. Spent evening in usual manner and place.

16/8/17

Black heavy clouds fill the sky this morning. The month of August is by no means a pleasant one, so far as weather is concerned. The day passed off without rain, but an extremely high wind has maintained until late in the evening. Nothing of especial note occurs in our daily routine in this depot.

17/8/17

Beautiful morning, the clear fresh air is quite charming. Day passed in the same sort of drole way as usual.

18/8/17

Nice morning. Posted a letter to my aunt Ada. I have become quite anxious as have not relieved a single line from my aunt or my cousin, all the time that I have been in this depot, although I have written several letters myself. Some showers during the afternoon. Passed the evening at my usual rendezvous.

19/8/17

Pleasant sunny morning. In the afternoon (being Sunday) I went for a stroll and later went for tea at a restaurant in the town, accompanied by a young girl, to whom I was introduced, at the cafe where I usually frequent in the evenings. I met her there on the first day of my arrival in the depot. A dozen or more khaki girls with their soldier friends were also partaking of tea at the same place, and there were too a few officers (British). My friend proved a gay little talker and she seemed to be the centre of attention for all eyes. Returned to camp shortly after 8 pm. passing the "P.O.W" prisoner of war camp, I stayed for a while to listen to a large body of Germans singing, it is a usual Sunday evening practice with them and to give them credit they do sing most beautifully.

20/8/17

Glorious morning. Received a letter from Monsieur Hunel of Querrieu, with whom I formally rented a bedroom. It contained many expressions of goodwill and friendship, which to me is very gratifying as of course I am both a stranger and a foreigner to him and his wife. Spent a pleasant evening at my usual place of retreat.

21/8/17

Weather still continues beautifully clear and fresh, during the day the heat became extremely intense. Was happy to see the good news, which is reported in the papers of today's date, from the Verdun and Italian fronts. How I do trust and hope that these successive and successful blows at the enemy will eventually culminate in a decisive and overwhelming victory for the gallant allies. Day terminated in the same manner as customary.

22/8/17

Night rather chilly but the morning has brought in its train, the glorious sun and freshness of yesterday. Was too late to be paid at pay parade this afternoon, so must wait until next week, which is unfortunate as I am down to my last franc. The heat is quite tropical and in the evening, behind heavy banks of clouds, vivid flashes of lightening struck through the blackness in rapid succession. This storm however was very far away and did not approach in our direction.

23/8/17

Cooler this morning. Went through a test in telegraphy during the morning and passed everything comfortably. Met a man who had gone to Stafford shortly after I had left about 10 years ago. He was familiar with my name and recognised it when it was called out. Rain fell rather heavily at intervals from teatime onwards.

24/8/17

Cold night, morning windy and penetrating, but otherwise fine and sunny. Well " mon petite cahier gris" things are to open up again apparently for you and I. Have been put on draft for tomorrow morning. Mais, mon petit, I am still unwell so that perhaps I may have to go into dock again. I am sorry that this might be my lot once more and I am sure that I have your sympathy too. Under the circumstance however the stoutest heart could not avail, in the meantime we will converse together upon our journeyings and experiences. This afternoon have drawn my kit, had my tunic patched and mended, and boots soled. After tea went to the military post-office in Abbeville to change into French money a couple of one pound postal orders which most fortunately had arrived at midday today from my good, kind and most reliable Aunt Ada. I met with a good deal of opposition to payment on account of the fact that I had not got my pay book with me, same being in the orderly room. In the end I managed to persuade the clerk of red tape, that I really was the person I pretended to be, which was proved by exhibiting my disc. Going straight back I spent the evening at my good friends cafe, where I indulged in a good meal of eggs and bread and butter.

25/8/17

Rose at 6 am. Breakfast at 6.30 am. Finished my preparation for departure to the 38 the division and paraded at 7.30 am with the draft. Marched to the station at 8 am. Entrained shortly before 10 am and soon afterwards started upon our way. Arrived at Etaples at midday, but could not get no further this day, and in consequence am now housed in the "FBD" near to the station. There are only two of us going to the aforesaid division and we have received instructions from the RTO to parade at the station at 8.30 am tomorrow morning. These journeys are indeed trying, while they last, bully-beef and biscuits are our staple nourishment, after a rest had a walk round the camp and as far as a certain open place, which goes by the high title of "market". It is composed of lines of small stalls, covered with fruit and sweets, or perhaps embroidered postcards and souvenir rings. There are chip cabins, which do a roaring trade, charging half a franc per packet. I bought some to help me keep going and at another stall I purchased a packet of picture postcards and dispatched by the French civil post to my Aunt Ada. Well my little friend my journey hear closes.

I am fairly broken up again and judged it best to see the M.O and I am being sent into hospital here, I shall perhaps have several chats with you upon occasions during my term in hospital, for the moment I must say au revoir and good luck for the future, whatever that may be.

21/9/17

I am opening your pages once more "mon petit cahier gris". I am now at another address, where I arrived yesterday about teatime. It was a long journey but on the whole it was made somewhat comfortable on account of the fact, that I did the journey in a hospital train. My address is for the present no 18 casualty clearing station, which is situated at a little village called La Pugnoy. It is an awfully nice hospital, not very large, and well laid out. The most important feature however is the "grubbing", which is both abundant and good. There is a hill behind and above the village upon which, stands a large crucifix, which is plainly distinguishable for some distance. The sky is continually filled with aircraft and the throbbing of the engines goes on unceasingly. I shall have to do light jobs during the short time that I am here. Have written and dispatched 4 letters today 3 in French and one to my Aunt Ada. I am really feeling much more like myself at the present time than I have been for many a long day. I am trusting with all my heart that I shall never again decline from the standard I have now reached. In the evening I attended a concert in the hospital, which was given by the anti-air gunners. The sisters were also present. Another big push appears to be on the move, but official news is extremely scanty here. I really do not know what is expected, but personally I expect very little indeed, with the present army chiefs. Still it is rumoured that we shall have peace by Xmas perhaps.

22/9/17

Sunny brisk morning. Day passed rather quietly. Just carrying on doing light work and carrying a few stretcher cases from the reception room to their respective ward. This latter employment is not however included in the category of light jobs, not indeed by any means. Wrote a letter to my brother Harry, also wrote a letter in French for a comrade.

23/9/17

Cold night. Artillery firing extremely violent during the early hours of the morning. An enemy aeroplane also flew at a great height over our locality at 6 am just as we were washing. Light fatigues during the morning and washed out a shirt, pair of socks and a couple of handkerchiefs. Weather continues "bon".

24/9/17

Brisk and sharp in the early morning. I have been tent staining all through the day. Am feeling very fit again thank heavens. Received three letters at dinner time one from my friend Miss Dorothy Roberts of Southport, one from Monsieur Hunel of Querrie, with my letter to him enclosed, which had been corrected by his daughter Marie, there were very few mistakes. I was also very happy to receive a letter and a beautifully nice post card from my recently acquired little friend Mademoiselle Danielle Hangard of Rouen. I have replied to the latter this evening.

Guns are still somewhat active, but there appears to be little of note, doing upon this particular front. Drafted a letter for a friend of mine, a Corporal in the A.S.C.

25/9/17

Glorious weather still prevails. Helped to load up a train with wounded and sick Tommies immediately after breakfast. Daubing tents rest of morning. Spent afternoon writing and studying. Wrote a letter to Monsieur Hunel, afterwards watched the sports, which were being held in the field adjoining the hospital. Watched one of our balloons come down in a ball of flame and column of smoke in the evening.

26/9/17

Weather still "beau". Received a letter from Aunt Ada and a written a long epistle to her. Have remitted 7 pounds (army credit) to my aunt. I was quite surprised to learn that I had so much to my favour, I do not believe however in allowing any money of mine to remain in the good care of the army pay corps. I've had some. In between times I do a little studying, but get very little leisure indeed for that purpose. Wrote to my friend Miss Dorothy Roberts.

27/9/17

Drizzle and dull during the early part of the morning. Stretcher cases were coming in rather frequently during the night. Many cases of gassing are being brought down. Their eyes are bandaged up and their faces are very flushed. Daubing tents during the morning and afternoon.

28/9/17

Rose very early this morning, was carrying stretcher cases to the train shortly after daybreak. Rather a cold and dull morning but I think it will soon give place to brighter weather. Daubing tents all day. Received a letter enclosed in a parcel from my cousin Ethel, which contained a lovely cake, French and English pocket dictionary's, a box of gold flake cigarettes and a pair of braces, also received a letter from my friend at Abbeville, Mademoiselle Germaine Cherel. Have written a letter to each in reply. I have got a very bad headache tonight, I have never been subject of this sort before.

29/9/17

Dull morning. Daubing tents again today. Day passed as usual. Studied French a little, had a game of football in the evening, and a game of cards before getting into my blankets.

30/9/17

Foggy cold morning, but later sunny and warm. Very heavy drum fire bombardments during the night and early morning. Fritz has made repeated excursions over these parts lately, particularly today and our anti-aircraft batteries have been kept very busy. Received a nice letter from my friend Mademoiselle Danielle Hangard of Rouen. Wrote a letter to my sister Doris.

Being Sunday I had a nap on the grass in the afternoon. Just after lights out (9 pm) Fritz came flying round again and dropped several bombs not very far away. I was glad to hear that my good friends at Rouen, were sending to my Father, views of the interior of the cathedral there, in accordance with my request.

1/10/17

Very nippy misty morning. Daubed tents in the morning. Sun came out blazing and hot shortly after 9 am. No mail arrived for me today. Have written a long letter to Mademoiselle Danielle and one to my friend Miss Weeds. Artillery activity still continues and during last night was excessively severe. A letter did arrive for me in the evening from my dear Aunt Ada, to whom I have sent another long letter and a post card to my sister Doris.

2/10/17

Cold in the early morning but very warm later on. Tent daubing in the morning and have finished off the job. Rest of day putting straight different parts of the camp. Received a letter from Mrs. Wright of Sally-Park, Birmingham to say that she would continue to look after my things, which I have left with her care, until after the war. This is a good piece of news as they are all I had left from the wreckage of my home, and it is encouraging to know that they are in the care and safe keeping of someone. No great artillery activity, characterised either yesterday or today. Have written a letter to Mrs. Wright of Sally-Park and also one to my friend Miss Weeds. Am on stretcher bearing all night tonight. Am feeling very tired too, so don't know how I am going to get through it.

3/10/17

Rather a heavy nights work, most of the casualties, which came in during the night, were stretcher cases, an entire platoon had been made casualties by shell fire (shrapnel) and some of the cases were in a very pitiable plight indeed. I must say however that they received excellent treatment from the medical officers as soon as they arrive. Slight rain fell during the night. Rather damp cold morning. With another "temporary base" fellow cleaned out the "reception tents" and then knocked off for the day. A privilege accorded to those who have been on night duty. Received a nice letter from my friend Mlle Danielle Hangard, also one from Miss Winnie Hedge. To both of whom I have replied this evening.

4/10/17

Very cold windy morning. Am on a tarring job now, as anybody can easily see at a glance. Received a nice letter from my cousin Isabel and two arrived from my brother Harry. Have sent a long letter to my bro and have answered my cousin's. Rather a good deal of rain fell during the day and it was boisterously windy too. Two thousand prisoners are reported to have been captured today as well as 5 villages round about Ypres.

5/10/17

Cold night and brisk. A large number of casualties came in during the night. Tarring all day long. No mail arrived for me today.

6/10/17

Night cold again. Raining nearly all morning and afternoon. Tarring all morning, have got a "jocks" cap to wear while I am working to save my own and I find it excellent protection against the tar sprinkling over my face and hair. Have obtained also a thick pair of leather driving gloves, and with my overalls and khaki-drill jacket I make quite a workmanlike appearance. Had bath and clean change of linen in the evening. It was a very cold business bathing in our small ever-wet bathhouse. Loaded a train first thing this morning with sick and wounded cases.

7/10/17

Heavy frost during the night. Time was put back an hour last night so had an hour extra in bed. Did all my washing in the morning. It has rained practically all day. Posted a couple of pretty picture postcards to my friend Mlle Danielle Hangard ant her young sister Giselle. Had a short nap before tea. In the morning I attended divine service in the chapel. One of the sisters who was present helped us along with the singing.

8/10/17

Raw morning. Am back again on my old job of staining the new tents, which are being put up throughout the hospital camp. Rain again fell very heavily during the evening. Loading up a hospital train first thing after breakfast.

9/10/17

Cold raw morning. Staining during the morning. A lot of rather bad cases were brought in during the night. One poor gallant fellow passed away this morning, the first casualty to die since I came to this hospital. Football match on in the afternoon so we are all excused work. Have received a letter today from my friend Mlle Danielle Hangard.

10/10/17

Raining hard all the morning. Wrote a long letter to Mlle Danielle Hangard at Rouen. Stained tents during the afternoon, which turned out quite sunny and warm. Put a stove in our tent, but it is rather too small for the marquee, Cavalry have been on the move through the village (La Pugnoy) today. We heard last night that the 1st and 5th British armies and the 1st French army had attacked and taken successfully all their objectives, including more than 4,000 prisoners. I do hope that things are going well for the allies. I long for peace and I think everybody else wishes the same as I do myself.

11/10/17

Sharp brisk morning, and later sunny and exceedingly pleasant. Received a letter from one of my French friends in Abbeville. Played in a football match after tea, we lost however by 2 goals to 0.

12/10/17

Day passed as usual.

13/10/17

Wet morning. Stained tents in the morning. Very wet in the afternoon. Received a nice welcome letter from my friend Mlle Danielle Hangard of Rouen, to which I have replied with a long epistle in French.

14/10/17

Brisk sharp morning. Attended divine service in the morning. Received a letter from Mlle Hunel. Have written one to Miss Dorothy Roberts. Very little to talk about now a days.

15/10/17

Rather nice day. Was on stretcher bearing all last night. Did a little tent staining in the morning until 11 am. Rest of the day had to myself. Despatched a letter to my friend Miss Dorothy Roberts and a sketch, which had been done of me in profile, by a soldier, I sent to my sister Doris. I do not think it was a very good resemblance however.

16/10/17

Not quite so cold this morning. Tent staining all day. Received two nice cards from Mlle Danielle Hagard and one from her little sister Giselle. A nice letter also came from my dear aunt Ada. Did a little studying and writing.

17/10/17

Very nice day, but windy. Staining marquee's in the morning. Football match in the afternoon, so did no work. A little study and a game of cards and a letter in French to my institutrice Mlle Marie Hunel completed my days toil.

18/10/17

Weather nice. Staining marquee's during the day. No mail arrived for me today. A number of bad cases of gassings come in today, three of whom died. A very good and successful was held in the hospital in the evening, which commenced at 8 pm.

19/10/17

Cold night and morning. Staining marquees during "la journee". The heroes who died here yesterday, were buried today. They were taken away to the military cemetery under the undying colours of old Britain. Received a registered packet from Melle Danielle Hangard, which included my wristwatch, which unfortunately she had been unable to get mended for me, without forwarding to Paris for the necessary repairs. The glass is broken and also the metal circle around the face, I shall have to perforce to send it to Blighty. There were also a few sweets enclosed. Short sharp shower in the afternoon, which entirely spoiled a football match, which was on between Rame staff and ourselves, who are all temporary basemen. Wrote a letter to Melle Danielle Hangard.

20/10/17

Nice bright day. Had a warm shower bath in the morning. A good deal of straffing was going on all night, when according to some casualties, the Germans came over the top. Received a nice letter from my friend Melle Danielle Hangard, to which I replied in the evening.

21/10/17

Nice day but rather cold first thing. Attended divine service in the morning. No mail for me today. Watched a football match in the afternoon.

22/10/17

Cold damp morning. Loaded up a hospital train first thing after breakfast more marquee staining. Helped to carry another batch of poor Tommies badly gassed, who arrived about 11 am. Received a nice letter from my aunt Ada enclosing 2 pounds, which represented my credit in the army up to the present. Bought a box of dainty handkerchiefs and despatched per the French civil post to my friend Melle Danielle Hangard, also bought some pictorial postcards. Wrote a letter to aunt Ada.

23/10/17

Cold rainy morning. Loaded up another hospital train after breakfast this morning. Received a nice letter from Melle Danielle Hangard enclosing a few picture postcards of Rouen and its environs. I have written back to her this afternoon, a packet reached me also from my dear little sister Doris, enclosing a French grammar book.

24/10/17

Cold again this morning. Assisted in dismantling a marquee in the morning and stretcher carrying. Very heavy bombardment commenced early this morning somewhere upon our front and has continued extremely violently throughout the day. Evening miserably wet and cold. Wrote a long letter to my dear little sister Doris.

25/10/17

Windy cold morning, but sunny. Constructing marquees during the day. Received a nice card from Melle Danielle Hangard, also I sent one to her and several, which I had received from her I forwarded to my little sister Doris for safety. Did a little studying.

26/10/17

Wet morning. Loaded up a hospital train. Note much work to do today. A little studying.

27/10/17

Cold stingy morning. Had a warm shower bath and did a little washing. At 1 pm got my marching orders for another CCC (no 6). Paraded at 2 pm and was taken with a few more to our destination in a lorry, a distance of about 7 or 8 kilos I should think, a place a short distance out of a little mining village called Ruits. A new hospital is being erected here in the middle of a sugar beet field and we are deep in mud and water everywhere. We are much nearer to the line too and have a good view of Fritz's gasbags as well as our own. Where we have to sleep is more like a death trap.

28/9/17

Cold night, very difficult to keep ones self warm. After breakfast did a little word. Dinner early and afterwards went in a lorry with a working party to the railway sidings at Barlin to unload a number of trucks filled with hut parts of iron and timber for the hospital, which we transferred into lorries, it was a good afternoon's hard work. After tea went down to the village of Ruitz and spent evening in different cafes. Sent a postcard to my friend Melle Danielle Hangard.

29/10/17

Another very cold frosty night. Marched to Barlin railway sidings after breakfast. Where we repeated our job of yesterday afternoon. Our party was allowed to have the afternoon off, as we were kept employed all day yesterday (Sunday). Wrote a long letter to Melle Danielle also one to my aunt Ada. It is beastly cold and I am perished to the bones. Spent evening walking to different villages and dropping in to have a drink at cafes by the way. Received 10 francs payment in the afternoon. The continual variation in the lights, which are to be seen nightly upon this front, are very interesting and fascinating. I get very little spare time for studying, and certainly convenience whatsoever. I will be standing up against a railway wagon, or walking up and down with my French notes in my hand, for few minutes at a time. This in fact is the sort of method I have employed a great deal, so as to guard the benefits of passing moments in my desire to make at least some little progress with my pet study, needless to say I fall considerably short of all that I would be glad to accomplish, still nevertheless, I do my best to regain the time, which I must perforce lose, while I have not the privilege of calling any time my own.

30/10/17

Extremely cold bitter wind. I miss sorely the glad flicker of the welcoming flashes of a British fireplace, with its comfortable and inviting homely hearth. Working on different jobs during the morning. Raining and blowing furiously, practically throughout the day, am afraid that the cold has got a hold on me as I feel decidedly below the mark. As soon as possible after tea (a slice of bread and butter) and by the way no dinner to speak of, I went to a cafe in the village, where I spent the evening, had a good meal of eggs and fried chip potatoes.

31/10/17

Weather considerably improved. Have got a bon job as tent orderly. So that if I keep it, I shall always be in the dry. Have received no mail for the last few days, which is exceedingly disappointing. Did a little studying. Saw one of our captive balloons come down in flames just before tea. Spent evening at a little cafe. Am feeling slightly better today. I believe however that I am suffering not a little from the effects of this long unnatural life, and I am decidedly war-warn.

1/11/17

Rather cold and damp today. Again no mail arrived for me. Spent evening in usual manner. A few shells were popped over at intervals by our friend Fritz in our vicinity.

2/11/17

Dull day. Day divided between work, study and a little pleasure. No letters again today.

3/11/17

Dull miserable sort of day. Am doing post orderly duty as well as tent orderly. Today I had the great delight to receive five letters, three from Mlle Hangard and one from her mother, while the fifth came from my little sister Doris, enclosing some snaps of herself and of the pater. I was really most happy to get them. Have written a long letter to Mlle Danielle Hangard.

4/11/17

Very cold dull day. Wrote a letter to Madame Hangard, a card to her daughter and a letter to my sister Doris, also received another nice letter from Mlle Danielle and one from Miss Hedge. Had a good meal of eggs and fried chips in the village of Ruitz in the evening. Very severe bombardment commenced on our front at about 8.30 pm which lasted for about an hour.

5/11/17

A distinct improvement in the weather today. Received a letter from my brother Harry, wrote one to Mlle Danielle. Day passed in usual manner.

6/11/17

Weather still dull and rather cold. Received a letter from Mlle Danielle. I also got a letter from my old friend at Querrieu, Somme and another from their daughter enclosing one of mine, which she had corrected grammatically for me. Have sent off a box of 12 packets of gold flake to Monsieur Hunel of Querrieu, as per his request, for the benefit of his soldier son, who is ill in hospital. They are only poorly well off and it is a pleasure to me to be able to do some little kindness on their behalf in recognition of their untiring care of myself, whilst I was with them as their lodger. On guard at 6 pm. My turn being from 12 midnight to 2 am.

7/11/17

Fine moonlight night. Very dreary cold and wet during the day. Spent most of my two hours on guard learning French in the sentry box by the aid of a lamp, which I took from a lorry, which was standing in the road. Received a nice letter from my sister Gladys, wrote a letter to Monsieur Hunel of Querrieu, my brother Harry and a card to Mlle Danielle. Spent evening in the usual cafe where I visit in the evenings. The Germans continue to shell Barlin, which is over in the hill from here, and today there were 9 casualties. One shell fell on a house there.

8/11/17

Cold night and dull during the day. It is awfully slippery everywhere. I am coated all over, with mud. Wrote letters to my sister Gladys and brother Harry. Spent day in the usual manner, with the same program of work, study, writing and an evening in a cafe.

9/11/17

Fine in the early part of the morning, but rained later. Wrote a letter to my father and sent off cards to Mlle Danielle and her little sister Giselle.

10/11/17

Terrible wet day, and mud, bags of it, nothing else but mud everywhere. Wrote a letter to my dear aunt Ada.

11/11/17

Still wet. Firing of heavy pieces still goes on at intervals throughout the night and day. Went to Barlin in the morning for a bath and clean change of linen, at the divisional baths, also got a new pair of khaki trousers and a new pair of boots. I had become quite black for want of a bath and it was quite a treat to have a good wash down, after so much work in the everlasting mud and dirt. No mail arrived for me, which was rather disappointing as I had quite expected to receive at least one from my friend Mlle Danielle Hangard.

12/11/17

Frosty in the early morning but gloriously bright and sunny during the day. The guns are rolling somewhere upon the front "sans cesse". I notice that long columns of lorries conveying troops are wending their way in an apparent opposite direction to the gun firing, which has been of a savage nature all day, at some point far away on our left. Barlin has been under the fire of a German long-range gun all day and I heard this evening that several school children had been gassed. No mail again today. Wrote a letter to my aunt Ada, Mrs Smith of Sally-Park, Birmingham and a card to Mlle Danielle and Mlle Berthe Caille of Abbeville. Spent evening in usual way.

13/11/17

Guns still pouring out their venoms. Fine day but dull. A number of men were arrested last evening, attempting to "flog" military articles, such as new boots and blankets to the French civil population in the villages round about here. Received a nice letter from Mlle Danielle but it was too of a somewhat disconcerting nature. Letters also arrived form Miss Weeds and one from my dear little sister Doris, enclosing a very pretty photograph of herself. The roar of artillery continued incessantly throughout the day. Wrote letters to Mlle Danielle and one to Miss Weeds.

14/11/17

Dry but dull weather is the order of today. By the way I was delighted and proud to see my old regiment the Warwickshire Yeomanry mentioned in yesterday's dispatches, in connection with a brilliant mounted charge, which they had executed against the Turks and Austrians in Palestine. It is something at least to have belonged to such a gallant regiment and to have endured with such an excellent type of soldiers, the hardships of soldiering. Received a very pretty card from Mlle Danielle and a short letter, which latter was rather disconcerting, owing I believe to an unfortunate misunderstanding in one of my letters. Received 10 francs payment in the evening.

15/11/17

Nice pleasant day. Received a very nice letter from my little friend Danielle, to which I have replied with a long one, also was glad to receive a nice long letter from my dear aunt Ada, to whom I have also sent a long letter of 12 pages in return. The bombardment of which I spoke about the other day has recommenced with violence today. I hear that 8 spies; 5 men and 3 women have been apprehended in Barlin. It seems that quite a large number of these people exist behind the line.

16/11/17

Dull but not too cold. Heavy artillery firing still in progress. It appears by this mornings paper, that all this heavy firing is the outcome of a fierce attempt on the part of the enemy to break through our line on the high ground north of Paschendale.

Received a very nice letter from my dear little sister Doris. Wrote card to Mlle Danielle and her little sister Giselle. We have now a recreation marquee and I spent the evening playing chess and had the luck to win all games.

17/11/17

Nice sunny day. No mail arrived for me today. Wrote a long letter to Mlle Danielle and another to my dear sister Doris.

18/11/17

Once more very dull. Received 2 nice cards from Mlle Danielle and her little sister Giselle. Have also sent one of to my very dear friend Mlle Danielle. Spend my time each day just as usual. It is an extremely quiet and sad sort of existence. What a blessing indeed will it be for all the world, when this folly finally comes to an end. Went down to my cafe, where I usually resort in the evenings. I had not been there for several successive nights and they thought that I had gone away in consequence. There is very little French spoken about these parts, it is all pat, fearful head aching sort of stuff.

19/11/17

Weather still dull. Shells still continue to whistle overhead as they pass over on their way to the railway near Barlin. We learned today from a notice that a number of letters were accidentally destroyed by fire on Sunday morning. This is really a great misfortune to myself as I had written a long letter to my friend Mlle Danielle on the Saturday evening, in which I had said several things, which I was anxious she should know. Spent evening in a cafe at Houchin, a small mining village a couple of kilometres or so from here. Received a letter from my aunt Ada enclosing a Bradbury for 1 pound and also a French book (Hugos) from my dear sister Doris. Wrote a letter to my dear aunt Ada.

20/11/17

Dull day. Enemy continues to bombard Barlin, with his long-range pieces Heavy gunfire, again distinctly audible in the direction of Paschendale. Received a lovely letter from my friend Danielle, to which I have replied with a long missive, also received one from my friends at Querrieu, Somme, stating that they had safely got the box of cigarettes, which I had sent to them. It was too a letter full of praise, and they were very glad to hear that I had had the good fortune to meet a nice girl for whom I had a deep affection. Had some fried eggs at Houchin in the evening and a couple of drinks. The old lady told me a tale of how she had heard two German spies were apprehended. The story goes that a Canadian noticing foot steps next to a hay rick, made some investigations and unearthed a couple of the enemy. The supposition is that they were dropped by an aeroplane with a valise for the purpose of sleeping in the hayrick and which contained too the uniform of a British officer.

21/11/17

Very wet night and dull and cold during the day. Dispatched a postcard to my little friend Danielle. Had some fried eggs for supper and a couple of games of chess afterwards, both of which I lost. News comes through that we have made a successful advance over on the new Somme front, I trust that it is true in every respect, especially as regards the number of prisoners which it is said have been captured.

22/11/17

Still dull and miserable weather. Wrote a long letter to my dear friend Mlle Danielle and one to my dear aunt Ada. Spent day in usual way. Played chess in the evening and lost three games.

23/11/17

Much brighter today. Received a nice box of biscuits from my aunt Ada and also a letter which has greatly upset me. Have written a long one in reply. By todays paper I learn that our recent victory on the Hinderberg line, was carried out according to my recommendations, which are embodied in the plan which I drew up last winter and forwarded to the Earl of Shrewsbury and Talbot begging his Lordship to use his power and influence in having it carried out for the sake of our country. The plan in question I have still in my diary of that time. I suppose as usual according to the depraved usage of English justice, that all the credit will go to those who do not merit it. Have written to the Earl of Shrewsbury asking for the return of my letter and the photograph which accompanied it. Have also written a long letter to my aunt Ada, as she declines to oblige me in a most important respect. Spent evening at a cafe in Haillicourt, where I bought also a quantity of illustrated postcards.

24/11/17

Have written to my Father and have expressed my indignation at the wilful disregard of my share in the recent successful military operations. The press too wants throttling as it has no moral or legal right to print half that it does. The attack too is spoken of as a product of a mastermind, but that is not so, it was simply a common sense plan which needs a master hand to carry it through and to develop it. A little item, which I am afraid we do not posses on our side. To me, the whole thing is a terrible tragedy and makes the cares and fortunes of my country hang heavily upon me. It is extremely boisterous and cold weather today. Received letters from Abbeville, Mrs Write of Sally-Park, Birmingham, and a packet containing a book and a couple of letters from my friend Miss Weeds, have written letters to Miss Weeds and Dorothy Roberts. On guard from 8 pm until 10 pm. Am suffering again with my stomach, I do not like the presence of these particular pains, I feel sick and run down.

25/11/17

Fearful boisterous night and very cold. I can't keep myself warm at all. Eggs for breakfast this morning, but I have very little appetite indeed.

With regard to the war, it looks very much indeed as though they are making a complete mess of things, it was not so that I intended the plan to be developed, and of course should the enemy posses a competent general he will know at once the counter-stroke, which none of or generals would know in the least how to cope with. No mail arrived for me today. Spent evening in a cafe at Ruitz. It is St Catherines day today which as everyone knows is a day, which is kept up in France in honour to the Jeunes filles.

26/11/17

Bitterly cold day, am absolutely perishing through. Received letters from Mlle Danielle and her mother, also one from Mlle Marie Raoul, with one of mine to her father corrected. Have written in reply to Mlle Danielle. Spent evening as usual.

27/11/17

Rained heavily all night and has continued all day. It is really most atrocious weather. Received a nice card from my pretty friend Danielle also sent one to her together with a letter to her mother. Bought a couple of nice Xmas cards in the evening. Very heavy bombardments still in progress. I suppose they are still trying to do their best and making a terrible hash of things. Thousands of lives are daily being wasted, simply because we have not a single general in the field. Have drawn up another plan, which would be as successful as the first should have been. The plan in question has for its object a number of important factors, which would bring about the immediate and direct result as follows. A victory of incalculable moral worth both at home (especially) and abroad. Sir Douglas Haig's and the French font would be relieved of any anxiety as to the disposal of any spare enemy troops from the Russian front. Baghdad would be freed from menace and Palestine liberated. I might also add that I believe, if this plan were properly conducted, it would be carried out and prove an accomplished fact, within 24 hours, without taking a single man from the western front.

28/11/17

Much milder today. Wrote cards to my dear Danielle and one to her little sister Giselle, also one to Germaine Sherel t Abbeville. Nothing worth noting today.

29/11/17

Windy but sunny day. Sent a long letter to my lovely little friend at Rouen.

30/11/17

Nice day. Still no mail arrived for me. It seems quite evident from the newspaper reports that our offensive before Cambrai has come to a permanent standstill. It is a very sad thing, and I cannot half but full profoundly disgusted with those who were responsible for the carrying out of the plan. It is good strategy wilfully reduced to suicidal tactics. I knew perfectly well what would be the ultimate result of that particular advance, for the simple reason that we have no general, who possesses in the remotest degree, the simple elementary rules of war.

We have in fact lost a great and splendid army, through no other reason than that there has been no one to lead them poor soldiers. I love them all, every one of them. Poor England you have been sold by your politicians and the military cast which now dominates your life and fortunes, is perhaps the most useless the world has ever seen.

1/12/17

Very cold day. Have received a most beautiful letter from my dear little friend Danielle, to which I have replied.   .

2/12/17

Extremely cold weather. No mail for me today. Don't understand it at all. Am quite perished to the bones, it is a great shame that we are not provided with some sort of means, by which it would be possible to warm ourselves, all that we are allowed to have is a small oil lamp in a stove in the evenings. Sent a nice card to my dear friend Danielle. Spent day and evening in the usual way.

3/12/17

Still very cold and frosty. The ground is hard and the piercing wind simply goes through one. Received a couple of nice letters from my dear friend at Rouen, and have replied with a long one, also sent a short note to my aunt Ada.

4/12/17

Still frosty, but the wind has dropped somewhat. No mail again today. Can't think what has happened to everybody as no replies come to my letters. Wrote another letter to my sister Doris and sent cards to my dearest of all girls Mlle Danielle and one also to her younger sister Giselle.

5/12/17

Bitterly cold, had to break the ice for a wash in the morning. No mail again today for me. By todays paper it would seem that the Germans are walking into the plan, which was laid for them. My idea was to force the enemy to fight on a battlefield selected by ourselves, or retreat. He has apparently chosen the first named course and I trust that that he will be thoroughly beaten. The enemy still persists to shell in the direction of Barlin, his shells go whistling overhead at frequent intervals. There were again yesterday a number of victims including women and children, no soldiers have been injured so far as I have heard. Spent evening in the usual manner. Sent off a postcard to my loving little Danielle.

6/12/17

Still freezing hard, although the wind has dropped, so that the intense cold is naturally more easily born. Very heavy bombardment during the night. Received two nice postcards from my little Danielle and I have also sent one to her.

7/12/17

Thaw has set in during the night and in consequence the ground has become rather soft again. Received letters from Miss Winnie Hedge and Mlle Germaine Sherel of Abbeville. Have replied today to the former.

8/12/17

Rained heavily for a time during the night. I see from the paper that we have carried out what is called a successful retreat on the Hinbenburg line. Poor England I am so sorry for you. If only you had one soldier, that world would be yours. I had the good fortune and happiness to receive a long nice letter from my dear good friend aunt Ada this afternoon, to which I have replied with a long one, which took me about 3 hours to write, also had another nice one from my dear sweet Danielle. On guard at night.

9/12/17

Rained heavily all night. Received a beautiful letter from my darling Danielle and one also from her mother. Sent off letters to my little Danielle and one to my aunt Ada, enclosing the two from Danielle and her mother, which had translated in to English. Enemy still continues to send over a number of shells daily at targets round about Barlin.

10/12/17

Wet and dull. A lot of work to do today. Cannot do all I wish with regard to studying and writing for want of sufficient time. Wrote a letter to Madame Hangard and a card to my dear little Danielle. Also sent off a card to Mlle Germaine Sherel at Abbeville.

11/12/17

Hard frost during the night. Bitterly cold day. Fierce bombardments started late last evening and continued for a long while. Oh what joy today for I have received this evening a beautiful photograph from my darling little Danielle, strange to say I received at the same time a dozen of me from my dear aunt Ada, which had been taken from an original. Wrote two letters to my sweet Danielle, enclosing in the letter two photos, one for her and the other for her mother.

12/12/17

Still very cold but dry. Received a letter from Miss Dorothy Roberts, also I was greatly delighted to receive the handsome gold wristwatch, which I had ordered through my aunt Ada in London. Have sent it on to my dearest of all friends Danielle, to whom I trust it will reach quite safely and without injury. Sent a portrait of myself to Monsieur et Madame Hunel at Querrieu, Somme, also one to my dear little sister Doris, also wrote to my aunt Ada.

13/12/17

Dull damp morning. Fierce artillery engagements continue mostly at nights. The enemy also dropped many bombs in our neighbourhood during the night, I hear that a number of civilians have been killed in consequence of these operations. Wrote to my dear aunt Ada and sent a card to my precious little Danielle at Rouen.

14/12/17

Dull and wet today. I see by today's paper that a strict enquiry into the Cambrai affair is demanded. I hope sincerely that it will come off for my countries sake. There is unquestionably a good deal of rottenness and underhandedness, which requires to be uprooted and buried in a dung heap, its proper receptacle. Sent off a card to my dear Danielle.

15/12/17

Cold and frosty today. Received a very pretty card from my dearest of all friends Danielle, to whom I have sent one in return. Am feeling slightly worse in myself today. Have also dispatched a letter to my dear aunt Ada. More bombs dropped this evening from hostile aeroplanes in our vicinity.

16/12/17

Cold frosty day. Am put again on work outside, the result of petty spite on the part of a low bred A.S.C m t Corporal. Am not well at all however, the cold is attacking my stomach and chest badly and I am throwing up a good deal of frothy phlegm. Enemy still bombarding Barlin and vicinity rather severely. In an "Estaminet" at this place ten persons were killed today I hear. Am feeling ill this evening and have been vomiting.

17/12/17

Very bad weather, snowing and blowing. Had to report sick as have a high temperature. Am now in the bell tent with another sick patient. We have nice comfortable beds and a stove. No mail for me today. The guns are incessantly active.

18/12/17

Very bad night, could get very little rest, was like a furnace "et a" refrigerator combined. Temperature still high. Received a nice letter from my dear sister Gladys and another from my brother Harry. Severe bombardments are continually breaking out upon the front.

19/12/17

Much better night, but temperature still high. Freezing still very hard. No mail arrived for me today.

20/12/17

Temperature still up, my head nearly splitting all day long. Received a letter from Miss Dorothy Roberts. To say that the parcel, which they were sending to me, had been unfortunately delayed until after Xmas, as the P.O refused to except parcels after the 14th of this month. Received also a nice letter from my sweet little friend Danielle together with a couple of nice postcards which had been delayed on route. Have done no studying or writing since I have been laid up, absolutely feel too weak even to think. Still freezing very hard indeed.

21/12/17

Frosty weather still prevails. Am slightly better but my head is still painfully bad. Received a beautiful parcel from my dearest of all aunts, which comprised, a plum pudding, box of choice cigarettes, box of Turkish delight and other sweets, tin of herring, tin of sardines, a nice cake, some nuts, a fruitarian cake and a tablet of soap, what a dear good kind soul my aunt Ada is, I am deeply indebted to her for untold kindnesses, she has proved to be the best friend I have ever known, she has always been the one bright spot upon a dark horizon, a lighthouse of pure light and goodness, a haven of sweet refuge and safety. Aunt dearest from this dull tent upon the fringe of so much human wreckage and sacrifice, upon the site of the old world even now groaning in the throes of death, I send you aunt dear, from my heart all the warm heartfelt thanks and gratitude, which abides even yet in my torn and shattered breast, aunt dear I do love you affectionately, you are white, white all through. There are indeed so few like you nowadays, God bless you, keep you and preserve you.

22/12/17

Still freezing hard. Sent a postcard to my dear Danielle. Am still feeling very weak and exhausted. I was gladdened greatly to receive a nice letter from Danielle and another from her mother, both expressed their gratitude and thanks for the "petite itrenne", which I sent to Danielle in the shape of a nice gold wrist-watch. A nice postcard also arrived from Danielle, and letters from my father and Doris, my dear sister enclosed a pretty Xmas card, on which she had painted a handsome rose. German aeroplanes were very active directly it became dusk this evening and dropped promiscuously a large number of bombs everywhere, 3 fell in the field opposite, just over the road.

Diary Number 9

23/12/17

Very cold frosty night. Feel much better but lack an appetite and am decidedly weak and exhausted. Plenty of bombs dropped again "ce soir."

24/12/17

Very unpleasant weather still. Have been ordered up today although I am still well on the wrong side of normal health. Wrote a letter to my darling Danielle and I also sent a box of choice cigarettes to her brother Etienne for the New Year. Good deal of artillery activity. Spent evening in a cafe in Ruitz, where they were quite pleased to see me again after my long absence. Took my plum pudding down to them to boil for me tomorrow evening.

25/12/17

Xmas day. What a life indeed. I wonder greatly what will be my luck this time next year, trust sincerely that my fortunes will have turned by that time decidedly for the better. The day is less cold and started well, with an egg, piece of fatty ham, bread and butter, plate of bergoo and a bowl of coffee for breakfast. Dinner included roast beef, chicken, boiled ham, potatoes, brussel sprouts, plum pudding, fruit, nuts, crackers, jellies, cigarettes and lemonade. Tea as usual. Spent the evening at my new cafe at Ruitz, where I had my own plum pudding, which was boiled by the kind lady and she and her little daughter aged 9 or 10 shared with me our English Xmas dish. It was very delicious and I enjoyed this little remembrance of the old country very much indeed. I turned in early and was first into bed, although the cafe's were not closed until 9 pm and in fact many were going strong I heard afterwards until after midnight.

26/12/17

Ground still covered deep in frozen snow. Worked very hard all day until 4.30 pm. Received a very beautiful letter from my loving little Danielle. Stayed in camp in the evening to write a letter to her, also wrote a letter to my dear sister Doris. It is freezing hard this evening and I am very cold.

27/12/17

Still freezing hardly. Worked hard all day. Sent a postcard to my dearest of all friends Danielle. A tremendous bombardment is still in progress at some point some distance from here.

28/12/17

Awfully cold night still freezing hard. Put in a hard days work. Blowing a perishing cold blizzard all day long, am sticking it rather well however. Wrote a letter to Madame Hangard and a card to my darling little Danielle. Spent a couple of hours in a cafe where I usually resort in the evenings.

29/12/17

Not quite so cold today although the ground is still covered deep in snow and it continues to freeze hard. Sent a card to my little Danielle.

30/12/17

Thawed slightly during the night but it is still very cold. Oh when will this wretched beastly war come to an end. It is really a most terrible existence for everybody. If there is a God why does he allow such a crime to continue. This war has truly turned millions away from the cross. It makes one wonder whether we are all going to. It is no longer a war between right and wrong, not that I ever believed that it was, but between the commercial classes of Germany and her allies against the commercial classes of the rest of the world. The Tommies at the present time only see the war in this light. God help their taskmasters in the future, for as surely as they detest this particular class, so surely will they seek to revenge themselves upon them, for all that they have so unjustly suffered for their putrid selfishness. I write these words with reason as they convey much that is perfectly true. This war could have been fought out to a definite and quick finish had the commercial classes allowed us to prepare in time for the approaching conflict, which everyone with the smallest grain of reason knew would come, and now this same class, would sacrifice every man, woman and child in their own unscrupulous interests. Received a really nice letter from my own little Danielle, which proved her kind solicitude on account of my recent illness. How different such genuine kindness is to that, which I have been accustomed to, at the hands of those, who might at least have shown some little consideration for my welfare. Have sent her a long letter in return.

31/12/17

Very cold dull day. Received a nice card from my little Danielle. Also a small packet from my dear aunt Ada containing a tablet of soap, a stick of shaving soap and a tube of toothpaste. Sent a card to my darling little Danielle. My hands and feet are very cold indeed.

1/1/18

This the first day of the New Year has opened with the ground still covered with ice bound snow. A violent bombardment commenced on our front during the early hours of the morning and continued for several hours. It was probably merely a martial greeting upon the entrance into our much tired planet of a new era. All the world desires peace, God be merciful and grant to us poor creatures, peace and good will among mankind as soon as possible. Enemy aeroplanes were again busy in our area last evening, and they succeeded in starting a fire over in the direction of Houchin. I was not aware until last night that we had in our army a fairly large number of Japanese troops fighting in the ranks of the Canadians. In the cafe where I was a couple of these fine fellows came in one a Lance Corporal and the other was wearing the ribbon of our military cross. Some Canadians who were present told me that they had no fear whatsoever and that the Canadians themselves thought very highly indeed of their yellow Comrades.

They are men who apparently have made their homes in British Columbia and other parts of Canada. Received a nice card from my precious little Danielle and have sent one also to her. On guard tonight, my time being from midnight to 2 am.

2/1/18

Still very cold, but thawing slightly. Sent a card to my own little Danielle. Day passed as usual, plenty of work and in the evening I went down to my habitual "rendez vous".

3/1/18

Another sharp frost during the night. High power guns were active on our front last night. I am feeling rather ill again, on account of the cold and had in consequence a most restless night on account of coughing. Received another beautiful parcel this time from my faithful friends Mr. and Mrs. Roberts and family of Southport, it contained a large box of assorted biscuits, a box of chocolates and a tin of sardines. Received also a nice Xmas card from my friend Miss Weeds and a rather astonishing letter from my brother Harry. Sent a letter to Mr and Mrs Roberts and a card to my dear little Danielle. Spent evening with two of my friends at a cafe at Ruitz.

4/1/18

Freezing very hard. Severe bombardment is still in progress somewhere along the line. Received a letter from my aunt Ada to tell me that my stepmother and stepbrother had been knocked down by a train in America, and that my stepmother had died in consequence. It is really very hard lines on the little one, also had a letter from Mlle Hunel, enclosing one of mine to her parents, which she had kindly corrected for me, there were very few faults however and Mlle congratulated me on my progress in the French language. Sent a letter to my dear aunt Ada and offered to pay 10 pounds towards the fare for my step brother to travel to England, also sent my portrait to Miss Weeds.

5/1/18

Still very cold. Received 3 letters from that dear darling girl Danielle. Marched to Barlin in the afternoon for a bath.

6/1/18

Colder still than ever today. Working all morning digging a trench on the top of a hill. Wrote letters in the afternoon, today being of course a Sunday. Sent letters to my dear Danielle and one to my dear sister Gladys. Most atrocious weather at night raining and blowing a cold wind.

7/1/18

Water and mud is again with us. No mail arrived for us today. Sent a box of chocolates to my little friend Gisele Hangard of Rouen and a card also to my darling Danielle and a letter to my dear aunt Ada. Spent evening as usual.

8/1/18

Sharp frost during the night, heavy snowstorm during the morning and fierce penetrating wind. Received a nice card from my darling little Danielle which I have acknowledged with another, also sent a letter to my dear sister Doris.

9/1/18

Bitterly cold day. Received "une gentille carte de ma petite" Danielle "cherie". Sent a card to her this evening. Walked to Barlin after tea in order to buy some picture postcards. It was rather cold to commence with, but after walking sharply for a short time I quickly got up a good circulation. Managed to secure a good selection of cards.

10/1/18

Still cold and what is worse a very heavy thaw has turned the ground into a veritable quagmire. Received a nice card from my precious little girl and also a most charming letter. She makes me wish so much that I were free and that this cursed war were a thing of the past. Wrote a letter and a card to my dear Danielle in the evening.

11/1/18

Very muddy, windy and sharp showers. Nice card from my dear darling Danielle, also sent her one in return. The mud is simply terrible and my feet are wet through from morning to night on account of the poor quality of the material with which are boots are made at the present time.

12/1/18

Chief interest still lies in getting oneself out of the mud, which is everywhere and on everything. Very cold nasty weather. Received no mail today, sent a card to my own little Danielle. On guard in the evening. Absolutely plastered all over with undrainable mud.

13/1/18

Frosty during the night, which has mercifully hardened the ground. Work as usual until midday, when, being Sunday I knocked off for the day and took things easy on my bed. Received a nice card from my pretty little flower at Rouen.

14/11/18

Heavy snow storms during the night. Very cold, can't get warm at all. Sent a card to my own sweet little Danielle.

15/1/18

Raining and blowing most furiously throughout the night. Very miserable weather all day. Got drenched through going down to the village of Ruitz in the evening. Sent some of my photo's to my brother Harry and a letter to my aunt Ada.

16/1/18

Very high wind and a great deal of rain. Can hardly hold my pencil for the extreme cold. Pegging down the camp most of the time as the wind blows everything into the air including iron sheets, which are really a danger to passers by. Received a charming letter from my beautiful Danielle and also a pretty card. Have written a letter to her in return.

17/1/18

Weather still very bad, at times snowing and at others raining hard. This is the order of the day. I do not ever remember such conditions prevailing for such a length of time. My diary has become I am afraid, merely a record of the weather. Life here goes on from day to day much in the same way and my greatest if not only distraction is the arrival of the post and a letter or a card from the charming little girl, whom I have learned to love so much. Spent evening in the usual way.

18/1/18

Weather still wet and uncertain. My clothes, especially my great coat will not dry. No mail for me today. Sent a card to my own little girl.

19/1/18

Windy but considerably drier. Received a very nice letter from my dashing Danielle. Plenty of work as usual. Sent Danielle a nice card.

20/1/18

Much milder today. Worked hard all morning. Received three nice cards from my friends at Rouen, two from Danielle and one from Giselle. Wrote a long letter to my own Danielle. The enemy commenced at daybreak to shell pretty frequently in our neighbourhood, apparently they are after dumps which are scattered about in different places.

21/1/18

Dull and windy. A good days work. Received 10 francs pay in the afternoon. On guard in the evening. Sent a card to my dear Danielle.

22/1/18

Weather maintains rather moderate. Received a nice letter from my precious little girl at Rouen. Am invited out to supper this evening with my friends at the cafe where I usually frequent, I enjoyed my meal very much especially the salad, which I am particularly fond of, I have always thought it to be a great pity that this customary dish of our French allies is so rarely seen on an English table.

23/1/18

Hard days work. Wrote a long letter to my little darling Danielle.

24/1/18

Lovely spring like weather today. Received a nice letter from Monsieur Etienne the young brother of my own Danielle, who is back again in the trenches in Lorraine, I have replied to him this evening and also sent a card to my Danielle. Artillery activity has again been renewed after a considerable interval of apparent tranquillity.

25/1/18

Weather still holding remarkably good. Was greatly pleased to receive a charming letter from my own Danielle and also a card. which latter was enclosed in a nice letter from Madame Hangard whom I call "ma petite mere". Enemy aircraft very busy round our part in the evening. One of our captive balloons was bombarded with high explosive shells during the evening. The occupant threw himself out and I could distinctly see him falling slowly to the ground beneath his parachute.

26/1/18

Beautiful day. Am feeling extremely well and considerably more vigorous than I have been for a number of years. Received a letter from my dear aunt Ada, wrote a letter to my darling Danielle. One of our aeroplanes came down close to our hospital and by the light railway, which has recently been constructed principally by Chinese labour, and was smashed up. Several of our chaps were put to guard it. Spent the evening at my usual rendezvous in conversation with three Canadian officers.

27/1/18

Weather still holding good, but rather cold first thing in the morning. Received a packet from my dear aunt Ada, which contained an electric torch, steel looking glass, indelible pencil and a small pocket book in case. The torch however proved useless as it would not light and I asserted that the battery had become run down. A nice card arrived from my darling little Danielle and another from her little sister Giselle, which she had painted herself and I must say that the roses were very well executed indeed. Sent a card to my Danielle.

28/1/18

Today has brought yet another change and I have been sent now to no 57 Casualty clearing station, which is situated at artillery corner between the villages of Anzin and St-aubin about 4 kilometres from Arras. We arrived here in time for dinner and I would like to say that I had the best dinner that I have had since Christmas. The food at no 6 CCS was plentiful and good, but here it is decidedly better and the cooking is much superior. Worked in the afternoon. In the evening had a walk over to Maroeul about 25 minutes walk. Had a few beers and returned at 8 pm.

29/1/18

Very cold night and had little rest on account of not sufficient blankets. Lovely day however. Have procured three more blankets. Champion dinner which included plum-pudding, it appears that the latter dish is frequently dished up at midday as for some reason they are over stocked with it, probably on account of opening shortly after Xmas for patients instead of before as was expected. Spent the evening writing to my darling little Danielle and also to my dear aunt Ada.

30/1/18

Another very cold night and frosty misty morning. Worked hard all day. Wrote a card to my dear Danielle in the evening and also a letter to my dear sister Doris. Had a walk in the village for an hour. There are only a very few civilians in these parts, and the "estaminets", which are only ramshackled buildings are filled to the doors with soldiers. It is in fact very difficult to obtain a drink, and a glass of beer costs three pence and very poor stuff at that.

31/1/18

Still freezing hard and very cold indeed. Had the great pleasure and delight to receive a nice card from my darling Danielle to whom I have sent one in return this evening, have also written to my friend Miss Dorothy Roberts. At 8 o'clock I attended a concert, which was held at the camp, and which I enjoyed.

1/2/18

Weather still the same, cold and frosty. Am feeling very fit however and am eating far more than hitherto I have been able to do, owing to a bad appetite. In the evening wrote cards to my dear Danielle, her little sister Giselle and Monsieur and Madam Godel at Ruitz, with whom I became very friendly during my stay near the village.

2/2/18

Weather still the same. Worked hard all day long from 7.30 am to 4.30 pm, assisted in evacuating during the morning and afternoon. Received a letter from my brother Harry, also one from my dear sister Doris enclosed in a packet of notepaper and envelopes. Sent a card to my darling little Danielle, also wrote a letter to my brother Harry.

3/2/18

Still cold, but lovely weather. Am doing stretcher bearing now for a week, commencing today at 7 pm until 7 am in the morning. Had a "bon" supper at midnight, consisting of roast beef and mashed potatoes and beautiful rice pudding. However the cold or something has got hold of me and I am feeling very sick and ill. Wrote letters to my dear aunt Ada, my dear sister Doris and a card to my own little Danielle in reply to a letter card, which I have received from her.

4/2/18

Dry and less cold, but have got a bad attack of diarrhoea and am feeling generally rotten, as have completely lost my appetite. Found in the evening that I was feeling far too unwell to go on duty at 7 pm, so reported sick.

5/2/18

Nice day. Had a fairly good night but am still suffering from the effects of diarrhoea. Think I must have caught cold in my stomach, which is a very weak spot indeed so far as I am concerned, and is the cause of my persistent bad health. Received a nice letter from my darling Danielle to whom I have replied this evening, also had a note from Mlle Marie Hunel, who returned my letter to her parents, which she had corrected for me.

6/2/18

Not so cold today. Am feeling slightly improved in my health today, but have still pains in my stomach and am off my food. Still I did a good days work all he same. Wrote a letter to Mlle Marie Hunel at Touques, Calvados where she is a school mistress and I am getting indebted to her for the interest and the trouble which she has taken on my account, in order to assist me in my French studies, which I find to be an extremely hard and difficult task, especially as I have to rely absolutely upon my own efforts as I have no-one to give me any aid whatsoever. Sent a card to my dear Danielle in answer to a nice one, which I have received from her.

7/2/18

Had a good nights repose and am feeling less weak and out of sorts today. What funny weather we do have. Today is dull and slight rain. Have had the great good fortune and pleasure to receive two very nice letters from the little girl I love so much, and also a very pretty card. Have written a long letter to her in return. Danielle tells me that her brother Etienne has received my letter and that he too loves me already.

8/2/18

Dull rainy day. Feeling considerably better in my self however, no mail came for me today. After tea I went down to Marouell for the purpose of buying a few postcards to send to my dear Danielle.

9/2/18

Nice day. Am feeling quite well again. Had a bath after finishing work this afternoon and a clean change of linen. Sent a card to my darling little Danielle. Wrote a letter in French for a corporal in the South Africans.

10/2/18

A good morning's work. Put in an application for a pass to go to Arras, which was granted and I started immediately after dinner. Turned to the right through Anzin and taking what is called the blue road, I arrived in about half an hours walk at my destination. Arras is a much larger town than either Albert or Peronne, but I do not think that it has suffered quite so much from bombardments as is the case with the latter places, nevertheless the most beautiful monuments in this city of desolation have been totally and most cruelly wrecked. The town hall with its beautiful architecture exists only in crumbled masses of masonry and a few stark and badly wounded walls are all that is left to mark the spot where once it stood so elegant and so stately. On the right hand side, which had not received the full shock of the bursting shells there is just a few scraps of sculpture work still standing, which testify unmistakably to its former beauty and grandeur. The cathedral is likewise quite demolished, except for the stout supporting pillars, which happily bear only the traces of villainous shrapnel kisses. The main entrance is piled up 30 feet or more with the wreckage of this noble edifice. On the south side the great steps are in fairly good preservation. By this entrance I gained admission to in to this shrine of God, which in all truth bears quite a hopeless aspect. Two immense statues in representation probably of Peter and Paul, which stand in a chapel on the right hand side, had miraculously escaped the devil's hand of destruction. They were however smothered with the names and addresses of attentive Tommies, in fact that most indefatigable of human beings in the prosecution of anything he ought not to do, had climbed up in all directions for the purpose of making known to the world, that he had really paid a visit to the place and would like everybody to know it. Hundreds too of small stone square tablets, had been religiously placed in rows on the altars with names and addresses inscribed thereon. For my part I looked about until I found a small piece of granite, which had been broken off a holy water fount, to take away as a souvenir. A number of civilians have returned and have opened shops for the benefit of the troops and I suppose themselves too. The town was full of Tommies and --- officers, many of them sightseeing like myself. On my way back I called at the E.F canteen, which is a large building and is quite the largest I have seen in France, with electric light generated upon the premises. Had a tin of tea and a couple of pieces of cake at 4 d a slice, also bought in a French chop, a quarter lb of dates, which cost me a franc and an album of views, which were 1 franc 25. Afterward walked back to camp. Received a very nice letter from Etienne and a charming card from his sweet sister Danielle.

11/12/18

Good day. Hard work. Received a letter from my aunt Ada, which has ended forever our good relationship. Have sent it to my sister Doris for her and my Father to see, I shall never forget or forgive the insult, which she has offered to me.

12/2/18

Was pleased to receive a nice card and a most pleasing letter from Madame Hangard, whom I call my little mother. She is indeed very kind to me. Wrote a letter to my dear Danielle, also sent one of my French notebooks, several letters and card from my Danielle, and an album of views of Arras to my sister Doris. Went to a concert in the evening, which however was very flat.

13/2/18

Wet miserable day. Stretcher carrying all day until 7 pm. Sent letters to Madame Hangard and another to her son Etienne, who is in the trenches. Had a talk for a short while, with a French woman, who came to visit the doctor at our hospital, accompanied by her daughter a young girl. I learned among other things that after the battle of Marne and the French came up in pursuit of the retreating Germans, that round about the cemetery at Arras and other places in this martyred town, the troops of France and their enemy were only divided by single walls, and that those on one side could hear distinctly the talk of those on the opposite side. Got in a good days study, for the first time since I have been here.

14/2/18

Dull day. Took part in an exciting chase after a rat during the morning, which came into the open from beneath the tent boards of a marquee, which we were pulling down, it tried hard to escape, but was too large and fat to get over the ground quickly enough. He got under a row of duck-boards and ran furiously up and down, but we had him marked and upon dashing out he was quickly bundled into eternity with spades and mallets. He had made a comfortable little nest in a bunch of newspaper scraps. Sent a card to my dear Danielle and a letter to my dear sister Doris.

15/2/18

Dull and cold. Stretcher bearing all day. Received letters from my dear Danielle and my friends at Querrieu. Sent off a card to my own Danielle. There has been a considerable increase in artillery activity during the past few days. Freezing in the evening.

16/2/18

Hard frost in the night, but sunny clear healthy weather during the day. Afternoon off so after a bath and clean change of linen, I took the road for Maroeul. It was a beautiful walk. Had tea in the village in a building, which had once been a stable. The three fried eggs, a couple of small slices of bread and butter and a cup of tea cost me two francs. Spent the evening in a cafe then returned home.

179

17/2/18

Freezing hard again all night and very cold to commence with in the morning.
Several red balloons came over in our direction during the morning and it is thought that they carried propaganda from the German lines, which I am inclined to think was the truth. One of these air messengers dropped between our camp and the Arras to St Pol road, which runs along the high ground not far from here. Some of our men raced over to it and cut off the barrel which was suspended from the balloon and then let the thing go again. I could not ascertain, what it did really contain however. Stretcher bearing all day until 7 pm. Wrote letter to my dear sister Doris and to my friends at Querrieu, Somme. Received my S.B which contained deposits of 138.12.5 also 11 pounds in notes and 10/6 in silver, an unusual cheque also arrived, which have sent to the postmaster in Birmingham, requesting that it should be made payable to my sister Doris, whom I have made my nominee.

18/2/18

Weather still continues the same as the last few days. Received a charming letter from my dear Danielle, to whom I have sent a letter in reply. Guns still very active on the front.

19/2/18

Weather "toujours la meme". Guns and explosions were the order of the night. Received a nice card from my dear Danielle, which I have acknowledged, also written to my dear sister Doris to whom I have forwarded my S.B.B per registered letter post. Expect to go to my depot at Abbeville tomorrow or the day after. Drum fire bombardment commenced at about 9.15 pm and continued for some time. The Germans apparently made a big raid on this part of the line. We received 17 wounded cases during the night. A few days ago one of our fellows here gave a pint or more of his blood for a Sergeant who had had both his legs amputated, unfortunately however the man, who wore a D.C.M and was a Mons hero, succumbed to his injuries. The chap who gave his blood looks non the worse for the operation but he is required to go into a ward and has cooked for him special diets.

20/2/18

Got my things together in preparation for going down to my base start from here at 3.30 pm.

21/2/18

Arrived at my depot at 2 am after a cold miserable ride in a cattle truck. I find things are considerably changed her now, owing to a change of C.O and Sgt-Major. Have to work hard all day until 5 pm. No opportunity to dodge whatsoever. Got a bath in the morning at the new shower baths in the camp. Spent the evening at my usual "rendezvous" in a cafe.

22/2/18

Went through gas in the morning. In the afternoon a rotten dry lecture in the telegraph school. Sent a card to my Danielle. Spent evening as usual.

23/2/18

Weather fine. Lecture in the T.S until 10.30 am. From 11 am to 12.15 pm physical jerks. On pay duties with another chap from 1.30 pm to nearly 3 pm. Received 40 francs. Went into the town after tea and bought some large photographs of cathedrals etc. and had them forwarded to my dear sister Doris. Spent rest of evening at my usual place.

24/2/18

Sunday. Nothing much doing to day except church parade. Wrote a letter to my sister Doris and a card to my dear Danielle. Had a walk in the afternoon, with my friends from the cafe. Had tea at 6 pm of fried eggs at their home.

25/2/18

Day passed in technical study, physical jerks etc. Received a nice letter from my dear Danielle and also a card Also a letter arrived for me from my friend Miss Dorothy Roberts.

26/2/18

Frosty during the night. School and physical drill in the morning. Rather cold but sunny during the day. In the evening bought a present for my dear Danielle in the shape of a gold heart and necklace which cost 90 francs also a box of chocolates for "ma petite mere" for 12 francs

27/2/18

Day passed as usual. Nothing especial to write about. Received a nice card from my dear Danielle.

28/2/18

Very heavy storm during the night. Sunny day. Received two nice cards from my little Danielle.

1/3/18

Very cold windy day, with snow and sleet. Bought a nice present for my dear sister Doris in the shape of a cushion cover, with the grand old church of Abbeville on satin in the centre and a lace border of flowers.

3/3/18

Still frightfully cold. Wrote a letter to my dearest little Danielle and also to my own dear sister Doris.

4/3/18

Am not feeling at all well today. Have had four fearfully restless nights on account of the cold. Received a very nice letter from my little Danielle and her mother. They were both delighted to receive the little presents, which I sent to them.

5/3/18

Much better night and am much better in myself. Weather still however on the wrong side of pleasantness.

6/3/18

Beautiful spring weather. Day passed as usual. In the divisional signal school in the morning until 10.30 am. Physical jerks 11 am to 12.15 pm. Afternoon in divisional school. Had the great good fortune to receive a very nice letter from my own dearest little girl at Rouen, who had very graciously enclosed a few strands of her beautiful hair, which were tied with a bow of blue ribbon.

7/3/18

Sharp frosty and bright day.

8/3/18

Weather still continues nippy but clear and bright. Have passed my final exams in technical this morning.

9/3/18

Weather as usual. Received 20 francs pay this afternoon.

10/3/18

Very bad night indeed. Church parade at 10.40 am. Wrote a letter to my dear Danielle and one to my dear sister Doris. A marquee at the hospital was burnt down in the space of a few minutes, we had a fire alarm at 9.30 as a practice.

11/3/18

Still beautiful weather. Foot drill with rifles in morning and fatigues in the cable shed.

12/3/18

Night frosty as usual followed by perfect summer weather. Same drill and fatigues as previous day.

13/3/18

It is rather remarkable how well the weather is holding. I am afraid I am becoming distinctly tired of writing up my diary. I find nothing to say and I have nothing whatsoever of interest nowadays to talk about. Received a nice card from my gentle little Danielle, also sent her one in reply.

14/3/18

Weather has changed today for the worse. Fine rain nearly all morning. Rifle drill and bath in the morning followed by work in the cable shed. Received a nice letter from my dear sister Doris.

15/3/18

Nice day. Work and drill as usual. Received a nice letter and card from my precious little girl at Rouen, to whom I have written a card in return.

16/3/18

Weather still holding remarkably good. Received 20 franc's pay in the afternoon. On guard from 6 pm until 6 am Sunday.

17/3/18

Am feeling rather tired after my guard duty. Little or no sleep during the night. Fatigues in the morning in the Quartermasters store, cleaning rifles. Managed to wangle a new cap however. Wrote a letter to my darling little Danielle and one to my dear sister Doris.

18/3/18

Lovely day. Day passed with the usual fatigues and drill.

19/3/18

Raining all day. Weather seems to have broken up at last.

20/3/18

Weather conditions somewhat improved today. Received a nice card from my darling little Danielle, to whom I have sent a nice one in return.

21/3/18

Fine day but not very bright. Drill and fatigues as usual until 3.30 pm, when I was called away from my work on account of one in our tent having gone into hospital with chicken pox, and in consequence am now isolated together with the other two occupants. Received a nice card from my little Danielle and also a typewritten letter in French from my dear sister Doris.

22/3/18

Visited the doctor this morning for the purpose of being inspected, we are still isolated and likely to be so for some days. Fine but dull day. We are employed in digging during the day. Handed in an application for leave, which I wish to spend in Rouen, but it has been returned to me on the grounds that while I am isolated, such an application is useless.

23/3/18

Foggy cold morning again. Visited the doctor for inspection in the morning. Digging until midday. The sun came out strong in the afternoon, and spread its warming rays over all, one felt something of the true delight of living, to be able to bask in its soothing caresses. We have been informed this morning that we shall receive no pay this week, on account of being isolated. Damned hard luck I consider it, also my application for leave cannot be considered I am told on the same grounds.

24/3/18

Foggy morning, but which quickly dispersed when the sun began to mount in the heavens. Another dog shot after breakfast, quite a number of these poor animals have been destroyed lately at this depot, following a general order in respect to stray dogs. ****** Diary finishes for some reason half way through this day ******

Diary Number 10

26/12/18

I here once more take up my pen, to jot down the objects and scenes with which I may come into contact during the closing days of the titanic upheaval, which has rocked and badly shaken the whole framework of civilisation and indeed the very world itself. Many months have elapsed since last I made any notes and now as I am penning these I find myself sitting at one of the dining tables at the Salvation Army rest for soldiers in London, Blighty. Am on my way back to France after 14 days furlough and seven days extension which was granted to me by the Royal Engineer Records Chatham. In spite of many thing I have spent a really pleasant and enjoyable time, at the old home in Stafford, in the company of my father, Sister Doris and my little treasure boy Derrick. I left Stafford this morning with my little boy at 11.37 am and went first to Warwick where I left Derrick in the care of Mr. and Mrs. Kendrick at 48 Avon Street. I think that these forced partings from the little chap, who is so dear to me, have caused me deeper and more cruel pain, than all other pains that I have known. If there is such a thing as love in this world, it must be surely just like that, how little Dux is loved by me. Left Warwick at 5.58 pm and arrived at Paddington at 9.10 pm. Took a bus to Victoria station and passed by the Marble Arch and Saint James Park, which was profusely decorated with flags and bunting in honour I suppose of the visit of the American president, who arrived today. At Victoria station went into the free buffet, and had a sandwich and cup of tea. Wreaths in the evergreen and other laurel decorations were hanging up everywhere and welcome greetings to the soldiers were emblazoned in large letters upon the walls, one inscription ran something like this "We pray for all who have died and we thank all for bringing us victory and peace" another ran "Welcome home the nation thanks you". Was directed by a gentleman to board a small motor lorry, which had two seats down the centre and a roof, something after the style of the well known Irish "stage coach". This vehicle took a party of us to the pace where I am now and where I have engaged a bed no 182 for the night for the price of half a shilling.

27/12/18

Slept fairly well. Was awakened shortly before 5 am by some individual blowing loud blasts on a whistle and calling out "boat train", was very tired so I did not get up immediately. Later had a wash and partook of a good breakfast comprised of Ham, roast meat (cold), bread and butter and tea for 9 d. Walked down to Victoria station, where I found already assembled an immense crowd of soldiers returning from leave, and most of them appeared to be at least several days overdue, having preferred to stay in Blighty for Xmas. In consequence of this large number, the trains seemed to go anywhere, as eventually I found myself at Dover instead of Folkestone, where I stayed until after midday in the military barracks on the top of the cliffs. We were then marched off again to the docks and boarded a boat, which took us across to Boulogne, where we landed about 5 pm and marched up to the rest camp which also stands upon the summit of a steep hill and is well known to Tommies. Later went out and spent the evening in a cafe. Returned to billet at about 8.45 pm. It is now 9 pm and as blankets are being served out I must stop here and go seek my bed for the night.

28/12/18

Slept rather uneasily. Two of us had made down our kip together for extra warmth. Breakfast at 6 am, when we were provided with an excellent meal in more than sufficient quantity. My portion consisted of an ample slice of fish and bread and butter, we were afterwards dished out with a tin of sardines, a bun, two cakes and a small piece of cheese for the journey up to our units. Paraded about 7.30 am and then fell out to join the party for "q" train. It was a miserable day, with rain and wind and sludge, through which we had to march to the railway, a distance of about 5 kilometres. This long trudge was somewhat remarkable by reason of the great number of troops en route, in ascending the hill through the town, the road was black with moving troops for as far as the eye could see, half of them just returned off leave and the other half descending the hill on their way to Blighty. We were all packed into the train somehow and started off about 10 am. The journey proved long and tedious, the train moving "tres doucement" and stopping frequently. At 6.15 pm we were still 3 kilometres from Abbeville and in spite of the darkness I left the train and made my way to the road and followed it to Abbeville on foot. On the way I dropped into a barbers for a shave and then made my way to my favourite cafe in the Rue St-Gilles, where I endeavoured to appease my hunger and fatigue in the pleasant occupation of devouring a hot meal in the shape of mashed potatoes, fried egg, bread and a litre of beer. Reported at the depot at 9 pm. Obtained a couple of blankets from the guardroom and betook myself to the hut marked "night details", where I made my kip for the night.

29/12/18

Slept soundly. Paraded at 7.15 am for breakfast and issue of cigarettes and matches. Reported again at orderly room at 8.30 am and was told to report there again tomorrow at five minutes to ten am, on account of being "adrift" for one day, so suppose I shall be punished in some way for overstaying my leave one day. It was not likely that I should start back on Xmas day and for that reason I did not go back until the following day (Boxing Day). After dinner went into Abbeville to by a few things to send to my little nieces Ivy and Annie and bought a couple of small silver brooches for them as a new years gift, also bought a small brush for polishing my brown boots, and two pretty cards for my own dear little boy. This evening I am on guard from 6 pm until 6 am. My periods of duty are 10 pm to midnight and 4 am to 6 am. It has rained pretty heavily most of the day and the wind is still blowing furiously. There is nothing I hate more than doing guard, and it fags me dreadfully. Wrote a letter to Mrs Corbett and my sister Doris, also a postcard to Danielle.

30/12/18

7.30 am my guard is over and as usual I feel rather done up, my post was over the horse lines, but to speak truly I took very little interest in the welfare of the beasts. Despatched my letters on the 7 am parade. Paraded as ordered at the orderly room at 9.55 am and was awarded 8 days C.B and one days pay Royal Warrant. I appealed against this and requested a court martial, and was paraded before the commanding officer, who upheld the decision of the colonel and would not allow my demand for a court martial.

This procedure is of course quite contrary to military law and the C. O therefore guilty of a serious breach of justice. It is on account of nothing more than this sort of thing that my poor country is likely to be ruined at least so far as the army is concerned, and during the war has led up directly to the brutal death of many British soldiers. It is not improbable that all this may bring in its train a frightful reckoning. Should this day presently appear above the blackened horizon, then I trust that God will be with and aid the soldiers. My name is up on the notice board for the 62nd division and time of departure 7 am tomorrow, at 1.30 drew my full marching order kit and spent the afternoon in putting it together. Wrote to Mrs Kendrick in the evening and enclosed a card to little Derrick. Made down my kip and got into it early as felt I wanted a good rest.

31/12/18

Breakfast at 6.30 am. Paraded at 7 am and moved off shortly afterwards in full marching order to the station. The train was very late in starting and we were kept waiting until after midday. There are four of us going up to the 62nd division and we have been provided with six days rations. It is miserable wet weather so that taking all things into consideration, the journey ahead is going to be somewhat interesting. Arrived at Etapoles about 4 pm, where we are to stay in no 9 rest camp until further orders. Had tea in the canteen and afterwards my chum and me, went into the town and spent a really pleasant evening in a cafe in the company of French, Canadians, New-Zealanders and Tommies, songs were the order of the day and the gramophone played its part in dispelling morbid thoughts. Discipline has been relaxed to a remarkable degree in all infantry base depots and for very good reason, I think that the signal depot at Abbeville is the only exception to the usual order of things, which is probably due to there being so few men at present in the depot, and the well known docility of post office sappers, may have something to do with it.

1/1/19

Slept soundly our breakfast was hardly eatable, porridge all lumps and cold, tea ditto and the ham merely huge chunks of fat. I suppose like everywhere else, the only people who do well in the army so far as grub is concerned are the officers, Sgt. Majors and Sergeant, who of course have the pick of everything. I know that this is true, as have done fatigues in cookhouses, and have had the job of picking out the best for the different messes, and poor Tommy has to be grateful with what is left, after his "betters" have had their pick. Well here we are at the beginning of a New Year, it would be interesting to know what is hidden beneath its mantle of many folds, within each one is held the destiny of all and the world looks on anxiously to see the things, which are to be unfolded from this day to the coming of its successor. My friend and me walked out into the town at about 11 am. Answering the guard on the bridge in the affirmative, whether we had passes. Of course we have "passes" just as much so as officers and we do not intend to tolerate any more childish restrictions. There have been already quite a number of disturbances last night in no 6 rest camp, the guard-room was attacked and other damage done, because the R.S.M had had arrested an Australian for having dirty books. In the evening the men, who are very touchy at present, demanded the key to the guardroom, broke into it and released the prisoner. While the other went to seek the RSM round the camp and among other places at the WAACS dancing room. Luckily for him, he was not to be found.

Paid a visit to the old church, which from the outside looks almost in the last stages of decay. Many too of its stained glass windows have been smashed as a result of German bombs, as also a large number of houses in its vicinity have been totally wrecked by the same cause. Inside the church, the aspect is quite changed, and instead of dilapidation one is confronted with a host of interesting objects. I don't think that I have ever seen a place of worship anywhere, so densely crowded with church furniture, it is simply packed right up to the by these objects, which appertain to the Roman Catholic ritual. After dinner went with my chum to Paris-Plage by train. This seaside place is quite modern and architecturally typically French, although it is only in course of completion. Walked along the entire length of the promenade, which is broad and uniquely paved. Had a cup of tea etc in a WAACS club just behind "L'hospital Temporaire" at the extreme end of the prom. They have a really nice and comfortable club, with grun etc at moderate prices. On the door is note stating "This club is open to WAACS and their friends". Had a look around the town, bought a number of postcards of local views and sent them home. Returned to Etaples about 5 pm. Had tea in the Salvation Army hut and spent the rest of the evening in the same cafe as yesterday.

2/1/19

Paraded in full marching order this morning, but have still to hang on here. Spent morning writing, after dinner walked into the town and round by the docks where is moored a number of fishing smacks. This old fishing place is in a horribly dirty condition and together with the debris of fallen houses presents quite a morbid spectacle. Had a look round the cemetery, which is densely packed with tombs and little chapels after the French style. Bought a souvenir match box, embossed with the arms of the Somme as a new present for the old dad. Returned to camp for tea and afterwards spent evening in the same way and at the same place as before. At 9 pm when we returned to billet the rain was teeming down. Since I returned to France the weather has been most unfavourable.

3/1/19

Morning a little brighter, with welcome sunshine. Went for a stroll through the camps, which cover many acres of land. Later wrote a letter to my sister Doris and a postcard to Mlle Danielle. In the afternoon lay down for a nap. Went with my chum in the evening to the cafe, which we prefer and which is called "cafe de l'avenir". We are to continue are journey tomorrow, a long list of units to go on parade at 7.45 am is stuck up on the notice board. Shall be really glad to get a move on, as things are by no means pleasant here and the wretched weather does not tend to improve matters. Lying in bed, I cannot escape the drops of water, which come dripping down through the tent and splash my face incessantly. I consider this sort of thing is down right shameful, in all probability these old tents have sheltered Tommies since the war began and no effort even after 4_ years of war has been made to provide more suitable accommodation for the common soldier. What a difference to be sure between the lot of the poor Tommy and the luxurious billets of the German soldiers, and then again, why should officers be provided with all the best of everything obtainable. Some of these questions will have to be answered one day.

4/1/19

Owing to some reason the 7.45 parade was cancelled until further orders. The bugle sounded "fall in" at about 10 am and off we went to the 'new siding" to embark on route for Germany, am writing this en route. We have four days rations with us and we are packed into cattle trucks. We were allotted to truck no 118, but could not find an inch of room there, so I went back to the R.T.O and explained matters, he sent us then to no 127 and we have fixed up as comfortably as possible under the circumstances. I notice that several trucks have been reserved for officers only (six in each), while the Tommies are overcrowded and the floors of their trucks are in a most horrible filthy condition. A corporal of the Manchester's whom I heard complain to the officer in charge, that the truck he was in was not fit for men to be in, met with the usual reply, which useless British Officers generally give, which was to the effect that he could do nothing. He had he said been put in charge of a certain number of trucks, but he was sorry he could do nothing in the matter, and forthwith put an N.C.O in charge of the said truck and himself disappeared. Tommy may be hard done to, but he is perfectly capable of looking after himself, some go scrounging round for tins, or buckets, with which to make fires, while others go to seek for fuel, and it is necessary to say that they get all they want. Quite a busy scene may be witnessed on these occasions, amateur tinsmiths are hammering holes into improvised braziers, others buying provisions at the YMCA or canteen and some are filling up petrol tins with water for boiling. The train started off at 11.30 am and except for a few short stops, we went along at a good speed, running right through Boulogne and on to Valais without drawing up once, which is certainly an exception to the rule, as almost all trains stop at Boulogne. Picked up more troops at Calais and then resumed our journey to the frontier. We stopped at several places during the evening including Bethune. Our train of at least 134 wagons presents a remarkable spectacle as it rushes along through the country districts. From one end to the other, the glowing braziers hang just outside the doors, and behind these, clustered closely together are our khaki clad Tommies taking a dreamy but interested view of the ever changing landscapes.

5/1/19

Could not rest easily, owing perhaps to the heavily smoke laden air in the carriage, which is not at all pleasant at the best of times, and the absence of hot grub is another item, which produces a sickening effect, especially after 4 years of rough wear and tear in different climates and under all sorts of conditions. Was awakened about 7 am by my chum, who handed my a welcome drink of hot tea, at this hour we were standing in a suburb of Lille and now at 10 am we have only advanced a little further towards this well known city, the Manchester of France. For breakfast had a couple of slices of toast and bully beef with half a Dixie of strong pick-me-up tea. It is remarkable that wherever one travels in France there are sure to be littered about great numbers of discarded tins of every description, and all along the rails, one notices bully-beef tins, sardine tins and others, which have contained jam, pork and beans and other tinned stuff. Approaching Lille and beyond, one sees plainly the system of destruction, which the Germans carried out in their retreat. The rails for instance had been blown up by a small charge at the point where they are joined up, which either bend the two ends very badly or breaks off a portion of each. The telegraph poles for the most part have been thrown to the ground, while on others the wires have been cut. It is now midday and we have just crossed the Scheldt and standing outside Tournai, which is in Belgium.

The bridge over which we have just passed is a splendid bit of work constructed by our Engineers with massive wooden beams on concrete beds, which has been erected to replace the one destroyed, by the enemy. The countryside is terribly flat and marshy and one wonders how we could have crossed the Scheldt in face of any resistance. Entered Tournai station where we stayed for a while. Proceeding on our journey we passed through a number of stations all demolished by the barbarian in his retreat. At ATH where we arrived at about 5.30 pm several of us made a raid on an engine standing by in a siding, and took from it several boxes of small coal and also an oil lamp with its glass broken, which I commandeered for the purpose of illumination as we are without light. My friend and I made are way out of the station to a cafe opposite, where two bonny Belgium girls stood in the doorway. I asked them if they could oblige me with some bread and a candle, they brought a candle for which I paid them six sous and following their advice, I went to another cafe two doors away where an old woman, said she would be pleased to give me a loaf of bread, although she had not much herself as it was still difficult to obtain. I gave her 2 francs and she was satisfied. Had a last cup of hot tea and a piece of toasted bread before getting down to it for the night. A few visitors branded us during the evening including a tall Belgium youth of 18 years, who was returning to his family at Roux. He had been forcibly sent to Germany to work and is very bitter against his country's enemy's for the indignities inflicted upon his countrymen and especially his own personal experiences during his 12 months sojourn in Germany.

6/1/19

Fairly good nights rest was up at about 7 am, making preparations for breakfast and a much needed wash, the first since leaving Etaples. Had a long walk with our Belgium friend, who had be en route from Switzerland for 8 days. Among his souvenirs was the skin of a Chamois (wild goat) which he had shot (with a Winchester) on the mountain slopes of Switzerland. Passing by a German train, with German drivers, I saw for the first time, a visible expression of German hate, which was directed at my Belgium friend, who stood by my side. The German a fine looking young chap, looked a perfect picture of disdain as he fixed with his eyes our comrade in arms, for two or three seconds. Glancing from one to the other, I noticed that this untimely expression of feeling was dull reciprocated by this sturdy son of little Belgium, who in addition shook his fist menacingly. I may here make note of something, which has come to my knowledge recently. The Germans compelled everyone in Belgium to work, or they were imprisoned without food, for failing to salute German officers, two days imprisonment or a fine of 1 mark was imposed. The people it seems never submitted to this tyranny and preferred solitary confinement to paying fines. This I hear accounts for the number of broken windows in Lille, for example, where the friends of these ill-used people come to bring them bread and threw it through the windows of these private houses, which the Germans used as cells. I must not omit to mention, it would be impossible to describe, the terrible spectacle of destruction, which we witnessed on arriving at the big junction of LUTTRE. It would seem that the enemy had concentrated a vast number of ammunition trains and then blew them up. To give him his due he is certainly a master hand at systematic destruction and here the result of his handiwork is frightfully complete, never again perhaps shall we be permitted to look upon such diabolical devastation. The blowing up of so much explosive had fulfilled the double purpose of ripping up the metals and leaving large holes in the permanent way.

190

The station buildings and houses in the vicinity had shared in the general demolition, shells of every size lie strewn about not having all gone the way of their kind. Except for this our journey today has been through a country, which bears little or no evidence of the scorching breadth of war. Passed through Courcelles and Rous, at which place our Belgium friend descended and about midday we ran through the big station of Charleroi from there we passed through a great industrial and mining centre. At no time have we stopped for more than a few minutes and so must write these notes as we move slowly along. Fortunately the weather today has turned most fraciously in our favour, and at this moment the sun is giving to us the welcome pleasure of its radiant smiles. We are now at Montigies, a busy mining district and I noticed that women are doing the same work as men and pushing great trucks of coal in and out of the lifts, with as much agility as strong men. The number of towering slag heaps all the way along from Charleroi is prodigious and one can see the little trucks mounting to the summit, where they are relieved of their burden by men, who look to be mere specks from below. A noticeable feature of both the French and Belgium railways is its diverse rolling stock, which includes engines and wagons lent by Uncle Sam, engines belonging to R.O.D, and the vast number of German wagons and a few passenger trains. The trucks from the fatherland are easily distinguishable by their red coating of paint and the German eagle painted in black with brown skeleton markings on a white background. It must be noted that this once proud eagle has been erased on almost every coach by a cross of white painting the manner X. After leaving TAMINES a soldier, who had been drinking fell off the train and was killed. It is a peculiar fact that although the actual fighting has ceased, many men will lose their lives from one cause or another. At Namur we stopped for half an hour or so in the station. I managed to procure half a loaf of bread for a Franc at a shop near by. Shortly after leaving Namur we ran along the left bank of the Meuse, which in spite of a cloudy moon, we could distinguish out of the gloom, the beautiful scenery through which we passed. The massive rocks which guard its banks must present a charming spectacle in daylight. Stopped for a few moments at Statte and Huy. I then made down my kip and got down for the night.

7/1/19

Woke up this morning to find myself in Germany, with a German Engine and drivers. We are stopped for a few minutes at a place called Ronheide. Have just passed through aix la chapelle, which is a beautiful city and is the first large town in Germany over the Belgium frontier. The French tricolour is flying proudly over one of the big buildings in the city. The wide streets is a pleasant feature in the town planning system of this German town. Arrived at Duren shortly after 10 am, where we the 62nd and several other divisions had to change. We are due to catch the train for Mechernich at 1.12 pm. Am writing this in the warteraum, which I suppose means refreshment room. It is a spacious compartment and is full of Tommies, Belgians and German civilians, some of the later are beguiling away the time at a game of cards. Have just had a small tankard of beer, which I presume is really the favourite drink called lager for 2d. The people are remarkably friendly and the girls wave their hands to our troops - nearly as cordially as do the women of Belgium, although perhaps with not quite the same feeling of thankfulness, at this moment a German woman is showing photographs to one of my friends and everyone appears to be happy and contented. Our train which is a, passenger and contains a crowd of civilians started away promptly to the scheduled time.

We are travelling 3rd class and is of course decidedly inferior to our own comfortable coaches in Blight, the seats and backs are of plain wood, at one side there is a narrow opening, which gives access to the next compartment. For companions we had a Fraulein and her male friend, she was obviously what Tommy calls "hot stuff". She was pleased to accept a cigarette, which she smoked and it was noticeable that she was not content until by a number of dextrous movements quite feminine, she had succeeded in drawing her skirt a short way above her high brown boots in order to make visible her open work brown stockings, at which her friend placed his finger inside the said boots, which action the Fraulein resented greatly as of course she realised that she was found out. We arrived at Euskirchen about 2 pm, where we found that we could proceed no further as the train we were in was going on to Bonn. We marched to the local infantry barracks a distance of about 1 1/2 miles and there billeted temporarily. This building is comparatively new and of a very modern type, with wide clean passages and glazed walls. The beds unlike our own collapsible ones in the barracks at home, are strong wooden structures with thick but not hard mattresses, with springs underneath. The washing place is original, and the water instead of splashing all over one when the taps are turned on, flows directly into the trough. The first thing I did upon arriving here was to shave, have a good swill down, polish my boots and thoroughly brush my clothes, all of which I was badly in need. Had tea, then went into the town with my chum. There are quite a few khaki clad heroes walking about. Entered a large hall which the YMCA had taken over, where we found a throng of Tommies and someone was playing a piano. The whole place was gay with bunting and garlands in the good old Christmas fashion. Bought some views of Euskirchen, and one specially for my own dear little boy. Am at this moment in a cafe "for British soldiers only, N.C.O's too have certain cafe's set apart for them, the principal "draw" is a big organ, which makes as much noise as a full orchestra. To give it its rightful due I must admit that it is turning out some beautiful tunes and I am quite a delighted listener. Germany you are a wonderful and beautiful country, Germany you are intellectually highly efficient, you have erected a civilisation of unique ideals and polished cultivity, you are the first nation to lose by arms what you have acquired by skill. It is the verdict of progress, which has willed that you should not lose your incentive to accomplish yet higher things. Victory would have brought you too much power and instead of conquest in the field you must seek fresh fields of action and take your place of honour and of right in those particular spheres in which you excel and deservedly so. Returned to barracks at 9 pm. There are no restrictions whatever in respect to times for being back in billets, nor is there a roll-call at night or in the morning.

8/1/19

Weather beautifully fine following a slight frost during the night. Breakfast at 7.30 am. Paraded in full kit at 9 am to receive our marching orders to proceed to our destination. Have to catch the 1.30 pm train and dine at 11.30 am. My chum and I went out into the town for a couple of hours to see the sights. First walked up to the station where we saw several girls, presumably railway workers, dressed up in workmen's clothes. An iron statue in front of the station of a German soldier with drawn sword and gripping a flag in his left hand, which is unfurled behind him. Paid a visit to the church, which is quite modern and then proceeded to see a very old church. Which had been only recently restored. The shop woman, where I bought a view of the porch told me that it was six hundred years old. The interior is nicely adorned and has an extremely comfortable appearance, with tall high-back pews, with plenty of room between each. Had to change at Call on our way to Schleiden, which is our destination.

Arrived there about 3.30 pm and reported at the local postamt (post office) in which the signal office of the 62nd division is installed. After all particulars from birth to death had been duly taken, my chum and me took our kit up to the top story, where a room has been allotted to the operators. Went over to the station where the whole staff mess in the refreshment room, the grub being cooked in an out building at the end of the platform. After dinner returned to billet, had wash and brush up and accompanied by my chum walked out into the town and stopped at a hotel where we had several big cups of excellent coffee, plentifully sustained with milk and sugar. No beer is to be got unfortunately at present. There appears to be an abundance of food and every other necessity, meals are supplied at comparatively cheap rates and the tables are occupied all the evening in serving up dishes to hungry Tommy. There are no cafe's here, and of the big hotels, one the hotel Busch is out of bounds to British troops. I have heard that only British officers are allowed there in spite if the managers complaint to such an arrangement, which is easily understood as the Tommy does not generally spare his cash, on the contrary he spends lavishly. This reminds that in Euskirchen this morning I noticed that a stationers etc bore a notice on the door, stating that the shop was out of bounds to British troops "for charging excess prices" now that is the stuff to give em, what a pity the same procedure was not adopted in France. I must really remark on the prodigious number of men, who because they are employed in civilian jobs under the government wear uniforms. Even youngsters sport either the peaked or round caps worn by the military and it is one of their great delights, upon espying a British officer coming along to quietly await his approach, with a look of expectancy clearly visible in their eyes and then to dart forward and salute, which of course is politely returned and the child turns away contented with his little exploit. I feel I could write indefinitively of many things and I could wish for nothing better than to be able to express, to describe and to picture subjects in a way that other too could see and appreciate in the same way or better than I do myself, Germany there is much that an able pen might do and I am conscious that with more ability I had been given opportunities since the commencement of this war, now happily at an end, to speak volumes upon subjects and scenes of undoubted interest. Returned to mess room at the station for a little supper, and then reported at the signal office as per orders, where was given a test in the manipulation and told me duties for the morrow, wrote a short note to my sister Doris.

9/1/19

Got up at 7.30 am had breakfast then shave and general cleanup. Paraded at 9.30 am on the open space in front of the station. Went for a short walk with my chum into the village and bought several views, but which in my opinion quite fail to do proper justice to the magnificent scenery in which Schleiden is set. Dinner at 12.30 pm and on duty in the signal office from 1 pm to 5 pm. The German girls who are working in the same office are quite friendly towards us as indeed is everyone, with whom I have had anything to do up to the present. Have sent off all my cards to my sister Doris and have written to Mrs Kendrick adding a few words to my own little boy, whose tiny loving face is always in my thoughts and it is difficult to crush down the longing to be near to him again, also addressed to my darling a pretty souvenir card. Wrote a short letter to my friend Sapper South. After tea and wash betook myself to the same hotel as yesterday called "Hotel Pension" and had several glasses of lager. The village and houses are brightly illuminated by electric lights, even out of the way lanes have electric lights prominently placed, which is a great point in Germany's favour as compared with France's dark and gloomy streets.

The electric power is generated by the stream, which flows through the valley. What a pity we do not cultivate and make us of nature's possibilities a little more in our own country. The German's are really not even our equal, they have a fine country it is true and have raised a strong and formidable nation and their works are a great credit to their labours. But, and here we get right down to the root of the matter, for this must be noted, that all they have accomplished or achieved has been done by design, by force and by dogged perseverance. On the other hand the works and the civilisation, which have erected and diffused to every corner of the globe and of which we are justly proud is the outcome purely and simply of our superior nations character, which disdains dictation and has quietly worked out its destiny without interference in the warm and encouraging rays, which have for ever shone and lit up the watch-word of our race "liberty". Let me explain still further, a German is born a registered slave in his own country. True it is that the state accepts responsibility for the general welfare of the people, which commences right at the birth of a child. There is little or no unemployment in the country and the dwellings even in the poorer middle class are of a type distinctly superior to their prototype in England. Wages are not high but the workers live in comfortable surroundings, have food in plenty and fairly good prospects in life open to them, but all this is at a price, as may be clearly seen by the one example of an intending emigrant, after going through all the formula of a British Tommy getting demobilised, he receives a pass say to America, and he is shepherded across the Atlantic, where he is met and conducted to interview the German consul, who if necessary will find him a job, but it must be remembered that all this is full of purpose and services in kind are required to be rendered by every German slave in the interests of the fatherland. Returned home and to bed shortly after 8 pm. 10/1/19 Fine brisk morning and ground slightly frozen. On duty in signal office 8 am to 1 pm. Wrote a letter to Mlle Marie Hunel and received two from Mlle Danielle and her mother which had been on the way for several weeks, as they are both addressed to me at Saint Riquer, where I was on a months course of wireless at the latter end of November and beginning of December 1918. We are experiencing great difficulty in changing our French and English money here, for instance a 20 franc note is worth more than 32 marks at present but the German shopkeepers and hotels will only give 20 marks and we have no means of taking advantage of this great drop in the value of the mark. I think something should be done to force the difference in value of our money to be accepted and recognised by the Germans. Was looking at a German periodical this morning, which had published several photographs of bombed houses, but from Aix la Chaelle upwards, I have not seen even a broken plane of glass, why ?, it is incredible that after nearly 4½ years of ceaseless destruction in France that here, tranquillity has reigned undisturbed and the hot breath of war has not been even remotely felt. As there is a God some men in England must be brought to book and quickly for they stand convicted of the vilest criminality known to the human race, for none are so base or anything so despicable as those who are guilty of "national treachery". I notice that for agricultural work the Germans make great use of the ox as a beast of burden and the Belgians too employ the ox for work in the fields. The French small-holder on the other hand has any number from one of powerful and hard working horses of a particular breed and in this at least I think the French farmer can claim points. Had a hot bath and change in the afternoon at the Hotel Schleiden for a mark. After tea attended a debate at the divisional school rooms about 10 minutes walk from here, the subject of the debate was "should bachelors be tasked" and was discussed by a large audience, including three officers.

Afterward adjourned to a hotel where we spent the remainder of the evening and what is more had the pleasing satisfaction of a good square meal and well cooked of roast meat and gravy, as much asparagus and mashed potatoes as one could eat, and an ample serving of well sweetened stewed rhubarb as dessert, for the moderate charge of 3 marks 50 or at the present rate of exchange 1/10 in English money. Who said Germany was starving?, if these big establishments can lay out a meal of this sort and provide spotlessly white table cloths at such remarkably cheep rates, then most certainly there can be no truth whatsoever in the reports that the people in Germany are starving. I should have been on duty at 9 pm until 8 am the following day, but after working until 11 pm, arranged with the other chap who was on duty with me to go back to kip, so the next time it will be my turn to stay on duty all night.

11/1/19

Fine and frosty but sunny weather during the morning. Walked out towards Ober Hausen with a friend to get a blanket from the stores. Afterwards returned to Schleiden, bought a few more picture postcards and had a coffee and a slice of dry ginger bread sort of cake at a cafe. After dinner I went to the company stables to join a party for a ride round, I chose a horse, which was given a bad name as of course fools generally describe a good beast in that manner, and as it proved I had a most glorious ride going up the hill sides and along woodland paths leading through the forest, along the summit of these hills I was able to obtain most beautiful views of the surrounding landscape with charming villages nesting snugly in the deep valleys. Am rather sorry have not got my riding breeches with me, as it is not so comfortable in the saddle in slacks and I want to go on every ride there is if possible, which I think is intended for each Saturday afternoon. On duty at 5 pm to 9 pm during which time between intervals of work I wrote postcards to my friends at Abbeville, my brother Harry and sister Gladys, and did a little French studying. Cleaned my rifle before turning in, to save time on the morrow.

12/1/19

Paraded in clean fatigue dress at 9.30 am. Assisted in cleaning up mess-room and then walked out towards Ober-Hausen taking my haversack, water bottle carrier and bandoleer etc to the sores for exchange for infantry equipment, and was also able to get a small piece of soap for washing purposes from the Quarter Master, this very necessary commodity cannot be obtained easily by the civilians and for this reason they will not do our washing. Owing to a rather heavy fall of snow during the night the surrounding hills with their crests cloaked with dense forests are all mantled in dazzling whiteness and present an envious to the eye of a punter. This being a Sunday and the people strictly Roman Catholics there has been an endless procession of worshipers passing to and from the different churches since early morning. On duty in signal office at 1 pm to 5 pm, but as luck would have it, was released soon after going on duty as owing to things being so slack now it is not necessary to keep on a full staff so we take it in turns to be off duty. Took a stroll up one of the hills with my chum, which was delightfully pleasant, the snow had commenced to thaw but the valleys and trees still retained their white brilliance, came back feeling very hungry and my legs too a little stiff, the effect probably of my riding yesterday afternoon. Wrote a letter to my dear sister Doris after tea.

Spent the evening with a friend at "Hotel Hermanns" where we dined on roast beef, gravy, brussel sprouts and mashed potato, with apple pie smothered in sugar for dessert and two glasses of lager each, all for 4 marks per head. Sent off a card to Mrs Corbett.

13/1/19

Snow still lays upon the ground but it is thawing quickly. On duty 8 am until 1 pm in signal office. After dinner took my washing out together with a piece of soap, as owing to the scarcity of this very necessary item in the fatherland, it is essential to provide the said article for the purpose. I should have mentioned that walking yesterday along a path leading up a neighbouring hill my chum and me came across a small cemetery on the hill side, it has no boundaries and there is no evidence, except the large headstones, of the existence or position of the graves, at one moment the though would pass in ones mind that it was a relic of German barbarism, as some bear recent dates such as 1902, 1905 etc. I decided in my own mind to accept the theory or explanation, that these persons who have found their last resting place like outcasts upon the hill side and beneath the sheltering care of tall and stately fur trees, probably on account of their creed, for this being a Roman Catholic country and naturally only half civilised it may easily be believed that protestants would be refused internment in a churchyard. Attended a lecture on the new procedure for telegraphy from 2 pm to 3 pm. At 6 pm attended a debate in the divisional school on "can women be reasonably expected to give up their jobs to men returning to civilian life from the army". There were many comments upon the subject and some amusement, but at the close by a show of hands the great majority thought that they should. Had supper at the same hotel as heretofore and this time we had, rissoles, mashed potato and apple sauce and for dessert something nearly approaching pancakes in taste and shape and divided up into five hearts with sugar spread over them. On duty at 9 pm until 8 am tomorrow morning.

14/1/19

Off duty at 8 am and after breakfast and a shave and general clean up I pulled my rifle through and pocketing a couple of clips of cartridges, slung my rifle over my shoulders and accompanied by my chum went up into the forest on a shooting expedition. I don't suppose sport of this sort is permitted to a Tommy, although the divisional General was himself out shooting and we had to run the gauntlet of German keepers and British mounted military police. We came up with no one and neither did we see so much as a bird, although it is known that the forest contains both deer and game, and on emerging from the forest we spotted an M.M.P on the lookout and in spite of all our precautions we were forced to pass by him in the end, but fortunately for us he said nothing except to answer our good morning. In the afternoon I took a stroll alone and visited, what appears to be a monumental structure of a Greek type, which has been erected high up on a hill overlooking the town, upon reaching it I found that it had only been built recently and was not yet been completed, owing no doubt to the war, surrounding the main tower shaped body is a ring of arches and looking through the narrow framed windows (which are all broken) of the door, I could see an iron spiral staircase leading up to the roof, I could only imagine that the object for which it was being built was as an observatory. The view from this point is excellent, as it dominates completely the town, and nearly the entire length of the valley, with its winding swift flowing stream curling away into the distance.

A pleasant feature too is that more modern child of man, a train, which comes steaming rapidly down the valley and as it approaches our little station, its warning bell rings out continually, as is its custom and the valley resounds with these plaintive notes, which come floating up through the forest and over the hill tops. As it was my turn to be off duty at 5 pm to 9.30 pm I went with my chum to our usual "rendezvous" where we had supper, similar to those I have mentioned and which sufficiently prove that so far from Germany being in a state of starvation, she is positively abundantly supplied with food stuffs of every kind and in comparison she is I should imagine even better off than we were in England before the war, for, as I knew to my cost it was always a tremendous problem to make both ends meet, and in consequence even little pleasures were totally out of the question for me. Where as here in view of the cheap cost of living I don't think one would find life so hard or so difficult to live or with so much embarrassment or fruitless effort as has been my experience in old Blighty hitherto. While we were dining I noticed that one of the old gentlemen, whose custom it is to sit at one particular table for supper, had brought with him among other books and papers, a German book for learning English, to which he applied himself in a very serious manner. The closing time for hotels here has been altered to 8.30 pm, instead of 9 pm. I hear too that at Cologne an order has been issued forbidding British troops to fraternise with the German people.

15/1/19

Muggy damp weather. Attended lecture in our mess at the station, from 10 am to 11 am. Afterwards studied French for a short time. Handed in paybook with a request for 100 marks for the purpose of visiting Cologne. Also made out an application for my chum and myself for leave of absence from Reveille on the 20th inst to tattoo on the 21st inst to enable us to visit this famous hun city. On duty at signal office at 1 pm until 5 pm. Wrote a letter to Mrs Wright of Sally-Park Birmingham and cards to Miss Weeds and Mlle Renee Bellette. I think I am getting badly fed up with this country already and would like to get a move on, I find for instance that it is a distinct drawback to be totally ignorant of the language and for this reason I would much prefer to be back in France or Belgium. I am desirous of visiting Cologne of course, but after that and the possibility of a visit to Bonn, I am afraid that all interest and pleasure will become entirely exhausted, so far at any rate, as our present position in the country is concerned. One must have a grumble even though there be no legitimate cause and I'm sure that a good grumble never did anyone any harm and it is without doubt an excellent tonic for drooping spirits and further more costs nothing. At the moment the evening is fast drawing in and the crows, who have been all day seeking their food in far away fields are now returning and filling the air and forest with their rauking "bavadge". At 6 pm attended a lecture in our mess room by the mayor, who explained the system adopted by the army for demobilisation and he also expounded his own scheme for releasing the men in the company which is based on points, for instance a pivotal man gets 50 points, a married man gets 5, a ??? man or on compassionate grounds 40 points and 1 point for every 2 months served abroad.

16/1/19

Fine clear morning. On duty 8 am to 1 pm. Wrote a letter to Mrs Taylor at Westcliff on sea. After dinner took a walk to Glef, a little village about 1 1/2 kilometres away.

Along the route I was particularly struck by the fine scenery on all sides. In the valley itself it is nothing but orderliness, fine houses and mansions and the very terrain an absolute specimen of neat arrangement, which is a tribute no one can deny to these methodical Germans. The village of Glef is composed mostly of big black and white houses for the peasants, which are built in the French style of peasant dwellings in many of the small agricultural districts of that country, by the assistance of mud and plaster, but here they have the additional advantage, and especially so in appearance of whitewash on the outside walls and the wooden structure beams tarred. There is nothing of especial interest to be seen, except the old church with its slate tower, which is a common feature with German village churches and when I visited on horseback the village of Ober Haussen last Saturday afternoon I noticed that there too the small church sported a pinnacle tower of the same description. Looking along the valley and comparing mentally the work that man has achieved down in this lovely spot, with the unchanging grandure of damenature, I feel myself compelled to admit that she is still unbeaten and dwells supreme and radiantly defiant in the midst of her beautifully tinted hills and in the deep fastnesses of her majestic forests. At 6 pm had our rum ration and accompanied by two friends went out for a moonlight stroll until 8.30 pm.

17/1/19

As it was my turn to be off duty last night I only worked from 9 pm until 11.30 pm, so have the day to myself till 5 pm this evening. Walked as far as the quartermaster's stores and obtained some soft soap for washing purposes and also a set of brass buttons to replace those, which have come off my jerkin. Studied French until midday. I cannot make up my mind to tackle German and I am only sorry that here one is placed at such a great disadvantage for keeping up one's French studies. It is a beautifully sunny day and I am sincerely hoping that it will continue fine for my projected visit to Cologne in three days time. Don't feel quite up to the proper mark lately and after dinner today lay down and slept until tea time, when to my astonishment on looking out of the window, I saw that it was snowing rather heavily. On duty at 5 pm to 9 pm. wrote a letter to my dear sister Doris and cards to my cousin Isabel and Mlle Danielle Hangard.

18/1/19

Snow lies thickly upon the ground this morning. At dinner time owing to the heat of the sun the roads were fearfully slushy. At parade this morning the Sergeant Major informed me that the mounted paper chase, which had been arranged for this afternoon was cancelled until tomorrow. On duty 1 pm to 5 pm. I gather from reports of men who have visited such places as Cologne and Bonn that in spite of British official air reports, neither of these places were ever bombed and there is not the slightest evidence, so far as even a brick knocked down that these reports were anything but fictitious and merely sent out for public consumption at home. This is a very terrible thing and I have repeatedly touched upon this shameful subject. To me there is proof positive that right from the beginning until the close of hostilities, there have been persons in high authority deliberately turning aside the swords of justice of my countrymen, along the entire German frontier the inhabitants have never tested the bitter wine of war and have carried on in quite the usual way, with business as usual the keynote in the daily life of the people. What a contrast even now to the conditions which prevail in England and France.

While on leave a few weeks ago, I could not fail to remark the obvious strain, which the stress of war has brought, not only into the commercial world, but also into the homelife of every citizen in the country. How truly shocking this is especially to one, who is prouder of his country than of all else yet my country's most evil enemies are still at liberty and at large to work even more harm against the best country in the world. France has shot better men than these disreputable devils and I trust that even yet they will be brought to answer for their many crimes, at the bar of a peoples justice. Became dull again in the afternoon and more snow fell. Wrote a letter to my dear sister Gladys and a card to my father also posted a pretty coloured card to my own dear little boy who is always in my thoughts. Another heavy snow fall in the evening.

19/1/19

On duty 8 am to 1 pm. Nice morning but snow still lies thickly upon the ground. No mounted paper chase again this afternoon on account of the bad weather and the hills being still deeply covered in snow. Received 50 marks pay in the morning, but as I did not think this sum sufficient to visit Cologne tomorrow I asked for a further amount and the Major kindly increased it to 150 marks. Had supper at the Hermanns Hotel. Got my pass for Cologne late in the evening.

20/1/19

Got up at 5.45 am and with my chum got down to the station in nice time to catch the 6.38 am train for Cologne. Changed at Call, where there was a 10 minute wait. Very cold journey and the train was packed with soldiers and civilians. Arrived at Cologne at 9.30 am. Reported at the Dom Hotel, where my chum and I were given a form to take to the Hotel Zum Storch about 9 minutes sharp walk from the cathedral, where we were shown to a bedroom with two beds for which by the way we pay nothing, being one of the little items which Jerry pays out of his own pocket. Had a wash and a shave and then started off to explore the principal streets and places of interest. Discovering the Hohenzollern bridge we passed along it and over to the other side, pausing for a moment at the now historical spot, where General Plumer received the British troops as they passed over the Rhine to occupy and take possession of German territory. This bridge is of massive proportions. On one side runs the railway and on the other the road, the width of the Rhine at this point would be I should imagine at least three times that of the Thames at London Bridge. Turning to the right my chum and me walked along the bank of the Rhine as far as the suspension bridge, which we crossed and overtook a battalion of Coly's (Coldstreams) doing garrison duties in the city. Both civilians and French poilus take a keen interest in our military ceremonies such as changing guard and paying compliments. Double guard are placed at each end of the Ho Henzollern Bridge and at intervals on it. They stand on each side of the road and opposite and as in the city, where guardsmen are posted, one on each side of the main entrance to some of the public buildings and do nothing else but stand and salute officers the whole day long. These thoroughly trained soldiers of old England carry on each movement in perfect unison, for instance a Major comes along and the soldiers on each side of the road or doorway come to the present at the same time and back to the slope absolutely in time with each other. Made our way back to the cathedral and went inside, but as mass was in progress, no one is allowed to walk about and so we waited in the rear until it was all over and the congregation, which I thought was an unusually large one, had dispersed.

If I could speak with authority upon the architectural merits, which this great church undoubtedly possesses, I should very probably soon fill a book, as it is I must perforce limit my remarks to a few simple observations. To speak of such a building just in ordinary common phraseology could not do justice even to the steps, which lead up to the main entrance. Comparing the whole thing to any French cathedral I should say that in my opinion that the latter is far more beautiful, more elaborate and more exquisite externally than the Dom. On the other hand I prefer the interior of the Dom for very sound reasons, in France there is far too much obvious attention paid to paltry finery, with the sole object it would appear to create a gorgeous impression. This 6 1/2 d bazaar trumpery is always conspicuously displayed both in the body of French churches and also in the little chapels, which encircle the buildings and which are a peculiar feature in all catholic churches on the continent. Here although the creed does not differ, there is a total lack of booby ornaments and instead we have simply the glorious majesty of mans great handiwork, a symbol of his triumph, which he has erected in honour and in glorification to the Christian God. In its simplicity there is a powerful impressiveness beyond the crude devices of man to change or to alter. This is indeed a holy shrine, which is an estimable credit to the common sense of the Roman Catholics in Southern Germany. At midday we adjourned for dinner at the Hotel Zum Post not far from the cathedral. The catering arrangements are controlled by the church army people, who provide meals for soldiers on a visit to Cologne out of army rations at 2 marks per head for dinner and 1 mark per head for breakfast and tea. The dinner is of a most fearful description and is merely stewed meat with gravy to greasy to swallow and a slice of bread, following this there is served up an unknown and unnameable dish of boiled biscuits and raisins with a goodly mixture of hair etc neatly interwoven with the said biscuits and raisins. After this sumptuous repast returned to our billet for a wash and clean up, purchasing on the way a "Guillermo Hoppe Solingen" razor for 14 marks and a map of Cologne. Later took a tram from the cathedral and visited the Zoological gardens (by the way travelling in trams, trains etc is free of charge for British soldiers) which are extremely interesting. The inmates, which are there in captivity include, Lions, tigers, leopards, wolves, foxes, camels, deer, bears of different species, birds, fishes and reptiles of all sorts. Tea at 4 pm at the Zum Post. Spent the evening in a large hotel which was crammed to the doors with Tommies and Fraulines and Fraus who have lost their husbands in the war, all fraternising to their hearts content in spite of G.R.O no something forbidding same. Wine at 11 marks at least per small bottle was being drunk like water, everybody appeared crazily happy and drinking, smoking, singing and embraces were the order of the night. Only at intervals when the string band struck up a popular song the tune would be taken up and go swelling in volume until it had reached the furthest corners of the halls. This went on until 8.30 pm, when everybody dispersed to their different dwellings as all the streets must be cleared by 9 pm. I have never before seen life carried to such altitudes of sensual pleasure. The Colognians certainly love a Bohemian life. One might see smartly dressed women in hotels ogling British officers with a "sang froid" obviously acquired at an earl date in their worldly careers.

21/1/19

Spent nearly all my time today riding about the city in trams of buying picture postcards or souvenirs, have got together a collection of over 80 postcards, but even then I failed to get a number of views I wished to have. Bought a silver broach, black enamelled with hand painted roses for 33 marks.

Went again into the cathedral and this time the organ was playing and a few priests chanting, which had a beautiful effect in this lofty edifice, I like too the rich deep and harmonious intonations of the Catholic bells, which ring for a short period at certain intervals during the day, and send sweeping over this beautiful city their mournful reverberations. Cologne like all German towns is remarkable for its stately buildings, no matter whatever else the Germans may excel in I don't think they have anything finer or better to show to the world than their houses. Even the poor are well housed and all public buildings, shops, hotels etc are built solidly and have the appearance of immense strength and durability. The German people both in manners and physiognomy resemble the English more closely than does any other nationality, I have so far met with and I may say that I think it may probably be for this reason, especially that the Germans themselves treat us everywhere in such a cordial manner. In a competition of beauty, I am strongly of the opinion that for pretty girls and women la belle France comes an easy first on the list of nations. Caught the 4 pm train back to Scheiden where we arrived at 7.30 pm. Snow still covers the hills and fields and it is considerably colder than at Cologne, which probably does not lie so high up as we do here.

22/1/19

Sharp frosty morning. On duty at 8 am to 1 pm. Received a letter from my dear sister Dot. Spent the afternoon writing etc and for a short while went up the hill facing the post office to watch the youngsters enjoying themselves tobogganing. Despatched all my Cologne postcards and a map of the city by registered post to my dear sister Dot to whom I have also written a separate letter. As I did not jot down many notes during my recent trip to Cologne I shall have to record some of my observations as they occur to me. There is for instance unquestionable evidence that Germany was particularly of leather, all the leather straps to the railway carriage windows had been cut away. High class shops have nothing else on view in their windows but boots and shoes with bottoms made of wood and uppers of paper, this must not be taken to mean that the people have no leather footwear, on the contrary almost all have, although they may be old ones for the part. I have heard that one family cut up the horses harness to make and mend boots. Fat too was scarce and some friend told me that when they came here first they exchanged the fat after cooking for potatoes. Food even in Cologne is not exceptionally dear, in one big restaurant I had soup and a dish of mashed potatoes and roast beef and greens for 4½ marks. There are no signs of poverty of hunger and business goes on just as usual. I might mention a novel device for road cleaning which I saw, it is a water cart and road sweeper combined and driven like a motor car. Quite a useful machine I am sure and which leaves the smooth well tarred roads beautifully glossy and clean. On duty at 9 pm until 8 am tomorrow.

23/1/19

Not much work to do during the night. After breakfast and clean up, my chum and I borrowed from the postmaster a coupe of nice toboggans and went up the hillside, where we enjoyed the morning tobogganing in a blinding snowstorm, I sprained my left leg slightly in shooting a bank, but it did not prevent me from continuing this exhilarating sport. In the afternoon I was merely an interested spectator of the young lads and lasses of the town, who are perfectly practised in the art of tobogganing. A number of British officer were there too either taking part in this old time winter sport or skiing. On duty at 5 pm to 9 pm.

I have yet something else to add in respect to the scarcity of certain articles and I must not fail to include chocolate, which has totally disappeared from the shops, which recalls to my memory the remark of a Belgian soldier with whom I had a few words in a station waiting room, when on our way up here, he said "One may have a German woman for a stick of chocolate". This is how he expressed his disdain for one half of the nation, which had for so long oppressed his compatriots, another expression , which was made use of by a French woman in speaking of her sister in Germany, was "one may have a woman in Germany for a morsel of bread". I cannot confirm the latter statement as being true, although the implied interpretation may be well found, with regard to chocolate there is a little more to be said, and as in the old saying "once aboard the lugger and the girl is mine" might easily be expressed in another way, such as "give a piece of chocolate to a girl and she is yours". While tram riding at Cologne I remember passing a large square choked up with German automobiles of every size and description and the following telegram from the 2nd army which came through to all units this evening, throw light upon the matter t begins, " large number signwriters required at once by D D S and T 2nd army for numbering large fleet of motor transport ceded by the Germans under terms armistice aaa Good opportunity for signwriters not employed as such to get practice prior to returning to civilian life aaa wire soon as possible numbers and names of suitable men aaa urgent aaa addressed groups". I might add here that all these lorries etc have iron wheels, the few bicycles too that one sees about have no tyres, and they make a great rattle as they pass over stone paved streets. Rubber must have been terribly scarce. Received a card from my friends at Saint Riquier and a letter from an old soldier at Warwick, who gave me the welcome news that my own little boy is well and happy.

24/1/19

Not a very good night owing to a cold, which I have somehow picked up. After parade at 9.30 am a friend and I borrowed a toboggan and we spent an enjoyable morning on the hillside, coming down singly and together and sometimes lying face downwards on the sledge. It is a very exciting and exhilarating pastime. Received a letter from my brother Harry. On duty 1 pm to 5 pm. Replied to two letters I received today.

25/1/19

Dry fine morning with snow still covering the ground. I hear that at Cologne no snow has fallen, which I presume is proof positive that we are at a far more higher altitude than Cologne, although it is at no great distance away. My turn to be off duty in the morning so spent practically the whole day tobogganing on the adjacent hillside and am now quite good at the game, am all aches and bruises it is true, which I got in practising tricky descents and on one occasion having failed to turn a corner at a rapid pace in a face downward position and blinded with snow could not distinguish the brink in time and throwing myself free was shot over the bank, but fell on my back and shoulders, but received no hurt on another occasion when shooting a bank with my chum, the shock to the bottom of my spine was rather severe. And very like the sensation one has when one's feet go from under one in descending some slippery steps. Received a letter from Mr Kendrick to which I have replied, also have written to my dear little sister Dot. I was particularly glad to hear from the guardians of my little boy the welcome news that he is very happy and in good health and that his little cheeks are getting fatter and redder.

I feel that at present I am pulled two ways for I am not particularly anxious to be demobilised yet while on the other hand the distant small voice of the little boy I love so well, is ever calling me back to him. I realise that as the days pass by my little love is getting older and that very soon I shall have no more the exquisite pleasure of his pretty baby ways and that I shall no longer be able to love and to guard him as I loved to do in the days gone by. His image both asleep and at play is fixed for ever in my memory and he is never entirely absent from my thoughts, poor little Ducky I have only you to love and I am afraid that you have only me.

26/1/19

Still freezing and inclined to snow. Have not done much during the day except to take a short walk. Towards 4 pm snowed heavily for a while and we expect to have more before tomorrow morning. I have a rider to add to some of my previous remarks on Germans houses and then I think I shall have quite exhausted all that I can say upon this or any other subject which might be a theme of interest to German admirers. I have said in speaking of he houses in Cologne that they have the appearance of solidity and durability. This equally applies to houses in all other parts of Germany, but upon a closer inspection one is greatly surprised to find that their merits exist only in appearance. The fact that they are build fairly tall with spacious rooms or a goodly number of smaller ones and fantastic designs covering the whole of the front of a building or in other cases lavishly painted over, all this has the tendency to impress strongly the imagination of the stranger and the blind who won't see. In a flat house or a hotel the partitioning walls between rooms are often found to be so thin that one can hear easily every movement of another person in an adjoining room. The civil post office, where we are billeted, which of course is a public building has a very good appearance both outside and in, yet I find that some at least of the inside walls upstairs are in reality nothing but plaster carefully painted over and although it is quite a new building these walls are giving way in places and one can look through the chinks into the next apartment.

27/1/19

Very wintry looking this morning. Having heard several reports that deer had been seen yesterday by a number of our fellows including my chum, I decided to go out again this morning to try my luck with my rifle and accompanied by my chum we set off in search of our quarry. We discovered many tracks across the snow, where they had passed from one wood to another but did not meet with any of the gentlemen themselves and in the end we were forced to acknowledge a fruitless hunt. Had a pot at a target on a tree from a kneeling position at 50 yards and made a good shot, which also passed through the trees and out at the opposite side. On duty at 1 pm to 5 pm. Am feeling in the best of health now and I trust that this great blessing will not again desert me. I hear that typhoid fever has broken out among the troops at Eurskirchen and has claimed already a number of victims. I do not think that any fever would find this place an ideal hunting ground, it is to high up and healthy for the cordial reception of such an unwelcome guest. Received a registered letter this afternoon from my dear sister Doris enclosing notebooks, pencils, holders etc.*** **Also included some sheets not in a diary ***

Diary Number 11
28/1/19

Weather still cold but fine and healthy. On duty 8 am to 1 pm. The horizon blue of the Poilus has made its appearance here and at the moment 10 am several batteries of 75's are passing by. The Germans last night had got the wind up properly and an engine from whom three of us went to beg some coal for our billet fire was quite pressing in his eagerness to know if it were true that the French were coming here to take our place and if they were going to Cologne to take over from the British. I told him that it was not true and he appeared greatly relieved and remarked that "Angleterre soldat was tres bon but that Francais soldat was nix gut", no love is ever lost between these ancient antagonists. Lately we have been kept busily employed while on duty at the signal office, writing up German slips for the benefit of the security officer. No trust is evidently placed by the powers that be that all telegrams are duly copied by the civil staff and this check on the Germans has been adapted for the purpose of recording each and every telegram sent over the German wires in the territory occupied by us. This afternoon a friend and I went tobogganing. I received an official form from the post office at Birmingham endorsed by the labour exchange, which qualifies me in the eyes of the military as a "slip man". Have handed it into the orderly room this evening. On duty at 9 pm until 8 am tomorrow morning. A thought for today "nothing is wrong and nothing right in this world, or, all is right"

29/1/19

After leaving off work this morning at 8 am, swept out our room and cleaned the stove and made a good fire, washed shaved and general brush up. Afterwards went to hotel Hermanns where I spent the morning drinking coffee and talking in French to one of the daughters. The Germans will have it that the civilian population is in urgent need of food stuffs and they say that the cause of what is commonly called Bolshivison, which has made itself apparent in different parts of Germany is directly in consequence of this need of food. They say that America has plenty but will not supply them. I pointed out this morning that we ourselves are short of food and that for sometime we have not received our full rations, in England this would hardly be believed, but it is nevertheless true, at the barracks at Eueskirchen a few days before we arrived, the troops there had been in a state of revolt, as they were starving, several weeks have passed since then and still things are not yet normal, there cannot be the slightest excuse for this state of things as we have full control of all railways and the lines are clear of all German traffic except passenger trains and the lines in Belgium are by no means so heavily worked as they are in France. Received a nice letter from Mrs. Taylor of Westcliff-on-sea, to which I have replied this afternoon. On duty 5 pm to 9 pm. A thought for today "all that may be wrong for some to do is right when others do it"

30/1/19

Paraded at 9.30 am this morning for pay, when I received 40 marks. Afterward took out my rifle into the forest my chum accompanying me. We had terrible hard luck for coming upon a deer scraping for food beneath some low fur trees.

I had almost got within sighting distance when a German coming from the opposite direction at this moment caused my quarry to bolt and I only saw him for a fraction of a second. This was most disappointing and during the rest of the morning nothing living mad its appearance. In lieu of live targets my chum and I fired off ten rounds at a target on a tree, which we hit a number of times. Received a letter from Mrs Wright of Selly-Park Birmingham, to say that she had sent my civvy suits to be cleaned as per my request. Snow still covers the forest, the hills and the valleys. On duty 1 pm to 5 pm. Had a good supper at hotel Hermanns. A thought for today "In all the painful trials in life, as in trials of strength, patience and endurance point out the victor"

31/1/19

Extremely cold night. My chum and I had arranged to get up at 5.30 am this morning and to go out deer hunting. I woke up at 5.40 am but it was so cold and pitch dark that I decided not to disturb my pal and instead I rolled over and went to sleep again. On duty 8 am to 1 pm. Had a lovely hot bath at the Schleidenhotel at 2.30 pm. Afterwards proceeded to watch the skaters and sliders on the lake behind the Schloss (German for castle), all is now bound tightly in the grip of frost and everybody appears to be making the most of it and indulging in all manner of winter sports to their hearts content. The civilians of the junior community are particularly clever in this branch of athletics. After tea adjourned with my chum to the hotel Hermanns where we partook of a right good meal and came away abundantly satisfied. A thought for today "Man is the greater of all animals and woman the greatest"

1/2/19

On duty all night and left off at 8 am. After breakfast and a clean up, pulled through my rifle and accompanied by a friend took the war path into the forest in search of anything to shoot. Good fortune still deserts me and nothing living presented itself for a shot except a few beautiful squirrels, which presumably had smelt powder as they had no sooner appeared than they vanished out of sight in an instant. To compensate this unsatisfactory state of things we, put in some good target practice before returning home. After dinner my chum and I with two other friends went to spend the afternoon on the lake sliding and we had some excellent fun especially on the biggest slide, which runs from one bank to almost the opposite side and there were many spills en route. One of my friends hurt himself rather badly, at least he got a bad shaking up. Received a card from Mlle Renee Bellett of Saint Riquier to which I have replied. On duty 5 pm to 9 pm. A thought for today "Woman alone has the power to influence man's destiny"

2/2/19

Paraded at 9.30 am and again at 11.10 am for church parade. The service was held in the protestant church, which is a comparatively new building. The pulpit and steps leading up to it are beautifully painted in white and gold. On the walls on each side of the church are affixed a number of cardboard plaques encircled in wreaths of holly, with the names and towns and villages printed thereon of soldiers fallen in the war, at least this is my assumption. My chum who went to buy some skates at Hellenthal this morning has brought me back a pair for 3 1/2 marks, they have presumably been made for dumping into England as they are marked "Sheffield pattern, club skate".

On duty 1 pm to 5 pm. Received a nice letter from my friend Ronald South, who is at home in Cambridge demobilised. Sent off a pretty card to my own little sweetheart at Warwick, although I am very far away from his dear little presence he is ever present in my thoughts and the old adage which is well expressed in French "loin des yeuse loin du coeur" is not true in my deep and sincere affection for my little one, who is all in all to me and he alone has never done me wrong, I pray that God will help me to do all I can for him and not ever to fail him in all that I should do on his behalf, in his best interests and in his future welfare. I want to love my boy in my own way and as in everything else I shall brook no interference whatsoever. I may be a savage and uncontrollable but in genuine tenderness and honest love I have left still enough and to spare for the little mite who alone remains to me shining brilliantly like an exquisite jewel of unrivalled magnificence out of the blackened debris of a mutilated past. Spent evening at the hotel Hermanns. <u>A thought for today</u> "The devil is well served on earth by his high priestesses and sorceresses.

3/2/19

Still freezing. The weather here is certainly far more consistent than in dear old Blighty. On duty 8 am to 1 pm. Received a nice letter from my dear sister Gladys enclosing a "church army gazette", poor dear girl she is always trying to think of something that may do me good. I seem to be the only lost soul in the family, yet in spite of all to the contrary I have been the recipient of many gifts and favours, which I should endeavour never to forget and the greatest of these is in the life of my own sweet little boy. A nice letter also arrived from Miss Weeds of Birmingham. Telegraphs, who inform me that several men in this branch have already been demobolised . Went to the lake in the afternoon for a slide. After tea scrounged some briquettes out of a truck standing in the railway siding on the right of the station, these brickets make a splendid fire but burn away very quickly. Had supper at the Hermanns with several friends. My turn to be off duty tonight so got down to it soon after 10 pm. Replied to the two letters I received this morning. <u>a thought for today</u> "Life's pleasures are not measured solely in a measure of happiness, but rather by those achievements well accomplished no matter how small they may be"

4/2/19

After breakfast I cleaned out our room and made the fire etc and when I was ready, went out along with my rifle into the forest. I did not unfortunately have any more luck than on previous occasions and returned at dinner time empty handed. Received a registered packet from my dear sister Doris enclosing Hugos German grammar and other books. Spent the afternoon on the lake sliding. The skates which my chum got for me are to small and I cannot get them on my army boots, for this reason I have sold them and a good thing too as my customer in putting them on had the misfortune to break off first a nut and then one of the heel clips, they are only made of cast iron and like a good many other things made in Germany are of inferior quality. I hear that my name has come through for the post office claiming me as a pivotal man. Rations are still very short, it would be interesting to know who is responsible for this abominable state of things.

On duty 5 pm to 9 pm. Wrote a long letter to my dear little sis Dot. <u>A thought for today</u> "In the wintry silence of the forest one is brought face to face with one's self and clearer than in the mirror we do see ourselves as we really are, poor little perishable creatures of circumstance, pitiable samples of frail humanity, savages without the semblance of dignity or pride and horrible hypocrites majesty of shame".

5/2/19

Weather still continues cold and frosty. Spent morning after parade at 9.30 am at the hotel Hermanns. On duty 1 pm to 5 pm. The disgraceful order which was issued a few days ago to the effect that all ranks would in future pay their fares when travelling by train or tram in the territory occupied by us, was stated in orders last evening to have been suspended. I consider this order a down right insult to the British Tommy and also to the British army, and those responsible should be dealt with in a very severe manner, an order of this description is calculated to lower British prestige in the eyes of the enemy, and besides we are not here to defray local expenses or taxation, also this order would not have effected officers in the same way as it would the common soldier as the former have it in their power to procure "duty passes" when on pleasure bent. I was sorry to see posted up in orders that the shooting of game with service rifles is strictly forbidden. This now puts the cap on my own little exploits and deprives me of an excellent recreation and one which appeals to me. Wrote to Mr and Mrs Kendrick. Had supper at the Hermanns. Drew rum ration at 6 pm, also a Dixie full of English beer, a barrel of which had some how found its way down our way and it was distributed free among the troop, not being able to drink it all at once my chum and I have bottled it for future use. <u>A thought for today</u> "On the hills man imagines himself supreme, he can raise himself aloft to the summit of the highest peak, but there he must stop. He cannot go an inch higher and he must be wary of his footing, for nature claims at all times undisputed sovereignty over all mankind"

6/2/19

Snow fell pretty heavily last evening and this morning it lies several inches deep upon the ground. On duty 8 am to 1 pm. I would like to make few notes upon female dress in Germany at the present moment. In the first place I have been struck everywhere with the universal simplicity displayed. The great majority of women wear dresses and blouses most decidedly out of date, and one can easily imagine an old English scene when feminine nature had no particular cut and was designed rather for comfort than for show. I have been told that cloth is very scarce and dear too, but this of course would not account for the popular styles which are in vogue at present and it is obvious that although the dresses are of old pattern, they represent the exact style which was worn before the war. Still as a dress never made a good woman any better I don't think that the German women are in any way losers thereby. The sun made its first appearance for weeks after 9 am this morning and its beautiful warm rays are most welcome after the many days of cold and snow that we have experienced lately. In the afternoon I went with a friend to the lake, but owing to a thick coating of snow on the ice it was useless to attempt either to slide or to skate. Have received a particularly unwelcome letter from Miss Cummins telling me of the sad news of Mrs Roberts death and of Dorothy's recent illness which was of a serious character and that she is not yet recovered.

This Southport family were awfully good friends to me during my stay in hospital there and since have always treated me with the utmost kindness. I feel that me too I have lost a good and sincere friend and now I am not a little concerned in Dorothy's condition, for she is an admirable type of the best and truest in English womanhood and I hope sincerely that she will shortly recover her health and strength and her bright girlish spirit. A thought for today " In the valleys man is free and there he lives and dies and nature to whom he owes his life nourishes him with parental care upon her bosom by the living spring, which gushes from her breast, she suckles him and by the fruits of her ample nourishment, ungrudgingly, unceasingly and for all time".

7/2/19

On duty all night, finished at 8 am. After cleaning up our billet and myself too, was given fatigue in the cook house pealing potatoes owing to one of the cooks being off on account of inoculation. Spent rest of the morning at the Hermanns, where I drank coffee and did a little studying of German until midday. The sun is shining brilliantly again today but the wind is piercingly cold and the best place is obviously by a good fire. In the afternoon went with several friends tobogganing but unfortunately for me I hurt the bottom of my spine for the second time in shooting a bank with a friend behind me and had to give up and return to the billet to lie down, but found little or no relief even then. A thought for today "What would life be without wine and women? and what would be a soldiers life without either."

8/2/19

Terribly cold night and piercingly out of doors first thing this morning. The water in the basin was frozen to the bottom and the rapidly flowing stream, which passes through the valley is frozen hard enough to skate upon. Paraded at 9.30 am and after doing a short fatigue cleaning out the mess room, three of us out of the same billet commenced to swab it out and quite a thorough spring cleaning did we give it. Rest of morning I spent at the Hermanns. On duty at 1 pm until 5 pm. A few remarks upon woman's life in Germany may not be out of place here. As in every other country except England the womenfolk take quite a back place, and do not receive either the same amount of respect or homage as they do in our own country. A woman in Germany appears to be brought up from childhood in one particular sphere, she is educated both to please and amuse, (singing, dancing and music) but above all she has bred into her to a very high degree the duties of wifehood. A frau although she may not be to a man on account of her training an ideal pal, she is on the other hand an ideal wife. To bear children and to take an especial interest in her home would appear to be the principal vocation in a German woman's life. German women as well as French are rather fond of giving their opinion upon the chivalrous treatment always accorded them by the men from Britain here in Germany, this type of courtesy does not seem to be quite understood, at least it takes time. A certain proprietress told me that she liked the soldiers very much as they are much more noble than the German soldiers. The afternoon turned out simply lovely and it is quite warm and pleasant in the sunshine. Spent evening at the Hermanns but was alone as all my friends were on duty. A thought for today "The things, which seem to matter most to us are not those we have, but those we want"

9/2/19

Still freezing hard. On duty 8 am to 1 pm. was on parade for pay at 10 am. When the OC Major Reid addressed to us a few words before his departure today for England to be demobilised. He was a very popular officer with the men of this headquarters and of the company, and all the men regret his loss. The sun again shone brilliantly towards midday and during the afternoon. Sent off a nice card to my darling little boy. Received a registered letter from my dear is Dot, which contained excellent news and I feel once more, more satisfied with things in general and I can hope that my affairs, which at present are in such a chaos, will eventually straighten themselves out. Have sent off a letter in reply this evening. Spent afternoon and evening at the Hermanns where I played a couple of games of chess and won both. Several of us in the billet secured a couple of sacks of briquettes out of a railway truck. On duty 9 pm to 8 am. <u>A thought for today</u> "absolute purity of mind and of soul exists only in the grave"

10/2/19

After leaving off duty at 8 am cleaned myself up and went out for a walk. Beautifully sunny weather and the pure white snow had quite a dazzling effect. Took the path leading to the lake but after a few slides came away as I was the only being present, and went to spend the rest of the morning at the Hermanns. After dinner went again to the lake with my chum who took his skates. It was surprising that although the sun was decidedly warm yet the snow and ice remained crisp and firm. Among the trees upon the hill slopes, where the sun has taken off their silvery mantle, the famished feathered world flock there in their thousands and may be seen o heard busily occupied in delving among the dead leaves for the food which has for so long been denied to them. On duty 5 pm to 9 pm. wrote a letter to my dear sis Doris. <u>A thought for today</u> "Good women there are even on earth but am personally only acquainted with a very limited number among them being Jeanne D'arc and my dear grandmother of beloved memory."

11/2/19

A bit nippy first thing this morning but afterwards delightfully warm and beautiful in the open air. Certainly one could hardly choose a more charming spot for a holiday even in winter and in summer I'm sure one could not easily imagine a more glorious or picturesque little place or more suitable or idealistic to those who specialise to those picnic jaunts when the balmy summer weather comes along. Went to the lake with my chum shortly after breakfast and afterwards had a short walk. On duty 1 pm to 5 pm. Wrote out an application for the territorial bounty and one months special leave to which I became entitled on the 28th February last, upon completion of five years unbroken service, not including 3 years and 118 days in the Denbighshire (Hassers) yeomanry in which regiment I enlisted on the 25th September 1908. Received a letter from the dear old dad who enclosed me a newspaper cutting which states that the postmaster general "has now decided not only to grant full civil pay in future with no deductions that have been made in the past". This concession should bring me in quite a handsome sum of money when I am paid up eventually. The action of the department was most illegal when it was decided to rob married men in the service in order to pay war bonuses to civilian clerks, personally I have several other accounts to settle up and I am steadily working to get back every penny which has wrongfully been taken from me and I do not intend to fail in my endeavours.

Was glad to hear too from the dad that my own little boy was well and that he is going to school. I do want to see him again and I wonder constantly how distant still is that happy time to which I look forward to with so much pleasure and hope. Bought a pair of skates for 2 mark's, but they are not the best sort. In the evening went to the Hermanns for supper and played a couple of games of chess both of which ended favourably for me. A thought for today "Love which is not unselfish, cannot possibly be true or sincere."

12/2/19

Weather positively most idealistic, it is really a shame to be indoors even for a moment. I am personally enjoying almost perfect health, and am feeling fitter both in body and mind than has been my lot for a considerable time. On duty 8 am to 1 pm. Wrote a letter to my dear father. Went on to the lake in the afternoon with my skates, to the surprise of the others and still more to myself, I did not do at all badly and did not have a single fall the whole time. I spent evening at the Hermanns with my friend playing cards and after supper my chum a friend and myself went for a moonlight skate on the pond. It was bitterly cold to start with but after a few rounds one's blood got circulating and we spent a most enjoyable hour or more on the ice by the light of the full moon and a perfectly clear sky. When passing by the old church by the castle on our way back to the skating area in the afternoon I noticed that the door of the former was open and of course I took the opportunity to go inside. I have on many occasions previously gone there especially to have a look round but each time the doors have been close and locked. The chief object of interest is an old black marble tomb with a figure of a knight in armour in a niche in the wall behind it. The description as given on the postcard photographs of the tomb is as follows " Grabmal der sybilla von Hohenzollern in der pfarrkirche zu schleiden" so the occupant would be I presume a member of the famous house of Hohenzallerns. A thought for today " No love is purer than that we bear for our children."

13/2/19

Summer like weather continues. Had an enjoyable morning skating on the pond and am rapidly becoming more and more proficient in the art. When returning to the billet had the misfortune to slip and fell, my right hand striking my skates, which made a gash of over an inch long in the palm between the thumb and forefinger. The postmaster's wife kindly dressed it for me but it was obvious that she did not like the sight of blood. Went skating again in the afternoon with my chum and I can say made still a slight improvement, which I hope to maintain. On duty 5 pm to 9 pm. A thought for today "The greatest gift of the gods to us poor mortels is a little child."

14/2/1
Big changes in the weather today, it is dull and cloudy and a thaw has set in, which to me at least is very disappointing as it will put an end to all the winter sports which up to the present, I have much enjoyed and was looking forward to becoming an expert on the ice very shortly. Spent the whole morning skating with my chum and progressed still more before finishing up at midday. I wrote a short note last night on a pretty postcard and sent it off to my dear little boy, also posted a picture postcard to Mrs Taylor. On duty today at 1 pm to 5 pm.

Wrote a letter to my dear sister Doris and enclosed her a small German calander a souvenir from Cologne. Had a nice warm bath at the Schleiden Hotel in the evening and afterwards went to the Hermanns for supper, but as my chum sappier Whitest a jock and other friends were all on duty, I was alone throughout the evening. My hand is healing up nicely. Thaw continued all today and to say the very least I am distinctly disappointed over it as perhaps I shall not again have such a favourable opportunity to make myself efficient in such winter sports as are loved so much by occidentals. There have been many rumours of late concerning the fate of this division (the 22nd), it is said that it is intended to break it up and send it back to England for a triumphal march into one of the large cities in Yorkshire this being a territorial West Riding Division, as yet it is difficult to say what may be done eventually but in any case I imagine that before another four or five months have elapsed, all those who are eligible for discharge from the army will be back at home and will have resumed once more their duties of citizenship. A thought for today " War is the natural consequence of natural causes aided and abetted by two great forces, power and ambition."

15/2/19

A little snow during the night, but the thaw which set in yesterday still persists in having its own way. On duty 8 am to 1 pm. My name and that also of my chum were up on orders last night for the visit to the "Urfttalsperre" on Sunday. We shall go with a party by motor lorry starting from the signal office at 9.30 am, that is of course if thaw precautions are not issued before then, which would cause the ride to be cancelled as motor lorries are not permitted under such conditions to run on the roads. Had a walk over to the lake after dinner but no one was there and it looked quite sorry for itself. The ice is almost all covered in water which would make skating almost impossible. I am personally deeply disappointed that the change in the weather should take place just at this time, as was looking forward to several more weeks of frost to enable me to finish of what had so well begun, still "c'est la vie" as the French say and there's an end on it. Had a game of solo and a nice supper at the Hermanns in the evening. On duty 9 pm until 8 am tomorrow morning. A thought for today "War can only be successfully waged when it is conducted by the best elements in a country (Soldiers and sailors) and properly supported by the common people (rich and poor alike)."

16/2/19

Left off work at 8 am. Had breakfast and clean up ready for the lorry trip to Urfttalsperre near Germund (Eiffel). To start off with much precious time was lost in vainly endeavouring to obtain the necessary special pass from the people at "a" branch to permit us to run the lorry in view of last night orders to adopt thaw precautions. In the end the officer in charge of the party decided to go without one and to risk the consequences and we started off finally about 11.50 am instead of 9.30 am, the time originally fixed to start. Our road led via Glef and Gemund which runs through the beautiful valley of which I have already so often spoken. Passing through Gemund the road begins to rise considerably and winds serpentine fashion to the summit of the surrounding hills, where we made a sharp turn to the left and shortly afterwards we descended from the lorry at a wayside hotel and provided ourselves with stout sticks for the purpose of assisting us in the long march down into the valley again, we started off on foot by a woodland path which led gradually down to our destination.

The weather was not of the brightest, being dull and thawing which tended greatly to make walking both difficult and uncomfortable. On the other hand such slight inconvenience was easily counterbalanced by the magnificent scenery through which we passed and as we moved along the landscape continually changed in aspect as new and fresh scenes opened up before us as we moved our position from one point of vantage to another. In some cases especially on some of the smaller island the picture before one is of that jagged, rugged type which personally I always admire deeply. as the going is all downhill we made good headway and quickly came into a partial view of the great lake lying away in the distance beneath us, with its vast stretches of water immobile in the rigid grip of its most powerful antagonist and the ice of an average thickness of about seven or eight inches, but which unfortunately had been rendered useless for skating purposes by the recent thaw. Several of us had looked forward to this trip for no other reason than the prospect of being able to take our skates and when we saw for ourselves the miles upon miles of immense stretches of unbroken ice our disappointment was real enough. Our path wound about eternally and after about 40 minutes walk we came within sight of our goal, which was the restaurant at the end of the dam and in another half an hour we had come up to it having completed the journey of about 8 kilometres in an hour and 10 minutes. We arrived muddy and fatigued but happily a good meal was waiting for us. Our rations had been sent on a day previously and the restaurant people turned us out quite an excellent dinner and comprised first soup followed by bully-beef nicely made up with potatoes and kidney beans, which we washed down with the assistance of white wine at 12 mark's per bottle. The principle feature of interest (excluding nature) is the great brick and concrete dam and waterfall which have been built for the purpose of supplying electric power to all the villages situated in the valley and it is undoubtedly a splendid piece of engineering work. To describe the whole thing would be I'm sure more than my pen could paint accurately, but will have a shot at a short description. In the first place the lake is studded with exquisite little islands, some thickly wooded while other are mere barren rocks and when the waterfall (which is really an overflow of the lake) is flowing it must be of considerable depth as the water at the time we visited it had fallen at least 20 feet owing to the fact that the water had been from beneath the ice in the interest of the electric power, coupled with the freezing of the water supply at its source. The banks all round were littered with broken masses of ice from under which the water had departed and had left no support. I noticed four house boats lying high and dry upon the beach of one of the islands. The little restaurant at the entrance to the dam is built of the red and blue stone, which is common in this district and hardly needs digging or blasting for. This lonely dwelling is the only habitation for miles around at least I could distinguish no other anywhere. Then comes the waterfall, which serves the purpose as a channel for an overflow of the lake and is built of concrete in the form of steps which go down to the valley on the other side to a depth of probably 130 or 140 feet. One can imagine what a gorgeous spectacle this waterfall must present when it is in full swing, both from the valley and also from the hills on the opposite sides. Passing on we cross over the dam, which has a drop roadway wide enough for one trap to pass over at a time and on either side there is a narrow causeway for pedestrians. These remarks are merely descriptional and are not intended to convey the impression that the dam is a thoroughfare, which is not so as it joins up on the far side with the side of an adjoining hill and one may only proceed further by taking to the hill paths, which overlook the valley into which drops the waterfall and it is both beautiful and extremely picturesque. One can only surmise what such a place as this must look like when nature comes into her own and has thrown off her dreary winter garments and adorned herself in all her summer finery.

I can only remark that in England such a beautiful spot would be held in reverence and made a place of pilgrimage by many thousands of nature lovers and instead of just one solitary restaurant of decidedly limited accommodation there would be instead many beautiful buildings of residential character besides hotels and other places, for the entertainment and pleasure of the visitors. Owing to lack of time we had perforce to turn our faces most reluctantly towards home after but a short survey of these unique surroundings. Arrived back at Scheleiden about 5.30 pm. After tea went on duty until 9 pm. <u>A thought for today</u> " He who reposes total reliance upon another, cannot expect himself to be relied upon."

17/2/19

Rain fell heavily all night and this morning very little snow remains, even upon the hills. Walked as far as Ober Haussen where I procured a few articles of which I was in need from the quartermaster's stores. Wrote a letter to the postmaster in Birmingham requesting a clear statement of my accounts as I fail quite to understand in the least the import of a memorandum statement, which I received from the post-office yesterday. To me it looks as though yet another attempt is being made to swindle me out of every penny they can get hold of. English bureaucracy would appear to have enlisted in its ranks all the first-class criminals and sharpers in the country. Still I will even with them yet. On duty 1 pm to 5 pm. A slight disturbance was created at the station this evening as a result of the apparent food shortage further up the line among the civilians at Cologne and district. I had noticed a big motley crowd of Germans of both sexes arrive here by an early morning train and it transpired that they had come ostensibly to buy potatoes, which are both plentiful and cheap in this area. When they returned in the evening loaded up with sacks of spuds they were prevented by us from boarding the train with them, which resulted in some others not interested trying to secure the potatoes for themselves, while our cook in the meantime looked after the interests of the headquarters staff. I noticed a big German armed with an axe, a railway employee, obviously threatening the cook with this implement and surrounded by a crowd of German swine and without hesitation I went up to the German hog and demanded to know what he meant by threatening to use his axe, but the cad slunk away. There were only three Tommies there at the time, yet I am ashamed to say one actually took the side of the Germans. It is strange but very true that Englishmen frequently show an utter lack of comradeship which, especially with uncivilised barbarians is a particularly dangerous practice. The A.P.M and the stationmaster eventually took possession of the sacks and I suppose that these were the only two to reap a benefit from the affair. Spent evening at the Hermanns where I dined, and played three games of chess and lost each game. Sent a picture postcard of the lake which I visited on Sunday to my own little boy. <u>A thought for today</u> " Natures most remarkable achievement is the creation of man."

18/2/19

On duty 8 am to 1 pm. The weather is now quite mild and in the early morning one is reminded of the coming spring by the cheerful singing of countless members of the feathered world. Received a letter from Mr Kendrick enclosing a short letter from little Dux together with a couple of his sketches, which show a decided improvement and I am inclined to think that my little man although only six years of age has undoubted abilities in this direction and that perhaps who knows? he may be budding into a real artist,

I was sorry to hear that he had been indisposed for several days with stomach troubles. I suppose he has been over crowding his little tummy, hence his indisposition. What troubles me is his cough and I am wondering if it would not be advisable to have my darling thoroughly medically examined. In the afternoon lay down for a nap. At 6 pm attended a lecture in the mess-room by our OC, which was primarily upon demobilisation and lasted until 7.30 pm. Supper at the Hermanns afterwards. On duty 9 pm to 8 am the following day. A thought for today "The capabilities of mother nature are limitless, while those of mere man are strictly confined and positively limited."

19/2/19

Finished work at 8 am feeling rather fatigued. It is still very dull but mild. Spent morning at our usual nightly rendezvous. Received a picture postcard from Mrs M. Taylor. Got my postcards of the "Urfettalsphrre" away by registered letter post at last this morning. Feeling tired after dinner, I slept until tea time. On duty 5 pm to 9 pm. received a card and photograph from Mlle Renee Bellette of St-Riquier. A thought for today "Life's heaviest burdens are often borne by those least capable of bearing them."

20/2/19

Muggy weather and no apparent prospect of an immediate change. On parade at 9.30 am and afterwards on a fatigue cleaning out the rubbish from a deep brick rubbish hole behind the post office and carting same in petrol boxes to a rubbish heap on the other side of the railway opposite the station. During our labours the German postmaster very graciously offered us a small glass of wine, which was gratefully accepted. On duty 1 pm to 5 pm. Wrote and sent off another pretty French postcard entitled "Les anges" (the angels) to my dear little boy Derrick, also a couple of picture cuttings from the "sphere" to my dear sister Doris. Played chess and had supper at the Hermanns in the evening. Scrounged a sack of bricquettes from a railway truck to use in our billet. A thought for today "It is surprising how easily life may be taken away and yet on the other hand how tenaciously it may fight against terrible odds."

21/2/19

On duty 8 am to 1 pm. Have received this morning the worst sort of news, which could possibly reach me for I hear that my most precious treasure in this world is down with influenza and that his temperature at the time of writing on the 15th inst was up to 105. Life does not seem to be made of nothing but misfortune, with but fleeting moments of real happiness and the rest, anxiety, pain and distress. Here far removed from my dear little one I am helpless and am left only with my thoughts. My darling does not know a mothers care or a fathers love and even now he is in the hands of strangers but thank God I can at least trust them to fo for the little mite quite all and more than I could do for him myself. I have only known an endless, pitiless war against the gods of fate and of the world from my childhood, but that my little boy should now be the object of such strife and he alone and quite defenceless is positively intolerable. It is for this that we are brought upon this damned earth of ours, to fight against such cowardly odds from cradle to grave.

Humanity cries pitifully for peace but for ever the reply comes back, no, there can be no peace and the struggle to live to exist, even for life itself is resumed more bitterly still. Yes we will fight on, without quarter, to the death. We shall be beaten in the end, c'est vrai, but we shall have many victories to our credit and emblazoned on our triumphal banner in bright red letters of blood. In the afternoon I had a walk with two friends through the forest and over the hills. It was delightfully fine and nature herself was becomingly bedecked one more now that she had cast off at least for a time her plain white winter mantle and for this occasion looked quite charming in her fresh green robe of early spring. Still I could not dispel from my thoughts the little fragile helpless picture in whom is centred all my hopes of future joy and happiness and who might even then have been in need of me. Poor little Dux if only my love alone could help you, no harm could ever come near you. Had supper and a game of chess at the Hermanns. I lay long in to the night thinking of my poor little boy and I prayed for him. A thought for today "The only master of man is death."

22/2/19

Rained heavily during the night and at intervals during the today there have been a number of sharp showers. Received a letter from Miss Winnie Hedges of Newport-Pagnell but no further news concerning my little boy. Seven days have now elapsed since the report of my darlings illness was posted to me and I am hoping that in the meantime he has recovered somewhat especially as I have heard nothing further, as no doubt I should have done had he become worse. Have little or nothing to talk about these days, today I have hardly stirred outside the billet, it is hard to know what to do to pass away the time. Until I hear again how my little Dux is progressing. On duty 5 pm to 9 m. A thought for today "Life is the passage in many colours and phases of a dream/film and death is the only, repose, or proof of."

23/2/19

Pay parade at 10 am, and church parade at 10.40 am. On duty 1 pm to 5 pm. I am deeply disappointed again today that no news has yet reached me respecting the condition of my little boy. I wonder if when it does come whether it will be for better or for worse. I had half the afternoon off and went for a walk alone up the hill side. After tea went to the Hermanns played three games of chess all of which I won and had supper afterwards. A thought for today " The human structure is a miracle of nature, her crowning masterpiece."

24/2/19

Pleasant spring like morning, though rather mild. On duty 8 am to 1 pm. I am still without news of my poor little boy, surely he must be getting well now or I must have heard before now. It takes so long unfortunately for a letter to reach me from the homeland, from 5 to 7 days and a letter posted in France takes 9 days, which is not easy to understand. I am quite sure that were the Germans in England it would not take a week for letters to go from Berlin to London and this little fact might refer to quite a large number of other little matters too, but so long as our administrative authorities are composed of all the University and public school duds and until the Officer click as a class is dumped and duly buried in the debris of their own wreckage, no hope can be entertained of better conditions either in the army, or navy or in civilian life.

From 2 pm to 4 pm practising the new procedure for all branches of the signal service, which is to come into force on March the 1st. There will be two classes held daily in the mess-room, to be taken for an hour in the morning and afternoon. I do not think I have ever come across such an obvious example of official stupidity, and bears distinctly the impress of noodles. The object, which was a good one and perfectly intelligible, was to bring all branches such as, line telegraphy, wireless and visual into line, so that they may all be worked upon the same lines in so far as procedure was concerned, instead of this they are all now out of line and out of step too and very much so at that. If these gentlemen who have had the honour of compiling such a heap of ridiculous nonsense and incidentally a cushy time in Blighty during the war, in cosy billets and with comfortable salaries at the countries expense, and wit much jam on their bread and butter, if I say these gentlemen of the intellectual class had been instead sent home to help their women do their washing, the army would have been well rid of a very grave drawback. The finest cogs in the military machine mad of the best material, in sound British homes, have throughout the war forever clogged by down right ignorance and perfidious neglect. On duty 9 pm to 8 am the following morning. A thought for today "The wife of a Britisher as compared to the lot, or position of her foreign sisters is really the most fortunate woman in the world."

25/2/19

Received a letter from Mrs Taylor. Owing to the bad weather could not go for a walk and instead went to the Hermanns where I spent the morning ensconced in a comfortable chair by a warm fire and as a break had a game of chess. On the way to the above I should mention a little incident which took place a short distance before I arrived there, I noticed an armed picquet of three artillery men ambushed behind trees. A moment later a German vehicle with a German pony and inside what looked like a German girl with her German male companion came galloping down the road and as they came up the picquet dashed out and placed themselves in front of the carriage, which by the way had its hood up, but the driver who was a real German simply smiled and drove on, whereupon the soldiers levelled their rifles and fired at the animals head at point blank range, still, no impression was made and the party continued on their way, at this stage not being aware of the meaning of such a scene I thought it time to take a hand in it myself and went off down the road in hot pursuit of the runaways and by calling out as loud as I possibly could managed to get another trap driven by British Tommies and drawn by a couple of mules, to draw up across the road, and so our quarry was compelled to stop. I was now made aware of my mistake as the whole affair was prearranged and was merely a scheme to see if spies could pass through a cordon of picquets, which had been placed out on the roads and the two occupants of the carriage were merely British Tommies dressed in civilian clothes for the occasion. The cartridges are blank ones. Received a Registered letter from my dear sis Dot which contained some more provoking complications of a legal character. Dots own letter was very interesting and most acceptable, have spent several hours replying to letters and other business today and am feeling fagged out. Not a word of news has yet reached me from those who have the care of my own little Dux and I cannot help but feel deeply disappointed. On duty 5 pm to 9 pm. Afterwards I read a little of my book, which I picked up the other day called "running water". A thought for today "All that we do remains with us and lives after us."

26/2/19

Dull day but mild and fine. Received a nice letter from Miss Weeds. On parade at 9.30 am from 10 am to 11 am, in the mess-room practising the new signal procedure. At 11 am went to the Hermanns where I remained until midday. Here I learned from two German young women, who came here from Cologne and whose brother is the chauffeur to the general, that all we troops at present at Schleiden would move up to or near Cologne sometime next week, of course I do not give much credence to such a rumour myself, but I make a note of it here to show how difficult it would be to prevent spying, when British officers of high rank engage Germans to drive them about. On duty 1 pm to 5 pm. Another day has come and almost gone yet I am still in the dark as to how my Dux is progressing, I am all impatient to know the facts and this continued silence is most annoying and can have no object except to make me very miserable indeed. Replied to Miss Weeds letter and also wrote a picture postcard to my dear sis Doris. Passed away the evening at the Hermanns in the usual way. A thought for today "Of all the animals of god's creation, mankind takes precedence in lying, in hypocrisy and in every form of vice and corruption."

27/2/19

Dull but very pleasant morning in the open air. On duty 8 am to 1 pm. I am still anxiously waiting for news of my little boy. I am totally unable to comprehend why I am so persistently kept in the dark as to his condition. I might be the person least concerned in my Dux's welfare and it is hard to believe that anyone could have failed to keep me posted in all that transpires to the detriment or in the interests of the only little being of whom I should trouble to concern myself, and in whose life I am so earnestly interested. Despatched a small souvenir of Cologne to Mrs Taylor by registered post. Two to three in the afternoon at the class for new signal procedures which commences on Saturday 1st March. Afterward had a hot bath at the hotel Schleiden. In the evening played chess at the Hermanns and was successful each time. A thought for today "The truth is not in any man and is nothing that he fears or dreads so much to face."

28/2/19

On waking this morning we were surprised to see that snow was falling again and my hopes were at once raised that we should have some more frosty weather after all, although I must confess I have my doubts as the civilians are of the opinion that the winter is now practically over. Walked to Ober-Hausen to the stores and obtained a new pair of boots, a pair of braces and some washing soap. From 11 am to midday was at the Hermanns. I am still without news of my little boy, yet I cannot give up hoping that my darling is still on the right side and that I shall soon hear of his satisfactory progress towards recovery. After dinner walked out again, with a number of friends to Ober-Hausen to watch a big football match, but unfortunately we all got lost upon the hills and failed to find the pitch which was situated on the summit of an adjacent hill, which we did not succeed in locating.

Upon arriving back at our billet I was greatly pleased to find the long looked for letter for which I have been so anxiously waiting and I was furthermore more than relieved, more than happy to read such a favourable report, and I can hope now with renewed confidence that the next time I hear, the news will be still more satisfactory. The letter runs as follows. "Well I am pleased to say that now I think he (Derrick) is out of danger, but I can tell you that he has had a very narrow squeak according to the doctors. I think it was fortunate that he was, where he was, as the least neglect at the commencement would have been fatal. The doctors say that he is a very poor delicate chap indeed and will require great care." Poor little Dux I am so sorry for you, when you once remarked "What should I do without my daddy" you really expressed my own thoughts, for I do not know what I should do without you. On duty 5 pm to 9 pm. Have got four French novels from the circulating library in the village. Replied to Mr Kendrick's letter and sent off a picture postcard to Mrs. Taylor. A thought for today "The difference between a soldier (or sailor) and a civilian is that the former does something for nothing, while the latter does nothing for something."

1/3/19

More snow had fallen during the night and the fields and forest are once more beneath a light coating of snow. After parade at 9.30 am played football on our ground till dinnertime. On duty 1 pm to 5 pm. received a letter from the financial secretary of the T.C.A (G.P.O) in reply to mine and stating that I am in debt to the association to the tune of 2 pounds 1 shilling and 2 d. I have written to Doris requesting her to refund the said amount, also was glad to receive a French book called Andre by George Sand from my dear little sister Dot. Played drafts at the Hermanns in the evening, a disgraceful scene took place at this hotel at about 8.15, practically all the evening half a dozen or so Tommies belonging to the artillery and A.S.C had been breaking glasses etc. and making a disturbance generally. The climax came when the police intervened and commenced to put them out-of-door. The word was passed to be careful of shots as one of the intoxicated artillery men was armed with a revolver and the windows outside were promptly assailed with stones, which put the wind up the Germans and most of the troops too who were still inside and were crouching underneath the tables and behind the pillars. The police now made a determined effort to cope with these half bred savages and several were soon in their hands but others had decamped and were supposed to be hiding in the fields. Their unit was rung up on the telephone and the police in their neighbourhood were informed and I hope that they will be severely dealt with as it is on account of these sort that good places are so often put out of bounds. A thought for today "The difference between soldiering and working is that the soldier must work and suffer that the workers may play."

2/3/19

Clear bright frosty morning. On duty 8 am to 1 pm. In the afternoon I strolled out alone and went up along a valley path through the forest. It was very dismal and lonely and the little brooks which go racing down the valley on all sides are the only audible sounds which strike a pleasant note upon the ear and in a very friendly sort of way they seem to say we are happy, why aren't you? Have received a nice letter from Miss Cummins of Southport, also a packet of notepaper and envelopes from my dear little sis Dot.

Rumours are very strong now that before very long we shall move to Duren, which place is considered a pretty town and it will be a change for all of us, although we are perfectly comfortable where we are and many do not appreciate the prospect of a change. I have to admit in justice to the powers that be that since a week back we have been having excellent rations, I refer more particularly to the bread allowance which is now on a liberal scale. The poor German Mark has come another cropper and from five marks as the equivalent of 2/7 it has dropped to 1/11, it will be readily seen by this to what an extent we gain the advantage over the Germans when making a purchase in the fatherland, if the mark drops much more we shall be buying from the enemy at a cost of practically Nix. A German prisoner captured by us in a submarine, who escaped from Blighty by working his passage over as a stoker and who can speak English fluently was caught the other day at Mechernich not far from here and was lodged in the civil prison. He has again succeeded in making his escape. Sent off a nice card to my dear little Dux also letters to my dear little sis Dot and Miss Cummins. I received a telegram late this evening from 6th corps stating that they could not take us over on the 4th inst owing to Q reasons. This proves beyond doubt that we are about to shift our quarters and that being so, the sooner it takes place the better so that we may get settled down comfortably again. A thought for today "Neither nature nor time can ever heal all the wounds of life."

Diary Number 12

3/3/19

Finished duty at 8 am this morning. The weather is beautifully bright and clear although a little keen. The snow has all disappeared so I suppose we must give up all hopes of another spell of wintry conditions and instead look forward with hope to a spring, which will bring at least to some of us new ideals and brighter prospects. Had a walk to the Hermanns before dinner. In the afternoon played football, am feeling in fine trim at the present. On duty 5 pm to 9 pm. The new signal procedure, which comes into force on the 1 st inst is, working fairly smoothly, although as could easily be foreseen we are not following out all the rules as laid down in the book, as they are, at least a number of them are too impracticable for practicable purposes. Am taking a renewed interest in French and read a few pages each day of my French novels. Before finally putting out the light read a couple of chapters in the book called " Running Water" by A.E.W Mason. A thought for today "Marriage is an institution instituted by man for the purpose of raising woman and himself too to a higher plain than that which is supposed to exist among the rest of other animal creation, but through out the ages it has proved a dismal failure."

4/3/19

Mild and showery today and in consequence could not have the ball out. I went for a short walk before dinner taking the road to the lake, I was surprised upon reaching it to find that its banks simply swarmed with frogs and toads, which upon my approach dived precipitately into the water. There was abundant proof that someone had been here before and had slaughtered these extremely inoffensive creatures wholesale, one poor beggar with its leg broken but still alive although unable to move I assisted gently with a stick back into the water. On duty 1 pm to 5 pm. continued my French and English reading today, I have done so very little reading since the war began and now I feel that I have lost more time than I can ever hope to regain. Posted my diary No 11 by registered post to my dear little sis Dot. On leaving work at 5 pm I found all the postmasters children, four girls and two boys, the eldest is fourteen and a nice sort of girl, there was also a girl friend and they were having a lively talk with my friends in the billet, the two eldest girls the postmasters daughter and her friend can both speak English very well indeed and the conversation turned on several subjects. I was shown their English reading and grammar books and I must admit that the system of education is both practical and original. The official books contain many passages of English history and also well known poems. The "friend" was obviously a zealous patriot and remarked with evident pride and pleasure " I am a Prussian" and when I questioned her right to make such a statement, seeing that she is a native of the Rhine provinces, she became at once extremely indignant and drawing herself up to her full height and with her head thrown back disdainfully, proclaimed with most determined convictions that she was a Prussian. I should not have believed it possible for a child of her years to have acquired such sound and firm convictions and to uphold which, she would undoubtedly make willingly any sacrifice and confound her adversaries with profound contempt. Spent a quiet evening at the Hermanns. It has rained sharply all day long. A thought for today " Thoughts are but passing fancies and action the consummation or fulfilment of deliberate design."

5/3/19

Pleasant but dull morning. On duty 8 am to 1 pm. Played football in the afternoon. Played drafts at the Hermanns in the evening. Continued my French and English reading. A thought for today " The evil that women do never dies."

6/3/19

Rained most of the day. Finished reading a French book, which have returned to the library, it was in two parts and called respectively " Le scarabee d'or" and " Le double assinnat de larue morge", I could not exchange it for another as all arrangements have been made for quitting the present premises prior to moving to fresh ones at Duren. Played football in the afternoon for a time, but had to give up on account of the bad weather. Received a nice letter from my friend Roland South of Cambridge. On duty 5 pm to 9 pm. A letter also reached me from Elinor and its contents pleased me greatly, I was pleased to hear that she had spent several hours daily at the bedside of dear little Dux during the time the little man was so ill. Have replied to her directly this evening. A thought for today " People do not judge others as they appear to be, much less as they are, but rather in comparison to what they conceive themselves to be."

7/3/19

Fine but very windy. Played football for an hour of so in the morning. On duty 1 pm to 5 pm. Wrote to my friend Roland South. Received a picture postcard from Mlle Renee Billette. Day passed in the usual way, finishing with a supper at the Hermanns. A thought for today " To try to be what we are not is the pastime of fools, to try to be better than what we are is a preachers pastime, to try to be exactly what we are is the hardest task of all."

8/3/19

Cold but fine morning. The spring birds are rapidly increasing and their early morning song is gradually increasing in volume. On duty 8 am to 1 pm. Played football in the afternoon. We have good games daily and the exercise tends to keep one very fit indeed, have been picked to play in a team against the rest of the company in a match on Monday. After tea had a bath at Schleiden hotel, these baths and a clean change of clothes are something I look forward to in the army and are much appreciated. For a long while I have been anxious to procure one or two good specimens of German pipes and while waiting my turn for the bath I noticed that the proprietor had just received a good selection, I at once made a critical inspection of them and chose four at a cost of 24 marks, as I imagine they will make admirable souvenirs and I particularly wish to send one to the dear old dad, unfortunately I could not pay for them on the nail, so requested that they may be kept aside until tomorrow when I shall have been paid. I hardly liked doing this as I do not trust Germans, but it was my only alternative. Played cards in the evening with my friends at the Hermanns. Reinforcements to the number of 14 are expected to arrive here sometime during the evening.

I must not fail to mention that yesterday we suffered a great loss when our Sergeant Major an old contemptible left us to take up his new appointment as sergeant Major of the 10 th Corps, he was very popular with us and for that reason, discipline was good and everyone did their particular job conscientiously. On duty 9 pm to 8 am tomorrow. A thought for today " A weakness for women is live inviting the devil to accompany one to church."

9/3/19

Dull morning but nevertheless pleasant and there is quite a strong note of approaching spring in the air, which cannot fail to renew one with fresh hopes and new aspirations. I don't think anything can so favourably impress one and revivify ones drooping spirits so effectually as an early spring morning. Claimed my pipes from the Schleiden hotel people, and they very kindly gave me a couple of cardboard boxes and sufficient brown paper in which to pack them. Have handed the two packages into the orderly room to be censored by an office prior to despatching same per registered post to my sister, to whom I am writing to explain that it is my wish that the dear old dad should chose one of them for himself and to send another to Mr Kendrick as a souvenir. Had a long talk in French with two of the postmaster's daughters who came up to our billet as I was packing up my pipes this morning. The postmaster himself gave me a cigar when I went into the kitchen to fetch water to wash, this is not by the way the first time I have received favours form him in the shape of either cigars or wine. Watched a football match in the afternoon. On duty 5 pm to 9 pm. Sent off a letter to my dear little sis Dot enclosing a sample of German cloth made of paper, which tears remarkably easily. We are very busy in the signal office lately on account of the Brigades moving to their new quarters near Duren. We expect to follow sometime during this week. Received a letter from Mrs Wright of Selly-Park Birmingham to say that she had received back my suit, which she had sent to be pressed and cleaned sometime ago. A thought for today " Love with a little practice becomes quickly an accomplished though acquired habit."

10/3/19

Dull morning and inclined to rain. Posted the two packets containing pipes and a novel to my little sis Dot. Swabbed out our billet during the morning in anticipation of moving out very shortly. Played in a football match, Schleiden against Oberhausen, we the former team lost by 4 goals to one, I did not play as well as I had done in practice matches, although I can say I mad no glaring faults, we were dressed in light blue jerseys and blue shorts. Received a communication from the poor persons department and wrote to Messrs Jeffertt and co. solicitors, London E.C.2. Wrote a long letter to my dear sis Dot and one to Mrs Wright of Sally-Park Birmingham. Played chess in the evening at the Hermanns and won each game, am getting back my old play now and have not been defeated for sometime. A thought for today " Germans are probably the most unique copyists in the world."

11/3/19

Dull with strong wind today. On duty 8 am to 1 pm. The reinforcements have arrived and some of them began their duty in the signal office yesterday. Watched a football match in the afternoon. Did not stay long at the Hermanns this evening as was alone.

Have been foregoing suppers lately as I need what money I have for other purposes. Wrote a long letter to Mrs M. Taylor. Carried on with a little French reading and studying. <u>A thought for today</u> " When tearing up 'scraps of paper' I wonder if the Germans had in mind a probable shortage of cloth."

12/3/19

Beautiful sunny morning after breakfasting and cleaning up the billet I packed up my traps in preparation of moving off tomorrow to our new quarters at Duren an advance party has already left for there this morning. At this moment I am seated in a narrow alley buried away in the forest and high up on the hill sides, I can just see through the tops of the trees the village of Scheuren, which crowns the plateau upon the opposite range of hills. This is indeed a glorious spot and how regretfully we shall leave it. In the future I shall look back with sincere pleasure to the happy hours I have spent in this delightful country. No one can deny that we are about to bid goodbye to many objects which have become dear to each one of us, for the friendships which one makes with nature are indissoluble and become indelibly written upon one's memory so long as life may last, I am one who believes that poetry is not dead that can never die, it is the deep things in nature, which appeal to us, and speak to us and which lie but partly hidden even in a blade of fresh green grass. As I came round a bend of the woods a few minutes ago I came into full view of a couple of deer, standing majestically in the middle of a clearing hardly fifty paces from where I stood to look at them. We took stock of each other for a good half a minute, my first though was if only I had got my rifle and then almost immediately it changed to one of admiration for these superb creatures of the mountains. The colour of one was deep brown and that of the other a lighter shade. They turned and entered the wood behind them, I continued on my way and at the next turning they were just emerging again from the wood and right in front of me, this time they scampered away as though the devil himself was on their heels. The Germans are cutting down the trees in some places and these monarchs of the forest are now lying prone upon the ground, shorn of all their glory. Making my way homewards down the thickly wooded hill-sides I disturbed a number of beautiful yellow butterflies, which were gaily sporting in the sun, I thought it remarkably early for these heralds of approaching summer to be on the wing, but there they were and they gave an added charm to the picturesque surroundings and enhanced by reason of contrast the unnumbered beauties of dame nature. Lay down after dinner for an hours nap. Afterward washed and shaved and had my tea. On duty 5 pm to 9 pm. <u>a thought for today</u> "One can never have enough knowledge either of the good or bad side of life."

13/3/19

Up at 6.45 am. Rolled up my blankets, washed, breakfasted, cleaned up billet and paraded at 8.30 at the station for entraining to Duren. Did not leave Schleiden until 10.30 am and in the meantime another chap and myself cleaned up the mess-room. We travelled in German cattle trucks, which were cleaned and nicely fitted up with seats down the centre an innovation of the Germans in consideration for their troops, when upon long railway journeys, which is quite a contrast to many experiences I have had in the well ventilated animal coaches graciously provided for the sole use of troops of his Britannic Majesty. Judging by appearances we certainly had a most triumphal send-off by the population of Schleiden, especially the female portion.

They crowded their bed-room windows and lined up in front of their doors to wave a last adieu as the train steamed down the valley, passing the Hermanns the last house out of Schleiden we could distinguish a large group standing on the steps and in the road and even table cloths were brought into play the better that we might notice them. I'm sure we were as loathed to quit the place as these people were sorry to lose us and I'm sure they could not have expressed their regrets more forcibly even had we been their own well known field-greys. Just prior to arriving at Kall I noticed high up on the face of some rocks a huge iron cross with an inscription underneath in German and the dates 1870 and 1871, at Kall we shunted onto another line and proceeded on our journey, after about half an hours halt. Passed through remarkably flat country to Euskirchen and arrived at Duren about 3.30 pm. It was very cold travelling and when the train stopped as it did at rather frequent intervals, we amused ourselves by playing football with tin-cans on the permanent-way or throwing stones at each other or some other object to keep warm. We marched from the station at Duren to the school where we are billeted and where the signal office is also installed. We have no beds and contrary to right and justice are compelled to sleep on the floor, for some inexplicable reason the quartermaster (acting Sergeant Major) gave orders that we were not to have our dinner issued until the rest of the company arrived. This irritated me excessively especially as our last meal had been at 7 am in the morning. At 6 pm I headed a deputation to complain of this shameful treatment to the C.O and after a round of words I got my way, at least so far as I was personally concerned, on the grounds that I was on duty all night. Afterwards went into the town and after a short walk round entered a large cafe with two friends, where an orchestra played rag time and other well known tunes at 8.30 pm returned to billet and went on duty at 9 pm to 8 am the following morning. We have a great deal of work to do in the S.O. a thought for today " The good that is in one is too often strangled almost to death either by too much adversity or by an over abundance of good fortune."

14/3/19

Nice day. Off duty at 8 am after a poor breakfast I cleaned up. Afterwards I went down to the town to look round and to a little some shopping. Bought a razor for 20 marks and then selected a good collection of local postcards, bought another razor for my father which seemed a better one than I had already got and for which I had paid 6 marks more, being suspicious I showed these people the first razor I had bought and they said I had been overcharged. I there upon went back and demanded that they should refund me 3 marks, which after a bit they did although in a most ungracious manner. Two Tommies who happened to come advised me not to bother about it, but I said I was not going to be done down by these people and it is not in me to lie down calmly, as Tommies always do when someone tries to do the heavy on them. Walked round the town, passing by Bismarck's statue, he is figured as holding a sword in his left hand and a scroll in his right. One would imagine that German statesmen never wrote with anything but the sword, at the base upon the steps sits Germania reclining on the body of a lion. Turning to the right I arrived in a few minutes at the water tower, which is a unique example of German lack of originality. I will explain, at the foot of the tower there is a waterfall, which runs into a huge concrete basin in the centre of which are a number of sprays for creating a fountain effect.

This is very nice and quite creditable to the German architects ingenuity, but it is the rest of the pile of masonry of which I complain as it is difficult to understand, what is the intended imitation, a semi circle Grecian arches spread out on either side from the water-tower, while on the outer walls cut out of the stone are figures of a knight - crusader on horseback at one corner and at another an Egyptian with sword, other figures and heads of an Egyptian character adorn the walls, while on each side of the basin there are placed a stag and buffalo respectively, What in the world all this signifies is beyond me to understand, but it leaves one with the impression that with a little travel and less reading on the part of those responsible for the structure would have resulted in something considerably more comprehensible. Returned to the "Sudschule" our billet for dinner. In the afternoon took my chum round to see the sights. We entered first of all the church, which is of course a modern building and is of Roman Catholic pretensions. Interially there is nothing out of the ordinary to note, when we entered there was a small congregation of two or three men and several women sitting in the pews in contemplation, as the clock on the wall struck 2 pm a man past middle age suddenly commenced to pray aloud and taking out his rosary repeated by heart a number of prayers and at the end of each the rest of the worshippers answered in refrain, this continued all the while we were in the church and was the first impromptu service I had ever witnessed. The day was beautifully fine and sunny, rather too warm for a day in spring. Spent half an hour or so in a tobacconists smoking cigars at half a mark apiece and talking to the young ladies behind the counter. They told us they had 7 brothers in the war and two had been killed, one a sailor had lost his life in the Falklands Battle, when Admiral Spee and all his ships had been sent to the bottom. We were shown the photographs of the five vessels which the admiral commanded and which were preserved in a nice frame for hanging upon the wall. We then proceeded to inspect all the monuments in the town including Kaiser William the 1st and two others of a religious character, one of which is in the market place and is almost hidden by British notice boards relating to speed etc. We took the direction I followed earlier in the morning down Bismarck Strasse, with the statue of the statesman at the top, just to the right from this and at the side of a house is a big trough with fonts cut out of a piece of solid stone and cut into the back portion are the well chiselled figures of girls, or perhaps they may be water nymphs. Passed on to the right and into the main road, turning to the left passed the cemetery, where at the time a burial was in progress, to the water tower. Had another look at the grotesque figures carved upon the outer walls and the knight on horseback riding over the dragon, which was probably a misrepresentation of St-George and the dragon and on the further side the Egyptian soldier, with broad sword and shield. On the way back I bought a pair of gold cuff links (in anticipation of demobilisation in the near future) for 38 marks, the original price was 42 marks but a reduction of 10 per cent luxury tax is deducted to British purchasers. Was not on duty in the evening as it was my turn to be off so went out into the town with my chum until 8.45 pm. All civilians must be indoors at 9 pm or they are fined heavily. A thought for today " There is always time enough to do everything and anything even in the army."

15/3/19

Another beautiful sunny day. Paraded with the company at 9.30 am on fatigue cleaning and brushing the stone steps in the school, about 3/4 of an hours job. Afterwards went for a short walk into the town and spent the rest of the morning talking in a tobacconists. Received a short note from my dear sister Doris enclosing Territorial long service ribbon.

We are on very poor rations indeed here and to aggravate the position still more the bacon, which we should have had for breakfast this morning was stolen from the cookhouse sometime during the night and instead we had each a slice of cold bully-beef. On duty 1 pm to 5 pm. Spent evening with my chum down the town. This division the 62 nd is now the Highland division and in future we will be known as such. Have sent a razor as a present to my father and also a pair of gold cuff links for myself per registered post. I was informed this evening at the orderly room of the good news that the Territorial bounty of 15 pounds would shortly be put to my account and that I was entitled to a months special leave, I have requested that this should be given to me upon demobilisation, which would give me in conjunction with the months army furlough a nice little holiday of 8 weeks at full pay. A thought for today " One should be careful when trying to do a kindness, not to cause any harm thereby."

16/3/19

Dull and rather cold, in fact a short sharp shower of snow fell at 7.30 am. On duty 8 am to1 pm. yesterday I received a notification from the post office that I was entitled to draw 23 pounds the amount illegally deducted from my weekly drafts 2 years of so back. Have requested that this sum should be paid to my sister Doris. My luck was properly in yesterday as with the Territorial bounty in addition I came into the nice little sun of 38 pounds all without to mention an extra months special leave. Went for a walk in the afternoon, being Sunday all the shops were shut, which is quite a contrast to France. Sent off a card to my dear little Dux. Later in the afternoon I went to watch a football match between two German teams. They did not play badly but like the French teams they have not yet reached the standard of play, which one is accustomed to see in dear old Blighty. The grandstand was crammed with excited Tommies who kept up a continuous shout, first for one side and then for the other and their laughter could be heard for a mile or two around. Four huge navel guns drawn by giant tractors steamed in to town in the evening accompanied by their Khaki crews. I would like to mention here that the cost of living is undoubtedly very high in this place, a pair of leather boots cannot be bought under at least 100 marks, which to the Germans is equivalent to 5 pound in English money. It is rather sad too to watch the youngsters both girls and boys come flocking round the cook house at meal times carrying enamel jugs and basins in which the Tommies empty what otherwise they would throw away, and one sees stew, rice and porridge all mixed up together. A thought for today " There are none so blind as an Englishman."

17/3/19

Still cold and dull, towards midday it rained and snowed together rather heavily. I saw the four big guns, which came here yesterday evening pass out of the town this morning in the direction of Cologne. Wrote a postcard to my dear sis Dot. I was to play in a football match this afternoon but owing to the bad weather it has been cancelled. After dinner went through the museum with my chum, although it is not a large building the frontage is sufficiently imposing. The chief objects of interest so far as I can remember, include old Roman relics such as keys, rings etc all iron, roman and other coins. The most beautiful collection of butterflies I have ever seen. There is also an excellent collection of pictures, but not being naturally an artist I can pass no comment on them. A set of wine glasses made in Duren for the crown prince of Germany is on view.

Tipping the old gentleman who kindly took us round we took our departure after about an hours inspection. It was raining hard when we left so decided to go to one of the civilian cinemas where we spent the remaining part of the afternoon, a lot of jocks were there too and several who were drunk made some commotion for a short time. I have heard that the first troop to enter Duren were jocks and that they raided some shops jewellers I believe and in consequence they have earned for themselves a very bad name indeed among the civilians, who repeatedly tell you the Scotch are nix gut and that the English are better. This as it maybe I am not quite of this opinion myself. On duty 5 pm to pm. A thought for today " Love is not a language of the mouth."

18/3/19

Cold and dull. Paraded 9.30 am, cleaned up our part of the school afterwards. I would like to make a note of certain observations with respect to the Germans as a type and one or two other matters. The best description I imagine that I have ever heard is that he is a squarehead, pretty children are remarkable for their absence, which is a feature strongly in contrast to the great number of pretty boys and girls both in our own country and in that of France. I am constantly struck by the old appearance of German children, their little faces bear quite an old look, which is strange to see in such young people. There is too a great amount of infirmity, more so than I have notice anywhere else, one can hardly pass down the street without meeting a hunch-back, or person with cross-eyes, or another who has one limb to short etc etc. When one sees for instance a little girl with deep wrinkles lining her small forehead and so much physical suffering in this vaunted country, ones thoughts naturally incline to the belief that something is wrong somewhere and if the fault does not lie in the brain or intellectual portion of the social system then it must be in the blood. Another factor which, which is by no means common in England or France, is the custom in Germany to have large families, six, seven, eight or more is not considered abnormal, personally I am of opinion that this alone would account for much of what I have already mentioned, in so much that people who lack some of the essential qualities in bearing sound healthy children are permitted even encouraged to propagate their species without any check. On duty 1 pm to 5 pm. In the evening after clean up and taking my washing out to be done and posting back to my dear Dot the French book called "Andre", which she kindly lent to me, and which I have read with deep pleasure, I went alone to one of the civilian picture houses opposite the 6 th Corps cinema. I was greatly impressed by one picture especially which dealt with class prejudices and class hatred, and was very appropriate to the times we are now living in, representing as it seemed to me some true episodes in the ghastly scenes of which we have heard so much about recently, as almost daily occurrences in the German capital. It is a thousand pities that one is not able to understand the writing on the screen as of course it is all in German. A thought for today " Much love is lost in seeking it."

19/3/19

A distinct change in the weather is recorded today and it is now clear and frosty. On duty 8 am to 1 pm. Played in a football match in the afternoon, kicked of at 2 pm, it was a hard game and the sun somewhat powerful, as usual my side lost, by 4 goals to nil.

During the first half I played inside left but at my own request I fell back to left half towards the close of the game, was charged in kicking the ball out of touch and was caught on one leg and went down heavily on my face, injuring my left arm at the elbow, managed to play on without the game being stopped. Spent evening with a German family with whom I have made friends. The husband is a soldier or at least has been and is working at some post on the railway, this evening he was engaged upon making picture frames out of zeppelin stays. His wife pointed out to me that since my last visit they had taken down the picture of the Kaiser and the pope and had replaced them with others. Returned to billet at 8.30 pm. My arm is swelling up and becoming troublesome. A thought for today " Man and woman are the same all the world over, with just one single qualification in that some are a little worse than others."

20/3/19

Find it rather difficult to use a pen today as my elbow is turning blue and a little painful. Visited the M.O at 10 am who excused me duty and have now a tight bandage round my arm. Spent the morning at my German friends and the good woman made me up a nice dish of meat chopped up into small pieces. In the afternoon was a spectator at a great game of football between the 62nd division signals and the guards. We won by six goals to one, which is a great take down for the raunted guards. The game was played in a blinding snowstorm, but the play was excellent and the guards had no chance whatsoever against such a team as we put up against them. A thought for today " As we desire so do we live."

21/3/19

Sharp frosty morning. Saw the M.O again and got "m and d" although I cannot use my arm properly and it is quite blue or black still. Spent morning at my German friends. On duty 1 pm to 5 pm. I have been fortunate enough to secure a bed, three came into our billet and I took possession of one. They came in parts. There are two ends with two sides, which have to be nailed together and the bottom is formed by placing strips of wood across, where they are held in place by a ledge on the inside of each frame piece. By placing a German pallias made of paper and stuffed with straw inside this box bed affair, which stands about 3 feet high, quite a comfortable couch is produced and I am very pleased indeed with it. Spent evening at my German friends. The youngest child is down with the flu, he seemed very ill this evening and to make his case worse he had on only a thin cotton vest. Woollen articles or even flannel is not obtainable so I took off my own undervest, which is made of wool and very long and the father and mother put it on the little sufferer. Wrote to Miss Lily Cummins and Miss Winnie Hedge in reply to theirs, also to my solicitor in London to acknowledge their letter, which arrived today and which I forwarded to my dear little sis Dot with instructions. A thought for today " Without adversity there could be no hope and without hope life would not be worth living."

22/3/19

Dull and cold morning. A telegram has just come through cancelling all leave and stopping demobilisation owing to strikes in England. Received a long letter from Mrs Taylor and one from Mr Kendrick, which told me that my little boy was well, but the Dr. would not allow him to go to school for fear that lung trouble might develop.

I am thankful for small mercies and I am happy to know that my little darling is well and with god's help I trust that my little Dux will pull through safely and that I shall be able to assure his future. Wrote a long letter to Mrs Taylor in reply to hers. Spent afternoon and evening at the home of my German friends. I found the master and the little one still unwell, although the latter showed signs of recovering. I had tea with them, which consisted of black bread and very salty butter, I did not find the bread to be so repulsive as report has it, although I do not suppose that it contains so much nutriment as does our own, for drink we had coffee, which the lady ground in a "Moulin a cafe" exactly as the French do, and with plenty of milk and sugar it was quite a nice drink. Supper was a better meal and consisted of soup with peas, potatoes etc, followed by a tastefully cooked dish of mashed potatoes mixed with herrings chopped up into tiny morsels etc and spiced with a little vinegar and onions. The whole washed down with several glasses of beer. It will be seen that slowly but very surely I am becoming not a little reconciled to the fact that outwardly at least German's are not so bad as they are painted and that in all probability I may change some at least of my former views concerning them. As in all things where judgement is required I prefer to do all the judging myself and to believe in my own opinions only so long as I see them to be right and proper, and in this way I pride myself that very often I have been able to see things clearly that to others have been a total blank. Lately I have been feeling rather down, but the good hot soup this evening has put me on my feet again. A thought for today " One can never lose all hope so long as just one ideal is left to us even though all our gods may be overthrown and lie crashed irretrievably upon the ground."

23/3/19

Brisk but sunny day. Received 100 marks as pay at 10 am. Spent rest of the morning with my German friends, smoking cigar's and cigarette's with the husband, was pressed to stay for dinner, which I did. At 2 pm I went to the cinema with the lady while Monsieur stayed at home to look after the family. The picture was very good indeed. It is not an easy arrangement to go to a place of amusement accompanied by a lady, and one cannot be seen in the street's either talking or walking with a German woman, as she would be arrested immediately, hand cuffed and taken off to the police station, where she is fined heavily, a circumstance which has been of frequent occurrence in the large towns in the occupied area. On duty 5 pm to 9 pm. Wrote to Mr Kendrick and enclosed a card to my little Dux. A thought for today " Vice is a moral cancer."

24/3/19

Snow still falls at intervals as it has done for some time past. Paraded at 9.30 am. Afterwards on different fatigue's until nearly 11 am. Spent rest of the morning at same place as yesterday. I took with me a bar of carbolic soap and ten packets of players cigarettes the latter for monsieur. The little one was considerably improved this morning and wanted badly to get up. On duty 1 pm to 5 pm. Received an extremely long letter from my dear sister Doris in which she expounds her views on several important subjects and I must admit that she possesses more than the ordinary ability to express very forcibly her own. I have replied to her with an equally long epistle but I must confess that my efforts fell far short and decidedly inferior in quality and in reasoning to the well thought out arguments, advanced by my little sis.

Spent evening at the house of my friends and enjoyed some games with the young girls, who were highly amused. Had supper with them and returned to my billet at 9.30 pm. A thought for today " Riches and poverty may be said to have some little moral value and resemble in their effect good and evil, for the one cannot exist without the other."

25/3/19

Cold and dull. On duty 8 am to 1 pm. Received a letter from Mrs Wright. Have changer one of the P.O's that I received yesterday from my dear little sis 52 mark's 20 at the divisional post-office. Snowing at intervals during the day. Spent afternoon and evening at my customary German address. The little one has had another relapse and was very ill again. Had supper before leaving and a bottle of wine hot with sugar. Sent cards to my dear little boy and to Mrs Wright. A thought for today " For ridiculous imbicilities and ambiguous unreasonableness and senseless idiotism, a giggling young girl takes the biscuit, other young girls can make their own deductions."

26/3/19

Cold with some snow storms again today. At 9 am went for a bath in the town and fortunately got in with little time wasted in waiting. One feels to have got rid of an unpleasant load, after so refreshing douche, and one might even say that with a clean body one has a clear conscience. I find the in Germany bathrooms are rarely installed in private houses and even in the larger ones this very necessary commodity appears to be almost entirely absent. The place I went to this morning is used frequently by the civilians. I went afterward on a shopping expedition in the town as I wished to purchase a few presents for my sisters and my little boy. I finished up not very contented as some things, which I judged to be suitable were too highly priced, jewellery is quite out of the question here and the Germans do not neglect to offer their wares as being genuine gold or silver and one has to exercise great caution, as a matter of fact both gold and silver articles are very expensive luxuries and in spite of the immense drop in the value of the mark, I am thoroughly persuaded that such articles can be bought much cheaper in England even at this present day. First of all I went to the bazaar, which is a huge place, with a gallery above, running round the entire building and looking down to the ground floor. Quite a host of young women are employed behind the numerous stalls and a few Tommies were already making love to some of them although the morning was little advanced. Did not see much that presented itself to me as desirable except a few picture postcards and a penknife with the Dom at Cologne embossed on each side. These constituted the whole of my purchases at this place. Entering another shop I bought some envelopes and inspected some rosaries but as in the bazaar I found that none were silver. At a bookshop where I enquired for a French book I was informed that we had forbidden the sale of French literature here, although books by British authors were on sale , I wonder who is responsible for this latest piece of brainless intimidation. Bought a number of pretty postcards elsewhere which I propose to send one by one to my dear little Dux. The last shop I went to I selected a little model in metal of Cologne cathedral for Derrick, a small wooden stand with the virgin Mary in metal relief for my sister Doris and a small round picture of Christ in a wooden frame for my dear little sister Gladys.

Have packed them all up and handed in to the orderly room for the censor's signature. After dinner I betook myself to the outskirts of the town, where the house of my friends is situated and remained there until teatime. The little boy was decidedly better again today. On duty 5 pm to 9 pm. a thought for today " The old saying that every question has two sides is quite wrong, for who can judge either the one or the other to be the correct one? When judging a point one should endeavour to pass right between the opposing sides without touching them and go straight to the core, for only in the heart of a subject can a true and reliable solution be found."

27/3/19

Frosty and brighter this morning but changed to dull and windy later. After parade and a short fatigue went to the bazaar where I bought an English German dictionary and the proceeded to my usual rendezvous where I stayed for the rest of the morning. On duty 1 pm to 5 pm. Received a nice postcard from Miss Weeds to whom I have replied with another. Spent evening in the same way and at the same place as this morning and before coming away had 2 plates of soup. Nothing much to talk about these days. A thought for today " Love is a game, which like chess can be played in a million different ways."

28/3/19

Snowing, blowing and raining, rather treacherous sort of weather. On duty 8 am to 1 pm. Received a letter from Mlle Renie Bellette of Saint-Riquier, Somme, to whom I have replied with a picture postcard. In the afternoon I went to the cinema with my friend Fran and her lady friend and in the evening I went to her home and spent an enjoyable time with the family, having before I departed a much appreciated supper, with two hot cups of good milk and sweetened with sugar. "c'est bon ca". On duty 9 pm to 8 am the following morning. A thought for today " Of course it is only natural to suppose that a woman may love one man alone, but it is equally true that she can love two better."

29/3/19

Snowing all day long. Leaving off duty at 8 am I prepared to go out to my friends and arrived there at about 10 am, and returned to the billet for dinner. Received a nice letter from Mr Kendrick acknowledging the German pipe, which I sent to him sometime ago, I was happy to hear that my own little boy was going on well, he is taking viral and eating well, his weight to date is 3 stone 4 lb 4 ounces. Three doctors have thoroughly examined him, and as I have not been given to believe otherwise I presume that their opinion is not adverse, at least this is what I choose to hope and believe, and I do not think I could possibly do otherwise, than to follow the inclination of my belief in all that concerns the welfare and interests of my little one. Returned to the same address in the afternoon and when I left at their instigation I embraced both the wife of Monsieur in front of him and her friend a big finely built woman. The latter giving me her lips as though she had done so before a hundred times and she is the mother of grown up children. This is not mentioned to the detriment of Madame personally, not by any means for to be honest with myself I must own that were I not to receive such marks of feminine regard at all I should be inclined to entertain much better feeling against them, whereas, as it is I am much indebted to them for innumerable kindness and mutual sympathetic consideration.

On duty 5 pm to 9 pm. Replied to Mr Kendrick and sent a picture postcard to my dear little boy. <u>A</u> <u>thought</u> <u>for</u> <u>today</u> " France is the home of love and poetry. Germany is the abode of materialism and progress, England is the heart of the world."

30/3/19

Weather still continues wretched and cold with alternate frost and snowstorms. Paraded at 9.30 am. Fatigues brushing the school steps and passages. For some reason unknown there was no church parade for the C of E's but only for the non-conformists and in case any extra fatigues come along I was not slow in disappearing and went to my friends, where I surprised Monsieur still in bed and his wife working hard as usual in the kitchen. Swallowed something very big, which was in my porridge at breakfast and since have had a painful throat. On duty 1 pm to 5 pm. As dinner was not ready I declined an invitation to stay Chez mesamis but had a couple of plates of soup, which is always acceptable. As there was very little work to do we tossed up who should go off duty and I won, this was fortunate, as I had promised to accompany mesamis into the town for a quiet drink together at a restaurant. Accordingly I quickly put myself in gala trim and was not long in arriving back a la maison de meamic, although I had to brave a very heavy fall of snow, which appears quite determined to refuse admittance au printemps. Monsieur had a friend to see him, an ex-member of a zeppelin crew who had made several excursions to England, ate pasty and smoked cigars and cigarettes until 6 pm. Then accompanied by Madame and her friend we all went down the town catching a tram at the top of the street. The restaurant selected for our carrousel is in the Phillipper Strasse, and is both large and well ordered. It has been set apart for warrant officers and Sergeants only, but the manager did not object to me, but suggested that I should not take of my great coat, after a round of beers, we started on white wine and went full steam ahead until closing time. Supplying ourselves with four more bottles of mother's ruin at 13 marks a bottle we wended our way home, myself following until clear of the main thoroughfares and then arm in arm for the rest of the way. The night was fine and frosty and the good supper, which was soon prepared for the company was delightfully acceptable. The husband of Madame's friend had now joined us and the drinking recommenced with gusto, and with some little flirting avec mesdames the evening wore on in a perfectly pleasant manner, until some hour in the early morning. I have a faint recollection of a fierce tussle which took place between myself and the ladies, which terminated favourably for me, but only after quite a lot of furniture and ornaments had like us become effected and had lost their equilibrium. In fact if my memory can be relied upon the other gentlemen, who were spectators to the foregoing were holding in their arms some of the more valuable household goods. The little else which did or might have happened it is not my intention to narrate here. A nice bed was made up for me in the front room and there I lay until wakened at 6 am, as I had to be on parade at 7 am and on duty at 8 am, and here ends a little episode, which, though not much in itself, was nevertheless, quite thoroughly enjoyed and exquisitely pleasant, and the cost which was high, about 150 marks, was really worth it and more. <u>A</u> <u>thought</u> <u>for</u> <u>today</u> " All women are assailable and none are inaccessible."

31/3/19

Fine frosty morning. Except for a somewhat heavy head am in the pink of condition. I came home a 6 am, it was piercingly cold and the roads were hard with frost. After wash, shave and clean up went on duty at 8 am to 1 pm, which did not tend to improve the top portion of my anatomy. After dinner I went back again to my friends of last night, where I found some of the party talking over all the events and they were considerably amused. The Frau bore evident marks on her wrist and arms where I had taken hold of her. Stayed for tea and supper. On duty 9 pm until 11 pm. <u>A thought for today</u> "Marriage is a public license under the cloak of which, two people are permitted and entitled to carry on an immoral life to any extent whatever, without fear of molestation, or risk of ridicule or contempt from others."

1/4/19

Good night rest up at 7 am and after breakfast and clean up, went off to spend the day with my friends. On the way I bought another dictionary this time "Deutsche - English". Helped Frau in her household duties, with which I have become intimately acquainted in the army, such as peeling potatoes, brushing floors etc, etc. Stayed for dinner. I might mention that Frau like the German himself does not lack the power of inventiveness and in the matter of coffee, which is dear and scarce, she has found a good substitute in wheat which she roasts and then grinds up in a moulin a cafe like the French grind their coffee beans. The drink made in this way they are pleased to call cafe and indeed while the grain is roasting the smell is certainly not unlike the genuine article. On duty 5 pm to 9 pm. Another bit of good luck has come my way today, for I now become entitled to the 10/6 a week bonus under the new pay regulations for the army of occupation. The slip that has been posted inside my pay book reads as follows, " granted bonus (as machinery of demobilisation under a.o 14 dated 29/1/19 of 10/6. Ten shillings and six pence per week payable from 1/2/19." This means 8 weeks back pay, which amounts to over 200 marks. Really I have no wish for immediate demobilisation as I am not blind to the fact that I shall never get such a good job as this again. <u>A thought for today</u> " Free love is an institution dictated by the laws of nature."

2/4/19

Good sleep, which I needed badly. It is a fearfully ungracious sort of morning, with fog, some ice and a good deal of slush. On parade at 9.30 am. Requested to interview the C.O for the purpose of obtaining a new tunic and was successful in procuring a chit, but could not get a proper fit. Have taken it this morning to Frau, who has promised to male the necessary alterations, but it will be nevertheless too short. I cannot understand why our uniforms are so shoddy and poorly made in comparison to the Germans and French. A German soldier has four uniforms all of good quality material and extremely well put together. The pockets are even lined. Returned for dinner at 12.15 pm and on duty at 1 pm to 5 pm. When going up to visit the house of my German friends this morning I overtook the funeral of a student, but in order to proceed on my way I was compelled to stand for a while until the procession has passed, another soldier and myself who were standing together, as the processionists walked slowly along, we both came to a salute as the hearse passed by.

233

German burials are remarkable in one certain particular in so much that they are thoroughly representative off the station and age of the deceased. The one I saw this morning included many students who walked in front. A former one which I saw was obviously the last journey of a little girl, for preceding the hearse and carrying wreaths were a number of her former schoolmates. Did a little French and German study. Spent the evening in the usual manner, I had a hard scuffle again with the Frau, her daughter aged 16 years and Madame, but got the upper hand of them in the end, although I broke my watch face in the attempt. We have high jinks sometimes and nearly die of laughing. Had some hot soup and then returned to billet. Roll call has been extended from 9.30 pm to 10 pm and lights out 10.15 pm commencing from today. In the Duren paper of yesterday it stated that food for the civilian population is on its way from England for the benefit of the occupied territory, which appears to have given a good deal of satisfaction to the inhabitants. A thought for today " In the gloaming of life one is confronted only with past remembrances, and many turn with vain regrets to seek in quiet slumber a peaceful and unburdened hereafter."

3/4/19

Fine dry frosty morning. Paraded at 7 am. On duty at 8 am to 1 pm. I should do well to mention one item of interest, which came before my notice sometime ago. I came across a Fraulein a short while back in a tobacconist here, who was wearing an ordinary metal ring with the inscription " Varterland dank 1914" (the fatherland's thanks 1914) inscribed around the band, she explained to me that all the women in Germany who gave up all their golden trinkets in 1914 for their country's service, received a ring of this description in return and she was I must say extremely proud of her poor metal ring and rightly so I should imagine. Spent the afternoon and evening with my friends at 6 pm I went with them to Merzenich, a village about 3/4 hours walk from Duren, and I assisted them in drawing a bag of wheat in a small carriage on four wheels, to the above village for the purpose of grinding it into flour. Had some hot soup and then returned to billet and went on duty at 9 pm to 8 am the following morning. A thought for today " When counting the lessons of life, it would be well to remember that the foremost and best, which were ever taught us, are those which we learned at our mother's knee."

4/4/19

A fit of shivering came on me during the night, and during the day I have become gradually worse and weak. Went to my friends after breakfast. Had some hot tea and two cups of hot milk and went to sleep on the sofa until 4 pm. Was excused duty at 5 pm and instead I made my kip and got into it and there I stayed. A thought for today " All are not happy who smile."

5/4/19

Was much refreshed this morning, after a long sleep and rest. My head which yesterday was terribly heavy with cold, is now considerably clearer. Like yesterday the weather is gloriously fine, it is a shame to be indoors. Had two plates of really excellent gruel at the house of my friends in the morning. On duty 1 pm to 5 pm. In the evening returned to my friends and before leaving at 9.15 pm had a good plate of gruel.

For some unexplained reason we are not to be paid tomorrow as was customary and this has caused some little discontent, I think it is only right to expect regular pay and every week instead of once in a fortnight or three weeks. A thought for today " To really understand anything correctly one must be able to appreciate
fully and whole-heartedly the subject in question.

6/4/19

Dull morning. Am still not quite my usual self, but undoubtedly I owe very much indeed to the kind and considerate attention of my friend Frau, otherwise had I only to rely on the M.O. here, who would have palmed me off in the first instance at least with a few cure-all pills, I should have quickly become a genuine candidate for the hospital, which I am extremely anxious to avoid. On duty 8 am to 1 pm. Received a letter and important communications from my dear little sister Dot. Spent afternoon and evening at my friends in York-Strasse, near the hospital at present in the occupation of the British. A thought for today "Dress makes the man but cleanliness makes the woman."

7/4/19

Most beautiful sunny day, and one is very forcibly reminded of the old ideal Easter holidays in the far dim past in old England. I am still very much on the wrong side of perfect health especially my head, which is heavy and aching a great deal. I was glad to get out into the warm welcoming sun as soon as I could this morning and walked slowly in the direction of the cemetery, opposite the British hospital. I had heard yesterday that 54 of my comrades were buried there already and I wished to verify this statement for myself. It is a large cemetery and I had almost given up the search, when I espied two British Tommies at work on a grave at the end of a little avenue forded with small fir-trees, approaching the soldiers I quickly learned all I wished to know. The remark of one of them was characteristic and full of indignation, and was to the effect that after all these poor lad's had gone through against those damned people, they now found their last resting place here in the midst of their foes. The graves are arranged in two rows with a path down the middle, most of them bore good crosses at the head and all were profusely covered with beautiful wreaths. I counted the graves and found, including several officers, that the number above given to me by the German's was correct. Have received a long expected and greatly welcome portraits of my little boy, although taken but shortly after his resent illness the little mite looks remarkably well and I am indeed most happy to have his precious picture always with me. Spent most of the day at the usual rendezvous, where I had some more gruel etc. Had my hair cut by a lady barber who, as is her custom with everyone, took great pains with my poor show of hair, and she did not complete her task until well over 20 minutes had elapsed, and without the slightest doubt, it was the best hair cut I have ever had, and all for 7 d, where as in France I have been charge 2 franc's for a couple of minutes clipping etc and remarkably bad results, while yet again in England while on leave I was perfectly hideous in less than 3 minutes.

On duty 5 pm to 9 pm. I am hoping sincerely that I shall be at least a little improved by tomorrow, it is hateful to feel unwell. <u>A thought for today</u> "In books we find all that we ourselves feel and hope for and which we lack in ability to translate into writing or convert into fact."

8/4/19

Ideal weather still prevails. Paraded at 9.30 am followed by short fatigue. Walked out to York-Strasse. Returned for dinner at midday. On duty 1 pm to 5 pm. Am feeling considerably better today and my head is far less painful. Wrote to my dear little sis Dot and enclosed Mr Kendricks letter, which I received yesterday, with the request that she should send it on to my solicitors with an explanation. At 6.30 pm went to York-Strasse, where I spent a pleasant evening until 9.30 pm. We drank a couple of bottles of red wine between us which was boiled and sweetened with sugar. I might note here with reference to the attitude of the German's towards ourselves, that contrary to all other reports I am of opinion that their apparent friendliness is prompted primarily by a consciousness that they were not decisively beaten in the field and secondly that all honour is due to them for having withstood the onslaughts of overwhelming foes in a brave and honourable fight. In short they imagine themselves to be at least equal to their conquerors, I like this sort of spirit and I admire them for it. <u>A thought for today</u> "There is no music more pure or exquisite than the early morning spring song of birds."

9/4/19

Beautiful day, it is a great shame to be indoors. On duty 8 am to 1 pm. Yesterday I received 90 mark's in pay, which owing to lowering funds was most acceptable. Wrote to my sister Doris requesting her to forward me on behalf of my friends here half a dozen collars, and two yards of elastic for the purpose of making garters for the youngsters, who go about tied up in all sorts of injurious bandages on account of the total absence of the last named very needful article in Germany. Went to the cinema at 2.30 pm where I met Frau, afterwards returning to the school for tea and then to my friends house, where I spent a pleasant evening until 8.30 pm. Had a good plate of soup and a cup of excellent boiled milk with the added luxury of chocolate boiled with it. On duty 9 pm to 8 am tomorrow morning. The old screecher formally used by the Germans as a warning signal to the inhabitants of approaching enemy aircraft, is now used by us each night at 9 pm as a warning to all civilians that they must be in doors. Its rauky voice is unmistakable and to hear it for the first time it is apt to create quite a creepy sort of feeling. <u>A thought for today</u> " All things come to him - who gets them."

Diary Number 13
10/4/19

Weather still continues fine and healthy. I am back again in the enjoyment of good health for which I am genuinely thankful. At 9 am I went on a short shopping expedition with the object of buying something, which I had mentally noted several days ago and which I judged would appeal to the fine religious instincts of my dear sis Dot. The objects selected are a pair of embossed paintings representing a nun playing her violin on the convent veranda at sunset and its fellow is that of a monk listening by his open casement to the stains of music which come floating to him through the still air. A similar embossed imitation painting of Doren showing also the museum and water tower I bought for myself and have taken the whole bundle to the orderly-room for censoring. Rest of the day I spent at York-Strasse. On duty 5 pm to 9 pm. <u>A thought for today</u> " An opinion is often a selfish argument."

11/4/19

When visiting the cemetery the other day the following thoughts of " British graves" passed through my mind and I have committed them to paper with all due respect and sincere regards to nobler and better men than I am.

"British graves"

" People talk of blood soaked fields, of battlefields drenched with the life-wine of brave men, of gullies and ravines converted into running streams of the rich red life-blood of our soldiers on far distant rocky shores and on fairer fields in Flanders and elsewhere, where brave men have fought and died. But of graves, British graves, those immemorial monuments of Britains might and fame, which lie scattered broadcast from pole to pole, from east to west, in an unending chain from continent to continent and beneath the waves of every ocean. Linking up with their bodies all the corners of the earth to their beloved and native motherland. How very little do we hear of Britains worldwide grave-yard whose confines are limitless and brooks no boundary line whatever, and how little do we appreciate the great work accomplished by such stalwart sons of Britain before they paid the greater sacrifice. One might be constrained to believe that Britishers have left, no living interest in the dead. Wherever the sun may shed its rays from moment to moment through the ages yet to come, it will seek out and salute with a kindly glance the sacred tombs of Britains dead. Never for the smallest fraction of time will the light from heaven ever set upon the fair fame of Britains greatness and by her consecrated monuments shall future generations learn, know and understand many things which were the practice of her noble son's. Although all die and her temples and monuments of brick and stone may be overthrown, and rot into dust, yet the power and influence of this mighty people can never perish. For high up on the mountains in the full blast of natures wrath, on the slopes of desolated hills, in the shade of jagged rocks, in the arid wastes of barren lands, where all of god's creation wither and succumb, deep down on the uneven bed of every sea, in regions for ever unexplored, by the shore of every lake, in loneliness and peaceful calm, in the wildernesses in the midst of pestilence where reaps unceasingly the hand of death but never sows at the base of treacherous ice-slopes and at the bottom of fathomless dreary crevices ------ Be Britains best in silent sleep.

But, it is in the land of Britain's foes in the midst of Britain's most ruthless enemies the tale of " British graves" is yet untold. In the care of fickle nature on the mountain's summit, in the desert of hopelessness, or among the dwellings and habitations of reptiles the immortal son's of the motherland are at least assured of rude respect, but, what ignominy, and what awful and terrible destiny has so decreed that graves of Britishers should at least be set and mingled with the bones of Britain's would be assassins and among those who worship the hellish doctrines that assent to butcher babes and defenceless women. God, this is a crime against humanity, against the laws of nature and religion, but then it may be that those men are here to serve a purpose in due course, which will do good even to the Huns. Then in this case too, it may be said that British graves have purified, humanised and civilised the world." On parade at 9 am afterwards at York-Strasse. It is dull today but not cold. On duty 1 pm to 5 pm. Spent evening at the aforesaid address, where Frau altered a new tunic, which I had managed to get, and it now fits me like a glove, she also changed the buttons off my old tunic and affixed my decorations, completing the job by ironing out all the creases. The Germans are expecting peace to be signed within the next few days, but they say they will only sign it if the Rhineland is allowed to remain an integral part of Germany as they have a loathing to be associated in any way with the French, who they fear have designs upon all the districts west of the Rhine. A thought for today "All men have their superiors and also their inferiors. The former reverently bow the knee before their god - creator, while the latter cannot raise themselves above the level of dogs."

12/4/19

Dull and close. On duty 8 am to 1 pm. Wrote to my dear little sister Doris, making several more requests. Spent a very pleasant afternoon and evening at my friends house in York-Strasse. For supper we had pancakes, without eggs but very tasty and Frau and I drank hot wine mixed with sugar. My good chum Sapper Whittett is on orders tonight for demobilisation so that tomorrow I shall lose my friend and this is undeniably a big disappointment. He will also be keenly missed in the football team in which he never has failed to give a good display. A thought for today "The graves of Britishers, which be scattered broadcast thought the earth, will be lasting monuments of a great and mighty people."

13/4/19

Raining almost all the day. Had dinner and tea with Monsieur and Frau. They are really very kind indeed to me, and although the weekly meat allowance is positively only enough for one robust mans meal, yet, I am entreated to share with them in what they have, which goes strongly against the grain, although of course I try to make up for their kindness in many ways. Men, women and young girls have been working industriously on the land for some days now and the numerous smallholdings are looking quite ship-shape and one might imagine promise well later on. On duty 5 pm to 9 pm. A thought for today "By the tombs of Britains sons shall future generations throughout the universe, know, learn and respect the colossal works of this world's greatest people."

14/4/19

Very windy day. Paraded and rifle inspection at 9.30 am by our new O.C, who took over yesterday. Went to York-Strasse in the morning. I am feeling very crocked again as from yesterday. Posted pictures to my dear little sis Dot yesterday morning and I hope they will reach her safely. On duty 1 pm to 5 pm. From 6 pm to 9.30 pm at the home of my friends. A thought for today "The sepulchres of Britains dead shall serve for ever as sacred shrines, and marking along the road of progress for the guidance of future peoples the mile-stones of perfection."

15/4/19

Pleasant sunny morning. The high wind of yesterday has happily abated. Have still the unpleasant stomach troubles of which I complained yesterday in spite of an abundance of fruit salt and some antidotes graciously administered by Frau. On duty 8 am to 1 pm. Received a letter-card from Mlle Hunel and a letter from Miss Lily Cummins. Had an enjoyable afternoon and evening with my good German friends, in spite of the fact that I have quite failed so far to eradicate the evil, which is playing the deuce with my stomach. On duty 9 pm to 8 am the following morning. A thought for today "Adversity is not merely sent to try us, but rather to compel us to appreciate fully those fleeting moments of good fortune, when they arrive."

16/4/19

Am still very much indeed on the wrong side of good health and it is extremely disappointing and deprives one completely of all joy in life. Went for a bath in the town at 9.30 am. While waiting in the room set apart for the purpose, there came a number of civilians and among them, were two young Frauleins who sat down beside me and quickly became friendly. I quickly learned who and what they were, but I was confessedly surprised, as until this moment I was perfectly unaware that we had in Duren what are called " Controlled women" as interpreted for the German. They voluntarily showed me their "medical inspection books" which are printed both in German and English, and include such particulars as name and address, age etc. Their photographs are affixed at the top of the first page. On the front cover is a warning notice to the effect that the book must not be mislaid or lost, as the owner would be liable to sever punishment in such case. I was further informed that there were about 50 controlled women in Duren and that they must visit periodically both an English and German doctor for the purpose of having their cards signed and verified. Both these girls, from whom I obtained the above information were only 20 years of age and one confided to me that she had been a mother by a German officer during the war, but that her child had died. She came from Frankfort, was an orphan, had no sisters and her four brothers were all killed in the war. All this may or may not be accepted as a fact, but still if it is true of one case it certainly is of another. Afterwards went to York-Strasse where I remained until teatime. On duty 5 pm to 9 pm. A thought for today "the beggar is well off -- in the enjoyment of good health."

17/4/19

My luck is clean out again and I am only too afraid that I must report sick as I am much worse today. Paraded at 9.30 am and did a short fatigue. Afterwards went to York-Strasse taking with me as usual a number of different articles in the food line. It is a very wet day and one's feelings are even more depressed by such atmospherical bad conduct. On duty 1 pm to 5 pm. Returned to my habitual abode, when off duty at 6 pm, where I stayed until after supper. A thought for today " Bitterness is sweet in comparison to ill health."

18/4/19

As I have so greatly feared these past few days I found it impossible to carry on without medical attention and decided to report sick. Being Good Friday the M.O at the barracks did not put in an appearance until 10.30 am. So was obliged to wait about for an hour of more. I strolled out and sat down on the bank, which runs along the street opposite the Caserne, in which are placed a number of German surrendered motor lorries, all these vehicles were in course of having their iron wheels removed and replaced by British wheels with rubber tyres, but these latter had obviously seen much better days as many of them exhibited perfectly evident marks of old age. Here I sat and pondered for truly my thoughts at present are anything but bright. On the lorry facing me was the one word "fertig" and its meaning seemed significant to my own case. It is a nice warm sunny day and in two more days it will be Easter Sunday and here I am for ever a prey to misfortune, with every happy prospect cruelly snatched away from me, at all events temporarily. We had planned several little outings during the Easter holidays and these have been thrown overboard. Now I am in Hospital at the bottom of York-Strasse and am quartered in the surgical ward. I paid a visit to my friends of course before finally giving up my freedom. Had dinner with them and at 3.30 pm most reluctantly parted from Frau and Monsieur. My own sorrow at the turn of events was markedly shared by Frau, and yesterday after hearing how I was and the counselling me to go into hospital during my visit in the morning, she did no more work that day whatever, nor even take a bite of anything to eat. Poor old Frau you are a dear old thing and already I miss very much your pleasant smile and many kindnesses. I do hope I shall soon be well again and free. A thought for today "A single breath of love is worth a thousand kindnesses."

19/4/19

Life is still changing I saw the M.O at 10 am this morning and he has marked me for evacuation to the C.C.S, which is in the town and was formally the blind school. I went to say goodbye to Frau at about 11 am and at 1.30 pm I came on here together with a number of jocks in a red-cross ambulance. Have had a lovely tea, but unfortunately I lacked a sufficient appetite, it constituted bread and butter, jelly, apricots, cheese and sardines, and an excellent cup of Sergeant majors. At this moment 6.30 pm the church bells are clanking out the sonorous notes intermingled by the sweet evening chorus of birds love-songs. Spring is here and these little creatures are very happy for, life to them is pleasant and pure and cares are quite unknown or not allowed to enter into their scheme of joy and good-will. I am hoping most earnestly that in a few days I may be able to join in once more with that part of life, which alone makes life worth living for.

<u>A</u> <u>thought</u> <u>for</u> <u>today</u> " There are many useful lessons that we might all learn and profit by, if we would but try to follow in the spirit and the letter, the beautiful examples for ever set before us by the minor creatures of creation."

20/4/19

Easter Sunday and here I am a prisoner and clean out of all the good times, to which I had looked forward with so much hope and pleasure. Saw the M.O at about 10 am and I politely put the request to him not to send me away from here as I have no wish to be sent down to the base hospital or even to England just yet, and under the circumstances this is probably what would happen if I am evacuated. The M.O quite a decent sort of chap, replied in these terms, " I don't know old thing, depends on how you behave yourself, I can't make any rash promises etc etc". It seems to me that they can't decide whether I have slightly ruptured myself or perhaps it is only a sort of strain. I fancy myself it is all the cause of the throw I had at the last football match as truly I have not been properly well since that happened, and I have come to firmly believe that I am still suffering from its effects as it is the whole of my right side, which is effected, and even my right arm which I sprained at the time, continues to send out little pain spasms when moved into certain angles. We are having especially good grub here, a few eggs and some milk, would leave nothing else to be desired, at any rate for the moment. This is a lazy sort of life and terribly uninteresting. One loses all touch with the outside world and to everyone, with the slightest inclination for activity, it is horribly boring. Day passed in the conventional style of reading, a very little French and German study and a fair amount of sleep. A friend kindly called at our orderly room this evening and brought back for me three letters from Mrs Taylor, my dear sister Gladys and Miss Weeds. <u>A thought for today</u> "All things are worthwhile although sometimes they may end badly."

21/4/19

Nice warm day. Am still about the same and I cannot help but feel somewhat disappointed. Fate seems so often to be set dead against me, and in consequence I seem forced to maintain a running fight against big odds. I wonder how much longer I must pass away the precious hours in this manner. Although terribly weak for the moment my caged spirit is not by any means enfeebled and to ease the ache of its confinement I allow myself to relapse into a semi-coma and do nothing, say nothing and think nothing from morning until night. <u>A</u> <u>thought</u> <u>for</u> <u>today</u> " All are not good who preach."

22/4/19

What a glorious day. The sun has been shining brightly since early morning and the birds are even yet singing joyously in the trees, oh how much I wish I could go out and enjoy the fresh air and clear skies. After dinner I could restrain myself no longer and put on my cap and went out and sauntered along but very painfully in the direction of our headquarters. Passing on the way the German war memorial of 1870-71, which had been badly mutilated by the British troops soon after the occupation was completed.

It happened in this way, on or about new years eve a number of soldiers led by an officer, as the result of elated spirits I presume, requisitioned a motor-lorry and with the assistance of a long rope, which was fastened tightly around the figure of a German soldier, who bore in his right hand a standard, and the whole was dragged bodily off its high pedestal and crashed to the ground in pieces damaging in its decent other parts of the monument and bursting through the surrounding palings, where a big block, all that is left of the German soldier, being minus legs and head still encumbers the footpath. I heard that this little spree cost the officer quite a round sum of money and that the division was called upon to pay a heavy fine. I called at our orderly room for letters but there were none. I quite fail to understand Doris's silence and further I quite expected to receive a registered letter from her several days ago. Was very glad to get back to hospital again and to lie down, and I was thoroughly exhausted when I returned. <u>A thought for today</u> " The best type of men are to be found in every shade and grade of society from Bishops to burglars."

23/4/19

Yet another beautiful glorious day. The M.O in spite of my previous request not to do so has marked me for down the line, which of course has only increased my miserable position as this means Boulogne and most probably Blighty. I have very particular reasons for not wishing to be sent away from here just yet, and they are that my pay at records has not yet been adjusted. That my months special leave (time expired) and the Territorial bounty of 15 pounds are not yet confirmed and duly entered in my pay book. Have only a short while to go to complete four years service abroad and am still waiting for the Territorial efficiency ribbon, besides all this I am anxious as far as possible to make good a little of the black ruin, which now stares me in the face at any rate for my boys sake and I know well enough that I can do this far better by remaining out here a little longer. In the afternoon I walked out, bought a mark's worth of sweets (about a dozen for a mark) and sat me down on a small grass patch in a triangle just against the railway bridge, where there are two or three seats and kid's go there to play and I endeavoured to conjure up an interest in the passers-by etc. A little boy came up to me in quite a frightened sort of way and nervously asked if I would not like to sit upon a seat, not wishing to be disturbed by youngsters I gave him a decided no and he at once ran back to where a woman, presumably his mother and several kiddies where sitting upon one of the seats. After a short while I returned to the Hospital. <u>A thought for today</u> "Nothing dims so acutely the sight and senses as keen disappointment."

24/4/19

Dull and rain this morning. When the M.O came round I asked him once more to allow me to remain here, instead of being sent down the line and happily he acceded to my request, I pointed out that I was waiting for several things coming through, which would be to my advantage, including one month's special leave and that I would much prefer to return to my own Division. He mentioned that I was not in very good health to go on leave, but, he added with a smile it can be done I suppose. My cards, which were marked for down the line were thereupon cancelled much to my relied.

After tea I strolled out for half an hour, but owing to a strong feeling of weakness I was glad to come back and lie down. <u>A thought for today</u>
" Surely something good will yet turn up in spite of all contrary appearances."

25/4/19

Dull morning. Am feeling slightly better today. I do hope it will continue and that I shall rapidly regain my normal health. As no more letters or even the registered letter which I expected at the end of last week, have yet reached me I decided to go myself to our headquarters and to personally interview the postman, which I did, but without any success. I am quite unable to fathom this mystery as this is the first time my little sis Dot has failed me. After tea I went for a short stroll and got into conversation with a Fraulein outside her house, later I accompanied her to a neighbours, where there is a good gramophone, and at 9 pm I came away, Fraulein walked with me part of the way back to the hospital. <u>A thought for today</u> " Ones greatest friend and enemy is oneself."

26/4/19

The sun is still disinclined to show itself this morning. Shortly after dinner I received the long expected letter, at least an envelope containing two 1 pound postal orders from my dear little sis Dot, there was not a word of news and so I am left still to wonder at the silence. I do not even know if she has safely received any of the things I have sent to her of late. I went immediately to cash the orders but got caught in a heavy storm on my way back. Had a bath before tea and afterwards decided to pay a visit to my friends at York-Strasse. On the way I bought a silk collar to fit on a blouse as an Easter present for Frau. Both Monsieur and Frau were very glad to see me again and indeed I was glad too to be back once more with them. Frau told me that she and her friend had walked to the hospital yesterday afternoon, but that they had seen nothing of me, which was not likely as at the time I was at tea. Had some soup and came away at 8.30 pm so that I might arrive back at the hospital in good time. In consequence of a disturbance, which took place the other evening over a girl, which was traced to the men in this hospital, all men have now to wear the hospital blue dress, but as yet the ward I am in has not come under the ban so far as I can gather. The row started when a Fraulein a worker in the hospital was leaving the grounds accompanied by a Tommy, several jocks intervened apparently thinking they had as much right to the girl as her companion, they followed the pair home near to the hospital and it is said that there a fight took place and some windows were smashed. <u>A thought for today</u> " Come what may there is always something worth living for."

27/4/19

Clear bright morning but somewhat cold. A notice has now been posted up to the effect that no patient is allowed to leave the hospital grounds. This will not do at all as I have promised to be up at York-Strasse at 2 pm. After dinner I discreetly went for a stroll round the grounds and was presently through a hole in the hedge and away on my way to the other end of the town.

As usual I was very kindly received by my friends and Monsieur gave me his house slippers to wear instead of my heavy army boots and was soon installed comfortably on the sofa where I remained until I came away. Had some tea and a nice supper. Received a picture postcard from Mlle Renee, but at present I have not a sparkle of inclination to write to anybody and in fact since I have been laid up I have not done so. A thought for today " Church-bells are a masterly inspiration."

28/4/19

Am gradually recovering but oh so slowly. Did not attempt to go out until after tea although on the whole the weather has been fine today. Called at our canteen and bought a few things including a box of woodbines of 250 for Monsieur, a table of coal-tar soap and a cake of chocolate for Frau. With regard to cigarettes I may say that civilians are open to be heavily fined if caught smoking English cigarettes in public, as an example I may relate the following authentic case, which occurred here, while ravelling on a tram a young man handed round his cigarette-case, which was filled with English cigarettes, an English detective in plain clothes on the look-out for things of this sort arrested the individual in question, when the tram came to a halt and he was fined 250 mark's for his generosity. To enlarge upon our system of secret spying I may remark that at Cologne station our friend Frau was accosted the other day as she got of the train by an English woman, who proceeded to carry out a quick search over her person for any contraband, which she might be trying to smuggle into the cathedral city. I believe a large number of arrests have been effected in this way. Had some supper with my friends and then returned to Hospital. A thought for today " I think that the hardest work of all is when one has to think."

29/4/19

Rather dull but fine during the morning. A military funeral took place from here at about 10.30 am. An artillery officer had died and the preparations to accord him the last honours were solemn and imposing, a firing party of artillery men with arms reversed marched at the head of the procession (I always understood that they should march behind the coffin) followed by buglers and the artillery brass-band, the drum draped entirely in black. Then came a 4.5 drawn by six blacks and above the muzzle of the weapon was raised a small platform painted black on which rested the remains of the dead officer, encased in a German coffin, with the usual elaborate metal decoration on the outside and the union-jack lying caressingly over all. The officer's charger a black, led by a soldier created in itself an impressiveness quite indescribable and as he stepped proudly immediately in the wake of his departed master, whose jack-boots stuck in the stirrups, with the heels pointing to the front and swaying limply to the movements of the horse, one realises that in life there is death which is waiting ever so patiently for each one of us. Bringing up the rear was a good muster of artillerymen. Wrote a letter to Mrs Taylor and a card to my dear little boy. Finished reading " As in as looking glass". After tea I went to spend the evening with my friends. A thought for today " Life is death without light."

30/4/19

Dull and cloudy today. After dinner I went out and after visiting the YMCA and waiting for something in a long queue, only to find in the end that they had nothing, no woodbines, no players, no tobacco, no soap, no chocolate, no nothing, of all the institutions for the supposed benefit of the troops the YMCA is beloved least of any by the vast majority of Tommies and for good and sufficient reasons. The chief fault lies in the fact that the YMCA is essentially and first and foremost a money making concern whose chief object is profits, this sort of thing is directly opposed to the best interests of the individual soldier and he has therefore ample grounds for complaint. I once heard a lecture by the principal of the YMCA who had come over from London for the purpose of making a round of visits to some of the YMCA huts. He explained to us vast schemes, which he and his confederates proposed to carry into effect, such as the erection of a hut in every town and village in England (United Kingdom) which was to take the place of the public house, and these social halls would be supplied with every sort of indoor and outdoor game and amusement. I know too that the profits from the thirty YMCA cinematogtaps in France went to support YMCA farms for the incapacitated soldiers, which again I presume would be run for a profit. It is downright scandalous that soldiers probably but a few hours before they were killed in action should be robbed even indirectly for such purposes as these which in any case, it is the duty of the state to fulfil and should not be left to the seemingly charitable YMCA, which exists purely on charity and by what it can make out of the best man in the world "Tommy Atkins". Spent the afternoon and evening at York-Strasse. A thought for today "The English language is a cross between German and French. The root of a great number of English words are obviously German, Which makes it much simpler to pick up than French, which latter is far more difficult even in the elementary stage. On the other hand a large number of French words have been absorbed bodily in our language but with a noticable falling off of the original pronunciation."

1/5/19

Dull and raining. Was marked for discharge today the M.O said that I should probably be a long while in completely recovering and that I must not over exert myself in the least. I am glad to be at liberty once more and I can only trust in the happy ending of the M.O.S assurance.Spent afternoon and evening at York-Strasse. It has been a big day here for the Democratic Socialists, who marched in procession through the town with a German brass band leading. They were escorted by British military police armed with revolvers and British aeroplanes circled just above the house tops in case of emergency. All the processionists wore the red-roseatte and many people flocked into the town, many of whom wore also the red ensign, I stopped to watch one party marching into the town to the appointed rendez-vous and one individual turned to eye me most venomiously, his ugly eyes spoke hate and his wretched mouth twisted about frighfully, he reminded me of the Bull-ring orators (socialists) in Birmingham before the war. Creatures with horrible decayed teeth, nasty holes for mouths, which twisted uncontrollably into shapeless contortions, noses which signified nothing and eyes that glared like the germs of fell diseases. Quite a terrifying spectacle I used to think. It is a holiday for everybody but unfortunately the weather is most unkind and the processionists were obliged to carry umbrellas to protect their tall silk hats. a thought for today There are no joys without pain."

2/5/19

Left hospital at about 10.30 am and went first to the orderly room where I handed in my hospital papers to the sergeant major and I was informed that 5 pounds had been put to my credit and that 10 ponds was accredited to me and which would be paid to me on demobolization together with 5 % interest. I was surprised to learn that all the signal staff had gone with the divisional headquarters to Kreuzau a village a village at the tram terminus half an hours run from Duren. I decided to go out at once and to get fixed up. Arrived by tram about 12.30 pm and after dinner went round the village in search of a billet and after a good deal of trouble I was fortunate with the aid of our sergeant and a corporal who speaks German to procure an excellent billet with lovely bed and electric light. It is not a big house but extremely comfortable. There are two old gentlemen and a Frau and two daughters, as soon as I was fixed up I returned to Duren and went to York-Strasse taking with me my hospital rations, which I did not require, which included two tins of bully beef, half a loaf, some cheese and tea and sugar. Returned to Kreuzau at 8.30 pm and to my astonishment Frau whom I call mamma had a big plate of baked potatoes and some delicious rice-cake ready for me and some good hot coffee. Taked and smoked for an hour or more with my new acquaintances and then tumbled into my snug little bed. a thought for today " All are not bad, though badly painted."

3/5/19

Good night repose. After breakfast and clean up had a game (peculiar German) with fraulein in the sitting room and she won. No one is working as today is a religious feast day and is observed like a sunday. All have been to church in their Sunday best. Went to Duren and arrived at my friends at about 11.15 am where I remained until 3 pm. Bought four bottles of wine in the town on my way back to catch the tram, in view of Monsieur and Frau coming to visit me in my new quarters tomorrow evening, which at my request they have kindly consented to do. Frau I may say seems quite disheartened at my leaving Duren and indeed I am sorry too to be so far away from my old friends. Arriving back I was persuaded to have some cake and coffee etc with the family and at 5 pm I went on duty at the signal office until 9 pm. Had a busy evening and did not have the time to do several little things, which hitherto have been in the habit of doing in working hours, such as letter writing etc. Mamma had a big plateful of baked potatoes ready for me and some coffee on my return. Retired at 10 pm and wrote a letter to my dear little sis Dot in answer to her's, which I received this morning, which to say the least has caused me some little anxiety still it takes rather a good deal to entirely smother my hopes and I think I have successfully treated the occasion at least I hope so. a thought for today " The best thing about a women is her clothes only provided they are clean"

4/5/19

Good nights rest got up at 7.50 am. I know the time because there is a big clock on the wall of my bedroom. Breakfast and cleanup and then went for a short walk and at the moment I am seated upon the grass a little way out of the village by the bank of the vast flowing stream, which wends it winding way through the centre of the village. This particular feature and the hills round about bring back to my memory the lovely spectacle of beautiful Schleiden, although of course one cannot compare here with that charming place.

Looking round from where I am writing these few notes my eyes rest on several pleasant objects, which form a tolerable picture, such as the three-arched spanned bridge of concrete over the river, and on the opposite bank rough those same arches there are a number of black and white cows quietly grazing. On my left is a murmering waterfall, whose waters rush in a small semi-circle to join the main stream and in the back ground the trees and bushes are all bursting into life and beyond the grey low lying hills of cultivated fields. The cows are now all on this side of the bridge and facing me but the two tall chimney stacks and oldish looking factory and buildings in the rear do not appear to sympathise with the rural surroundings. The sun is shining, and it is warm, but thick dark clouds are hanging low and threatening. Returned to my billet and at 11.30 received 200 marks in pay. Had dinner and on duty 1 pm to 5 pm, I cannot help but feel extremely upset and more than anxious over the news I received yesterday form my sister Doris. It was undoubtedly a terrible blow for me as I had hoped so much for a good time to come in the near future and it now seems all dashed away from me and after reckoning up affairs it seems that my position is even much worse than at first I thought and things look hopeless enough. it would seem that there is no one in the world that can be trusted and I think I am beginning to hate everybody and there is certainly not a living soul who is not a damned liar and often the deepest dyed criminal is purer of mind and more honest of purpose than the most fiendish religious fanatic. At 5 pm went to meet my friends from York-Strasse at the tram terminus. They had come apparently at 3 pm and had visited some friends of theirs. They came with me to my billet and my mutter provided them and me with an excellent tea of sponge, cake, rice cake and apple tart, with real good coffee, afterwards we drank our wine and at 7 pm went for a short walk calling at the home of my friends friends and one of the daughters came with us along the same route I spoke about this morning and crossed the bridge into another little village, where we spent the remainder of the evening in a large hotel drinking wine. Many civilians were there and at the back there are lovely grounds for walking in and dancing on the second floor. We were all in high spirits when the time came for departure at about 8.40 pm, but arrived at the terminus too late for the tram and so we all returned to the house of fraulein to await the next and last tram at 9.40 pm and there was much merriment and laughter, which was responsible for missing the final tram into Duren. Things now changed rapidly and what had been a very pleasant evening was suddenly changed into one of a very different description, a sergeant and a couple of artillery who were in a spiteful mood came up and were shamefully insolent to my friends and wished to fight and even stuck Frau in the face. The sergeant and I were then in the dispute and after a few exchanges I got a black eye and it's a miracle how I come of no worse as I could not possibly stand to fight. The women screamed and frau hung onto me as if for life, frau had no pass for the night so we all returned once more to frauleins home and her mother and sister all took part in bathing my eye in cold water. Monsr went back to Duren on foot on account of the children, which distance takes 2 hours to cover. I was ensconced on the sofa and frau and fraulein stayed with me for sometime, after they had retired I got up and went out for a stroll up and down in the coal air and turned in about 2 am. Here ends a day out in Kreuzau. a thought for today " There is many a slip between drink and one's kip."

5/5/19

Was wakened at 5 am by frau and fraulein who were dressed and ready to catch the tram back to Duren. The morning was gloriously fine and presently monsr turned up to take Frau back home.

I accompanied them back to the tram and after it had left I wondered my weary steps home. Mamma was up and seemed greatly upset at the tale I told her. She had waited up last night until midnight for my return and my supper, which she had cooked was still on the hob. I set about cleaning myself up and after breakfast went on duty from 8 am to 1 pm. After dinner as I had promised I went to the tram terminus to go to Duren but had to wait an hour, owing to a curtailment of the service and in consequence I did not reach York-Strasse until 4 pm. On the way I went almost to sleep on the tram and when I got to the above address I quickly took advantage to get into bed there for a couple of hours. Again at 7 pm I was compelled to wait until 8 pm for a tram and arrived back at my billet at 8.45 pm, where mutter had some beautiful hot soup mad of goats milk of which I partook copiously. She also made me up a couple of sandwiches as she said "for the night" and then I proceeded on duty at 9 pm to 8 am the following morning.

6/5/19

Another beautiful morning. The countryside presents a charming picture and the fruit trees are overburdened everywhere with a mass of sparkling blossoms. I did not go to Duren today as I am not feeling quite equal to it. After breakfast and clean up I went out with my writing pad and sat down by the wide waterfall, with its fluffy spray dancing in the sunlight and tall green flanking hills showing up green and white in their fresh spring clothing in the background. On the other side the picturesque dwelling of the German peasants. Here I wrote some letters. Whatever else Germany may be, it is certainly a most beautiful country and the people are by no means so bad after all, as they have been painted. As the clouds began to gather and it grew cold I went on further and called at the home of fraulein of Sundays acquaintance and stayed there learning a little German with her young sister. After dinner wrote a letter to my friends at Duren explaining my absence and gave it to fraulein when she came here in her dinner hour to take back with her to hand it to monsieur at the office were they both work. I then went back to my billet and into bed until 4 pm. On duty 5 pm to 9pm. a thought for today " All is well that does not turn out badly."

7/5/19

Dull and somewhat chilly today. I reach my 30 th year and as I look back through the long years I can see nothing except much that I would rather forget. Have come out to the same place as yesterday morning as it is quiet and I need not fear being disturbed, while I write and think, principally of nothing. After writing for something more than an hour I went to visit fraulein and had a lesson in German. On duty 1 pm to 5 pm. After tea I caught the tram at 5.50 pm for Duren, bought some cigarettes, brown boot polish, matches etc. Went up to headquarters to get my pay-book totalled up and to see how much I could draw for Sunday our next pay day. Arrived at York-Strasse about 7.30 pm where dear old frau was delighted to see me, and gave me as usual a good reception. She had been awfully disappointed at my not turning up to see her yesterday. I think she is a little jealous. The collars for monsieur which I took with me proved to be much too large and are therefore useless to him, was persuaded to stay the night and I slept on a bed made up by Frau on the sofa and she came and tucked me in before she herself retired.

Her mother has come over to see her from Aachen(aix-la-chapelle) which is in the French area, and she and monsieur returned from the cinema at 9.30 pm. After supper I played games with them until midnight. a thought for today " Love and let love."

8/5/19

Monsr called me at 5.45 am and I had a cup of coffee and some French bread and butter, which frau's mother had brought, before catching the tram back to Kreuzau at 6.26 am. It is a most glorious morning and this afternoon frau and her mother are coming here for a walk into the country and we are taking our food with us. On duty 8 am to 1 pm. After dinner and a cleaning up I went to meet my friends with my haversack over my shoulder in which I carried my tea and a packet of chocolates. I arrived at the terminus as the tram came up and we all three started off on our walk into the country. Taking the road over the bridge and past the hotel of Sundays acquaintance and on past orchards in full blossom and fields and gardens beautifully fresh and green. Striking the main road again we walked along for a short distance and then took a bye path up a small hill shaded with diverse trees including many cherry-trees exhibiting a glorious picture in their dense masses of bright white blossoms. Here we sat down in a suitable place on the grass and talked , surveyed the landscapes, listened to the birds singing and watched them fly from branch to branch, while squirrels gambolled happily among the dry dead leaves of autumn last. This day has been undoubtedly the finest so far of the year and in the fresh spring air I feel already remarkably revigorated. Broke into the contents of our knapsack about 4.30 pm, after which frau and I went through the undergrowth to gather flowers and break off some sprigs of cherry-blossom. Seven o'clock came all to quickly and I know we all felt that we were breaking off with something which delighted us all. My friends caught the 7.50 pm tram back to Duren. While I went home to mutter, who provided me with a good meal before going on duty at 9 pm to 8 pm the following morning. a thought for today " It is astonishing how fast ones troubles stick to one."

9/5/19

It is again a beautiful day. Matter fried me an egg with my beacon for breakfast and since I came here I must say I have enjoyed an excellent appetite. Washed and shaved and then took my towel and soap for a hot bath at the big baths by the river here, which have been allotted to us for Fridays. They are beautifully arranged and I enjoyed yet another enjoyment before 10 am in the morning. I am now at my old place by the water fall which is both cool and refreshing as the sun is gaining still more heat as the days advance into summer. Personally I am feeling quite a different person to what I did a few weeks back and am getting a healthy colour into my cheeks, which is an unusual occurrence for me. My black eye too will soon have vanished completely, so I have at least something to be thankful for. Remained lounging about until midday. Had dinner and caught the tram for Duren at 1 pm. Where I went for the purpose of buying several things I needed such as matches, cigarettes, shaving soap, brown boot polish, soap etc, which I succeeded in getting. Got back to my billet at about 3 pm, had a cup of coffee with mutter and some of her own baked bread. Wrote a letter to Mr and Mrs Kendrick. Bought six lbs of rice from our cook for five franc's and gave it to mutter. On duty 5 pm to 9 pm. a thought for today " love that is painless is no more than affection."

10/5/19

Good night's sleep. Got up at 8 am. It is much warmer even than yesterday. After breakfast and clean up sat in the garden writing etc till 1 am then I went to a neighbours to have my jacket altered as now that I have left off wearing my cardigan and vest my tunic is much too large to look respectable and the fraulein who kindly obliged me made a very good job of it. The sun became extremely powerful towards midday. At about 12.30 a bridal procession passed slowly down the street here, all were walking and in pairs and wearing either black or white. The men in black and silk hats. The bride and bridegroom were at the head of the procession the bride dressed in black with a long white veil hanging from her head down for the back. They none of them seemed to be in much of a hurry. On duty 1 pm to 5 pm. After tea I borrowed a bike from one of our jock orderlies and cycled to Duren. Bought a few fags and a cake of chocolate at the corps canteen and then rode on to York-Strasse where I had supper and started my way back at 9.30 pm, arriving at my billet soon after 10 pm. Where I found a lovely plate of soup made of goats milk left on the hob for me by mutter, who had retired. a thought for today " Birds and flowers are perhaps the sweetest of all god's creations."

11/5/19

Nice morning, though inclined to be dull. On duty 8 am to 1 pm. Before midday the weather had definitely turned to rain and we were treated to some thunder-showers, which gave me to wonder if our trip to Nedeggan would be spoiled. After all got through my dinner quickly and with my haversack over my shoulder, with what eatables I could get, (there is no butter issued at present owing to stock going bad) I went to meet my friends from Duren, who had already arrived together with frau's mother. We started off at once although the sky was overcast threateningly and indeed we were soon overtaken with some sudden sharp showers. The roads too were very bad in places owing to the recent rain, still we went ahead on out two hour walk, but owing to an error of route we did not arrive at our first stopping place, a restaurant until 1 1/2 hours after starting. Here we found a good company already assembled and we ourselves partook of the rations we had brought with us, and a pot of coffee. We had also a bottle of wine and then renewed our journey but owing to the lateness of the hour, we were not able to take the more pleasant but longer route at a restaurant in Nededdan we met as arranged our old friends Frau and her husband and soon the place was filled by a large number of tourists who had come by the road we had intended to take among the hills. It is surprising that in Germany all although strangers to one another make themselves happy in company and to the accompaniment of the piano nearly all took part in the singing of popular songs, which were rendered with great gusto. Returning to the station, which is some distance away and by way of a steep incline they continued to sing and in passing through the village I was asked by some jocks if I knew what the song was, as apparently it was not at all agreeable to the keen senses of the Scots, but like their English brethren, who like to lord it over anyone whom they think cannot hit back, although during the war they ran away from the German soldiers often enough and I think that there present attitude, or at least that of the so called young soldiers is distinctly cowardly.

Was persuaded to return to Duren although fraulein got out at Krouzain station, bought some more wine and spent the rest of the evening talking and drinking and eating at York-Strasse, where I slept on the sofa. Nideggan is a charming little place on the side of a hill and there are the remains of some very old houses and buildings. a thought for today " Woman is a most peculiar creation even in love."

12/5/19

Said ou-revoir tio frau at 9.30 am as I had to catch an early tram back to Kreuzali to receive m pay which was 600 marks this week, the equivalent to 10 pounds credit which I had or 25 pounds before the war. It is dull but warm and fine. Had a drink with the young chap out of the orderly room who arranged for me to have the above sum of money. After dinner went to fraulein's house where I spent the afternoon with her sister and mother learning German. Had tea and the uncle gave me a cigar. On duty 5 pm to 9 pm. Wrote a card to my little boy and a short note to my dear sis Doris. a thought for today " None are so little versed in merry-making as the English."

13/5/19

Slept soundly until 8 am when I was awakened by the frauleins laughing. It is another dull day. Wrote a long letter to Mrs Taylor in reply to hers of yesterday in which I enclosed 500 mark's for safty. Spent rest of the morning with Matilda at her home learning German. On duty 1 pm to 5 pm. After tea made some small purchases from our midget canteen such as cigs, tobacco and chocolate all of which except 2 packets of cigs I distributed to the members at my billet of both sexes. Afterwards registered 500 mark's to Mrs Taylor and then went to spend the rest of the evening with fraulein and her sister Matilda, where I had some supper, chiefly of potatoes and in the meantime I lightly embarked on a dissertation of some of Germany's wrong-doings and on such occasions I never fail to take advantage of the situation. Returned to my billet at 10.10 pm but found all had retired and the key left on the inside ledge of the window which was left open. a thought for today " All is not fair though good to look upon."

14/5/19

 Beautiful sunny day. On duty 8 am to 1 pm. After dinner went to Duren by the 1.50 pm calling on the way down to the terminus for fraus jersey, which she left last Sunday at fraulein's home. The latter travelled with me to Duren, where I stopped to get some cigs at the corps canteen but found it closed and the YMCA opposite had nothing that I wanted but bought a tine of fruit and a box of biscuits which I gave to frau when I got up to her house. It was plain to see that she was at best a little hurt at my absence yesterday, but she treated me well all the same. At 6 pm we all went up to the allotment to see a few plants etc, but I lay in the grass and enjoyed the warm sun and fresh pure air. Caught the 8 pm tram back to Kreuzau. Had some supper and mutter gave me a couple of slices of her delicious home made bread with which to go on duty at 9 pm until 8 am the following morning. a thought for today " There is no such thing as love except in peoples imagination."

15/5/19

Grand day. As soon as I got myself ready, went out into the fields with my writing pad etc and here I am in my favourite spot near the waterfall, which is glistening in the sunlight. A couple of Germans are swimming in the river, which is running very slowly in that part above the fall, owing naturally to the dry weather. Have written to Mr James Cullen of Liverpool asking if he is still willing to favour me with one of his photographs of the Dardanelle's landing, which is quite the best I have ever seen, but very gruesome. Am feeling delightfully better in myself these days and I trust I shall continue to improve. Had an hours speech with Matilda before dinner after which I went to the riverside and lay down for a nap under a willow, close by a party of Jock NCO's were being put through the intricacies of gas-drill by an officer and a number youngsters looked on. On duty 5 pm to 9 pm. a thought for today " Honesty is not one of the strong points in the character of the great majority."

16/5/19

The sun continues to ride triumphant in the heavens and all the earth is resplendent in it gorgeous outlay of beautiful colours and the birds in sweet concordant acclamations mingling with the joyous shouting of the children at play in the village school-yard complete a soul inspired picture, which so readily accepts is true that all is well and good in the world. I have come into the fields and am seated under the kindly shade of my friend of yesterday, near to the bath-house and close to the calm and peaceful river. On my way here I observed a man carrying the framework of a bicycle on his shoulder and I recognised it immediately as a British army bicycle and I requested the individual to follow me, I took him to our Sergeant and he explained that he had dragged it out of a river. It proved to be the one which was missed a few days ago from our signal office, and it had been stripped of its wheels and the leather seat cut off. Besides this 50 gallons of petrol had been stolen. I am rather inclined to believe that Tommies are having a hand in this looting, which is carried on everywhere. Had a lovely hot bath at 11.30 am. On duty 1 pm to 5 pm. Borrowed a bike after tea and went to Duren taking with me over 5 lbs of rice which I had obtained from our cook for 5 franc's and which I gave to frau, also bought some cigs and chocolate at the corps canteen. I found that frau had been rather badly indisposed and was still unwell. Had supper and then returned to Kreuzau, where mutter had ready for me some splendid hot milk soup. a thought for today " England is a country of sensual viciousness, France is a country of love and Germany is a country of lost souls."

17/5/19

Weather still superb. On duty 8 am to 1 pm. Marshal Foch came on a hurried visit to Duren from Cologne today. After dinner I went by tram to Duren taking a slice of bread and some cheese and a tin of maconicies in my haversack, of which as is my custom I gave to frau, also some chocolate, tablet of soap and a tin of cigarettes which I managed to obtain from the corps canteen in Duren. Had my photograph taken at a photographers close by the latter place, at 6 mark's for half a dozen, but I shall be surprised if they turn out good or even fair. Had tea with frau and monsieur and in the interval before catching the tram back to Kreizau at 8.30 pm which is the last.

We drank a couple of bottles of wine, which frau boiled and served up with sugar. Mutter had some fried potato's ready for me on my return. I also brought back with me some tobacco and cigs for my host. a thought for today
" Of all the nations on the earth the English love the truth the least and are the biggest liars.

18/5/19

Lovely and warm. At 10 am paraded for pay and received 80 marks. Have come to sit at my favourite spot by the river, which is wide and very beautiful just here, on the further side the bank rises up precipitately and is cloaked with trees and bushes massed together and at intervals in the midst of this superb bank of green can be easily distinguished the vivid whiteness of the cherry-blossoms, although now it is rapidly fading away to give place to the forthcoming fruit and the fulfilment of natures task. Many aeroplanes are flying over Duren and the air is filled with throbbing engines interspersed with the dull sharp rattle of their machine guns. On duty 1 pm to 5 pm. After tea cycled to Duren taking with me a small bag of oats for frau and buying some cigs, chocolate and soap at the corps canteen on the way. The latter for mutter. When I came to start back found my back tyre very soft and had to walk it to the school where I borrowed a pump, but did not reach home until nearly 11 pm. a thought for today " The worst a man can do is to waste time."

20/5/19

Warmer again today. Elizabeth, mutters daughter is apparently very ill, ever since she had the Spanish flue she has suffered with her lungs, and yesterday morning mutter showed me a handkerchief which was covered in blood, and now she is compelled to stay in bed. On duty 8 am to 1 pm. Caught the 1.50 pm tram to Duren visited the corps canteen and the YMCA for the usual commodities and also with the object of buying some tinned fruit for Elizabeth, who has expressed a wish for some, but as is often the case under such circumstances there was none to be got anywhere. Walked up to York-Strasse only to find that frau had gone to Kreuzau with Ludolph the youngest child. This was the outcome of a misunderstanding and owing to distance and poor tram service I did not get back to Kreuzau until after 4 pm, where mutter informed me that my friends were waiting for me at Sneidhuen, and that was where I found them by frau. We all then went for a walk into the woods and a pleasant evening passed away all too quickly. On duty 9 pm to 8 am the following morning. a thought for today " Days may come and days may go, but love goes on forever!"

21/5/19

Had a ripping good breakfast comprised of an egg fried, (1 mark) one small sausage, (out of mess fund 5 mark's weekly) bacon and bread and dip. Elizabeth is still in bed and I hear her coughing at intervals. After cleanup, betook myself to the fields by the river. One cannot imagine better ideal conditions or better weather and I am feeling in the pink and indeed I look it, I think. Lounged about in the open air all the morning. After dinner borrowed a bicycle and went to Maubach a couple of villages away from here for the purpose of visiting the YMCA there in hope of obtaining some tinned fruit and this time I was successful and returned with two tins of peaches and eleven packets of players cigs.

It is a beautiful run out along by the river side and on the right there are some big red rock boulders which jut out, not unlike the rocks along the sea shore, on the top most pinnacle of one of these, the highest, is an iron-work cross, which is such a common feature in catholic countries and by the way-side I noticed a very old brick shrine covered with verdure and I could dimly distinguish through the aperture, the religious emblems of catholic observance. From 3 pm to 4 pm I lay under a tree. 5 pm to 9 pm on duty.

22/5/19
Good weather maintains. Spent morning lounging about in the fields near my favourite….**entry stops**

Diary Number 14

28/5/19

At frequent intervals the fish in the river jump out to catch the insects flying over. The wooded bank opposite is simply ringing with the joyous notes of happy birds, in the large open space in front of the bath-house, swing boats etc. are being erected in preparation of tomorrows festivities, which is a holiday for the Germans and they are all talking about it. Today is Kaiser Williams "namenstag". Wrote to Miss Cummins and Mrs. Taylor enclosing to the latter 500 Marks. On duty 1 pm to 5 pm. In the evening went to Duren by tram and returned by the last at 8.30 pm. Received a letter from Mlle. Marie Hunel. <u>A thought for today</u> "Jealousy springs solely from lack of confidence."

29/5/19

Beautiful morning and ideal weather for the holiday. On duty 8 am to 1 pm. Am looking forward to the trip to Nideggin this afternoon, with Fraulein and Frau and their husbands. The arrangement is to go by train and to return on foot. I went to the tram at the station her at 1.21 pm, which was obviously packed out with holidaymakers. I was unable to get to my friends until the journey was nearly completed Ludwig accompanied his mother and we walked first of all up the hill from the station to Nideggen and out again towards the church on the cliff where we stopped at a restaurant to eat some lunch, which we had brought with us. At 4 pm we started to walk back and struck off from the dry and dusty road along the most glorious woodland paths. I cut down a stick for each of the ladies and one for the young lad and myself. The hillsides resounded with song and laughter by unseen parties and all the world seemed happy careless. Such beautiful scenery as is here to be met with I would prefer to leave to greater pens than mine to describe. I only know that I enjoyed it all immensely. At frequent intervals we would step out onto the edge of dizzy boulders and survey the lovely wooded valley beneath and the charming hills beyond. At last we reached the favourite half way house where everybody calls and we took possession of a little harbour in the garden with table and chairs and began at once to quench our thirst with excellent wine and five bottles were quickly disposed of and were placed in the centre of the table, with one turned upside down standing in the middle supported by the other four "cadavres". At this juncture when passing through the restaurant to the bar an unwelcome occurrence as so often happens took place. Three Scotch soldiers, 2 Sergeants and a Lance-Corporal kindly pointed out to me, that after all we had suffered at the hands of the Germans, it was a pity that any one should condescend to be friendly with them, and pointing to another Tommy seated at a table with two women and a couple of men, remarked that if he had been a prisoner in the hands of the Germans he would not now be sitting where he was. They also added that the previous week they had effected the capture of 3 R.E. Corporals for the same thing and had quite a lot to say to the same effect. It would be as well to add here some of the reasons which actuate the noble Scotsmen and others in this particular attitude. The Germans say and I am inclined to agree with them, that the Scotch are jealous of the English as the former are so hopelessly out of the running where females are concerned.

255

They have too earned for themselves quite an unenvious name among the people by their conduct. But the real foundation lies I believe in quite another direction, all the troops here now, whether NCO's or not are retainable in the army of occupation and on this account they imagine that it is Germans who are responsible for their present position and love them accordingly, whereas as a matter of fact the fault lies solely with themselves, for having failed to join the army earlier and waited instead to be dragged into the army, when the forces long before the war started were even then badly in need of men and more men. Still this is merely an instance of the Britishers lack of sport and fair play. We continued on our way after this and the young fellow with his friends, who had of course overheard the remarks above related came away too. When I spoke to him he said he did not wish to get into trouble now as he was due for demobilisation next week, another case of self. It is always No. 1 first with almost every one of Britains civilian soldiers. We were a merry party on the way back and went along singing and dancing and from woods to glens and the hills around came the ringing notes of happy singers. I have never seen a people so fond of singing in my life (and I have lived in Wales for 3 1/2 years). They form themselves into bands and march along to the strains of mandolins and other instruments at a swinging pace and sing heartily. Dropped in at a wayside inn and had some more wine. I gathered May and other flowers by the wayside including a parsons garden, with which I decked the Fraus and with blossom of the horse-chestnut and ferns stuck in their hats and round their waists and great bunches in their hands they looked the picture of happy spring -- perhaps. Arrived at Kreuzau, had more wine and then caught the last tram back to Duren. I remember a fine looking dark eyed girl sitting on my right and beautifully dressed with whom I had just a mild flirtation, she spoke very kindly in whispers and sighed a good deal, but I had to be careful as Frau, who sat on my left repeatedly nudged me. Monsieur who was very happy indeed gave us a song standing at the further end of the car, which was full of civilians. Arrived at York-Strasse without any untoward incident and after a little supper Frau made me my bed on the couch and I was soon asleep.

30/5/19

Woke up with a bad head, and worse appetite. After dinner I returned to Kreuzau and had a lovely warm bath and a change. On duty 5 pm to 9 pm. Nothing worth talking about today.

31/5/19

Very warm day. Changed another 10 pounds in Postal Orders for Marks, which I intend to send to England. Spent the morning in the usual way at usual rendez vous. On duty 1 pm to 5 pm. Went to Duren on a cycle after tea and returned after supper at York-Strasse. Frau was very busy baking and cooking all evening in anticipation of tomorrow which is another holiday of a sort in Germany. <u>A thought for today</u> "Honesty is rarer than the most precious of jewels."

1/6/19

Magnificent weather continues. On duty 8 am to 1 pm. In the afternoon went to Duren again by tram and on my way to York-Strasse I called for my photographs which were ready, but still I did not feel satisfied with them. There was a party to tea at Frau's house but as I was on duty at 9 pm on the all night turn I was reluctantly compelled to come away at 8 pm.

Frau made me up a bundle of rice cake etc. to take with me to the office and Mutter had some fried potatoes ready when I returned and she also wrapped up several slices of her delicious milk and sugar bread, which I took with me at 9 pm. <u>A thought for today</u> " All is not sweet that tastes nice."

2/6/19

Very dull and rather cool and threatening rain. Gathered a big bunch of flowers from the beautiful grounds of the kindergarten, in which is situated our Headquarters and took them with me at breakfast time as a present to Mutter. Later went into the fields to write and read but owing to a shower of rain I was forced to return home and sat down to write.

"Springs song"

"What is spring, what is its meaning and what does it convey to us the mere children of poor mortals. To use we think it is a time for great rejoicing, when our hopes sore voluntarily upwards and our fears and misgivings pass away. To us we think that life is worth living, indeed, that Spring installs within us new life and pleasant dreams of approaching happiness and contentment. To us we think how much in truth there is to live for and fresh and nobler aspirations fill our thoughts and hearts. But to what do we owe so much for all this and to whom are we so deeply indebted for such renewed awakening, which at this time enters deeply into our souls but one only in all the year. Honestly we cannot congratulate ourselves, for souls that lie dormant only to be awakened by Springs song through the graciousness of the mother of nature and by the love and tenderness of sweet nature herself, we feel bound to admit that in the world of God's creation we are by no means foremost but only form a part in the great work of the creator. When in the reposeful slumber and quiet peacefulness of the night watch, the Nightingale in a labour of pure love makes sweeter still the hours of peace to all who will or won't at break of day, a spectacle most wonderful is unfolded. The air, the fields, the woods, the hills and valley all unite and with one accord salute in happy friendly greeting the monarch of the universe, with joyous song and pleasant smiles, which acclaim beyond all doubt the fervid genuineness in the love of life, which is the soul of nature. There is not a flower both great and small nor a leaf or blade of grass, that fails in obedient felicity to greet with smiling gratitude and pure delight the object of this universal homage and yearning adoration. The vast concourse of the pretty feathered world combine with jubilation overflowing in their little hearts to herald with a morning hymn of praise to the new born day and never has and never will the ears of man hear finer music than that which is so gloriously rendered by this heavenly choir of little angels. Here then is that to which we owe our all, the appealing notes that swell the morning breeze cannot fail to thrill and drive away our cares, for here and these and none but these are Christians pure and true, who know no guile and live as all should live and die as they have lived, an unspotted, untarnished, heroic band of little martyrs. Then too from the very bosom of fair nature the lessons of life, which we do never learn are known all by heart from birth by everything that lives and breathes, and in the sparkling blossoms, which crown and glorify the distant woods or be thickly clustered in beauteous dales and valley, we who are but the poorest of poor mortals do see and yet do not, that there a least life and love are not misunderstood. How much happier we should be if but our lives were such as these, they live and are happy and only die but to live again."

Cycled over to Maubach after dinner and bought at the small YMCA there, 500 Players cigarettes, a box of chocolates and seven tins of sausages, the latter for our mess. On duty 5 pm to 9 pm. <u>A thought for today</u> "One can never be disappointed in nature's love."

3/6/19

Dull with sharp showers, but pleasant nevertheless in the open air. Strolled up into the wood on the further side of the waterfall after breakfast. Received a letter last evening from Mrs. Taylor. On duty 1 pm to 5 pm. Finished reading " A welsh singer". I think Mifanwy is an ideal character, I wonder if I shall ever meet her. Wrote to Mrs. Taylor enclosing a copy of "Springs song". After tea I went to Duren on a cycle but it teemed down with rain all the way, and at one place gliding into the tramlines I came a cropper and fell on the ground, but fortunately sustained no injury to myself or bike. I arrived at York-Strasse very wet and hot. Gave Frau 2 1/2 lbs. of rice, which I am in the habit of taking to her on my visits. After supper I mounted my iron horse for the return journey, the weather had cleared up but it was very chilly. Mutter was still up when I got back and she had some lovely baked potatoes ready on the hob for me, but I could not eat much, as I am always eating since I came to live here. Getting into bed I read for half an hour and then switched off the light. <u>A thought for today</u> "If love were painless it would be loveless."

4/6/19

Dull and cold morning. On duty 8 am to 1 pm. Got myself ready quickly after dinner and went to Duren by tram for the afternoon and evening. I was persuaded to stay there the night by Frau and Monsieur so did so as I do not like to offend anyone, when asked to do things although it would have suited me better to return as I always feel so cramped sitting for long hours in a house and my nature seems to rebel against it, although of course I don't go seeking work of any description for that also goes distinctly against the grain. But I do love the fresh pure air of Kneuzau and it is always a relief to me to get back to it. Had a good tea and supper with my friends and spent yet another nigh on a bed made up on the sofa and a few chairs. <u>A thought for today</u> "I wonder if anyone has ever yet discovered the best way to live."

5/6/19

Did not trouble to get up until the morning was well advanced, somewhere between 10 am and 11 am. After breakfast, which I partook with Frau, went across the road for a shave soon afterward caught the tram back to Duren, where I bought a camera, which cost me 100 marks. I don't know anything about cameras, but I am very willing to learn. Got back at Kreuzau shortly after 1 pm. Had dinner and then cycled over to Maubach where I bought two boxes of 500 Players cigarettes each for 30 marks and a box of chocolates for 12 marks. Sold one of boxes of cigs to Mutter. Had a few hints in photography by a friend, but have still exceedingly much to learn. Did a little reading and German studying. On duty 5 pm to 9 pm. <u>A thought for today</u> " If one could remember only half what one learns, one would be wise beyond his generation."

6/6/19

Very dull today. Got up at 7.45 am. Paraded at 9.30 for an inspection of gas-masks and afterwards took my camera and accompanied by a friend who has also recently taken up the art we proceeded to the river, where I learned a few points in photography and took snaps of the waterfall and of my friend and he took one of me. It was a pity that the light was so bad, but I must hope for better conditions and good prospects in the future. Have finished reading "Three men in a boat" and am now diving into " The last cruise of the majestic", which has of course a personal interest and have commenced "The hunchback of Notre Dame" by Victor Hugo, which book I have a faint recollection of having read a long time ago. On duty 1 pm to 5 pm. Cycled to Duren in the evening. Bought a new glass for my camera, having broken the other, also got a stock of paper fixing salts and finishing stuff. Had a good supper with Frau and then returned home going first to the kindergarten for any letters and at the same time picking a great armful of glorious flowers which I took for Mutter. <u>A thought for today</u> " A man cannot do worse than waste time."

7/6/19

Dull but with short intervals of bright sunlight. On duty 8 am to 1 pm. After dinner shouldered my haversack, which was very full and which contained a bag of meal, a book (for reading in the tram), some chocolate, my camera, a chunk of spotted dick pudding for the kids, chunk of bread with butter and cheese and bully beef etc. By this time the sun was predominant in the heavens and a beautiful Whitsuntide is practically assured. Called at the Quartermasters stores and obtained a new pair of trousers as I was all out behind partly by genuine wear and tear and partly otherwise and am now quite a swell in brand new clothes. Bought a necklace as a present for Frau on her inamenstag, with which she appeared highly pleased, I had a terrible misfortune with my camera. I had taken two snaps of Frau and the kinder in the garden when in replacing the black plate it crumpled up the last film and of course would not go back into position. I caught the tram back to Duren and handed in the apparatus for the shop people to deal with it, but all the films which had been used were completely ruined. This is my first disappointment in photography, I hope there will be no more like it as besides the useless cost, there is much time and still more hopes all shattered on the instant. Returned to York-Strasse with my camera made ready again for fresh work and I used the remainder of my films on Frau, Monsieur and the children in the garden. Almost missed the 8.10 pm tram back to Krauzeau as it seldom waits as it should for the junction of my tram with it and I had to run and spring up behind onto a ledge, all the cars were crowded out and people and soldiers clung to anything and everything all round them, in between them and on top. On duty 8 pm to 9 am the following morning.

8/6/19

Bright sunny day but terrifically hot. Played cricket for a time with the boys and also took some snaps of them. Later snapped Elizabeth my hosts' daughter and again of her and her sister's child and one of her uncle. After dinner waited at the tram terminus until Frau and Ludwig arrived and we all went up into the woods which overlook the village, where we sat down on the grass, surveyed the scene. I took some snaps and we had something to eat. The clouds gathered thickly for a time and thunder became audible, but fortunately passed us by.

As I had to be on duty at 5 pm it was with reluctance that I pulled myself from the spot and accompanied by my friends went back to my billet where I handed over a bouquet of flowers to Frau, which I had collected early this morning in the grounds of the kindergarten. Here we parted company, Monsieur and Frau to return to Duren and myself to duty from 5 pm to 9 pm. After a little more thunder the clouds dispersed and the evening resolved itself into a pleasant and peaceful attitude. A thought for today " Perhaps the most impossible of impossibilities is to persuade or discourage a woman in the pursuit of a possible lover."

9/6/19 and 10/6/19

Day dawned beautifully fine. Have changed duties today to enable me to go with my Duren friends to Hideggen this afternoon. On duty 8 am to 1 pm. Caught the 1.21 pm train from here, which was terribly packed as usual and could not arrive anywhere near my friends so went into a coach at the rear end of the train, reserved for soldiers. Arrived at Hideggen, we all proceeded of up the Baurge which is a steep climb but is well worth the trouble and energy expended. It is a charming spot and from the top one has a splendid view of the surrounding landscape. The old building which crowns the summit is interesting and novel but its thick grey walls have been quite spoiled by resent restoration. The sun shone brilliantly all day and I was deeply grieved that I could take no snaps on account of lack of films and my failure to procure any owing to all the shops being closed in Duren today. Going on we passed through the village and came up with a great procession, issuing from the church, carrying banners and chanting prayers as they went along. Arrived at the same restaurant as on the previous occasion of our visit. We settled down for tea, and then resumed our walk back to Kreuzau by the same route as last time, stopping at a restaurant en route to sup and eat again, here we were joined by another family a Frenchman and his German wife and two boys who were friends of Frau and Monsieur. We drank wine and beer together and I conversed with Monsieur le Francais for a while in English and afterwards I glided of into his own tongue. He teaches German and French and he told me after a time that he had not discerned a single fault on my part and that I spoke his language better than any of his English pupils, which included officers. This is certainly very flattering considering how long I have been out of France with no opportunity of keeping up my French. On the way back I was in conversation the whole time with Monsieur le Francais much I imagine to the annoyance of Frau. We boarded the train at a little way-side station and returned to Duren. It was fearfully hot in the coach and the sweat simply poured out of us. The brother of Monsieur and his fiancee who had accompanied us had to wait about 20 minutes for their train back to Cologne and we all adjourned to the waiting room and whiled away the time drinking more wine etc. Giving to the dense crowds we thought it advisable not to attempt to board a tram but to go home on foot and this very soon resulted in my downfall. We had not gone very far when I was accosted by two military policemen with notebook in hand, who asked me where my puttees were and pointed out that I was in the company of civilians(the civilians by the way were Monsieur le Francais and his wife). They allowed me to pass on however, but followed at a distance behind and presently came up to me again and demanded my pay-book, which I was not able to produce, as it was at the moment in the orderly-room for pay. I was there upon arrested and escorted to the police station, from which place I was sent to the prison house and searched from head to foot and everything I had on me was taken away. I was then ordered to take off my boots and thrown forthwith into a cell where I was told I should find a bed and three blankets and then the lock was turned and I was left alone.

Needless to say I could not sleep a wink and I could think of nothing but the indignities, which have ever been my lot since I had the misfortune to leave the old army for the new. My bed was exactly like a coffin, there were three all joined together placed on a raised and sloping platform, inside the coffin was a hard mattress and three small worn out dirty blankets. I spent the night listening to the chimes of the church and the many clocks in the town faithfully registering each quarter of an hour. My cell was so dark that it was impossible to tell, whether or when the day had broken. Shortly before 9 am I was relieved somewhat to hear the key turned in the lock of my cell and the jailer entered with a piece of bread and some bully beef and some tea. I drank the tea with a relish but the bread and bully beef stuck in my throat and I could not swallow it. At about half past nine the door was again opened and I was released for a few minutes for the purpose of cleaning up my cell and a wash and then I was thrust back again into the horrid gloom and stillness of a criminal's cell, with not even the luxury of a cigarette. It was so dark that one could only dimly discern the four whitewashed walls, upon which had been written in large printed characters some gibberish in German of a moral nature, but one had to go up quite close to be able to read it. Other prisoner's too had left their traces in the shape of drawings representing heads, ships and beef barrels. I lingered on here, pacing to and fro, or sitting in my coffin, thinking and cursing the English for their well know foolishness, when at about 10 minutes to 11 am my peaceful existence was again disturbed and the door opened. I was ordered outside and stood before the APM himself, I complained to him that I had been wrongfully imprisoned, that I was with an allied subject at the time of my arrest, and that I had his address in my wallet. The police sergeant when questioned answered that I was not properly dressed, and the APM responded that he would not imprison me for that alone and he ordered my release from the cell for which I was indeed grateful. The rest of the time until 3 pm I wasted upstairs in a nice room used as an office by the police, when the escort arrived and I was conducted through the town to the school billets. Where the Sgt. Major dismissed my armed guard and I was left to wait my trial by the CO at 6.30 pm. I explained my case to the CO and I was remanded for my statement to be verified. In this case as in many other of a similar or dissimilar nature the army is clearly wrong, but as it is English I can expect no satisfaction and I shall very probably have to undergo an additional punishment, in order to prove of course how very sincerely the army has at heart the best interests of the soldiers. Mutter was very pleased to see me on my return she had heard several different yarns but had not heard all the truth. Could eat very little supper and went to my room early and was soon in a sound slumber.

11/6/19

Very hot day. Spent part of the morning beneath the willows at my favourite spot on the river, where it is both cool and shady and before I came away and took a snap of the landscape as it appears up river. After dinner I was told I was wanted to go to the orderly- room for my pay, which I missed yesterday and I received 380 marks as per my request. I bought a couple of film packs, cigarettes and chocolate. Half a dozen knives and forks for 33 marks, half a dozen picture postcards for my little Dux and I also took my used film for development and a single print of each one. Am feeling much better today and my thick head of yesterday has now entirely disappeared. It is still extremely warm and the sweat pours out of one in a most persistent manner. I should not fail to mention with respect to Whit-Mondays "spectacle" that when I was get arrested, Monsieur followed up behind until he saw me disappear into the lock-up.

Frau did not sleep all that night as she expected to hear e knock on the door and all the children including Arnold cried when they heard what had befallen me. Should an exhibition of genuine and real concern would not be understood in England and it is very strange but no less true that I have far more sincere friends in foreign countries than I ever had in England and certainly far less enemies, even counting them in hundreds. On duty 5 pm to 9 pm. <u>A thought for today</u> "All the misfortunes that befall each one of us are peculiar to the character of the individual concerned."

12/6/19

Did not get to sleep until late or at least I should say until well past midnight, probably owing to the heat. It is again a glorious day but awfully warm. Am still under open arrest and have heard nothing more so far regarding my case. Am down by the river at this moment and verily I don't think a cooler place could be found anywhere than beneath the shade of my kind old friends the willows. Like myself the cows too know well enough which are the best places under the circumstances and they are browsing or idly chewing the cud beneath the neighbouring trees, but strangely enough they have never one taken up a position under my trees or attempted to usurp my place. Went through my daily exercises in German, read my book "The hunchback of Notre Dame" and afterwards took some snaps including youngsters bathing in the weir and the village church. On duty 1 pm to 5 pm. Towards tea-time the weather suddenly broke into a thunder storm, but except for one big crash and a little rain, and a good deal of wind it soon passed off. Went to Duren by tram and called at York-Strasse where I learned that no enquiries had up to then been made to certify with whom I was with at the time of my arrest on Monday evening last. Returned to Kreusau by the last tram. <u>A thought for today</u> "An honest man in civilian life is often a criminal in the army."

13/6/19

Windy but fine and sunny. On duty 8 am to 1 pm. Went to Duren after dinner taking with me a bag of rice for Frau and half a loaf of bread, some butter and a tin of bully beef. Called for my negatives, which were done and proved that I am really only an amateur photographer, although a few were not bad at all, some of the caused a good deal of laughter especially those of Frau and Monsieur. Returned to Kreuzau by the 8 pm tram. I had a beautiful warm bath in the morning and as usual changed my things for clean at York-Strasse. On duty at 9 pm to 8 am the following morning.

14/6/19

Fine day, but windy. Endeavoured to print some of my snaps but did not have much success, and even with help I got very little results. Went out with two others and took a few snaps. In the afternoon cycled to Maubach and bought a thousand players cigarettes at the YMCA there 500 of which I sold to Mutter. Carried on with some more printing and obtained better results. Something which puzzled us this morning with regard to the paper, which is not self toning. I think I now understand better. On duty 5 pm to 9 pm. It seems dreadfully long since any letters reached me, each day I look through the mail but in vain. <u>A thought for today</u> "By the labour of others do we derive our pleasures."

15/6/19

Again gloriously fine. Spent morning taking and printing photographs and with the aid of better paper and a little more experience, I have obtained some better results than yesterday. I have still a great deal to learn and being so far away from Duren I am at a disadvantage in that respect and for the present I am obliged to borrow some things in order to carry on. The only thing to do is to peg away and I know that I shall eventually become proficient, at least I hope so. Photography is a remarkable hobby in so far that, it has a really large mouth, always gaping wide open and seems to swallow with a decided relish every penny of ones pocket-money. On duty 1 pm to 5 pm. At 2 pm went off duty as there was not much doing and on such occasions we take it in turn to relieve each other. I did a few more prints, which were decidedly good -- for me. After tea bicycled to Duren taking my camera with me, and first went to the cemetery near the hospital, with the intention of photographing the avenue of British graves there, but owing to the presence of so many people I decided not to make the attempt, but to leave it for a more favourable opportunity. Spent the evening talking and drinking beer in the garden at 8, York-Strasse, with Monsieur and Frau. I also took some snaps of them. After supper returned to Kreuzau and went to bed at 10.30 pm but sat up reading for half an hour.

16/6/19

Very warm today. On duty 8 am to 1 pm. After dinner I went to Duren by tram. Bought a number of photographic articles in town and am I find getting together quite a big shop. Spent the day at York-Strasse. Missed the last tram home but went by another to Lendersdorf from which place I had half a hours walk to Kreuzau. Mutter thought I had been made prisoner again as I did not turn up at the usual time. Finished reading "A story of a passion" in bed.

17/6/19

Was awakened shortly after six am by our Sergeant who came to tell me that orders had come through to march over the Rhine, they had been working hard all night and I got up and went to relieve them. This is somewhat of a shock, it means a great deal too, at least as far as I am personally concerned. I must perforce leave a good bed, good food and a beautiful country. Pleasant associations and friendships must necessarily become broken, and one knows not what lies ahead. Was busy all the morning packing and cleaning up. Have dispatched by parcel post the litre jug, which Frau gave to me the other day, to my sister Doris. Have also sent another 1000 marks to Mrs. Taylor for safety. After dinner I went to Duren by cycle, and with the object of taking a snap of the old cloisters, with the ancient pulpit on the corner of the building, I managed to gain admission to my prison of a week ago, where a good view of my intended object is obtained from the upper windows. I was doomed however to disappointment as I had the bad luck to break off the first film before I could withdraw it and I was in consequence obliged to take the whole thing to the shop to get it fixed up again. This done and again in possession of my two film packs, which would not be developed in time before my departure. I again returned to the old cloister and taking up a position on the steps of the old church opposite, took a couple of snaps of the pulpit with a crowd of children standing on the pavement beneath it.

I then hurried away and cycled to the cemetery where I took three snaps of the avenue of British graves there, from here I went to pay what might be my last visit to Frau. She was alone and I could see she was in deep distress. I had thought that a woman had no feelings except jealousy or hate, yet I know that for the first time in my life I shall be genuinely missed and me I shall lose a true and sincere friend. Rushed back to Kreuzau to be in time for tea and to go on duty at 5 pm to 9 pm. We have been very busy all day, the telegrams alone numbering more than 800. After supper and a chat with Elizabeth and Josephine I went to bed and read my book "The Hunchback of Notre Dame" for an hour.

18/6/19

The whole of one relief is due to leave here for Solingen this morning. I have come to rest myself and to read at my old and favourite spot by the river, beneath the cool shelter of my dear willows. On duty 1 pm to 9 pm. We must work 12 hours a day, while one relief is short. relieved for tea from 5 pm to 6 pm and as arranged yesterday monsieur and frau come at 5.30 pm to visit me and to spend the evening together, bad luck prevented this and I had to leave them shortly after 6 pm to go back to duty. I had just gone to retire, when the Sergeant came to inform me that I was to leave for our new quarters at 2 pm tomorrow, so I finished my pack got into bed and read my book for a while. I am very disappointed with the course of events, I feel that I am leaving and losing such a lot.

19/6/19

I had the pleasant satisfaction to hear first thing this morning that our move was temporarily cancelled, so we have still another day or two of grace. On duty 8 am to 1 pm. Today is another festive holiday here and there have been numerous processions during the morning. Directly after dinner I went to Duren by tram. Spent afternoon with my friends at York-Strasse, smoking cigars, cigarettes, drinking wine, eating, talking, and taking photographs of the family and as usual making the best of a miserable existence. I should like to remark re the religious festival today that Duren was bedecked with flags, but of a very different description than were formally used on such occasions, in so much that the colours displayed were only either black and red or white and red, a combination of black, red and white or yellow was not allowed, nor even black and white, which are I believe are the symbols of the Prussian state or something, along the route taken by the processionists, flowers and leaves were scattered and walked over. Returned to duty 9 pm to 8 am the following morning.

Diary Number 15
20/6/19

Not much work to do during the night. Received a letter from Miss Weeds and one from my dear sister Doris with this pocket notebook enclosed. The fields are looking extremely gay and fascinating at this moment, especially at those spots, where, among the tall and graceful corn the blood red poppies and deep blue cornflowers (the Kaiser's favourite flower) are mingled together in such surprising vividness. The wild flowers which served yesterday as a processional carpet, still lie where they were strewn, and although withered and sadly crumpled up, one can still easily recognise the blue cornflowers and the white marguerites, which composed the greater portion of the colour scheme. Have finished reading "The hunchback of Notre Dame", which though of so grotesque a character, impresses one very forcibly with the ever recurrent fact that even now we are so further advanced and that all are subject to the same principals which governed the lives of our forefathers from the beginning and right through the ages. On duty 1 pm to 9 pm. was ordered to report to headquarters by 6.30 pm to interview the CO in connection with last whit-Monday's affair, when I was wrongfully arrested, illegally imprisoned in a dark cell and in every way treated (as usual) as a confirmed criminal or as an escaped convict. When I was paraded before the CO he commenced at once a most disgusting, disgraceful and unjust harangue. I really thought I must be guilty of some new offence. He said that on the face of it and really it was a very serious matter, that it was just my sort who was ruining the army (my opinion of course is that the army was ruined before it came to Germany by my sort perhaps, but in this case the culprits were officers). He said I was just the sort of chap to get at (an expression of vindictiveness is quite in keeping with a certain class of English officer). Thing's years old were brought up to prove what a worthless fellow I am. The remarkable this is that I kept my peace though it all. He said that I was only to happy to make friends with any German and all but told me that I was a German, I objected that he was taking a wrong view of me altogether, but it was obvious that he was pre-prejudiced against me. To write all that was said would take too long and if it were not downright disgusting it would be highly comical. I can or could write heaps on the conduct of officers, but as it is so well known and in fact common talk among the soldiers and civilians alike it is hardly worthwhile, except I may say, that one officer who was billeted with the very same people I was arrested for talking to was ordered to quit the house on account of his conduct towards Monsieur Lebrun's wife who complained of his unwelcome attentions. She was also obliged to dismiss her servant as she objected to her relations with another officer in the house. I have myself seen English officers walking out with German women of all classes, yet this was actually brought up against me by the CO, which of course was a deliberate lie as I make a point of avoiding such particular company. To finish off with I was awarded 4 days CB and was told to think myself lucky in getting off so lightly. We shall see however what may the sequel be. After supper a friend came to help me develop some of my films in my bedroom. We worked until nearly midnight but as usual I bungled several during the process of developing, and several others were failures. I hope to do better the next time as of course one has to pay for learning.

My poor bedroom was in a terrible condition at the end of the business, still we were happy enough drinking lemonade, and smoking cigars and cigarettes the while.

21/6/19

Dull and rain. Hung up my negatives to dry first thing this morning. On duty 8 am to 1 pm. Received a letter from Mr Kendrick in which I was glad to learn of my little boy's welfare. Wrote to Miss Weeds. At 2 pm was on cookhouse fatigue, later developed and printed my films with some success, my bedroom presents a weird spectacle during these operations. The windows are blocked with blankets, my coat is over a small window in the door, and the chinks round the door are stuffed up with paper, the electric light is encased in a small red lantern, which is very cleverly affixed with the help of string, and a khaki handkerchief is packed in round the top effectually preventing even the smallest ray of light escaping. I'm sure I must resemble the devil himself working away in the gloom of hell in the interest of diabolical art and corruption on souls. It lay between two of us to go on duty tonight, I lost the toss and worked from 9 pm to 8 am.

22/6/19

Considerably brighter weather today and hot, too hot. Spent morning and afternoon printing my snaps and have been rewarded with some excellent results, which proves that am making some progress in the art. Did a cookhouse fatigue from 10.30 sawing up wood in pursuance of the punishment relative to my most resent crimes, to which there will in all probability be a sequel. It is now presumed that all who have gone forward in anticipation of advancing further into Germany may shortly return, but at the moment it is purely a matter of conjecture. Wrote a card last night to my dear little boy and this morning I received a letter from Elinor who has been to see the little man and her report was good. On duty 5 pm to 9 pm. Pinned up all my snaps to dry during the night.

23/6/19

Very windy and dull. Received 800 marks in pay. On cook-house fatigue at 10.30 am. Too dull to do any printing, so contented myself with arranging etc and placing the best in the album. On duty 1 pm to 5 pm. Several snaps, which I endeavoured to print in the evening failed on account of bad light.

24/6/19

The unfavourable weather of yesterday continues. On duty 8 am to 1 pm. Short fatigue in the afternoon and afterwards strolled away for a walk alone, Not feeling quite up to the mark these days and quite off eating, still it is always refreshing to get out into the country although it rains hard and blows a hurricane, After tea attempted to do some printing but owing to insufficient light, it was not quite a success, so whiled away the time inking in some scratched negatives. Read some 20 pages of my French novel, which my dear little sis Dot has kindly sent me called" La Tulipe noire" by Alexandre Dumas. I am also reading a book on "Famous modern battles". Was on duty for the third time in succession from 9 pm to 8 am the following morning, owing to shortage of personal.

25/6/19

Wretched miserable weather. After breakfast and clean up I went by car to Duren and visited my friends at York-Strasse, who were glad to see me reappear after so long an absence. Returned in time for tea and proceeded on duty at 5 pm to 9 pm. Am feeling quite down today probably on account of the weather, which usually affects me adversely, but I think too as a result of so much excitement recently the substance of which I have omitted to note here, but which may have a sequel before long, at least I hope so. Read my book in bed for an hour after retiring.

26/6/19

Somewhat improved weather conditions today. Managed to print some snaps in the morning and afterwards went for a stroll with my book. On duty 2 pm to 5 pm. Went by tram after tea to Duren but returned at 8 pm. I fancy I shall be demobilised very shortly now, as a result of my application to that effect. Read my book for an hour before turning down for the night.

27/6/19

Dull and cold. On duty 8 am to 1 pm. In the afternoon went to Duren and bought some glass-wire in the shape of six tumblers at 3 mark's each and a set of 4 wine glasses at 5.50 mark's each, got them all packed in the shop and am trusting good fortune that they will get through safely. Afterwards went to York-Strasse, where I stayed until 8 pm. Read my book on war in bed for an hour.28/6/19Windy and dull with occasional bright intervals. Trammed to Duren in the morning for the purpose of buying some more useful articles for civilian life. Purchased a couple more razor's one for 30 mark's and the other for 20.50 mark's, as I am obliged to shave every day I am rather keen on a decent set of tools. Bought an alarm clock for 25 marks and 20 pencils of different brands, including some "Koh-i-noors" the lot costing over 13 marks. Have managed to start off by post the glasses and alarm clock this afternoon. Had a hot bath before tea. Called at the quartermasters stores this morning and changed my cap and puttees for new. On duty 5 pm to 9 pm. This is supposed to be peace day. I can't say if it is yet an accomplished fact and nothing definate has come through. Now I suppose my time in the army is drawing rapidly to a close. So far as length of service goes, I have something at least to my credit, but as far as anything else I am as usual the victim of fatality, apart from the fact that I am the real victor of Cambrai or at least the originator of the plan, I have nothing to recommend me and when I step back again from the army it will be into oblivion. Finished reading my book " Famous modern battles" before turning out the light.

29/6/19

Tried one of my razors. The 30 mark one, this morning but did not find it very satisfactory considering the price. Went for a stroll and coming up with a Frau attending her cow while she grazed, I had a long conversation with her on topical subjects. On duty 1 pm to 5 pm. The day is very dull and boisterous. No trams ran from here after 1 pm so was prevented from going to Duren as was my intention and instead went for a walk. My name was not among the list for demobilisation as I had expected.

If proof were needed this is just one more of English duplicity, it is no exaggeration to say that so far as my personal experience goes it would be hard to beat the English in tearing up " Scraps of paper", their unwillingness, even refusal to carry out an honourable bond. Swindling and lying, which must necessarily accompany the former. At the moment I am being swindled out of leave, demobilisation, war pay, about 28 pounds war gratuity, and the long service territorial ribbon. These are only a few of my grievances, which have gone on ever since the war began and indeed long before it began.

30/6/19

Windy but fine. Received a letter last evening from Miss Winnie Hedge. On duty 8 am to 1 pm. Was at York-Strasse in the afternoon and evening. I disclosed to Frau the fact that I expected to be demobilised very shortly and as I feared she took it badly. On duty 9 pm for the night.

1/7/19

Went to Duren after breakfast ostensibly to buy a number of articles of which I had written out a list, but after much examination and enquiries came away unsatisfied. I did buy four photograph frames, postcard size and have posted them and the two new razors and pencils. When I got back to Kreuzau I was informed of the surprising news to pack my kit at once and report to the 4 th corps signal's in Duren by 3.30 pm. I need not say that it came as a shock and I felt acutely this sudden severance from mutter and my cosy billet, and I realised perfectly well that my new abode would lack much that I had become accustomed to in this ideal place Kreuzau. This move is of course the outcome of recent events and the result merely of the peculiar working of the English mind, which revels in petty annoyances and attacks of this kind. I must of course make the best of it, but I feel it will take me sometime to settle down to my new conditions of life. I parted from mutter and all, with deep regret. Reported at 4 pm to the orderly-room 4 th corps and was conducted to my quarters in a large building close by. Am attached to no 3 relief. Had tea in the large mess-room, a drastic change from the old conditions when I had all my meals on a table by myself at mutter's with a plate and cup. Have got the bed vacated by the man who has gone to Kreuzau in my place. It seems obvious by all this that instead of demobilising me as requested, they intend to stick to me at all cost. I suppose I should take the insult as a compliment and consider myself fortunate to be held in such high estimation by the powers that be. Am still on the strength of the Highland division being only nominally leant to the 4 th corps. On duty in the evening until 9.30 pm.

2/7/19

Today no 3 relief has a holiday and all are going by lorry to Nideggen for the day. I have declined to accompany them as I have other arrangements. In the first place I interviewed the CO at the highland division headquarters and asked him when and if I could expect demobilisation. He told me that I should take first place in the next batch and asked me if that was satisfactory. I was rather surprised at the good reception I received on this occasion. It seems odd that no mention has been made as to my claim to be the real victor of Cambrai, it seems to be tacitly acknowledged in certain quarters, but why it should be kept such a mysterious mystery is beyond my comprehension.

I then went shopping and bought a set of skittles for my little boy, also purchased other articles at the canteen and proceeded to York-Strasse where I remained for the rest of the day and slept there the night. The party included the sister of Frau and her boy and we regaled ourselves during the afternoon and evening drinking white and red wine. But fraud's sister was terribly afraid lest she should drink too much.

3/7/19

Was up at 6.30 am, washed and boots blackened by 7 am and after a cup of cocoa betook myself to my billet. Had a shave and breakfast and at 8.25 am paraded with rifle and marched to the post-office for duty from 8.30 am to 1.30 pm. It is a nice fine day, but owing to the sudden change in events I feel very unsettled. I hardly know if I am taking the best or proper steps in seeking my discharge from the army. I feel I am about to part with a long loved one and to think of it is to border on agony. The only bright spot in fact is that I shall have the pleasure and good fortune to see and be with once more my little Dux, whom I love always and as much as my black heart will allow. Yes I shall have Dux to fill up the big gap, which is about to enter my life. After dinner (which was rather good for the army, plenty of meat and nicely cooked with desiccated potatoes and cabbage, I was hungry so enjoyed it) went into town and bought a tin of preserved apricots, some chocolate and two pounds (German) of cherries for 2 mark's 20 per lb. For rest of day until 8.45 pm was at York-Strasse. Marched on duty at 9.25 pm with rifle but at 10 pm I was released to go back to billet for which I was extremely grateful as I was dead tired.

4/7/19

As soon as I was ready went into town and bought a set of carver's with steel for 45 mark's, also got away by post the skittles for Dux and a box full of photographic apparatus and some books. Then took my camera to the cemetery and took 5 snaps of the British graves there, as the others I took sometime ago proved quite a failure. Spent an hour at Frau's before dinner. At 2 pm paraded in the schoolyard for the usual silly inspection after which I went again to York-Strasse. Came back for tea at 4 pm and on duty 4.30 pm to 9.30 pm.

5/7/19

Sunny warm day. On fatigues brushing up the corridors, while the others of my relief were paraded with gas masks and afterwards on the mess-room fatigue, which is a big job. I shall be heartily glad when the time comes to throw off all these useless parades and fatigues, which of course are only conducted for the purpose of discipline, while on the other hand the result is quite on the contrary and the men are dangerously dissatisfied. In any other unit, where the men have more spirit there would be an immediate uprising. Bad officership ruined our army in the war and now I don't think a man could be found here who is willing to stay in the army and one hears on all sides nothing but bad of the army, I think this alone amounts to the strongest condemnation of the officers responsible. The buttons which I have worn since the war started have been found fault with for the 1 st time and have been ordered to get fresh ones, although mine are an army issue and quite good. This is how the men are victimised daily in the 4 th corps signals, yet the men themselves are allowed to walk about in dirty uniforms and many in fact have holes in them.

The whole presenting a scandalous disgrace to the British army, for besides being unclean, and few if any of the men's clothes fit them properly. Bought an inkstand and some film packs and printing paper, which I intend to send to England. Have posted my carvers this morning. Marched on duty at 1.30 pm to 4.30 pm. Tea at 5 pm. posted the inkstand and films which I bought this morning. Had supper at York-Strasse and then returned to billet. Was very tired and not feeling well.

6/7/19

At last it is a fact that I am to be demobbed. Have been to the school to ascertain for myself and have seen my name heading a list of three other names for demob on Wednesday. Well I have seen the war declared and peace signed as a soldier, so that in spite of much to the reverse, I have this at least to my credit. Bought a big post-card album to hold 800 cards for 27 mark's and despatched same. 2 pm parade and was again checked for buttons and cap-badge. I took no notice of course but contented myself with an inward smile, and with a firm conviction that the English officer is a born idiot. Afterwards went to see Frau and to tell her the news. Tea at 4 pm. On duty 4.30 pm to 9.30 pm. The Supt Highland division rang me up to tell me that I was to report to company office at 8.30 am tomorrow morning.

8/7/19

Today is Thanksgiving Day and is a general holiday for the troops, for me it marks the turn point in my military career in so much that my service virtually ends. Left the 4 th corps (with not the slightest regret) shortly after 8 am and reported at Highland division at 8.30 am. Where I as given a medical form to be filled in at the M.O's, after the M.O's inspection I handed into the quartermasters stores ground sheet, 50 rounds of ammunition, 1 shirt, 1 pants and 1 pair of socks, exchanged my old great-coat, which I picked up on the Gallipoli peninsular for another nearly new one and which I intend to keep. Went to York-Strasse to spend the few remaining hours and when the time came to take my departure at 9.30 pm I suddenly found myself in the centre of a weeping family. I had observed that Frau had previously left the room, and returned with eyes very red, now she was bathed in tears, her old mother who had returned from Bonn today also joined in and all the children cried while monsieur discreetly left the room. I don't think I have ever been in such an awkward position, and I realised that the circumstances necessitated some little tact on my part. Went back to the billet in the school and managed to secure a bed.

9/7/19

At 8.30 am went to the concentration camp by the station. At 10 am drew 100 marks from the cashier on the opposite side of the road. The order to parade at 10.20 am was cancelled as no special train was being run for us on this day. Stew was provided at 11.30 am and directly afterwards we were marched to the station and boarded the 12.07 pm train for cologne at which place we arrived at about 1.30 pm. Boarded a train car which took close to the demobilisation barracks. I was attached to "A" coy my dispersal camp being 6 B (Clipstone). Waited a considerable time in a long queue to hand in my papers (which include, A printed document, signed Major General Campbell commanding Highland division, voucher for suit of plain clothes, certificate of employment during the war, medical certificate and dispersal certificate, the duplicate of which is retained until one has had a bath and can only be reclaimed a bath ticket as proof of having had one. my chum a Jock waited for me and together we went souvenir hunting in the city, I bought a tiny inkstand with pen for Dux and 3 bottles of eau do cologne. Afterward went into a restaurant, where a good concert was in progress. Ordered dinner of chicken rice and potatoes and had some good wine. At 9.30 pm we left for home and very pleased with ourselves, although the temptation to make a night of it was particularly strong as we were in select company and anyone who is acquainted with continental glamour van readily understand how alluring it is. As so often happens however. Little Dux will come into my thoughts and though I love myself so much, I do love my little boy too.

10/7/19

Was up before 6 am and by 7.30 am had washed, shaved, breakfasted and was ready for moving off. The time ordered to parade was 8 am, but by this time B coy in which is my chum had not moved off and they should have left at 7 am as they are going by train. Paraded about 8.30 am and were told off into groups and for an hour at least we stood in our ranks waiting to move off. Eventually the officers condescended to put in an appearance and we got a move on. Marched to the Quay, handed over our rifles as we passed onto the boat the "Express dampser Bluche" and told off into messes, mine being no 4 mess. Bought a book of views of the Rhine, a packet of picture postcards of the same and a book of Rhine legends. At 11 am prompt the bell rang and off we went in the right direction. For dinner we had Macoricies and pork and beans, and later being very tired I went off into a short slumber. It has been very dull and windy all day and I have seen nothing whatever, which can claim to prettiness or beauty all through the journey, except perhaps the big buildings of Dusseldorf. At about 6 am we arrived at our destination, a number of barriers moored in the middle of the Rhine. We ran alongside one of them and disembarked, walking over the covered top and descending by a trap door into the hold allotted to each group. These holds into which the barge is divided is accommodated with a double row of iron beds one above the other and sufficient accommodation for 40 men. I was standing alone on the deck, when I was recognised by two men, one remembering me from my school days. The bad weather interrupted a long interchange of confidences, but it does seem strange, that here in the middle of the Rhine on an old barge, one renews an acquaintance of 16 to 18 years ago. The rain continued to pour down heavily all the evening. In order to have my decorations sewn again on my tunic I knocked at the bargeman's cabin and asked his wife to do the job for me, and in this comfortable little home I spent the evening, while the rest where at the impromptu concert held in the Blucher, which still lay alongside the barge. I was shown over the house by Fraulein, the bargeman's daughter and to my great surprise I was admitted into a beautiful cosy sitting room, with thick soft carpets on the floor, splendid ornaments of cut glass and furniture of true elegance, showing refined taste on the part of the occupants. Two beautiful bedrooms, their walls painted a gay green and white. The majority of workmens houses anywhere cannot boast such luxury as here presented. They were also the possessors of a house in Coblens. At the other end of the barge another family (Dutch) was in possession of similar quarters. Truly life on the Rhine under such conditions has more than one bright side. Returned to my bunk about 9 pm. The rain was coming in through the trap door and though chinks in wooded covering in ample quantities.

271

The Germans told me that they had suggested to the OC in charge of the barges that it was advisable to have a tarpaulin or some other covering put down, to prevent the rain coming in, but the officer had had said it was good enough for soldiers, of course it was good enough for soldiers, but the gentleman himself did not sleep there, Oh no.

11/7/19

Up at five. Got a bit of a hoarse throat through the wet. The 270 who make up our party all washed in the same water in the old bath, which was nevertheless refreshing. Very dull misty and cold. Went back on board the Blucher with our kit and at 6 am prompt we were off. A run of six holos brought us to the Dutch frontier and we came up alongside a jetty and took on board a pilot or somebody. The weather continued very unpleasant and it was quite impossible to take photographs as I had intended. The chief features which I was able to note during this second stage of the voyage, were the vast number of brick works lining the left bank of the Rhine and also the large number of ships in different stages of completion on the stocks right up to Rotterdam. Another feature is the number of cattle (black and white) which graze upon the banks of the Rhine both in Germany and Holland. For the rest the landscape is terribly flat, but the Dutch churches have quite elegant spires or sturdy square towers of stone, which contrast very favourably to the everlasting similarity of the German church spires. The houses too though small and pretty and I took a liking to them from the distance. Arrived at Rotterdam about 2 pm and we were all shoved on to another barge and two tugs took us for a long trip through the docks accompanied by a police patrol boat. The size of the place and the enormous number of ships was a big surprise indeed. And I heard others expressing the same thing. Eventually we came up to the S.S Lutterworth which is to take us on our last voyage to Blighty, and crossing her decks we were taken to the quay store houses opposite where we are to remain until 1 pm tomorrow morning. Beds have been placed on the floor touching each other each man is allotted to one. It is really a shameful arrangement, everything is dirty and looks it. I went directly to the canteen and a long queue was soon in my rear. It was first necessary to change my German money into Dutch and for 20 marks I got in return 320 centimes which sounds a lot but really is very little indeed and after purchasing 10 packets of Goldflake cigarettes I had very little left. A basin of tea costs 10 cents. We are not allowed to pass out of the gates and a soldier caught out will be placed in isolation for 2 weeks. This of course applies only I believe to men on demobilisation. Dinner was served up at 5 pm in the mess-room, which though not good was acceptable, and consisted of sausages not very nicely cooked, peas even worse and unscraped new potatoes, a small chunk of bread of a particularly good bake and a mug of tea. Afterwards lay down for a while, then as the sun came out I went on to the quay and snapped our boat the Lutterworth and also one of the docks showing three Tommies in a rowing boat, I afterwards persuaded one of them to row me out too and took another photo of the Lutterworth from the water and another of the Tommy who was rowing me. Arriving back on the barge I went with him to his bunk, he is in sole charge of one of the German barges commandeered by us for military purposes. I then attended a good concert held in the YMCA. I might mention here that one mark only represents 16 cents. Played a game of chess in the YMCA, which resulted favourably for me after about 3/4 hours play. Lay down on my mattress until 1 am, when the whistle blew to put on equipment. Had a Dixie of tea and then filed on board. I found a bed and was soon asleep.

13/7/19

At 7 am I awoke and went up on deck. The sea was beautifully tranquil and the sun shining caressingly. We had done 40 knots so our speed is about 10 knots an hour. Had a scrounged breakfast of tea and bread and dip, as there is no ordered arrangements for messing and the troops simply helped themselves and left nothing for quite half the men. We ran into a mist but after a while it became gradually clearer again. We expect to reach Harwich by 1.30 pm. I shall be heartily glad when this journey comes to an end, but we have yet a great deal of travelling and humbugging about to do. Weather became extremely bad with rain and mist and the remainder of the journey was decidedly unpleasant. Reached Harwich about 2 pm and a special took us direct to Liverpool Street, from there we marched to London bridge and entrained for the crystal palace. To write in detail all that happened at this place would be absurd even if it were possible. It was 2 1/2 hours of continuous bustle and bewilderment and I should think twice about enlisting with a vision of demobilisation before one. At about 8 pm we left Crystal Palace free men and I caught a train back to Victoria and from there I went by tube to Euston just in time to catch the 7.15 pm to Stafford and arrived at my destination at 12.15 am. **Thank god for many mercies great and small.**

THE END

After the war Stapleton returned to Stafford and re-joined the Post Office, he later moved to St. Asaph, North Wales where he died in 1971. His son Derek died in Stafford in 1969.

© Jon Wickett 2016

8355734R00158

Printed in Germany
by Amazon Distribution
GmbH, Leipzig